WORLD BANK STUDY

Reforming Education Finance in Transition Countries

Six Case Studies in Per Capita Financing Systems

Juan Diego Alonso and Alonso Sánchez, editors

THE WORLD BANK
Washington, D.C.

Copyright © 2011
The International Bank for Reconstruction and Development/The World Bank
1818 H Street, NW
Washington, DC 20433
Telephone: 202-473-1000
Internet: www.worldbank.org

1 2 3 4   14 13 12 11

World Bank Studies are published to communicate the results of the Bank's work to the development community with the least possible delay. The manuscript of this paper therefore has not been prepared in accordance with the procedures appropriate to formally-edited texts. This volume is a product of the staff of the International Bank for Reconstruction and Development / The World Bank. The findings, interpretations, and conclusions expressed in this volume do not necessarily reflect the views of the Executive Directors of The World Bank or the governments they represent.

The World Bank does not guarantee the accuracy of the data included in this work. The boundaries, colors, denominations, and other information shown on any map in this work do not imply any judgement on the part of The World Bank concerning the legal status of any territory or the endorsement or acceptance of such boundaries.

Rights and Permissions

The material in this publication is copyrighted. Copying and/or transmitting portions or all of this work without permission may be a violation of applicable law. The International Bank for Reconstruction and Development/The World Bank encourages dissemination of its work and will normally grant permission to reproduce portions of the work promptly.

For permission to photocopy or reprint any part of this work, please send a request with complete information to the Copyright Clearance Center Inc., 222 Rosewood Drive, Danvers, MA 01923, USA; telephone: 978-750-8400; fax: 978-750-4470; Internet: www.copyright.com.

All other queries on rights and licenses, including subsidiary rights, should be addressed to the Office of the Publisher, The World Bank, 1818 H Street NW, Washington, DC 20433, USA; fax: 202-522-2422; e-mail: pubrights@worldbank.org.

ISBN: 978-0-8213-8783-2
eISBN: 978-0-8213-8784-9
DOI: 10.1596/978-0-8213-8783-2

Library of Congress Cataloging-in-Publication Data has been requested

Reforming education finance in transition countries : six case studies in per capita financing systems.
   p. cm.
  ISBN 978-0-8213-8783-2 -- ISBN 978-0-8213-8784-9
  1. Education--Developing countries--Finance--Case studies. I. World Bank.
  LB2826.6.D44R44 2011
  379.1724--dc23

2011020610

Cover photo: "Original graffiti by SP£ND, anonymous street artist, Oxfordshire, United Kingdom," by Kate Mellersh.

Contents

Foreword xi
Contributors xiii
Acronyms and Abbreviations xv
Executive Summary xvii

1. **Reforming Education Financing Systems in Transition Countries: An Introduction to Six Case Studies** 1
   1.1. Introduction 1
   1.2. From Input-Based Financing to Per Capita Financing 2
   1.3. About This Book 7

2. **Per Capita Financing of General Education in Armenia** 10
   2.1. Introduction 10
   2.2. Background 11
   2.3. The Design of the Funding Formula 13
   2.4. The Implementation of the Funding Formula 15
   2.5. Assessment of Outcomes 18
   2.6. Conclusions 28

3. **Per Capita Financing of Education in Estonia** 33
   3.1. Introduction 33
   3.2. Background 34
   3.3. The Design of the Funding Formula 36
   3.4. The Implementation of the Funding Formula 53
   3.5. Assessment of Outcomes 60
   3.6. Conclusions 82
   Annex A. Additional Statistics 87
   Annex B. List of People Interviewed for the Country Case Study 98

4. **School Vouchers in Georgia: Implementation of a Simple Idea in a Complex Environment** 101
   4.1. Introduction 101
   4.2. Background 102
   4.3. The Design of the Funding Formula 110
   4.4. The Implementation of the Funding Formula 115
   4.5. Assessment of Outcomes 120
   4.6. Conclusions 127

5. **Student Basket Reform in Lithuania: Fine-Tuning Central and Local Financing of Education** 133
   5.1. Introduction 133
   5.2. Background 135
   5.3. The Design of the Funding Formula 141
   5.4. The Implementation of the Funding Formula 151
   5.5. Assessment of Outcomes 170
   5.6. Conclusions 177
   Annex A. Methodology of Student Basket 182
   Annex B. Complete Table of Allocation Coefficients for Student Basket in 2007 ... 189
   Annex C. List of People Interviewed for the Country Case Study 192

6. **Per Capita Financing of General Education in Poland: A Case Study** 198
   6.1. Introduction 198
   6.2. Background 199
   6.3. The Design of the Funding Formula 204
   6.4. The Implementation of the Funding Formula 212
   6.5. Assessment of Outcomes 222
   6.6. Conclusions 238
   Annex A. Additional Statistics on School Funding 242
   Annex B. List of People Interviewed for the Country Case Study 249

7. **Per Capita Financing of General Education in Russia: An Assessment of the Financing Reform in the Chuvash *Republic* and the Tver *Oblast*** 252
   7.1. Introduction 252
   7.2. Background 253
   7.3. The Design of the Funding Formula 255
   7.4. The Implementation of the Funding Formula 257
   7.5. Assessment of Outcomes 264
   7.6. Conclusions 272
   Annex A. Factors Influencing the Implementation of PCF in 72 Regions 275
   Annex B. List of People Interviewed for the Country Case Study 277

8. **Per Capita Financing of General Education in Europe and Central Asia: Has It Delivered on Its Promise? An Overview of Six Country Case Studies** ... 280
   8.1. Introduction 280
   8.2. Different Objectives of Per Capita Finance Reform in ECA—But in the Context of Decentralization 280
   8.3. Great Variation in Design, Structure, Coverage and Reach of Funding Formulae 284
   8.4. Assessing the Reform: What is the Evidence? 289
   8.5. Main Lessons Learned 300
   Annex A. Per Capita Financing Formulae: A Comparative Analysis 302

Boxes

Box 1.1. What is Decentralization? 5
Box 3.1. The Funding of Private Schools in Estonia 42
Box 3.2. Per Student Funding: Efficiency Effects on Private Schools in Estonia 67
Box 3.3. A Look at the Effects of the Financing Reform on Quality: Equality of
    Outcomes in Estonia 79
Box 5.1 Teacher Qualifications and Salaries in Lithuania 169
Box 6.1. Non-Public Schools in Poland: Federation of Educational Initiatives..............229
Box 8.1. To Pilot or not to Pilot? Issues in Introducing the Per Student Finance
    Reform..290

Figures

Figure 1.1. Decline in the Proportion of School-Age Population in Selected ECA
    Countries: 1990-2004 2
Figure 2.1. Per Student Expenditures by School: Historical Input-based (1999) vs.
    Formula-based (2000) Allocations...14
Figure 2.2. Formula-Based Per Student Unit Cost by School Size, 1999-2007 17
Figure 2.3 Kotayk Region: Budgets vs. Actual Expenditures by School, 2006
    (consolidated picture) 23
Figure 2.4 Kotayk Region: Budgets vs. Actual Expenditures by School, 2006
    (breakdown of key portions of picture) 24
Figure 3.1. Number of Schools and Student Enrolments: 1980 to 2005.........................35
Figure 3.2. Education Grant as a Proportion of Total Municipal Education
    Expenditure, 2005 53
Figure 3.3. Education Expenditure as a Proportion of Municipal Total
    Expenditure, 2005 54
Figure 3.4. Municipalities: Sources of Revenue, 2005 54
Figure 3.5. Municipal Tax Revenues Before and After Equalization Grant, 2008............55
Figure 3.6. Percentage Change in Students Enrolled in Grades 1 to 12, 2006
    Compared with 1992..61
Figure 3.7. New Formula (2008): How Per Student Allocation Varies with Number
    of Students per Grade 71
Figure 3.8. Average Salaries Compared: Teacher vs. Other Workers, 2006......................72
Figure 3.9. Distribution of Municipal Tax Revenues Per Student, 2005..........................74
Figure 5.1 Student Basket Allocation to Initial Schools as a Function of Student
    Numbers 163
Figure 5.2. Per Class Allocation for Grades 1 to 4 by Class Size 166
Figure 5.3. Average Per Class Allocation by Class Size 166
Figure 5.4 Average Class Sizes and Actual Student Basket Allocation Per Student......167
Figure 5.5. Average Class Sizes and Actual Per Class Student Basket Allocation 168
Figure 6.1. Number of Schools by Type..224
Figure 6.2. Primary Schools in Poland by Size 225
Figure 6.3. Student-Teacher Ratio (Full-Time Teachers) and Average Class Size..........226

Figure 6.4. Distribution of Current Expenditure Per Student in *Gminas* in 2005 232
Figure 6.5. Subvention for Education as a Proportion of Total Expenditure on Education in 2005 232
Figure 6.6. *Gminas'* Per Capita Income 233
Figure 7.1. Chuvash Republic: Per Student Normatives—Urban vs. Rural Schools, 2001-2007 (at nominal and 2001 prices) 260
Figure 7.2. Cheboksary Municipality: Per Student Education Budget—Regional Subvention and Municipal Budget (at 2004 prices) 260
Figure 7.3. Tver Oblast: Diversions from the Per Student Normatives, by Municipality 262
Figure 7.4. Tver Oblast: School Budget Adjustment Coefficients Applied by Municipalities 263
Figure 7.5. Cheboksary Municipality: Number of Students and Teachers— 2001/02-2006/07 265
Figure 7.6. Cheboksary Town: Per Student Wages and Salaries by School—2004-2007 (at 2004 prices) 266
Figure 7.7. Vishny Volocheck Municipality: Per Student Unit Cost Relative to the Normatives by School, 2006-2007 268
Figure 7.8. Zubtsov Municipality: Per Student Indicators by School—2004-2007 (at 2004 prices) 270

Tables

Table 2.1. Key Events in Education Financing Reforms in Armenia 15
Table 2.2. PCF Participating and Non-Participating Schools and Protected Schools 16
Table 2.3. Number of Protected Schools by Year and by Region 16
Table 2.4. Per Student Unit Cost and Fixed Cost for the PCF formula, 1999-2007 in Armenian Dram (AMD) 17
Table 2.5. Key Statistics of General Education Schools: 2001-2007 19
Table 2.6. Key Statistics of General Education Schools: 2001-2007: PCF, Protected and Non-PCF Schools 21
Table 2.7. Distribution of General Education Schools by Size, 2001 and 2006 22
Table 2.8 Indicative Average Monthly Salaries (incl. Benefits), in AMD 26
Table 2.9. Indicative Average Monthly Salaries (incl. Benefits) for School Directors and Deputy Directors, in AMD 27
Table 2.10. Indicative Average Monthly Salaries (incl. Benefits) for Teachers by Categories, in AMD 27
Table 3.1. Summary of Key Events in Estonian General Education: 1989 to 2008 34
Table 3.2 General Education Grant: 2003 to 2007 39
Table 3.3. Per Student Coefficients in the Funding Formula in 2007 40
Table 3.4. Number of Students by Category, 2006 40
Table 3.5. Additional Factors in the Per Student Funding Formula 41
Table 3.6. Grants for General Education to Municipalities by Type of Grant, 2007 42
Table 3.8. Minimum Number of Students Needed to Bring in Sufficient Funds to Pay for Teaching Costs 46

Table 3.7. Calculation of Per Student Funding Amount 46
Table 3.9. Additional Funding in Stages I to III for Small and Under-sized Full Classes 47
Table 3.10. Additional Funding for Grades 1 to 6 with Fewer than 7 Students 48
Table 3.12. Allocation for School Directors and Deputies 49
Table 3.11. Funding for Additional Lessons and for Enhanced Costs 49
Table 3.13. Allocation of State Education Grant to Sub-categories of Grant, 2008 51
Table 3.14. Case-Study Municipalities: Descriptive Statistics 56
Table 3.15. Tallinn City: Formula for Determining the Part of the Municipal Budget Allocation that Goes to Schools, 2007 58
Table 3.16. Tallinn City: Method of Allocating State Budget for Teaching 59
Table 3.17. Number of Schools, by Type: 1992-2006 61
Table 3.18. Distribution of Public Schools by Size Categories: 1992 to 2006 (Percentage of Total) 62
Table 3.19. Average Class Size in Estonian Public Schools: 2000-2004 62
Table 3.20. Student-Teacher Ratio in Estonian Public Schools: 1990-2006 63
Table 3.21. Tallinn City: Distribution of Schools by Size (Percentage of Total), Selected Years 63
Table 3.22. Tallinn City: Classes and Students in the Two *Gymnasium* Schools, 2007 64
Table 3.23. Tallinn City: Distribution of General Education Expenditure by Category, Selected Years 68
Table 3.24. Municipalities' Education Expenditure Per Student and Fiscal Burden on Residents, 2005 75
Table 3.25. Determinants of Education Expenditure Per Student, by Type of Municipality, 2005 76
Table 3.26. Comparison of Per Student Expenditure in 7 Schools in 4 Municipalities, 2007 78
Table 3.27. Estonian National Test: 2006 Results (Average Student Marks) 79
Table 3.28. Constraints and Flexibilities in the Estonian School Funding System 83
Table A1. Calculation of State Grant for Funding a School in a Municipality with Less Than 1600 Students in Each Language Medium, according to the 2008 formula 87
Table A2. Numbers of schools in Estonia, 1981 to 2006 89
Table A3.1. Budget of Prangli Basic School (2007) 90
Table A3.2. Budget of Viimsi Secondary School (2007) 91
Table A3.3. Budget of Juri Gymnasium School (2007) 92
Table A3.4. Budget of Mustvee Russian Gymnasium School (2007) 93
Table A3.5. Budget of Mustvee Estonian Gymnasium School (2007) 94
Table A3.6. Budgets of Tallinn's Gymnasium Schools: School 21 and Russian Gymnasium (2007) 95
Table 4.1. Timeline of Key Events Related to the Education Finance Reform 102
Table 4.2. Number of Schools, by School Size 106
Table 4.3. Number of Students, by School Size 106
Table 4.4. Change in the Average Size of Schools 107

Table 4.5. Number of Teachers, by School Size 107
Table 4.6. Student-Teacher Ratio, by School Size... 108
Table 4.7. Average Number of Teaching Hours per Week per Teacher,
   by School Size.. 108
Table 4.8. FTE Teachers, by School Size 109
Table 4.9. Students per FTE Teacher, by School Size... 109
Table 4.10. Administration Staff, by School Size.. 110
Table 4.11. Administration Staff per School, by School Size 110
Table 4.12. Values of the Vouchers in Successive Years.. 112
Table 4.13. Values of the Vouchers in Successive Years as Percentage of City
   Voucher 113
Table 4.14. Number of Schools in 2006, 2007, 2008, by Size Category and Voucher
   Type... 113
Table 4.15. Number of Students and FTE teachers in 2006/07, by School Size and
   Voucher Type 114
Table 4.16. Number of Non-Teaching Staff in 2006/07, by School Size and Voucher
   Type... 114
Table 4.17. Students per FTE Staff in 2006/07, by Size Category and Voucher Type 115
Table 4.18. Minimum Number of Students per FTE Staff, by Voucher Type................. 117
Table 4.19. Average Value of Student Voucher, by Size Category (in GEL) 117
Table 4.20. Minimum Required Expenditures and Their Coverage by Vouchers,
   by School Size.. 118
Table 4.21. Required Funding above Voucher, by School Size.. 119
Table 4.22. Average Class Size, by School Size and Voucher's School Location
   Categories 121
Table 4.23. Average Per Class Allocation, by School Size and Voucher's School
   Location Categories.. 122
Table 5.1. Timeline of Key Events Related to the Education Finance Reform............... 135
Table 5.2. Students by School Type: 2000 to 2005 136
Table 5.3. Schools by School Type: 2000 to 2005 136
Table 5.4. Students by Instruction Language, Selected School Years 137
Table 5.5. Founders by Type of School.. 137
Table 5.6. Students by Transportation Mode 138
Table 5.7. Expenditures of Teaching Process and Teaching Environment..................... 142
Table 5.8. Education as Part of Lithuanian Public Finances (million Lt)........................ 144
Table 5.9. Education as a Proportion of the GDP, Central, and Local Budgets............. 144
Table 5.10. Structure of Education Spending in Lithuania... 145
Table 5.11. Revenues of Panevezis Budget, 2006 145
Table 5.12. Expenditures of Panevezis Budget, 2006... 145
Table 5.13. Structure of the Student Basket: 2002 to 2007... 146
Table 5.14. Simplified Structure of the Student Basket: 2002 to 2007 147
Table 5.15. Yearly Rates of Growth of the Student Basket: 2002 to 2007 147
Table 5.16. Major Components of the Student Basket: 2002 to 2007............................... 148

Table 5.17. Size Categories of Schools and Normative Class Size	148
Table 5.18. Initial Allocation Coefficient by Size Category and Grade Level	149
Table 5.19 Corrected Allocation Coefficient, by Size Category and Grade Level	149
Table 5.20. Per Student Allocation to Municipalities 2003 to 2007	154
Table 5.21. Student Basket Grant and Expenditures on Teaching Process (Thousands Lt.)	155
Table 5.22. Municipalities That Contribute Most to the Teaching Process above the Student Basket Grant	155
Table 5.23. Non-Salary Elements of the Teaching Process: 2003 to 2006	156
Table 5.24. Expenditures on Non-Salary Items in Student Basket Expenditures: 2003 to 2006	157
Table 5.25. Incoming and Outgoing Students in Panevezis Municipalities	157
Table 5.26. Reallocation of Student Basket Funds by Municipalities: 2003 to 2006	159
Table 5.27. Average School Sizes by School Type 2000 to 2005	161
Table 5.28. Allocation Thresholds for Initial Schools	163
Table 5.29. Allocation Thresholds for Basic Schools	164
Table 5.30. Allocation Thresholds for Full Secondary Schools	164
Table 5.31. Initial Per Class Allocation by Size Category and Grade Level	165
Table 5.32. Corrected Per Class Allocation by Size Category and Grade Level	165
Table 5.33 Salary Coefficients of Lithuanian Teachers, 2002 and 2007	169
Table 5.34 Distribution of Teachers by Career Level, 2002 and 2007	169
Table 5.35 Student-Teacher Ratios in Lithuanian General Education Schools[71]	171
Table 5.36. Private Schools: 2000 to 2005	177
Table 5.37. Value of Factors Used to Calculate the Basic Student Basket Amount	182
Table 5.38. Teaching Student Basket Coefficient: 2002 to 2007	184
Table 5.39. Non-Teaching Student Basket Coefficient: 2002 to 2007	184
Table 5.40. Complete Student Basket Coefficient: 2002 to 2007	185
Table 5.41. Stipulated Structure of the Student Basket: 2002 to 2007	186
Table 5.42. Stipulated Structure of the Average Student Basket: 2002 to 2007	187
Table 5.43. Official Lithuanian Allocation for Teacher Professional Development: 2002 to 2007	187
Table 5.44. Adjusted Structure of the Average Student Basket: 2002 to 2007	188
Table 5.45. Coefficients for Allocation of Student Basket (From January 1, 2007)	190
Table 6.1. Summary of Key Events in Polish General Education, 1989 to 2005	200
Table 6.2. Total Amount of Subvention for Education, 2000-2007	209
Table 6.3. Kwidzyn *Gmina*: Education Budget 2006	212
Table 6.4. Annual Per Student Funding of Each School in Kwidzyn (2007)	214
Table 6.5. Kwidzyn City *Gmina*: Number of Pupils, 1998 to 2006	215
Table 6.6. Kwidzyn City *Gmina's* Schools: Teaching and Non-Teaching Posts	215
Table 6.7. Kwidzyn City *Gmina*: Students and Classes at *Gimnazjum* 2	216
Table 6.8. Kwidzyn City *Gmina*: Budget for *Gimnazjum* 2 (2007)	217
Table 6.9. Czosnów *Gmina*: Education Expenditure and Budget Revenue	218

Table 6.10. Czosnów *Gmina*: The Composition of Total Teachers' Salaries (2006) 219
Table 6.11. Czosnów *Gmina*: Total Actual Expenditures of Schools (2006) 220
Table 6.12. Czosnów *Gmina*: Student Rolls, 2001/2 to 2006/7 221
Table 6.13. Staffing Ratios at Czosnów Schools Compared to Kwidzyn Ones (2007) ... 221
Table 6.14. Comparison of Per Student Expenditure in Czosnów and Kwidzyn (2007) 222
Table 6.15. Educational Expenditure per Student (Primary and Lower Secondary) in *Gminas* in 2005, in zł 231
Table 6.16. Factors Explaining Current General Education Expenditure Per Student in Different Type of *Gminas* 234
Table 6.17. Constraints and Flexibilities in the Polish School Funding System 239
Table 6.18. Shares of the Education Subvention by School and Student Type in 2000 ... 242
Table 6.19. Kwidzyn's Subvention for 2007 Determined by the Formula 243
Table 6.20. Kwidzyn: Calculating Part A of the Voucher 245
Table 6.21. Czosnów's Subvention for 2007 Determined by the Formula 247
Table 7.1. Key Events in Education Financing Reforms in Russia 254
Table 7.2. Adjustment Coefficients by Level of Education 257
Table 7.3. Adjustment Coefficients by Type of Class (Educational Program) 257
Table 7.4. Chuvash Republic: Adjustment Coefficients, 2003 and 2007 259
Table 7.5. Tver Oblast: School Education Budget—Total for 43 Municipalities 262
Table 7.6. Tver Oblast: School Statistics—Total for 43 Municipalities 269
Table 8.1. Policy Objectives of Per Capita Financing in Case Study Countries 281
Table 8.2. Details of Per Capita Financing Formulae: Main Features 286
Table 8.3. Details of Per Capita Financing Formulae: Adjustment Factors 287

Foreword

The year 2011 marks the twentieth anniversary of the independence of many countries in Eastern Europe and the former Soviet Union. The disintegration of the former Soviet Union and the former Yugoslavia alone brought about 20 new countries to the map of Eastern Europe. All of a sudden, these new states were faced with a change of paradigm for governing their territories. This was also a time when the transition "recession" imposed severe constraints on public spending. The ensuing years also saw significant demographic shifts that led to a sizeable reduction in the populations of these countries. Many of the countries in the region lost, in about a decade, 40 percent of their pre-independence population due to a combination of a reduction in the birth rates, an increase in mortality rates, and high rates of emigration to other countries.

The size and financing structure of the education system in these countries, traditionally the biggest employer within the public sector alongside health, quickly became unsustainable, as these had been designed for a different era and purpose. A declining school-age population started emptying schools across the system, and authorities began to realize that the generalized decrease in both average class size and school size needed a concomitant reduction in spending. When measured in per capita terms, though, educational expenditure kept increasing. Moreover, higher spending per student did not go hand in hand with improving the quality of education. Thus, reforming the way the system was financed became evident, not only for sound public finances but also for raising the quality of service delivery.

This book is about how some countries transitioning from former communist type of systems undertook financing reforms, and how such reforms moved the systems from norms to capitation-based financing or *per capita financing*. Six country case studies are the bulk of the book and are drawn from a study initiated by the World Bank in 2007. The choice of countries (Armenia, Estonia, Georgia, Lithuania, Poland and the Russian Federation) was motivated by the fact that the World Bank was actively involved in supporting reforms in these countries and, in some cases, played a fundamental role in bringing these reforms to fruition. Most of the background research and the chapters were finalized by mid-2008 but, for different reasons, could not be completed during that year. Juan Diego Alonso and Alonso Sánchez now bring this to completion.

This book brings about the personal experience of three experienced professionals in the field, Rosalind Levačić, Jan Herczyński and Sachiko Kataoka, who have actively worked with the countries they wrote about (two countries each), to help develop solid per capita financing systems. Their chapters document the historical background that preceded the reforms, the intricacies of the design of the formulas, and the challenges of implementing these systems. The authors also assess whether these reforms have improved efficiency, equity and transparency and accountability of education systems. Dina Abu-Ghaida summarizes the evidence in a final overview chapter that also details the lessons learned.

It is our hope that this book will be useful to both educational authorities and general practitioners in the field of education finance. We hope that this book will contribute to policy debates around significant structural reforms that can help free up fiscal space to allow for higher investment in quality-enhancing inputs in education.

Mamta Murthi
Sector Director
Human Development Department
Europe and Central Asia Region
The World Bank

Contributors

Dina Abu-Ghaida is a Ph.D. economist who has worked at the World Bank since 2000. Initially, she worked in the Africa region analyzing poverty in Niger before moving to the education sector in 2002. During 2002-2005, she worked as an education economist in both project as well as report teams (in particular poverty assessments), and co-led the design and training for a Bank-wide toolkit on analyzing the education sector in public expenditure reviews. In 2005-2008, she led education project and report teams in several Central Asian countries, as well as the present regional study on education finance reform in transition countries. Since 2009, she has worked in the World Bank office in West Bank and Gaza as Program Manager.

Juan Diego Alonso is an Education Economist working at the World Bank. He currently works for the Education Unit of the Human Development Department at the Europe and Central Asia (ECA) Region and is part of the World Bank Education teams working on Ukraine, Turkey, and Serbia. Juan Diego has been working at the Bank for 4 years and has also participated in a handful of projects in Africa (Mozambique, Democratic Republic of the Congo, and the Republic of Guinea) as well as in studies of the effectiveness of aid development. Juan Diego specializes in areas of education finance and holds a Ph.D. in Economics and Education from Teachers College, Columbia University.

Sergo Durglishvili is the school principal of Public School #150 in Tbilisi, Georgia. A professional mathematician and economist by education, he has been involved in education finance since 1985 as a deputy principal and later as a school principal. Between 1977 and 1985, he worked as a senior scientist at the Moscow Institute of Economic Research. In 2000, he joined the Georgian 'Ilia Chavchavadze' project funded by the Ministry of Education and Science of Georgia as a trainer. In the scope of this project, he had professional relations with school administration and related educational institutes. From 2006 on, he has worked as an invited trainer and expert on Management and Financing in 'The Center for Strategic Research and Development of Georgia'. He has also contributed to the Open Society Georgia Foundation as a trainer and to the Open Society Institute in Budapest as a researcher in education projects.

Jan Herczyński is an Adjunct Professor at the Interdisciplinary Center for Mathematical and Computer Modeling at Warsaw University in Poland. A professional mathematician by training, Jan has been working on education finance since 1998. In 1999 he supported the Polish Ministry of National Education in introducing a new allocation formula for education grant to Polish local governments. He has also been very closely involved in the introduction of per student allocation formulas for primary and secondary education in Macedonia in 2005. Since then he has worked in Albania, Bulgaria, Georgia, Kosovo, Kyrgyzstan, Macedonia, Moldova, Lithuania, Poland, Romania, Serbia and Ukraine. Jan has also worked as an international consultant for various USAID-funded project, for the World Bank, and for the Open Society Institute in Budapest. He is the author of many reports and country analyses focusing on education decentralization, education finance and education management. In 2009, together with Tony Levitas and Mikołaj Herbst he published a first major monograph on education finance in Poland, *Finansowanie oświaty w Polsce (Financing of Education in Poland)*. At present he is the coordinator of the EU-funded project *Strengthening of Strategic Role of Polish Local Governments in Education on Local and Regional Level*, and he is the editor of the forthcoming guidebook for Polish local governments on communicating their management of education.

Sachiko Kataoka is an Education Economist at the World Bank. She specializes in education finance, higher education, and early childhood development. Since joining the Bank in 2006, she has primarily worked on Southeastern European, Caucus, and Central Asian countries. She has worked with the governments of Armenia, Azerbaijan, Kosovo, Romania, Tajikistan, and Uzbekistan for designing and implementing school financing reforms, particularly formula-based financing. She holds a D.Phil. in Education from the University of Sussex in the UK. She conducted her fieldwork on educational decentralization in Sri Lanka for her thesis. Prior to joining the World Bank, she worked as an Education Economist for the Asian Development Bank and the Japan Bank for International Cooperation, covering Indonesia, Malaysia, Sri Lanka and Nepal.

Rosalind Levačić is Emeritus Professor of Economics and Finance of Education at the Institute of Education of the University of London. She has been teaching, researching, and consulting in the field of school finance since the late 1980s when England introduced decentralization of school funding and she advised several local authorities. Ros has been working on school financing reforms in Eastern Europe and Central and South Asia, in particular on funding formulae and budget management at school level in Poland, Azerbaijan, Bulgaria, Romania, Serbia, and Kosovo, as a consultant to the World Bank or to Ministries of Education. She is currently working as an international consultant for the World Bank-funded Institutional Development for Education Project in Kosovo and also for the Delivering Improved Local Services project in Serbia. She has undertaken various studies for the International Institute of Educational Planning and co-edited (with Kenneth Ross) their publication *Needs based resourcing of education via formula funding of schools* (1999).

Alonso Sánchez, a Mexican national, is currently pursuing a doctoral degree at the Harvard Graduate School of Education in the Quantitative Policy Analysis Program, and has interests in teacher quality, child development, and human capital. Before that he worked for several years as a consultant for the World Bank in various departments on both operational and research activities related mostly to the economics of education, including rates of return to education, school-to-work transitions and youth unemployment, school investment projects, and teacher education reform. He also collaborated with the Living Standards Measurement Study group. Alonso has two master's degrees—in public affairs and Latin American studies—from the University of Texas at Austin. He attended college at Texas Christian University, where he met Annie Laurie Sánchez, his wife. They currently live in Somerville, Massachusetts.

Acronyms and Abbreviations

AMD	Armenian Dram
ECA	Europe and Central Asia
EEK	Estonian Kroons
EMIS	Education Management Information System
EU	European Union
FT	Full-Time
FTE	Full Time Equivalent
FY	Fiscal Year
GEL	Georgian *Laris*
GER	Gross Enrollment Rate
GDP	Gross Domestic Product
GSE	General Secondary Education
ICT	Information and Communication Technology
IT	Information Technology
LG	Local Governments
NA	Not Applicable
NER	Net Enrollment Rate
NCO	Non-Commercial Organizations
NTS	Non-Teaching Staff
OECD	Organisation for Economic Co-operation and Development
PCF	Per Capita Financing
PISA	Program for International Student Assessment
PIU	Project Implementation Unit
PR	Public Relations
PRSP	Poverty Reduction Strategy Paper
STR	Student-Teacher Ratio
SY	School Year
UK	United Kingdom
UN	United Nations
UNESCO	United Nations Educational, Scientific and Cultural Organization
USAID	United States Agency for International Development
USD	U.S. Dollar
USSR	Union of the Soviet Socialist Republics
VAT	Value Added Tax
WB	World Bank
WBI	World Bank Institute
XS	Extra-Small

Executive Summary

In the last 20 years two key issues with significant implications for financing education in Europe and Central Asia (ECA) have been the major governance reforms following the end of communist influence in the early 1990s and a significant demographic transition. From the early 1990s to the early 2000s, a decreasing fertility rate and a considerable exodus in many of the region's countries caused a gradual decline in the population growth rate, which went from 0.64 percent annual growth in 1990 to 0.10 in 1995 to hovering around zero in the early 2000s. Consequently, schools in this period became increasingly inefficient and unequal in their relative spending as the population of school-age children diminished while the number of schools, classes, teachers and other school inputs generally stayed the same. This situation created pressure on central governments to reduce such inefficiencies and spending imbalances among communities.

Following the end of the Soviet era, countries in the region have gradually reformed their governance structures by decentralizing power and turning to a market-based economy. This gradual but major reorganization has required, at different stages, accompanying reforms of funding systems to successfully support newly empowered administrative entities and to deal with unfavorable financial conditions. While the specific country context and ultimate reform objectives differed, it is in this environment of demographic transition and governance reform that per capita financing emerged as a potentially successful approach to funding education.

This book reviews the experience with one specific though widely introduced approach to funding general education, namely per capita financing (PCF), in six countries in the Europe and Central Asia (ECA) region in an effort to learn which outcomes were achieved and how. *Per capita financing* is a type of *formula funding* of schools–funding characterized by a set of agreed objective criteria for allocating resources to schools–that provides schools fixed amounts of financing based on the numbers of students enrolled. Five of the six case study countries—Armenia, Estonia, Lithuania, Poland and the Russian Federation—were chosen primarily since they represent ECA countries with relatively long experience in implementing PCF schemes[1]. The hope is that, as a result, the likelihood of observing the outcomes of per capita financing is higher. Since per capita financing replaced a school budget allocation process (input-based or normative budgeting) that was non-transparent and conducive to inefficient use and inequitable allocation of resources, the main expected outcomes of the per student finance reform were improved efficiency, equity, and transparency and accountability of public education expenditures. Indeed, the case studies document a range of policy objectives of the per student finance reform in the individual countries, with a specific focus on the three types of outcomes just described.

Decentralization of responsibility for general education to either local governments or directly to schools features prominently in the reforms implemented in tandem with, or as precursors to, per student finance reform in the case study countries. These ECA countries were attempting to come to grips with financing schools in the context of ongoing decentralization reforms, and resorted to per capita financing of education as it promised to deliver on the many objectives policymakers hoped to achieve. The degree of decentralization and, by extension, the reach of the per student formula, varied. In some countries, recently elected local governments were charged with providing education services and the per student formula was used by the central government to allocate funding to local government, which in turn chose the approach by which it determined funding for individual schools. In other countries, the central government used the per student formula to determine the budget of individual schools, which it then either provided for all schools to the relevant local government or directly to the individual school.

The per student formulae encountered in the ECA country case studies show considerable variation in their complexity and hence desire to accommodate the different cost structures of schools. In general, the per student funding formulae observed in the case studies begin with an amount apportioned for each student enrolled and subsequently incorporate adjustment factors, either based on school or student characteristics. Examples of school characteristics that feature in the different formulae include geographic location, e.g. mountainous, rural, urban, or island; school size; school type, e.g. primary, basic, or boarding school; whether a minority school or one with migrant students; and whether a school with multiple languages of instruction or integrated teaching. Examples of student characteristics that feature in the country case study formulae include the grade level; type of special needs, if any, e.g. students with learning difficulties, mental disorders, or sensory or physical disabilities; adult, evening, or distance learning student; and specialized student, e.g. sports, music, ballet, or art student. The funding formulae in Armenia and Georgia include the lowest number of adjustment factors based on school and student characteristics, whereas the formulae in Lithuania and Poland contain the greatest number—a fact that is likely related to the different approaches to decentralization in those countries, as described above.

The funding formulae vary in the degree to which they cover the school budget, i.e. whether they include capital expenditures in addition to recurrent expenditures, and which elements of the latter. Thus, the formulae in Armenia and Georgia cover all recurrent costs–but not capital expenditures. Indeed, the Estonian funding formula alone includes a per student allocation for capital expenditures, though only as of 2005, having previously covered only teacher salaries and textbooks. Despite the inclusion of capital expenditures in the Estonian formula, not all recurrent costs are included, and municipalities are expected to pay for schools' operational costs and non-teaching staff out of own budgets. The situation is similar in Russia where municipalities are expected to cover utilities, maintenance, and repairs out of their own resources. Lithuania, on the other hand, distinguishes between expenditures on the *teaching process* versus the *teaching environment*, with only the first covered by the funding formula. The teaching process includes salaries of teachers, administrators and professional staff, teacher in-service training, textbooks, library books, and teaching aids, while the teaching environment covers the salaries of technical staff (e.g. cleaners, drivers, gardeners and cooks), utilities and communications (telephone and internet). Finally, Poland's formula is exceptional in that it does not stipulate what aspects of the school budget it is meant to cover, which may be interpreted as the formula covering the entire school budget in theory, but in practice municipalities supplement the formula allocation from their own resources.

Turning to an assessment of the results achieved by implementing per student finance reforms, beginning with improvements in efficiency of expenditures, it is important to describe the measures of efficiency in question. A broad definition of efficient spending is that it obtains the maximum social value of output from a given quantity of resources. More specific to education, an education system that enrolls a student at lower unit cost than another education system is, other things equal, more efficient[2]. Arguably, however, even this second definition remains too abstract and does not reflect the concrete priorities identified by ECA countries undertaking education finance reform. Instead, ECA policymakers found themselves burdened, at a time of fiscal constraint, with large school networks that included many small schools, small class sizes and low student-teacher ratios, and a financing system that provided no incentives for actors at the school level to save (whether in general or on certain schooling inputs versus others). Thus, it is changes in the above attributes of the general education system, in particular the size of the school network and the student-teacher ratio, that will serve as proxies for an assessment of improved efficiency of education spending as a result of implementation of per capita financing.

Regarding the rationalization of school networks, the country case studies demonstrate that closure of under-enrolled schools is by no means an automatic corollary of putting in place per capita financing and that local governments play a key role. The underlying logic is that per capita financing imposes efficiency measures on jurisdictions with under-enrolled schools, and falling enrollment causes further drops in school funding. Consequently, the need of local governments to find the most efficient means of providing education within the overall spending envelope available will result in closure of schools they can no longer afford.

- The case of **Poland** comes perhaps closest to this scenario: the initial 1994 design of the per student formula guaranteed individual local governments at least 100 percent of their inflation-adjusted allocation in the previous year, so that in those local governments where student numbers fell, allocation per student increased and efficiency gains were not realized. However, an important reform of the per student formula took place in 2000, which only guaranteed that the per student allocation could not be cut below or increased above certain levels. This meant that jurisdictions with declining student rolls could experience for the first time a reduction year by year in total allocation, leading them to economize and close down under-enrolled schools[3].
- **Lithuania** succeeded in rationalizing its school network by a combination of the incentives inherent in the funding formula as well as the obligation imposed on all municipalities by the central government to adopt network consolidation strategies.
- In the **Russian Chuvash Republic**, the Republican government required all municipalities to prepare a school-restructuring plan. These restructuring plans were then supported by improving roads and providing school buses through Republican and Federal programs.
- **Estonia** implemented a per student formula that put pressure on municipalities to close small schools and has recently decided to design a new formula that instead favors municipalities with 1,600 students or less.
- **Armenia** from the beginning excluded small schools from the application of the per student formula. In addition, the fact that regions (*marzes*)—with deconcentrated offices of the Ministry of Education and Science—have no authority to reallocate budgets between schools or to arrange for student transportation

to schools meant that they have neither the incentives nor the tools to promote school consolidation. Thus, for considerable school consolidation to take place within per capita financing reform, financial management authority between the center, localities and schools must be properly distributed, and the per capita financing arrangements must include earmarked financing, bonuses, or other adjustments that facilitate school closings.
- **Georgia**, on the other hand, conducted a centrally mandated massive school network consolidation process in preparation for and as a precursor to implementation of per capita financing.

In terms of increasing the student-teacher ratio—the other efficiency indicator this book considers[4]—the case studies demonstrate the importance of the correct incentives emanating from the funding formula, as well as taking into account political economy considerations. Thus, Armenia succeeded in increasing the student-teacher ratio primarily by making teachers redundant and providing a teacher redundancy package under the Education Sector Reform Program. As a result, 7,200 teachers were made redundant during 2004-06, which fell short of the original 2003 target of 15,000 teachers, partly as a result of growing political opposition. On the issue of teacher redundancy, political economy considerations were of particular importance in Poland. Initially in 1994, the design of the formula in Poland ensured that per pupil allocations were higher for local governments—known as *gminas*—with low pupil-teacher ratios. Naturally, this arrangement provided perverse efficiency incentives, which were removed in 1996 when the class size criteria were abandoned. Nonetheless, the Teachers Charter in Poland includes regulations that make the market for teachers very rigid. Consequently, in response to the decline in student numbers in the country, surplus teachers were absorbed by the system by creating more teaching hours by splitting classes. Poland has, therefore, experienced a 14 percent *decline* in the student-teacher ratio over the period 2000-07 as student numbers fell by 16 percent over the same period.

Regarding the equity[5] impact of per student finance reforms, the majority of per student formulae include adjustment factors based on school or student characteristics that seek to ensure adequate funding for good quality education for all students. The principle here is that there are structural differences in education provision for schools in different geographic locations, for example, that have cost repercussions that need to be taken into account to ensure equity of expenditures (e.g. the smaller average size of rural schools, the extra cost of heating mountainous schools, etc.) In addition, several of the formulae take into account student special education needs since such students require additional inputs to ensure equity, whether in terms of human resources or equipment. The Polish and Lithuania formulae additionally provide adjustment factors for minority students, and Lithuania further takes into account migrant students. Accounting for the minority or migrant status of students is probably the closest that any of the formulae comes to actually considering student welfare level, but none of the formulae reviewed makes explicit adjustments based on student socioeconomic status.

Beyond the actual formula, local governments again play a key role in terms of the equity impact of per student finance reform. On the one hand, it is arguably the case that per student funding allows the central government to ensure a *minimum* level of education financing in all jurisdictions. On the other hand, in most case studies, central government allocates funding based on the per student formula but dispenses it to the municipality. Once at the municipal level, different approaches are employed to allocate funding to schools, including, in the case of Poland and Estonia, the ability to supplement the central education allocation. In fact, the data show that one of the main factors contributing to differences in education spending per student is differences in the amount that *gminas* fund from their own revenues, with urban *gminas* tending to contribute the most. In other words, the equity impact of per student funding is mitigated by the impact of decentralization reforms, which give local governments the ability to influence the final per student allocation depending on local preferences but also on the size of its revenues. Nonetheless, this same leeway in funding, which resulted from strong decentralization efforts, has led to a process leading to improved equity within a few *gmina* in Poland that have chosen to adjust their per student funding across their own schools.

In terms of the impact of per capita financing on the quality of education, a potential tension exists between healthy school competition for students[6], on the one hand, and the incentive to increase student-teacher ratios, on the other. Thus, Armenia has increased class size and the student-teacher ratio and fostered multi-grade teaching to reap efficiency gains from per capita financing without collecting, in parallel, data on student learning. On the other hand, Lithuania does demonstrate improved education quality between 2002 and 2006, probably in no small measure as a result of its distinctive pro-quality per student formula. Thus, the funding formula expressly focuses on the teaching process, and apart from the basic amount for teacher salaries includes a number of components that contribute to the quality of the pedagogical process, including textbooks, teaching aids, teacher professional development, pedagogical and psychological services, career guidance, and cognitive development of students. Furthermore, the share of non-wage items of the per student amount increased over time, indicating a substitution away from pure teaching wages to the above-mentioned quality-enhancing inputs.

Per student financing offers, last but not least, the opportunity for improved transparency and accountability of education funding as the amount each school receives is calculated objectively and can be made available to the public. In addition, simplicity of the per student formula contributes to its transparency and accountability, while its growing complexity deters technical debate and therefore public oversight. In the case of Estonia, strong features of the old funding formula were its simplicity and the stability over time of its adjustment factors. While the process for designing the new formula has been transparent, with wide involvement of stakeholders and consultations with local governments and school directors, it is doubtful that the complex calculations entailed are equally well comprehended. At the local level, accountability and transparency depend on the process by which the local government determines school budgets and the availability and publicizing of the relevant data. Thus, in Poland, all local governments discuss the annual school budgets in council where they are agreed as part of the local government's annual budget. However, while school councils are presented with the school's annual budget plan and ratify it, they have no executive authority over the budget and do not monitor it at regular intervals. This lack of involvement of school council members therefore limits accountability. Furthermore, while schools and localities have greater financial authority and there is more availability of school-level information since the implementation of recent education finance reforms, the ability of stakeholders to fully exercise either their authority or oversight duties remains elusive because of their limited capacity or information. In Georgia, the budgeting and planning skills of school administrators are insufficient, which has led them to not take advantage of such opportunities as additional funding from donations or participation in projects. School boards also do not have the necessary skills to be active participants and full partners in school management, which makes them rely heavily on school directors and limits accountability.

Notes

1. In the case of Georgia, it was felt that the approach to implementing PCF in the country already demonstrated certain outcomes of interest despite the short period of implementation.
2. The concept of efficiency under discussion is referred to as *internal efficiency* as opposed to *external efficiency*. The latter measures the ability of education systems to produce graduates who can achieve positive labor market outcomes, and is outside the scope of this report.
3. Data from the Polish National Statistics Office indicate that between 2000 and 2005 the number of primary schools declined by 10 percent while the number of classes fell by 9 percent.
4. The potentially detrimental impact of increased student-teacher ratios on quality of education is discussed below.
5. This report looks at both *horizontal equity* (i.e. like treatment of recipients whose needs are similar) as well as *vertical equity* (i.e. differential funding levels for recipients whose needs differ) on the premise that equitable funding needs to ensure equality of opportunity.
6. Insofar as per student finance rewards greater student enrolment, it is assumed that schools will compete against each other by increasing the overall quality of education as a way to attract students.

CHAPTER 1

Reforming Education Financing Systems in Transition Countries: An Introduction to Six Case Studies

Dina Abu-Ghaida[1]
Juan Diego Alonso
Alonso Sánchez

1.1. Introduction

In the last 20 years two key issues with significant implications for financing education in Europe and Central Asia (ECA)[2] have been the major governance reforms following the end of the communist influence in the early 1990s and a significant demographic transition. In regards to the former, the appearance of democratic states on the ruins of the "communist camp," as it used to call itself, created an impetus for change unseen in the regions since the end of World War II. While not all the countries progressed equally, and many stalled in their democratic evolution, the peaceful transition to democracy and market economy of Central European and former Soviet republics is the dramatic background to all other reforms. In education, in particular, as we discuss below, democratization was accompanied often by decentralization and by making many voices.

At the same time as they embarked on their democratic journey, ECA countries faced major challenges due to demographic shifts. From the early 1990s to the early 2000s, a decreasing fertility rate and a considerable exodus in many of the region's countries caused a gradual decline in the population growth rate, which went from 0.64 percent annual growth in 1990 to 0.10 in 1995 to hovering around zero in the early 2000s (UN Population Division 2009). Consequently, schools in this period became increasingly inefficient and unequal in their relative spending as the population of school-age children diminished (see Figure 1.1) while the number of schools, classes, teachers and other school inputs generally stayed the same. This situation created pressure on central governments to reduce such inefficiencies and spending imbalances among communities.

Following the end of the Soviet era, countries in the region have gradually reformed their governance structures by decentralizing power and turning to a market-based economy. This gradual but major reorganization has required, at different stages, accompanying reforms of funding systems to successfully support newly empowered ad-

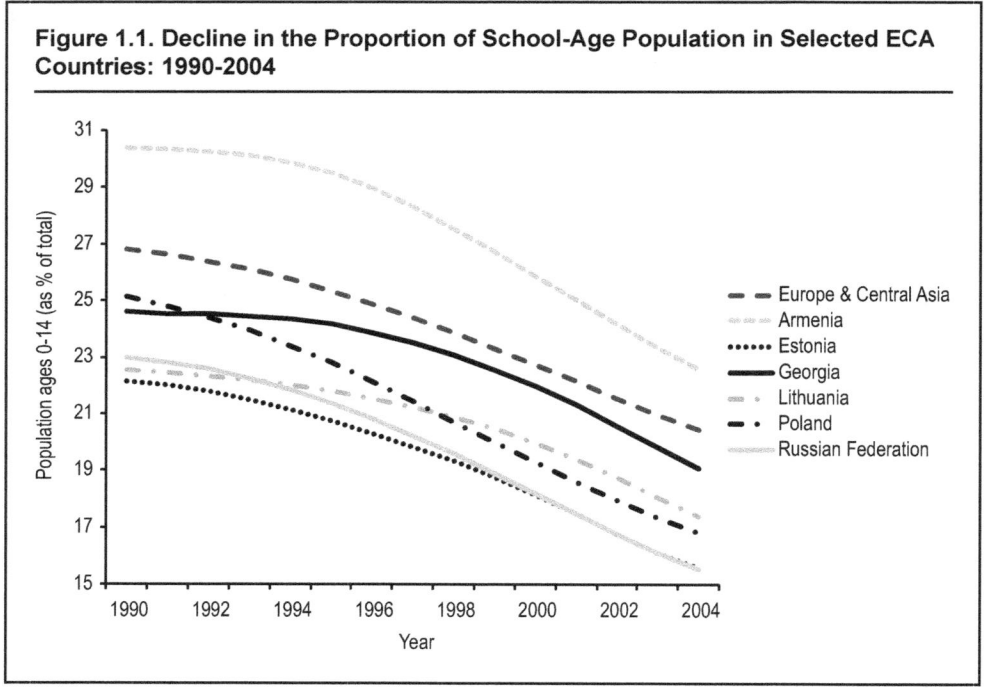

Figure 1.1. Decline in the Proportion of School-Age Population in Selected ECA Countries: 1990-2004

Source: UN Population Division (2009).

ministrative entities and to deal with unfavorable financial conditions. While the specific country context and ultimate reform objectives differed, it is in this environment of demographic transition and governance reform that per capita financing (PCF) emerged as a potentially successful approach to funding education.

1.2. From Input-Based Financing to Per Capita Financing

Per capita financing[3] arguably falls under the umbrella of *formula funding* of schools, which has as its main characteristic that it consists of a set of agreed objective criteria for allocating resources to schools that are impartially applied to each school (Levačić & Ross 1999). Thus, in 1988, the Government of the United Kingdom defined formula funding as "methods, principles, and rules of any description, however expressed. The formula does not have to be expressed in purely algebraic form, but it must apply a consistent set of criteria for distributing resources" (Department of Education and Science 1988 7/88 para. 103). Formula funding for schools has therefore arguably been a feature of educational management since the formation of systems of public education and has a history within Western schooling systems (Caldwell et al. 1999). For example, it is very common in administratively centralized school systems for the education authority to determine the teaching staff establishment of each school by means of a formula that relates the number of teachers to a specified student-teacher ratio, or to an assumed class size considered necessary or feasible, or to a specified teaching group size for designated subjects and grade levels. Similarly, education systems have used funding formulae with respect to supplies and equipment; and with the passage of time, have established formulae for different types of schools and for different kinds of educational programs.

In the case of ECA, the education finance approach in place prior to the transition is often referred to as input-based, or normative budgeting. It included staffing norms allocating teaching resources by number of classes, so that each class got a teacher and teaching aids according to the grade-specific number of lessons stipulated by the curriculum. This encouraged schools to minimize class size in order to maximize the number of teachers and teaching aids. Furthermore, a fragmented and specialized curriculum, with limited opportunity for teachers to teach across related fields, further inflated the need for teachers in all but the largest schools. Separate staffing norms applied to administrative and custodial staff. Furthermore, detailed space norms specified funding based on the area of school facilities and led to much wasted space, such as large lobbies and highly specialized laboratories and workshops that often were underutilized (Berryman 2000). The rules further encouraged jurisdictions to regard the building of new schools as beneficial, since more schools meant more classes, which meant more staff and more resources.

Although formula funding has a history in public education systems world-wide and in ECA in particular, it is important to stress that three alternatives to funding schools were (Levačić and Ross 1999) and continue to be more prevalent. These three alternatives are by no means mutually exclusive and can be described as:

- *Historic funding or incrementalism:* the school receives funding for this year, which is the same as it spent the previous year modified up or down by a few percentage points;
- *Bidding and bargaining:* the school presents a case for funding based on known criteria and is awarded financing according to how well the funding agency considers the bid meets the criteria;
- *Discretion:* the school receives funding according to the opinions and judgments exercised by the funding agency administrators.

Under any of the above three approaches to resource allocation, no clear relationship between the funding needs of the school and actual resources received arises. In the case of historic funding, the allocations to different schools may often seem illogical and unexplainable based on currently observed criteria. Allowing schools to bid and bargain for resources simply rewards the more entrepreneurial school heads and can bear little relationship to the needs of the student body. And the personal opinions and preferences of school system administrators, while ideally policy-driven, are by no means guaranteed to be so.

For ECA countries, there is much evidence that input-based budgeting created a budget planning process closely resembling a specific combination of historic funding, bidding and discretion (World Bank 2004). The starting point for budget negotiations always was the last year's funding level. The bidding and negotiations focused on incremental changes to the historical funding, where schools, which did not formulate their budget per se, used staffing norms to determine the number of teaching and non-teaching positions required.[4] The schools then submitted their estimate to the municipal administration where proposals were reviewed against actual resource availability. In addition, multiple bargaining processes took place at different levels of government. At the end, what different schools obtained above and beyond their historical budgets was based on discretion and favoritism of local or central level bureaucrats. Usually, the actual funding received by a school was less than that demanded. Often, it simply resembled last year's allocation with an adjustment for inflation and emergency needs (Fiszbein 2001). In other words, the actual application of input-based funding of schools was then tempered by a combination of historic funding, bargaining and discretion.

For ECA countries, the resulting school budget allocation process was therefore, and in many countries remains, non-transparent and conducive to inefficient use and inequitable allocation of resources. Schools receive their allotment on a monthly basis, by line item with no provision for any kind of monitoring, evaluation and feedback. This line-item budgeting procedure limits school directors' autonomy in making allocative choices. There is no incentive for schools to economize on particular areas of spending since the school is unlikely to benefit from the savings. School budgets are sometimes cut by the amount saved during the previous year. Indeed, there is an incentive for schools to inflate their "needs." For instance a school could create classes with low number of students, in order to increase artificially the relative number of teachers (see above). In some cases, recurrent deficits of local budgets and associated repeated budget amendments led to a perverse budgeting process called "deficit budgeting" in which institutions strive to achieve higher deficits since it will increase their additional allocation when the budgets are amended (Levitas & Herczyński 2001). In addition, inequities are more likely to be fostered since the poorest and weakest municipalities have less chance of making their voices heard in the bargaining process and thereby securing a higher allocation. Combined with the fact that a common feature of ECA countries is the wide difference in tax bases among localities, the result is that some jurisdictions are better than others at securing funds for education, whether in terms of the central allocation or their ability to generate revenues locally, leading to inequities in per pupil spending.

Yet in the West, starting in the 1960s, funding formulae using various indices of economic and social disadvantage were developed in order to allocate additional resources to schools serving disadvantaged communities. Following the recognition at that time of the relationship between economic disadvantage and poor educational attainment, policies to provide additional resources for schools with particularly large concentrations of disadvantaged students were introduced, for example in the USA, Australia, Britain and France (Caldwell et al. 1999). However, most of these early attempts at formula funding of schools were program-specific, usually targeted at special sub-groups of schools, and almost always confined to a relatively small proportion of the total budget that was available for schools (Ross & Hallak 1999). Examples include the Educational Priority Areas program in the United Kingdom and the Disadvantaged Schools Project in Australia, which had formulae that employed detailed social indicators based on income, education, occupational status, language spoken in the home and ethnicity. Different formulae were usually used for different programs. Additional resources were usually supplied in kind (i.e., additional teachers or auxiliary staff, equipment and materials). If additional money was provided, it was an earmarked allocation, so that transfers across different categories of resources were generally not an issue. Finally, although the focus in these early formulae was on the student, class, or school, these developments generally occurred in systems of public education that were centralized in respect to the locus of decision-making on most matters of importance.

Major advances in the conceptual and methodological aspects of formula funding in education emerged in the 1990s, when school systems in countries such as Australia, Canada, New Zealand, United Kingdom and USA started to implement radically decentralized approaches (see Box 1.1) to educational administration (Ross & Hallak 1999).

Box 1.1. What is Decentralization?

Decentralization—the transfer of authority and responsibility for public functions from the central government to subordinate or quasi-independent government organizations or the private sector—covers a broad range of concepts. Each type of decentralization—political, administrative and fiscal—has different characteristics, policy implications and conditions for success. While distinguishing among the different types of decentralization is useful for highlighting its many dimensions and the need for coordination, these concepts overlap considerably.

Political decentralization aims to give citizens and their elected representatives more power in public decision making. It is often associated with pluralistic politics and representative government, but it can also support democratization by giving citizens or their representatives more influence in formulating and implementing policies. Political decentralization often requires constitutional or statutory reforms, development of pluralistic political parties, strengthening of legislatures, creation of local political units and encouragement of effective public interest groups.

Administrative decentralization seeks to redistribute authority, responsibility and financial resources for providing public services among different levels of government. It is the transfer of responsibility for planning, financing and managing certain public functions from the central government and its agencies to field units of government agencies, subordinate units or levels of government, semi-autonomous public authorities or corporations, or area-wide, regional, or functional authorities. Administrative decentralization has three major forms—deconcentration, delegation and devolution—each with different characteristics.

Deconcentration, the redistribution of decision-making authority and financial and management responsibilities among different levels of the central government, is often considered the weakest form of decentralization and is used most frequently in unitary states. Within this category, however, policies and opportunities for local input vary: deconcentration can merely shift responsibilities from central government officials in the capital city to those working in regions, provinces, or districts, or it can create strong field administration or local administrative capacity under the supervision of central government ministries.

Delegation is a more extensive form of decentralization. Through delegation central governments transfer responsibility for decision-making and administration of public functions to semi-autonomous organizations not wholly controlled by the central government, but ultimately accountable to it. Governments delegate responsibilities when they create semi-autonomous school districts, for example.

Devolution is the transfer of authority for decision-making, finance and management to quasi-autonomous units of local government with corporate status. Devolution usually transfers responsibilities for services to municipalities that elect their own mayors and councils, raise their own revenues and have independent authority to make investment decisions. In a devolved system, local governments have clear and legally recognized geographical boundaries over which they exercise authority and within which they perform public functions. It is this type of administrative decentralization that underlies most political decentralization.

Fiscal decentralization: Financial responsibility is a core component of decentralization. If local governments are to carry out decentralized functions effectively, they must have adequate revenues—raised locally or transferred from the central government—as well as the authority to make expenditure decisions.

Source: Litvack and Seddon (1999), pp. 1-3

These school systems started to employ school-based management models in which the majority, sometimes over eighty percent, of a school system's available educational resources was placed under the direct control of schools. The arrival of these models generated a very strong demand for formula funding because this was seen as the only way in which to establish valid and defensible methods for making decisions about exactly how much each school should receive from a total school system budget. The most sophisticated approaches to formula funding to date have been associated with recent efforts to reform public education in a number of countries, especially where that reform involves a significant level of decentralization of authority, responsibility and accountability to schools within a centrally determined framework of policies, priorities and standards (Ross & Hallak 2004). If resources were to be allocated directly to schools as one line or lump sum budgets for local decision-making, then governments and their agencies were confronted with questions such as "What amount should be allocated to each school?" and "What factors should be taken into account in determining the level of resources that should be allocated to a particular school?" These questions raised others, especially when it became evident that existing approaches to resource allocation were unclear or inconsistent, or in some instances, open to manipulation on the basis of special pleading or political interference. Fair and transparent approaches were demanded.

Three main policy functions of formula funding emerged in Western countries in this regard: an equity, a directive and a market regulation function (Levačić & Ross, 1999). Here, two forms of equity need to be distinguished. On the one hand, *horizontal equity* implies the like treatment of recipients whose needs are similar, so that, for example, significantly different funding of comparable students in different regions is considered horizontally inequitable, unless the difference in funding is addressing structural inequalities among the regions, such as variability in costs that result from a region's geographic location, population density, or size. On the other hand, *vertical equity* implies differential funding levels for recipients whose needs differ, e.g. greater per student funding for disabled or socially disadvantaged students may be vertically equitable. Formula funding attempts, therefore, to determine the learning needs of each category of student and the cost of providing for those needs so that the allocation of inputs is equitable. In addition, a funding formula is used *directively* when it contains specific incentives or sanctions for schools that are intended to influence the behavior of school managers in ways consistent with the policy aims and objectives of the funding agency. For example, if the funding agency wishes to sustain small schools and to enable them to deliver the same quality of curricular provision as other schools, then the funding formula could give additional payments to schools with smaller enrolments. Finally, the market regulation function operates in school systems with emphasis on parental choice of school so that the education authority or funding agency uses a formula to allocate money to each school according to the number and nature of students in given grade levels that it has recruited. In other words, the school responds to the financial incentives linked to parental choice by providing a high quality of education so as to induce a sufficient number of parents to choose that school rather than an alternative. The above three policy functions of the formula may be at odds with each other at times, so that in practice the funding agency performs a subtle balancing act to accommodate different priorities and political pressures.

As the newly democratic ECA countries begun their reforms of inherited education systems, they could not avoid taking into account the discussions and models concurrently developed in Western countries. In particular, some ECA countries moved to per capita financing to achieve the above policy priorities, reformulated upon their specific conditions. They also hoped to improve the efficiency of education spending, seriously worsening under the impact of demographic changes, and made even more urgent by the fiscal constraints they faced. One way to define efficient spending is that it obtains the maximum social value of output from a given quantity of resources. More specific to education, an education system that enrolls a student at lower unit cost than another education system is, other things equal, more efficient.[5] Arguably, however, even this second definition remains too abstract and does not reflect the concrete priorities identified by ECA countries undertaking education finance reform. Instead, ECA policymakers found themselves burdened, at a time of fiscal constraint, with large school networks that included many small schools, small class sizes and low student-teacher ratios, and a financing system that provided no incentives to actors at the school or municipal level to save (whether in general or on certain schooling inputs versus others). Thus, it is changes in the above attributes of the general education system that will serve as proxies for an assessment on changes to the efficiency of education spending as a result of implementation of per capita financing.

1.3. About This Book

This book reviews the experience with one specific though widely introduced approach to funding general education,[6] namely per capita financing (PCF), in six countries in the Europe and Central Asia (ECA) region in an effort to learn which outcomes were achieved and how. Five of the six case study countries—Armenia, Estonia, Lithuania, Poland, and the Russian Federation—were chosen primarily since they represent ECA countries with relatively long experience in implementing PCF schemes.[7] The hope is that, as a result, the likelihood of observing the outcomes of per capita financing is higher. An attempt was made at geographic variation across the ECA region as well.[8] Naturally, the approach of relying on country case studies entails certain trade-offs: on the one hand, in-depth knowledge of the experience of the six countries[9] is available and documented in the individual case studies; on the other hand, any generalizations across the entire ECA region will require additional nuances based on individual country scenarios and specificities.

The rest of the book is organized as follows. Chapters 2 through 7 discuss the country case studies. For no specific reason other than a given sorting mechanism for displaying the chapters is needed, the case studies are presented in alphabetical order: Armenia (chapter 2), Estonia (chapter 3), Georgia (chapter 4), Lithuania (Chapter 5), Poland (Chapter 6), and Russia (chapter 7). All six chapters present a similar structure. First, an introduction is provided to motivate the discussion. Second, the historical background to the introduction of the PCF system is discussed. Third, the design of the PCF scheme is analyzed. Fourth, the peculiarities of the implementation of the scheme are described. Fifth, an assessment of a set of three main outcomes—efficiency, equity, and transparency/accountability—is presented. A sixth and final section provides a summary of the lessons learned in each of the cases. Chapter 8 presents an in-depth overview of the case studies within a common framework to compare these experiences.

References

Berryman, S. (2000); *Hidden Challenges to Education Systems in Transition Economies*, World Bank, Washington, D.C.

Bischoff, C. (ed.) (2009); *Public Money for Public Schools—Financing Education in South Eastern Europe*. Local Government and Public Service Reform Initiative, Open Society Initiative, Budapest.

Caldwell, B., Levačić, R., and Ross, K. (1999); "The role of formula funding of schools in different educational policy contexts" in Kenneth N. Ross and Rosalind Levačić (editors) *Needs-based Resource Allocation in Education via Formula Funding of Schools*, Paris: UNESCO International Institute for Educational Planning.

Department of Education and Science (1988); *Education Reform Act: Local Management of Schools*, Circular No. 7/88. London: Her Majesty's Stationery Office.

Fazekas, M. (2009); "School Funding Formulas: A Literature Review", Unpublished Manuscript.

Fiszbein, A. (editor). (2001); *Decentralizing Education in Transition Societies: Case Studies from Central and Eastern Europe*, World Bank Institute, World Bank, Washington, D.C.

Levačić, R. and Ross, K. (1999). "Principles for designing needs-based school funding formulae" in Kenneth N. Ross and Rosalind Levačić (editors) *Needs-based Resource Allocation in Education via Formula Funding of Schools*, Paris: UNESCO International Institute for Educational Planning.

Levitas, T., and Herczyński, J. (2001); *Education Policy and Finance in Lviv: Strategic Proposals*. Report Written for Lviv City Council under Largis Project, Lviv, Ukraine.

Litvack, J., and Seddon, J. (1999). *Decentralization Briefing Notes*, WBI Working Papers, World Bank Institute, World Bank, Washington, D.C.

Ross, K., and Hallak, J. (1999); "Introduction" in Kenneth N. Ross and Rosalind Levačić (editors) *Needs-based Resource Allocation in Education via Formula Funding of Schools*, Paris: UNESCO International Institute for Educational Planning.

United Nations Population Division (2009); *World Population Prospects: The 2008 Revision*. New York, United Nations, Department of Economic and Social Affairs (advanced Excel tables). Available at http://esa.un.org/unpd/wpp2008/index.htm.

World Bank (2004); *Per Capita Financing of Education: Experience and Issues*, World Bank Russian Country Office, Moscow, Russian Federation.

Notes

1. The authors of this chapter have benefitted from many exchanges and conversations with the authors of each of the country case studies. Special thanks go, however, to Jan Herczyński for thoroughly revising it and suggesting further edits and changes. All mistakes and errors of interpretation or judgment are, of course, our sole responsibility.

2. The reference to the Europe and Central Asia (ECA) Region, in this book, alludes to the 30 countries which are World Bank client countries in this region, namely, Albania, Armenia, Azerbaijan, Belarus, Bosnia and Herzegovina, Bulgaria, Croatia, the Czech Republic, Estonia, Georgia, Hungary, Kazakhstan, Kosovo, the Kyrgyz Republic, Latvia, Lithuania, Macedonia, Moldova, Montenegro, Poland, Romania, the Russian Federation, Serbia, the Slovak Republic, Slovenia, Tajikistan, Turkey, Turkmenistan, Ukraine, and Uzbekistan.

3. "Per capita" financing is also referred to in the literature as *per student* or *capitation* financing.

4. Other school costs, such as utilities, were paid directly by the relevant municipality or local government.
5. The concept of efficiency under discussion is referred to as *internal efficiency* as opposed to *external efficiency*. The latter measures the ability of education systems to produce graduates who can achieve positive labor market outcomes, and is outside the scope of this report.
6. The term *general education* is used in this report to refer to primary, lower secondary, and upper secondary academic, i.e. excluding vocational or technical, education.
7. In the case of Georgia, it was felt that the approach to implementing PCF in the country already demonstrated certain outcomes of interest despite the short period of implementation.
8. The chosen approach means that some important countries or groups of countries within the ECA region, like the Western Balkan countries, were left out of the present book given that they either had very recent—and limited—or no experience or a very recent and limited one. For the interested reader, a recent review of education finance in Albania, Bulgaria, Croatia, Macedonia, Romania, and Moldova is provided by Bischoff (2009). For a comprehensive literature review on the worldwide experience with formula funding, see Fazekas (2009).
9. Note that in the case of the Russian Federation, the chapter in this book only refers to the experience of PCF introduction in two regions (the Tver *Oblast* and the Chuvash *Republic*).

CHAPTER 2

Per Capita Financing of General Education in Armenia

Sachiko Kataoka[1]

2.1. Introduction

After independence from the Soviet Union in 1991, Armenia's public education system was put on the verge of total collapse with spending plummeting dramatically. Until the late 1980s, total education expenditure in Armenia was supported by the general budget of the Soviet Union at an estimated average unit cost per student across all levels equivalent to approximately US$500-600.[2] Following the collapse of the Soviet Union, Armenia faced a severe economic recession, and the new government of Armenia was no longer able to allocate its budget to education at the same level as before. Public education expenditure dropped from almost 8 percent of GDP in 1989 to 1.2 percent in 1994. Teacher salaries dropped sharply—as low as US$3 per month in 1994, which forced many teachers to become part-time teachers and have a second job. Per student public expenditure on general secondary education (GSE)[3] declined from an estimated US$292 in 1989 to about US$33 in 2001.[4] With limited government resources, the education system could no longer survive without substantial contributions from parents.

The ever grimmer situation of education financing in Armenia was compounded by the lack of necessary adjustment of the system to the new demographic trends. Between 1990 and 2000, while the number of students declined by almost 6 percent (from 597,000 to 564,000) primarily due to the declining birth rate,[5] the number of teachers increased by 2.7 percent (from 55,500 to 57,000). Education spending was also distributed unevenly between schools. Many schools had idle capacity, while some in urban areas were overcrowded. Given the severely scarce resources and the rapidly deteriorating education system as a result, the government felt an imminent need to spend available budget more efficiently and effectively. To restore and improve the education system, the Ministry of Education and Science (MOES) singled out education financing as a key reform area in the overall general education reform strategy of 1997 and proposed to introduce per capita financing (PCF) as a major reform to start addressing the fiscal problems in the sector.

The rest of this chapter discusses how the introduction of a system based on capitation principles (PCF) played a critical role in the general education reforms. Section 2.2 reviews the Armenian school system and discusses the policy objectives of introducing PCF in general education. Section 2.3 examines how the government designed the PCF scheme on a pilot basis. It also discusses other key reforms which were running in parallel to the financing reform. Section 2.4 analyzes how the new financing system was implemented, and adjusted in the process of gradual nationwide expansion. Section 2.5 assesses the outcomes of the PCF scheme in terms of efficiency, equity, transparency and accountability, and some other outcome indicators, *i.e.*, school autonomy, academic effectiveness. The last section concludes with a summary of the key findings.

2.2. Background

2.2.1. The General Secondary Education (GSE) System

The management responsibilities for GSE are shared between the central government and its deconcentrated administration offices at the regional level. MOES is responsible for curriculum and textbook development, teacher training and qualifications, students' assessment, capital investment, and management of boarding and special needs schools. School administration and distribution of recurrent budget to GSE schools are the responsibility of the regional education departments. Regions, referred to as *marzes*, were established after independence as the deconcentrated offices of the central government, and their officials are not elected, but are appointed by and accountable to the central government. In the country, there are 11 regions (10 *marzes* and the City of Yerevan). Recurrent budgets for general education are channeled from the Ministry of Finance and Economy (MFE) to regional finance departments, which are responsible for disbursing funds to individual schools on the basis of budget line items. Regional education departments are responsible for appointing school directors, and managing the regional school inspectorate.

Armenia's GSE system is being extended from 10 to 12 years. Until recently, the GSE system in Armenia consisted of eight years of compulsory basic education (three years of primary and five years of lower secondary) and two years of upper secondary education. Currently, this Soviet-era system is being extended, in two steps, first, to nine years of basic education (grades 1-4 for primary and grades 5-9 for lower secondary) and, second, to three years of upper secondary education (grades 10-12).[6]

Over 96 percent of primary and secondary students are enrolled in various types of state schools. In the school year 2009/10, there were 1,368 public schools, consisting of nine primary-only schools (grades 1–4), 293 basic schools (grades 1-9), 999 full general secondary schools (grades 1–11/12), 19 lyceums (grades 5–11/12, and 48 high schools (grades 10–11/12). In addition, there were 46 vocational education schools. Finally, there were 53 private schools offering general secondary education. Altogether, 381,286 students were enrolled in these various types of public GSE schools and 5,992 in private schools, or 387,278 in total.

Compared to other countries at similar income levels,[7] basic (primary and lower secondary) education enrollment rates are relatively high, but they decline significantly at upper secondary.[8] Because children are not necessarily enrolled at the officially intended level of education, however, the net enrollment rate (NER) for basic education (grades 1-8) was much lower, only 89 percent, than the gross enrollment rate (GER), 114 percent in 2005. This is partly the result of variations in the entry age and cumulative repetitions throughout basic education. Similarly, while the GER for upper secondary education (grades 9-10) is estimated at 89 percent, the NER is only 70 percent. The GER goes up to 104 percent for higher secondary level if those in preliminary (secondary level) vocational training are included.

2.2.2. Policy Objectives

In 1997, the MOES adopted the Strategy for Reform of the General Education System in an effort to restore and enhance the quality, equity, and efficiency of the educational system.[10] The comprehensive strategy aimed at: (i) the diversification of education financing by concentrating public funding in core general education and promoting private investment in extra-curriculum activities and other levels of education; (ii) structural reforms of the education system based on decentralization, school autonomy, and rationalization, supported by a new information system; and (iii) continuous improvement of curriculum and teaching methods and upgrading of knowledge evaluation consistent with international educational standards.

The Strategy proposed to introduce PCF for general education as a tool to ensure greater school autonomy, to improve cost effectiveness, to facilitate the consolidation of the school network, and to eliminate staff redundancy. On education management and financing, the Strategy pointed out that school directors had no incentive to be efficient or cost-effective because they had received school budgets based on the number of classes and teachers and therefore opted for inefficiently low class sizes and student-teacher ratios, and because they were given no decision-making authority over financial management with very little non-salary budget. Therefore, *an important element of the education reforms was to transform schools from budgetary institutions to autonomous legal entities with the right to hold their own bank accounts and manage their own budgets.*

The introduction of the PCF scheme in Armenia was, therefore, accompanied by the enhancement of school autonomy and accountability in management and financing to achieve multiple objectives. The Government Decree No. 377 on the Approval of the Pilot Project on the Republic of Armenia General Education System Reforms dated June 1, 1999 envisaged the objectives of the PCF pilot project as follows:

- to assess possibilities of the general education system reforms and implement mechanisms;
- to establish favorable and promotional conditions by increasing the *rationalization* and *efficiency* of the education system; and
- to implement education reform innovations, particularly *decentralization of management and financing autonomy to schools*, and promotion of *efficient and sustainable mechanisms* for self-dependent schools.

In addition, under the Education Law dated April 14, 1999 and the new regulatory framework for school-based management, all schools were required to establish the school board, comprised of parents, teachers, and local government representatives, as an *accountability* mechanism by involving communities in school management. Decisions relating to the allocation of resources within the school, including the selection, hiring and firing of staff, became the responsibility of the school board, in compliance with the selection rules and procedures and standards established by MOES. The school director would implement the daily school activities and decisions of the Board.

2.3. The Design of the Funding Formula

2.3.1. The Design of the PCF Scheme

Initially, the PCF scheme was implemented on a pilot basis in three selected regions. In 1999, 154 schools (about 10 percent of the country's total) in Yerevan City and the Kotayk and Vayots Dzor regions participated in the PCF pilot project. The piloting of the system was supported under the World Bank-funded Education Financing and Management Reform Project (EFMRP) (1998-2003). The schools were selected by their respective regions to represent different types of schools and were based on the willingness of school principals to participate and the availability of an accountant in school.

The project tested the management capacities of the elected local authority, the *hamaink*, which is administratively the second level of jurisdictional authority below the region.[11] When the pilot project was being designed in 1998, the government passed the Government Decree No. 661 on Further Decentralization of the Management of the State General School System dated October 28, 1998, which aimed to decentralize significant responsibilities for delivering public services, including GSE, to *hamainks*. In order to test their potential roles and capacities in managing general education, one third of the pilot schools were transferred to the *hamaink* authority, while two thirds remained under regions. Most *hamainks*, being small and inexperienced, however, lacked administrative and management capacities to take on the new responsibilities such as school administration and distribution of recurrent budget to schools. Furthermore, some newly elected community leaders misunderstood their functions and misused power such as the appointment of school directors. Consequently, the schools under them were taken back to the regional level after the first year of the pilot project implementation.[12]

2.3.2. The PCF Formula

An inter-ministerial Working Group on Education Finance and Management developed a relatively simple formula based on the input-based budget of the 154 pilot schools, which was supplemented by a transitional mitigation measure. First, the government decided to exclude 18 small schools with less than 100 pupils from the formula-based financing completely and to continue allocating budgets based on the number of classes as in the earlier days because the potential budgetary gaps for these schools would have been too large.[13] Second, a simple formula was developed based on a linear regression analysis of the input-based budget of the remaining 136 schools. The formula consisted of only two variables without any adjustment factors as follows:

$$\text{Total School Budget} = A \times N + B$$

where A = Per student unit cost
N = Number of students
B = Fixed cost (informally called '*maintenance costs*'[14])

To avoid radical changes in school budget, and in particular, in terms of staffing, the government decided that no pilot school would receive a lower budget than the one in the previous year. As illustrated in Figure 2.1, out of the 136 schools, 41 schools were going to receive a smaller budget under the formula-based allocations than with the histor-

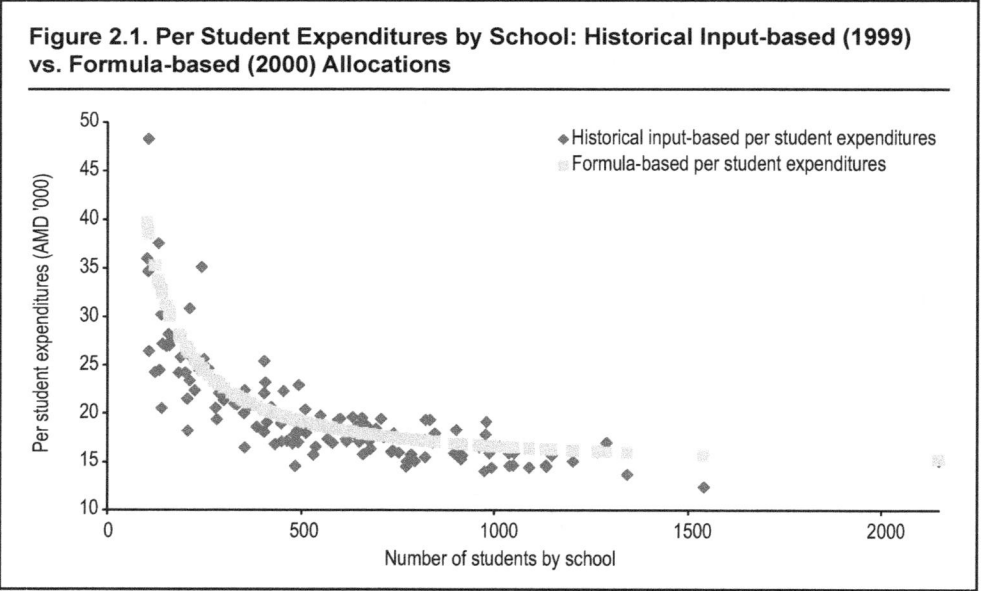

Figure 2.1. Per Student Expenditures by School: Historical Input-based (1999) vs. Formula-based (2000) Allocations

Source: Government Decree No. 377 on the Approval of the Pilot Project on the Republic of Armenia General Education System Reforms (June 1, 1999).

ical allocations. The biggest loser would have lost 29.5 percent of their budget, while the other 95 schools were going to receive more (even up to by 59.1 percent). As a remedial measure, the Ministry of Finance and Economy (MFE) allocated additional funds from the Contingency Fund to the 41 potential losers and filled the gap. The total contingency fund spent on this purpose was 2.2 percent of the total formula-based expenditures for the 136 schools. Together with the 4.0 percent net increase for the formula-based allocations for 136 schools, the total expenditures increased by 6.2 percent in total.

In September 1999, all of the 154 pilot schools—regardless of how their budget was calculated—started to receive a lump-sum budget from the central Treasury via the regional financial departments and to exercise school financial autonomy. The 154 pilot schools were required to: (i) establish a school board, comprised of parents, teachers, and local government representatives; (ii) open their own bank account(s); and (iii) receive training for school accountants and principals.[15] Schools were then governed by school boards, and managed by school directors selected by the school board. They were allowed to raise funds themselves from non-budgetary sources such as incomes from extra-curricular services, to make their own staffing decisions, and to allocate their funds according to their needs.

2.3.3. Other Reforms

In parallel to the PCF scheme, other reforms were also introduced, which were supposed to help enhance the effectiveness of the new financing system. Table 2.1 presents the highlights of education financing reform in Armenia. In 1998, MOES adopted the rationalization plan, proposing to revise norms for teacher wage rates, class size, student-teacher ratio (STR), full-time teaching hours, and non-staff inputs, and required each region to prepare a school and class consolidation plan to enable schools to meet the new staffing norms. Most regions complied with this instruction at least in part, but for political and other reasons it was not followed through then.[16] Subsequently, the school rationalization program, *i.e.*, consolidation of classes and schools was carried out systematically between 2003 and 2006. Moreover, the government planned in 2003 to make 15,000 teachers redundant and provided a teacher redundancy package under the Education Sector Reform Program.[17] The package offered the following options: (i) professional training for new jobs; (ii) relocation grants for those who wished to move from urban to rural schools; (iii) small business start-up support (not financial investment, but technical assistance for registration and training); and (iv) a cash payment equal to six months' salary for teachers within five years of the official retirement age of 62. Between 2004 and mid-2006, 7,200 teachers were made redundant. The reasons why the government could not meet the original target included (i) before consolidating small classes, teachers needed to receive training in multi-grade and multi-subject teaching, but there were no such programs available; (ii) the original target was estimated based on a common STR across the country, which overestimated the number of teachers to be made redundant because small schools in rural areas inevitably have smaller STRs; and (iii) there was strong political pressure from politicians not to pursue further redundancy.

Table 2.1. Key Events in Education Financing Reforms in Armenia

Year	Event
1997	MOES adopted the Strategy for Reform of the General Education System which proposed to introduce PCF for general education.
1999	The PCF reform was introduced in 154 schools in Yerevan City and Kotayk and Vayots Dzor regions on a pilot basis. Out of the 154 pilot schools, 18 small schools were protected by being excluded from the formula funding.
2001-2006	The government gradually expanded PCF nationwide, excluding protected schools.
2002	The government introduced geographical coefficients in the formula.
2003-2006	MOES carried out the school rationalization program—class and school consolidation—for all regions. The government provided teacher redundancy packages under the Education Sector Reform Program.
2007	The category of protected schools was abolished. Subsequently, the government introduced a new adjustment coefficient for schools in remote areas. The regions were given the authority to reallocate the budget between schools.
2007	The unified nationwide teacher salary scales were no longer applied, and each region and school started to pay different salaries, depending on their financial capacity, within a certain range.
2008	The high school reform began to make the school network more efficient and improve quality of upper secondary education.

2.4. The Implementation of the Funding Formula

2.4.1. Introduction of Protected Schools

After two years of the pilot phase, the government decided to expand the PCF scheme nationwide, and also to introduce a category of 'protected schools.' In October 2001, the government decided to gradually expand the PCF scheme nationwide and complete the transition by 2005. All schools were given a legal status as public non-commercial organizations (NCOs) then.[18] As in the case of the small schools in the initial pilot project, the government decided to 'protect' those schools with no other schools within a 5-km radius and those located in border areas from application of the PCF formula.[19] In 2001, 10 regions reported 284 schools to be protected. The protected schools continued receiving norm-based budgets as before. Table 2.2 shows the number of PCF participating, PCF non-participating and protected schools. The number of protected schools gradually increased up to 403 (about 30 percent of the total) by 2006[20] until they were totally abolished in 2007. On the other hand, the government did not provide additional funds to fill the gap for those which were going to receive less funding than in the previous year. That was because education expenditures were increasing every year, as shown later in the text, and therefore, there were very few schools which were going to receive less, and even if they were, the decrease was going to be small.

Table 2.2. PCF Participating and Non-Participating Schools and Protected Schools

	1999	2000	2001	2002	2003	2004	2005	2006	2007
Total No. of schools	1,407	1,407	1,389	1,392	1,392	1,359	1,354	1,362	1,362
PCF participating schools		136	200	301	506	792	953	959	1,362
PCF non-participating schools		1,253	905	799	551	232	0	0	0
Protected schools		18	284	292	335	335	401	403	0
Percentage of PCF participating schools		9.7	14.4	21.6	36.4	58.3	70.4	70.4	100.0

Source: MFE; Statistical Yearbook of Armenia (2001) for the total number of schools for 1999 and 2000.

The proportion of protected schools varies considerably across regions. Table 2.3 illustrates that, by 2006, while more than half of the schools were protected in the Syunik, Tavush, and Vayots Dzor regions, and more than one third in another three regions, there were no protected schools in Yerevan City. In practice, however, the City had allocated additional budget to small schools from its own revenues for about 20 to 25 schools in 2007 as these were unable to afford the necessary number of teachers.

Table 2.3. Number of Protected Schools by Year and by Region

Region	2001	2002	2003	2005	2006	Total number of protected schools (2006)	Total number of schools (2006)	Percentage of protected schools (2006)
Aragatsotn	10		20	23		53	121	43.8
Ararat	17			4		21	112	18.8
Armavir	13			2		15	118	12.7
Gegharkunik	46			8		54	126	42.9
Kotayk	7			5		12	101	11.9
Lori	14			7		21	161	13.0
Shirak	52			4		56	162	34.6
Syunik	57	8	23	1	2	91	117	77.8
Tavush	45			1		46	81	56.8
Vayots Dzor	23			11		34	51	66.7
Yerevan						0	189	0.0
MOES*						0	23	0.0
TOTAL	284	8	43	66	2	403	1,362	29.6

Source: Project Implementation Unit (PIU) for the Education Financing and Management Reform Project.
*Includes schools directly managed by MOES such as special education schools. These schools started to participate in the PCF mechanism in 2005. There were no protected schools under this category.
Note: There are noticeable discrepancies in the number of protected schools between this table and the set of tables in the section immediately below (Table 2.5 and Table 2.6), and the number converges only in 2005. It is unclear which data source provided more reliable data back then, but the data from the PIU is presented in this table to illustrate regional variations.

2.4.2. Revision of the PCF Formula

Although the structure of the formula remained the same over time, revisions to the formula were made annually based on the adjustment for unit costs. Indeed, MFE has revised both the per student unit cost (A) and the fixed cost (B) for the funding formula every year, as shown in Table 2.4.[21] Figure 2.2 illustrates the formula-based per student unit costs according to school size, which increased steadily over time. The relatively large fixed cost has made the unit cost for smaller schools, especially those below 300 students, much larger than that for larger schools.

Table 2.4. Per Student Unit Cost and Fixed Cost for the PCF formula, 1999-2007 in Armenian Dram (AMD)

	1999	2000	2001	2002	2003	2004	2005	2006	2007
A (AMD per student)	14,000	19,900	21,887	24,348	26,764	36,068	51,202	56,876	66,956
Increase (percent)			10.0	11.2	9.9	34.8	42.0	11.1	17.7
B (AMD '000 per school)	2,600	2,600	2,600	2,600	3,400	4,600	6,600	9,700	11,450
Increase (percent)			0.0	0.0	30.8	35.3	43.5	47.0	18.0

Source: MFE.

While the variables in the formula remained the same, in 2002 the government introduced adjustment coefficients for schools in mountainous (1.02) and high mountainous (1.20) areas.[22] The per student amount (A) was multiplied by a relevant coefficient for the schools in those areas. The rationale behind the weights of coefficients for high mountainous areas (the list of which is approved by the government) included (i) higher wages (there was a Prime Ministerial decree on salary rates of budgetary organization employees that stated that in high mountainous areas salary rates were 20 percent high-

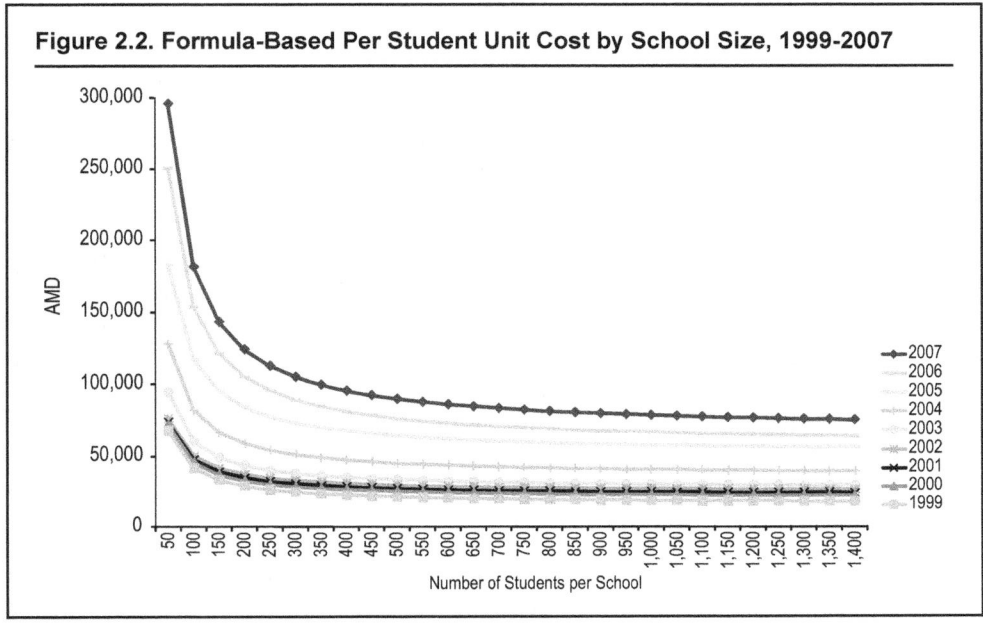

Figure 2.2. Formula-Based Per Student Unit Cost by School Size, 1999-2007

Source: MFE.

er); and (ii) higher estimated fuel consumption in winter. The formula did not include a coefficient for special education needs, which is often included in formulae in other countries, because it was funded separately outside the formula in Armenia.

Further adjustment coefficients to the general formula were introduced in 2006, when the government proposed to introduce more refined weights to better meet the needs of smaller schools.[23] These changes paved the way for the elimination, at the beginning of 2007, of the category of protected schools, which also led to the introduction of another coefficient for schools that were the only remaining schools in a given settlement and had less than 400 students (1.20).[24] In total, 691 schools met one or more of the three criteria (mountainous, high mountainous, or less than 400 students) for the FY2007 budget. In the case a school met two coefficients, a multiplication of the two coefficients was used; for instance, for a school in a high mountainous area with less than 400 students a coefficient of 1.44 (1.2 x 1.2) was applied. The MFE then proceeded to divide these schools into three groups: (i) schools that would have received more budgets in 2007 based on the new formula than in 2006 based on the old formula, (ii) those that would have received less, and (iii) those that would have received the same. Out of the 691, 464 schools would have received a higher amount than in 2006, 219 less, and three the same. At the same time, regions were given the authority to reallocate the budgets from the first group to the second group, without any ceiling on the amount of reallocation, depending on the actual needs of the schools. The new scheme was applied for the first time with the school year 2007/08 school budgets, starting in September 2007.[25] An analysis by the Project Implementation Unit for the Education Quality and Relevance Project suggested that adjusted school budgets through the manual reallocation resulted in almost the same amounts as the ones calculated by the more complicated formula.

The relatively simply defined formula has had obvious strengths in terms of transparency and simplicity, but also weaknesses in terms of its precision. The MOES' Working Group has identified the following major weaknesses of the formula:

- the formula did not take into account factors such as the level of education[26] and peculiarities of individual schools, including special needs, and building conditions (space, type of the building and utility requirements); and
- the formula had encouraged schools to become bigger and to expand beyond what MOES considered the optimal school size (around 700-900 students per school).

The Working Group has explored alternative formulae and an option to gradually decrease the per capita allocation for large schools beyond an appropriate level as well as their financial implications on the total education budget. However, except for an introduction of differentiated coefficients by the level of education (primary, basic, and secondary), the government came to appreciate the simplicity of the formula, and, as of 2010, no major further changes were made.

2.5. Assessment of Outcomes

2.5.1. Efficiency

The Armenian government made considerable progress in rationalizing the general education system since the introduction of the PCF pilot project in 1999, and achieved substantial internal efficiency gains without classes becoming overcrowded.[27] Table 2.5

illustrates the changes from 2001 to 2007 in key statistics pertaining to general education schools. As the number of students, driven by demographic changes, declined by over 20 percent, the number of classes was reduced by 24 percent, teaching staff positions by 35 percent, and non-teaching staff positions by 34 percent. The most dramatic reduction in teachers and non-teaching staff occurred between 2003 and 2005 when the optimization program was introduced, and it continued even after 2005. The teacher redundancy package also helped reduce the number of teachers after 2004. Even though the reductions were lower than the government's original targets, the rationalization program resulted in significant efficiency gains: the student-teacher ratio increased from 10.8 in

Table 2.5. Key Statistics of General Education Schools: 2001-2007

	2001	2002	2003	2004	2005	2006	2007	2001-07	2006-07
No. of schools	1,389	1,391	1,392	1,359	1,354	1,362	1,362	-1.9	0.0
No. of students[1/]	560,637	533,398	513,621	493,433	477,011	464,063	446,140	-20.4	-3.9
No. of classes[1/]	27,059	25,861	24,332	22,016	21,365	20,878	20,494	-24.3	-1.8
No. of staff positions	77,536	75,680	72,247	62,316	56,218	53,880	50,974	-34.3	-5.4
Teachers	48,666	47,280	47,411	37,338	34,204	33,496	31,765	-34.7	-5.2
Non-teaching staff	28,870	28,401	24,836	24,978	22,015	20,384	19,209	-33.5	-5.8
Administrative staff			3,913	4,476	4,355	4,358	4,297	9.8	-1.4
Support staff			20,923	20,502	17,660	16,027	14,912	-28.7	-7.0
Classes per school	19.5	18.6	17.5	16.2	15.8	15.3	15.0	-22.8	-1.8
Pupil per class	20.7	20.6	21.1	22.4	22.3	22.2	21.8	5.1	-2.1
Pupil teacher ratio	11.5	11.3	10.8	13.2	13.9	13.9	14.0	21.9	1.4
Pupil non-teacher staff ratio	19.4	18.8	20.7	19.8	21.7	22.8	23.2	19.6	2.0
Recurrent budget (AMD mils.)	16,575	17,330	19,121	25,167	34,925	40,784	47,599	187.2	16.7
Wages and salaries	10,207	11,469	13,180	18,753	27,424	30,664	36,293	255.6	18.4
Teachers	7,380	8,751	10,376	13,747	20,634	23,452	28,225	282.5	20.4
Non-teaching staff	2,827	2,718	2,804	5,006	6,790	7,212	8,068	185.4	11.9
Administrative staff			867	1,683	2,703	3,140	3,932	353.5	25.2
Support staff			1,936	3,323	4,087	4,071	4,136	113.6	1.6
Soc. sec. contributions	4,878	4,365	4,202	4,552	5,553	7,267	8,052	65.1	10.8
Goods and services	1,490	1,496	1,739	1,862	1,948	2,853	3,254	118.4	14.1
Office supplies	16	15	62	27	13	26	50	212.5	92.3
Fuel, energy and heating	1,154	1,118	1,272	1,602	1,637	2,341	2,317	100.8	-1.0
Communication services	53	53	39	39	46	93	93	75.5	0.0
Water and sewerage	33	91	80	98	147	199	389	1,078.8	95.5
Other G&S	234	220	286	95	104	194	405	73.1	108.8
Average salary (AMD '000)									
Teachers	151.7	185.1	218.9	368.2	603.3	700.1	888.6	485.8	26.9
Administrative staff			221.7	375.9	620.7	720.7	915.0	312.7	27.0
Support staff			92.5	162.1	231.4	254.0	277.4	199.9	9.2
Average salary (AMD '000 at 2001=100)									
Teachers	151.7	183.1	206.8	325.1	529.5	597.1	728.7	380.4	22.0
Administrative staff			209.4	331.9	544.8	614.7	750.4	258.3	22.1
Support staff			87.4	143.1	203.1	216.6	227.5	160.3	5.0
CPI, 2001=100	100.0	101.1	105.9	113.3	113.9	117.2	121.9		

Source: MFE.
Notes:
1/ Annual average.
2/ Changes between 2003 and 2007.
Notes: Data presented in the table are based on information used by MFE for planning central government expenditure in the general education sector. For 2001, 2002, 2003, 2005 and 2006 - total recurrent expenditure corresponds to the approved annual budgets for the respective years. For 2004 and 2007 - draft budget information of corresponding years is used for total recurrent expenditure estimate. Line item breakdown of total recurrent expenditure is done by MFE for planning purposes only, and it is not obligatory for schools to follow.

2003 to 13.9 in 2006 and the average teaching load increased from 18 to 22 hours per week.[28] The considerable reduction in staff positions allowed the government to increase nominal wages and salaries for teachers by 381 percent in real terms between 2001 and 2007, and for administrative staff by 258 percent and for support staff by 160 percent between 2003 and 2007. More importantly, due to the steady increase in the overall education budget, the per student budget (excluding capital expenditure) increased from AMD 29,600 (US$53) in 2001 to AMD 106,700 (US$305) in 2007.[29]

A comparison of these indicators between PCF-participating, non-participating and protected schools confirms the effectiveness of the new funding scheme in terms of improving the efficiency of the system. A comparison of the school size, as presented in Table 2.6 suggests that on average relatively bigger schools joined the PCF program first. Naturally, the student-teacher ratios for the PCF-participating schools were all higher than for both the PCF non-participating schools and the protected schools, and per student budgets were lower for the more efficient PCF-participating schools than the others. It should be noted, however, that PCF-participating schools succeeded in gradually increasing the student-teacher ratio, even when all non-protected schools joined the PCF by 2006. The student-teacher ratio dropped again in 2007 when all protected schools were included, but it was still higher than in 2001.

Internal efficiency gains at the school level were also largely achieved. An examination of class sizes of all schools in the Kotayk and Vayots Dzor regions in 2006 suggests that the general education system in Armenia achieved substantial internal efficiency gains without classes becoming overcrowded. Very little room is left for more efficiency at the school level. For instance, in Vayots Dzor, all of the 51 schools have merged classes up to the maximum level and 18 schools offer multi-grade classes. In Kotayk, only 6 out of 101 schools could still merge some classes, and 16 schools already offer multi-grade classes in 2006.

While there is little room left for further efficiency gains at the school level, the government's policies did not lead to more efficiency at the regional level. Despite the substantial reduction in the number of students and teachers, the total number of schools declined very little, from 1,389 in 2000 to 1,362 in 2007. Most of this decline was the result of school consolidation in urban areas between 2003 and 2005. The proportion of small schools with fewer than 300 students actually increased from 47 percent in 2001 to 55 percent in 2005, as shown in Table 2.7. These are not surprising outcomes for three reasons. First, it was a strategic decision of the government to protect small schools in remote and border areas from the application of the PCF formula, providing them with little, if any, incentive to merge with schools in their neighboring settlements. Second, regions have neither the incentive nor the tools to promote school consolidation because they had, as deconcentrated offices of MOES, no authority to reallocate budgets between schools, or budget to construct additional classrooms and arrange transportation programs for students and teachers. Third, MOES and the regions have yet to improve its analytical capacities to provide evidence-based performance information of schools for parents, so that the latter can make rational school selection decisions, which would drive bottom-up school rationalization.

It is important to note that the government of Armenia planned to limit protections of the small schools only at the primary and lower secondary levels but not at the upper secondary level. To make the GSE school network more efficient, the government

Table 2.6. Key Statistics of General Education Schools: 2001-2007: PCF, Protected and Non-PCF Schools

	2001	2002	2003	2004	2005	2006	2007
A. General education schools (total)							
Number of schools	1,389	1,391	1,392	1,359	1,354	1,362	1,362
Number of classes (annual average)	27,059	25,861	24,332	22,016	21,365	20,878	20,494
Number of students (annual average)	560,637	533,398	513,621	493,433	477,011	464,063	446,140
Number of staff positions	77,536	75,680	72,247	62,316	56,218	53,880	50,974
Teachers	48,666	47,280	47,411	37,338	34,204	33,496	31,765
Non-teaching staff	28,870	28,401	24,836	24,978	22,015	20,384	19,209
Recurrent budgets (AMD mils.)	**16,575**	**17,330**	**19,121**	**25,167**	**34,925**	**40,784**	**47,599**
Memo:							
Avg. school size: students per school	404	383	369	363	352	341	328
Avg. school size: classes per school	19.5	18.6	17.5	16.2	15.8	15.3	15.0
Avg. class size: pupils per class	20.7	20.6	21.1	22.4	22.3	22.2	21.8
Pupil-teacher ratio	11.5	11.3	10.8	13.2	13.9	13.9	14.0
Per student budgets (AMD '000)	29.6	32.5	37.2	51.0	73.2	87.9	106.7
		9.9	14.6	37.0	43.6	20.0	21.4
B. PCF participating schools							
Number of schools	200	301	506	791	1,024	963	1,362
Number of classes (annual average)	4,411	6,890	10,159	15,368	18,320	17,246	20,494
Number of students (annual average)	98,213	157,371	231,563	374,900	438,847	417,758	446,140
Number of staff positions	12,651	20,185	30,885	43,022	48,196	44,255	50,974
Teachers	8,104	12,776	20,349	26,033	29,618	27,483	31,765
Non-teaching staff	4,547	7,409	10,535	16,988	18,578	16,772	19,209
Recurrent budgets (AMD mils.)	**2,667**	**4,635**	**8,000**	**17,315**	**29,943**	**33,393**	**47,599**
Memo:							
Avg. school size: students per school	491	523	458	474	429	434	328
Avg. school size: classes per school	22.1	22.9	20.1	19.4	17.9	17.9	15.0
Avg. class size: pupils per class	22.3	22.8	22.8	24.4	24.0	24.2	21.8
Pupil-teacher ratio	12.1	12.3	11.4	14.4	14.8	15.2	14.0
Per student budgets (AMD '000)	27.2	29.5	34.5	46.2	68.2	79.9	106.7
C. Protected schools							
Number of schools				110	217	330	399
Number of classes (annual average)				1,059	2,009	3,045	3,631
Number of students (annual average)				13,268	25,735	38,164	46,305
Number of staff positions				3,080	5,863	8,022	9,625
Teachers				2,008	3,432	4,585	6,013
Non-teaching staff				1,072	2,430	3,436	3,612
Recurrent budgets (AMD mils.)				**860**	**2,331**	**4,981**	**7,391**
Memo:							
Avg. school size: students per school				121	119	116	116
Avg. school size: classes per school				9.6	9.3	9.2	9.1
Avg. class size: pupils per class				12.5	12.8	12.5	12.8
Pupil-teacher ratio				6.6	7.5	8.3	7.7
Per student budgets (AMD '000)				64.8	90.6	130.5	159.6
D. Other Non-PCF schools							
Number of schools	1,189	1,090	776	351			
Number of classes (annual average)	22,648	18,971	13,114	4,639			
Number of students (annual average)	462,424	376,027	268,790	92,799			
Number of staff positions	64,885	55,496	38,283	13,431			
Teachers	40,562	34,504	25,054	7,872			
Non-teaching staff	24,323	20,992	13,229	5,559			
Recurrent budgets (AMD mils.)	**13,908**	**12,695**	**10,261**	**5,521**			
Memo:							
Avg. school size: students per school	389	345	346	264			
Avg. school size: classes per school	19.0	17.4	16.9	13.2			
Avg. class size: pupils per class	20.4	19.8	20.5	20.0			
Pupil-teacher ratio	11.4	10.9	10.7	11.8			
Per student budgets (AMD '000)	30.1	33.8	38.2	59.5			

Source: MFE and author's calculations.

Note: There are minor discrepancies in the number of PCF participating and non-participating schools and protected schools between Table 2.2 and Table 2.5, but they do not change the overall picture of how the PCF scheme was expanded nationwide.

Table 2.7. Distribution of General Education Schools by Size, 2001 and 2006

	2001		2006	
	No. of schools	Percent of Total Schools	No. of schools	Percent of Total Schools
Below 100	286	19.8	320	22.4
101-300	393	27.2	471	33.0
301-500	271	18.8	297	20.8
501-700	235	16.3	206	14.4
Above 701	260	18.0	133	9.3
Total	1,444	100.0	1,427	100.0

Sources: MOES for 2001; Harutyunyan and Davtyan (2006) for 2006.

planned to reduce, in phases, the number of GSE schools offering upper secondary education (grades 10-11) from over 1,100 today to 350 or fewer.[30] In early 2007, an MOES Working Group completed a draft strategy paper on high school reforms and consolidation and developed a draft school mapping for the consolidated high school (grades 10-11/12 only) network for each region.[31] As a tactic, MOES started presenting the proposed reforms to regions, schools and the education community as a *quality-oriented* program to promote a better teaching and learning environment for students and teachers rather than as an *efficiency-oriented* program, even though, from the ministry's perspective, this was also an important objective of the reform. Facing popular resistance among parents and school staff to close the upper secondary section in rural schools, the government decided to keep about 700 of the general secondary schools with upper secondary section and established only 150 high schools. Pilot projects started in September 2008.[32] Unfortunately, the economic crisis in 2009 resulted in a slowing down of the reform due to severe budget cuts, but the reform is expected to continue at a slightly slower schedule.

2.5.2. Equity

The introduction of the PCF scheme for financing education in Armenia does not seem to have improved equity much compared to the system that preceded it. And this is valid both for vertical equity and for horizontal equity considerations. In terms of *vertical equity*,[33] the funding formula never included adjustments or special weights for addressing the higher cost of educating disadvantaged populations (e.g. children from low socio-economic background) or ethnic minorities. Special education needs are not included in the formula either, but are taken into account by funding from outside the formula. In terms of *horizontal equity*, while the formula does include geographical and small school coefficients, anecdotal evidence points out to these adjustments to being insufficient. In fact, there is a widely shared view among government officials as well as school principals that schools with 300-500 students have suffered most under the current PCF mechanism. Their argument may be explained as follows. The maximum class size is defined as 35 for primary and lower secondary education (grades 1-8) and 25 for secondary education (grades 9-10).[34] In theory, secondary schools with 330 students (35 students x 8 classes plus 25 students x 2 classes)—or a multiple of 330—in total are the most efficient in terms of class size, but schools with only one class per grade cannot be cost-effective due to the low economies of scale, for example, for financing part-time subject teachers. Schools with just above 330 students are also inefficient because they have two small parallel classes per grade. In sum, schools with less than 400-500 students would be considered disadvantaged if there were no remedial measures. However, most small schools were originally 'protected' from the PCF mechanism (403 protected schools as of 2006). If not protected, schools with less than 300 students would have been allocated a relatively high per student budget, as shown in Figure 2.2 above.

Detailed school budget data for the Kotayk Region seem to support the arguments above in regards to horizontal equity. Figure 2.3 and Figure 2.4 compare (i) the estimated 'input-based' (reflecting the number of teachers and other recurrent items required according to the norms) budget allocations, (ii) formula-based budget allocations, (iii) actual budgets that the region allocated to schools, and (iv) actual expenditures that schools incurred on—including own revenues—for all of the 100 schools in the region of Kotayk in 2006.[35] On the one hand, all schools except two with less than 100 students received budget as needed above the formula-based allocations and most schools with 200-350 students received formula-based allocations which were more than the norm-based allocations. On the other hand, most schools with 350-500 students received formula-based allocations that were lower than the norm-based allocations, suggesting that the formula was in practice disadvantageous to this particular group of schools. In short, the assessment of the horizontal equity of the formula by government officials and school principals—disadvantageous for the middle-size schools—seems reasonably accurate. The Kotayk data also suggests that by applying the formula with little adjustment at the regional level, schools of the same size seem to have been treated quite equally.

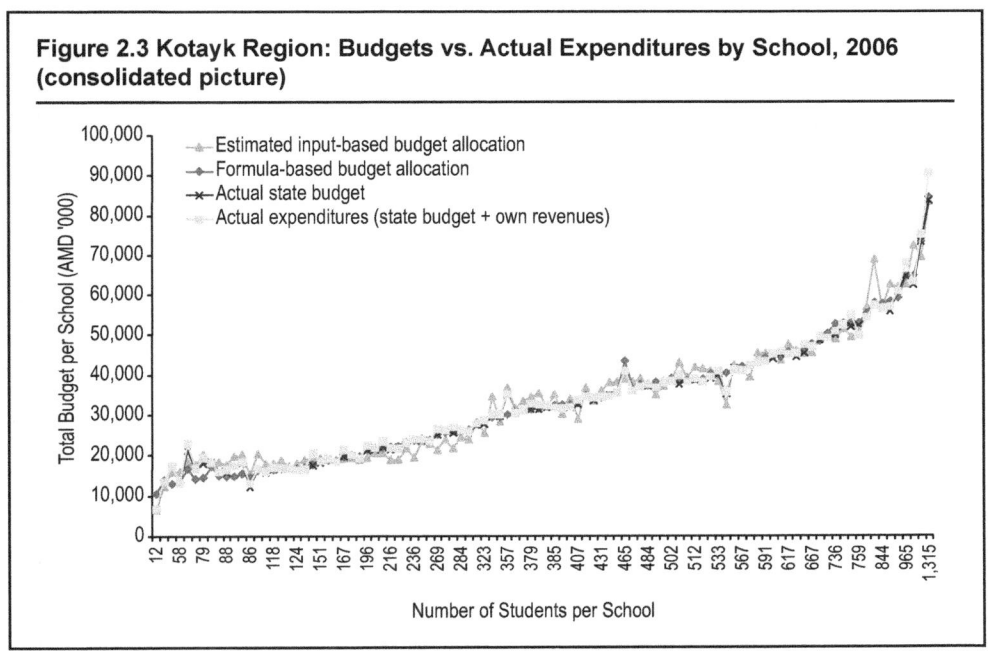

Figure 2.3 Kotayk Region: Budgets vs. Actual Expenditures by School, 2006 (consolidated picture)

Source: MFE for the norm-based allocations, Kotayk for the actual allocations and expenditures, and author's calculations for the formula-based allocations.

24 World Bank Study

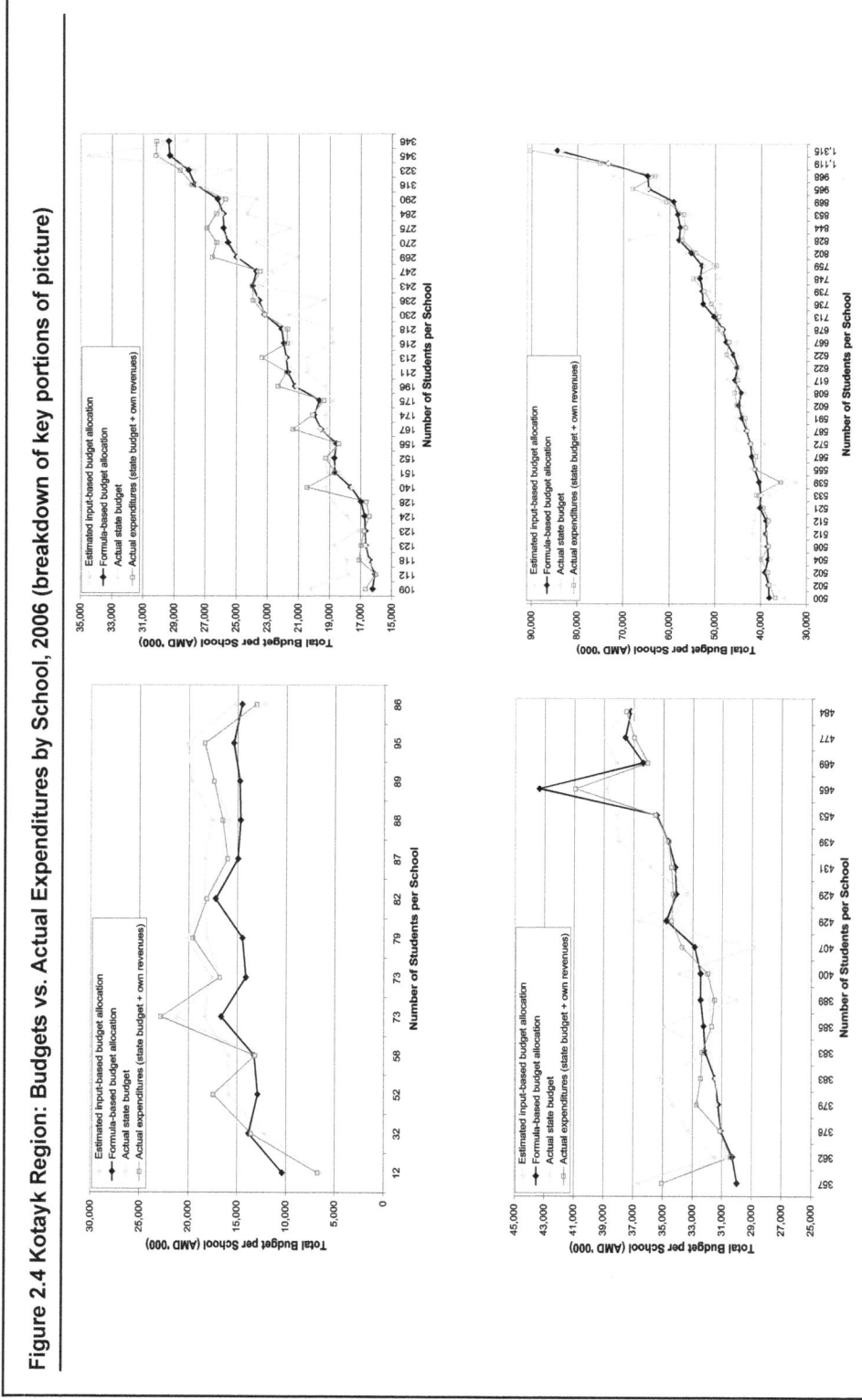

Figure 2.4 Kotayk Region: Budgets vs. Actual Expenditures by School, 2006 (breakdown of key portions of picture)

Source: MFE for the norm-based allocations, Kotayk for the actual allocations and expenditures, and author's calculations for the formula-based allocations.

2.5.3. Transparency and Accountability

The introduction of the PCF mechanism, accompanied by more school autonomy in financial management (see sub-section below), made the budget allocation and execution more transparent than in the previous system. Yet, despite the significant improvement in transparency, negotiation-based budget allocations still remain in some cases, which has allowed some degree of inefficiency by schools that probably have no legitimate excuse to continue having undersized classes. For instance, a school director in the Vayots Dzor region claimed that since the introduction of the PCF mechanism, her school had received insufficient budget to pay salaries for teachers and other staff because the formula was wrong. Luckily for her school, the director had somehow managed to get additional funding from the regional office. According to a regional official, however, the truth of the matter was that the school had lacked budget because it had too many non-teaching staff. This kind of non-transparent treatment of preferred schools is undesirable because it not only hinders efficiency gains but also undermines the legitimacy of the PCF mechanism as a whole.

The accountability mechanism at the regional level, in the meantime, remains still weak. The regional financial department quarterly collects financial reports and expenditure data from schools but it is not responsible for financial auditing. Schools are internally audited by MFE only every three years, and there is no external auditing. In general, it seems that regions are more careful for budget approval, but less so for monitoring and evaluation of expenditures. In Kotayk, officials assume that schools spend their budgets according to the approved budget and would seek further approval from the region for any reallocations.

2.5.4. Other Key Areas

2.5.4.1. SCHOOL AUTONOMY

Under the new PCF system, schools were given considerable financial autonomy on paper, but in reality, most schools did not fully exercise their financial autonomy. Even today, each school director drafts a budget plan based on a budget form provided by the MFE through the region, discusses it with the school board for its approval, and then submits it to the region for its final approval. Schools request reallocations in August, before the beginning of a new school year (September). While schools are required by various laws and regulations to meet various standards such as teaching hours according to the curriculum, hygiene and safety standards and labor conditions, schools are otherwise allowed to determine how to allocate and reallocate between budget lines, how many teachers and non-teaching staff to hire, and how much to pay for them above the minimum wage. In reality, however, when schools prepare and execute their budgets, most of them still follow indicative norms on staffing, even if they are non-obligatory (for instance, one cleaning staff per a certain number of square meters).

Schools had always adopted the same nationwide salary scale for teachers and non-teaching staff until 2006, but this practice changed in 2007; different regions and schools now pay different amount of salaries. The government has announced every year an indicative percentage increase for teachers, administrators, and support staff, compared to the previous years, as shown in Table 2.8.[36] School directors followed these indicative increases strictly until 2006. In 2007, however, when the government used a 27 percent increase in teachers' and administrators' salaries for budgeting purposes, different municipalities and schools responded to the government's guidance differently for the first time.

Table 2.8 Indicative Average Monthly Salaries (incl. Benefits), in AMD

	2000 Actual	2001 Actual	2002 Actual	2003 Actual	2004 Actual	2005 Actual	2006 Actual	2007 Budget	2008 Budget	2009 Budget	2010 Budget
FT teachers[1]	12,335	12,609	15,388	18,195	30,589	50,551	58,307	73,999	89,607	116,253	116,576
Increase (%)		2.2	22.0	18.2	68.1	65.3	15.3	26.9	21.1	30.0	0.3
Administrators[2]	7,852	7,852	7,852	18,470	31,317	51,762	60,092	76,295	136,012	176,143	176,143
Increase (%)		0	0	135.2	69.6	65.3	16.1	27.0	82.2	29.5	0
Support staff	6,932	6,932	7,979	7,718	13,517	21,181	21,185	23,131	25,436	36,563	30,525
Increase (%)		0	15.1	-3.3	75.1	56.7	0.0	9.2	9.97	43.7	-16.5
Memo											
Monthly GDP per capita[2]	27,942	31,966	37,097	44,244	51,928	60,982	68,744	85,417	96,634	83,870	93,880
FT teacher salary / GDP per capita ratio	0.4	0.4	0.4	0.4	0.6	0.8	0.8	0.87	0.92	1.39	1.24
No. of FT teachers	—	—	47,465	46,701	37,522	34,372	33,671	31,926	29,737	28,720	27,804
Decrease (%)				-1.6	-19.7	-8.4	-2.0	-5.2	-6.9	-3.4	-3.2

Source: MFE.
[1] FT refers to full-time.
[2] The average salary for school administrators had been very low compared to that for teachers until 2002 (64 percent of teachers in 2000 and 51 percent in 2002) because they were paid only according to the teaching load which was generally not full. The Poverty Reduction Strategy Paper (PRSP) aimed to substantially increase the average salary rates of administrative and support staff as well. In 2003, the average salary level for administrators was raised slightly above (1.5 percent) that for teachers and 3 percent above in 2007.
[3] GDP per capita divided by 12.

Table 2.9 and Table 2.10 compare indicative monthly salary scales for school directors and teachers in Yerevan City and Kotayk. In both cases (and in all the other regions), the salaries for school directors and deputy directors were determined according to the school size, *i.e.*, the number of students—(i) below 640, (ii) 641-1,120 and (iii) above 1,120. With regards to teachers, the salary scale was categorized by qualification—(i) high school, (ii) college, and (iii) university—and years of experience—(i) up to 1 year, (ii) 1-15 years, and (iii) over 15 years. In Yerevan, the Mayor's Office instructed all schools to raise salaries for teachers, administrators and support staff by 19.6 percent. Even though the City does not have such legal authority to instruct schools, all schools followed the instruction and adopted the salary matrices provided by the City Office. Unlike in Yerevan, Kotayk authorities only advised, but did not instruct, schools to increase salaries by up to 27.0 percent, and all schools responded differently according to their financial capacities and management decisions. Among three schools visited in the region, the salary increase rate varied from 15 to 27 percent.[37]

The implication of these different responses between regions and between schools can be contentious. On the one hand, some schools in Yerevan City have complained about the city's control over teachers' salaries, and this issue has been raised in the Parliament, but no action had been taken to stop the city from influencing schools as the time of this study. It is unclear why schools in Yerevan were compelled to follow the Mayor's instruction despite its lack of legal authority. On the other hand, salary variations in Kotayk have caused dissatisfaction among teachers who received a below-aver-

Table 2.9. Indicative Average Monthly Salaries (incl. Benefits) for School Directors and Deputy Directors, in AMD

	2006			2007			Percent Change		
School category	3	2	1	3	2	1	3	2	1
Number of students	Below 640	641-1,120	Above 1,121	Below 640	641-1,120	Above 1,121	Below 640	641-1,120	Above 1,121
Yerevan City									
Director	55,880	56,470	57,620	66,810	67,520	68,890	19.6	19.6	19.6
Deputy Director	55,070	55,680	55,880	65,840	66,570	66,810	19.6	19.6	19.6
Kotayk Region									
Director	55,888	56,492	57,632	70,978	71,745	73,193	27.0	27.0	27.0
Deputy Director	55,084	55,686	55,888	69,956	70,722	70,978	27.0	27.0	27.0

Source: Yerevan City (through a school principal), Kotayk Region Financial Department.

Table 2.10. Indicative Average Monthly Salaries (incl. Benefits) for Teachers by Categories, in AMD

Years of experience	2006			2007			Percent Change		
Level of Education	1 year	1-15 years	Over 15 yrs	1 year	1-15 years	Over 15 yrs	1 year	1-15 years	Over 15 yrs
Yerevan City									
University	46,450	47,370	48,740	55,540	56,640	58,270	19.6	19.6	19.6
College	46,450	46,450	47,370	55,540	55,540	56,640	19.6	19.6	19.6
High school	44,130	44,130	45,000	52,760	52,760	53,800	19.6	19.6	19.6
Kotayk Region									
University	46,466	47,387	48,767	59,011	60,182	61,934	27.0	27.0	27.0
College	46,466	46,466	47,387	59,011	59,011	60,182	27.0	27.0	27.0
High school	44,142	44,142	45,018	56,061	56,061	57,173	27.0	27.0	27.0

Source: Yerevan City (through a school principal), Kotayk Region Financial Department.

age salary increase and anxiety among school directors. For instance, a school director of one of the largest schools in Kotayk claimed that the existing formula was unfair because he could afford only a lower salary increase for his teachers from his budget, even with a significant amount of parental contributions. The different responses in Yerevan and Kotayk raise a question as to what is the right balance between school autonomy and local and/or central government control over teachers' salaries. While the flexible salary scale at the school level is in accordance with the principle of school autonomy, it is unclear whether it is 'fair' to introduce a differentiated salary scale when the basis for such differentiations often has little to do with the performance of teachers and/or directors and when a group of small schools receive more generous per capita allocations through protective measures than others.

2.5.4.2. ACADEMIC EFFECTIVENESS

There is no data to examine whether or not the PCF mechanism has contributed to improving students' academic performance. Teachers and students' performance is monitored by the regional education departments according to the state educational standards for curriculum and teaching/learning methodologies. However, no data have been collected to examine whether the PCF mechanism has resulted in changes in student performance. For instance, the PCF mechanism encourages schools and class sizes to become bigger, and some schools might have become too big to be pedagogically effective. It is unknown, however, how the bigger class sizes driven by pursuing efficiency gains might have affected teaching and learning processes and contributed to improving or worsening the quality of education in the classroom. Hence, MOES is currently trying to figure out the optimal size of schools to reduce the potential negative impacts on students, and discourage schools to become too large by adjusting the formula.

The impact of multi-grade teaching is also unknown. Multi-grade teaching has been conducted to make the system more efficient, but not in a pedagogically appropriate way in many schools. Many teachers divide one lesson hour into two and spend one half for one grade and the other half for the other grade. Surprisingly, however, an education officer of Vayots Dzor, where more than 40 percent of 51 schools conduct multi-grade teaching, explained that despite the shortened lesson hours, because multi-grade classes are very small and students are getting close attention from the teacher, those students often perform even better than those in large classes in urban schools who receive full lesson hours. There is no data to prove his argument, but this is an area worth investigating in Armenia.

2.6. Conclusions

The analysis in this chapter illustrates that Armenia has achieved many of the policy objectives of introducing PCF, as stipulated in the Government Decree No. 377 and the Education Law in 1999, to date. Facing the severe financial constraints in the early to mid 1990s, the government had no choice but to give more financial autonomy to schools and make school financing more efficient, equitable, and transparent/accountable. By introducing PCF, Armenia achieved, to some extent, many of these objectives. The government has succeeded in increasing the average class size and reducing the number of teachers in the system dramatically. It has made budget allocations to schools more transparent with limited subjectivity compared to the previous input-based budget allocation mechanism without clear rules in staffing. Enhanced school autonomy in financial management has also encouraged schools to pursue internal efficiency and use their budgets more effectively according to their needs.

The Armenian PCF formula has been very simple since its introduction, which certainly has contributed to improvement of transparency in education financing, but might have been too crude to accommodate different needs of different types of schools and students. The government also chose to keep small schools in rural areas by excluding them from the application of the formula. The simple formula is easy to follow, but may be difficult to reach an 'equitable' solution for all schools. The current formula seems to put middle-size schools in a most disadvantageous position. Having recognized the weaknesses, the government considered to revise the formula with more factors to differentiate types of schools and students. However, it has so far preferred to keep the simple formula, and let regions to make minor adjustments rather than introducing a complex formula. The additional budget allocations at the regional level appear to be determined in a less transparent way.

Considerable efficiency gains have been made at the school level through class consolidation. Many small schools have introduced multi-grade classes, and there seems to be little room to merge classes. The class consolidation strategy has contributed to improve pupil-teacher ratios while the number of students kept declining. On the other hand, the school network rationalization at the regional level has not made much progress, except for a small number of school consolidations mainly in urban areas. The government is fully aware of the inefficiency in rural areas, but it is a deliberate government policy to maintain rural schools to assure access particularly at the basic education level. To make the school network more efficient, the government has started the high school reform, but due to pressures from rural communities, the rationalization plan is still limited. As the new high schools begin demonstrating themselves as a place for better opportunities for students, the government may be able to pursue further high school network rationalization.

Schools have started enjoying more decision-making power over budget planning and spending and human resource management, but financial autonomy is still limited. Not only the Treasury system, but also socio-economic pressures to keep redundant teachers and non-teaching staff have limited schools to exercise their financial autonomy. Also, participation of the school boards is often limited to approval of the budget, and the budget planning process may still be carried out by principals and a small number of teachers. Financial monitoring by the regional government is weak, and needs to be strengthened to improve accountability. Differentiated teacher salary scales adopted by different regions and schools are in line with the principle of school autonomy, but it raises a question in terms of fairness because the basis for such differentiations often has little to do with teachers' performance.

Finally, the considerable achievement in school rationalization through class consolidation and teacher redundancy has resulted in social dissatisfaction among those negatively affected by the achievements, including many teachers and non-teaching staff who were made redundant. An official of MOES explained that it was not because the PCF was the wrong mechanism, but because the government has failed to address these people's needs. This suggests that any education reform needs to be closely linked with social protection programs in order to be successfully implemented and accepted in the long run by all elements of society.

References

Harutyunyan, K. (2002), *First Project Final Report for the Education Financing and Management Reform Project*, project manuscript dated March 14, 2002, Yerevan.

Harutyunyan, K. and Davtyan, N. (2006), *Education in Armenia: The Information in the Booklet Concerns 2005-2006 School Year*, Yerevan, Edit Print.

Ministry of Education and Science (1997), *Strategy for Reform of the General Education System of the Republic of Armenia*.

Monk, D. (1990), *Educational Finance: An Economic Approach*, Mc-Graw Hill College.

Perkins, G. and Yemtsov, R. (2001), *Armenia: Restructuring to Sustain Universal General Education*, World Bank Technical Paper No. 498.

World Bank (1997), *Armenia Education Financing and Management Reform Project*, Staff Appraisal Report, Report No. 16474-AM. Washington, D.C.

World Bank (2001), *Report and Recommendation of the President of the International Development Association to the Executive Directors on a Proposed Fourth Structural Adjustment Credit in the Amount of SDR 38.4 Million (US$50.0 Million Equivalent) to the Republic of Armenia*, Report No. P-7430-AM. Washington, DC.

World Bank (2006), "Education Quality and Relevance Project, Mid-Term Review", Washington, DC: The World Bank.

World Bank (2008), *Armenia Public Expenditure Review Education Sector*, Washington, DC: The World Bank.

Notes

1. I would like to thank Aleksan Hovhannisyan (Education Specialist, World Bank Country Office at Yerevan) for conducting the fieldwork with me in June-July 2007, and Melik Gasparyan (Consultant) for kindly collecting financial and educational data. The team is also most grateful to the officers of the Ministry of Education and Science, the Ministry of Economy and Finance, the Yerevan City, the Kotayk *Marz* and the Vayots Dzor *Marz*, and the school directors for their generosity in sharing their valuable experience and providing us with statistical data. All mistakes, errors of interpretation and judgments made are my sole responsibility.

2. World Bank (1997).

3. The term General Secondary Education (GSE) is a literal translation from a Russian expression that prevailed from former Soviet times. GSE refers to both primary and secondary education. For purposes of consistency with the usage in Armenian, however, the remainder of this chapter will refer to GSE.

4. Perkins and Yemtsov (2001).

5. Between 1989 and 1995, the total population dropped by 5.5 percent from 3.45 million to 3.26 million, but it has been fairly constant since then (3.21 million in 2001 and 3.24 million in 2009). On the other hand, the average birth rate per 1,000 females at age 15-49 sharply dropped from 48.5 in 1995 to 31.7 in 2000, which started to recover throughout the 2000s up to 44.6 in 2008, which was still lower than the level in the early 1990s (Source: National Statistical Service, *Yearbooks*, various issues, http://www.armstat.am/en/?nid=45).

6. First, in the school year (SY) 2001/02, compulsory education was extended to nine years, and the first cohort under the new structure will complete grade 11 in SY 2011/12. As a result, there will be neither grade 10 nor grade 11 graduates in SY 2010/11. Second, in SY 2006/07, the new National Curriculum Framework based on a 12-year GSE cycle was introduced, consisting of primary education (grades 1-4), lower secondary education (grades 5-9) and high school education (grades 10-12). While a half (6.5-7 years old) of grade 1 cohort in SY 2006/07 will continue in the 11-year GSE system, the other half (6-6.5 years old) will be the first to complete the 12-year GSE cycle in SY 2017/18.

7. GDP per capita was US$1,981 in 2006.

8. World Bank (2008).

9. Harutyunyan and Davtyan (2006).

10. Ministry of Education and Science (1997).

11. *Hamainks* were established in 1992 after independence.

12. Source: Harutyunyan (2002) and an interview the author of this report held with the Director of the Project Implementation Unit for the pilot project.

13. No data is available to observe the gaps.

14. The imprecise naming of the variables in the formula caused a general misunderstanding of the principle of PCF when the scheme was first launched. This happened, to a large extent, due to the government having called fixed variable costs as 'maintenance costs', even though the former were not meant to embed just maintenance expenditures. This unfortunate misnomer generated some controversy among groups of schools: while large schools tended to complain that the formula favored small schools with extremely generous budgets for maintenance, small schools claimed that their per student unit cost was too low and that they were forced to reallocate the maintenance

budget to teacher salaries. Neither of the interpretations was indeed correct and probably some of these misinterpretations could have been avoided if the formula had been adjusted to allow for more differentiations, for instance, by school size.

15. World Bank (2001), p. 18.
16. Perkins and Yemtsov (2001).
17. The First Phase of the Education Sector Reform Program was supported by the World Bank-funded Education Quality and Relevance Project, which was approved in December of 2003 and succeeded the 1998-2003 Education Financing and Management Reform Project, referred above. In parallel, a set of conditionalities under a series of structural adjustment credits (SAC) and poverty reduction support credits (PRSC) facilitated the implementation of teacher redundancy across the country (five SACs between 1996 and 2003, and three PRSCs between 2004 and 2007).
18. NCOs are regulated under the *Law of the Republic of Armenia on Non-Commercial State Organizations dated on October 23, 2001*.
19. *Government Decree No. 773 on Approval of the List of the Republic of Armenia General Education Schools to be Financed Irrespective of the Number of the Pupils dated August 25, 2001.*
20. The government approved the protected schools according to the reporting from each *marz*. It is unclear how the number of protected schools could have increased so rapidly despite the fact that the criteria had not changed over time.
21. There was no defined rule (mechanism) for calculating the unit and fixed costs, and the government revised those parameters based on the budget envelope for the general education sector. In 2006, additional regression analysis was conducted to justify changes in formula parameters.
22. As stipulated in the *Government Decree No. 377* that 'The Republic of Armenia Ministry of Finance and Economy and the Republic of Armenia Ministry of Education and Science shall differentiate the annual amount per pupil by the formula of the general education institutions involved in the pilot project on the Republic of Armenia general education system reforms also for schools located in high mountainous areas and schools with specialized courses at the upper secondary level.'
23. Letter of Development Policy for the World Bank's Poverty Reduction Strategy Credit (PRSC) II (2006).
24. *Government Decree No. 1262-N dated August 24, 2006* on approving the procedure of calculation of expenditures of the state general education institutions, reallocations made in the expenditures of state general education institutions, and canceling the Decree No. 773 of the Government of the Republic of Armenia dated August 25, 2001. The decree also stipulated that these coefficients might be revised annually.
25. The fiscal year in Armenia starts in January, but MFE makes budgetary adjustments for schools in September to reflect changes in the number of students. MFE will use this opportunity to allow *marzes* to make necessary adjustments between schools, if they deemed necessary.
26. According to the latest curriculum for SY2007/08, the weekly lesson hours are as follows: (i) Primary (Grades 1-4): G1-20; G2-23; G3-26, G4-27; (ii) Basic (Grades 5-9): G5-31, G6-30, G7-34, G8-34, G9-36; (iii) Secondary (Grades 10-11): G10-36, G11-35.
27. The maximum class size is set at 35 for grades 1-8 and 25 for grades 9-10.
28. The full-time (FT) equivalent teaching load was 21 hours until it was reduced to 18 hours in 1996. Then, it was increased to 22 hours in January 2005 (World Bank, 2006). When out-of-class activities such as lesson preparation, marking, etc. are taken into account the teachers' workload may have increased up to 27 hours per week (Harutyunyan & Davtyan, 2006).
29. Using exchange rates at US$1 = AMD 555.1 in 2001 and US$1 = AMD 350 in 2007.
30. It was agreed in the mid-term review of the Education Quality and Relevance Project in October 2006 that the government would study scenarios for the consolidation of upper secondary schools and would conduct preparatory work in order to finalize the consolidation strategy and scale it up to the entire country, preceded by a pilot in two communities (rural/urban). This would set the foundations for further efficiency gains and quality improvement.
31. Under the Education Quality and Relevance Project, there were 52 school centers across the country, which offered teacher training programs. These school centers were selected in such a way that all teachers could reach one of them within one hour of travel. Hence, with a careful planning of catchment areas, the planned consolidation of high schools would not require board-

ing facilities. At the same time, the country needed to have a limited number of specialized high schools, for instance, for arts and talented students, which were likely to require boarding facilities.

32. Aide Memoire for the Supervision Mission for the Education Quality and Relevance Project, April 2007.

33. Vertical equity is the 'unequal treatment of unequals' (Monk, 1990). In other words, it refers in particular to providing extra funding to those students with greater learning needs who therefore require more resources to support their learning.

34. General education is currently being gradually changed to nine years of compulsory education and three years of higher secondary education (grades 10-12) (see *footnote* 6 for details), which is not taken into account here.

35. The first series is used by the MFE for a budget estimation purpose and indicates how much budget each school would receive if it got budgets allocated on the basis of norms such as the number of classes and teachers. The second series is calculated according to the formula, even for small protected schools. The third and fourth are self-explanatory.

36. It should be noted, however, that these are indicative figures to estimate the total education budget, and are not necessarily the actual average monthly salary. For instance, an average salary for teachers in 2000 was AMD 8,000.

37. It was 15, 20 and 27 percent, respectively. One of the principals mentioned that the increase was 14 percent in her neighboring school. The lowest end in the *marz* may have been below 14 percent, although the highest end was probably 27 percent.

CHAPTER 3

Per Capita Financing of Education in Estonia

Rosalind Levačić[1]

3.1. Introduction

Estonia is a small country of 1.34 million people by the Baltic Sea and bordering Russia. It first gained independence as nation in 1918 but was incorporated into the USSR after World War II. It regained its independence in 1991. Since then Estonia has experienced rapid political and economic change. The first post-independence government was liberal, pro-market and keen to foster decentralization: it revived the pre-war municipalities as units of local government (Põllumäe 2002).[2] For its size Estonia has a large number of municipalities—227 in 2007. Although almost 70 percent of the population live in urban municipalities, over eighty percent of local governments are rural. Around half of the municipalities have less than 2000 residents, with the smallest in 2006 having only 70 residents. In contrast, the average size of an urban municipality is just over 26,000, with the largest–Tallinn–having a population of 396,000.

The structure of local government and the consequent political clout of the rural areas is important for education because the Basic Schools and Upper Secondary Schools (BSUSS) Act (Estonian State Chancellery 1993) assigned responsibility for general education to local governments.[3] The ownership of the vast majority of public schools was transferred to municipalities which began to increase the number of schools despite the rapid fall in the school age population. This Act also provided for municipality schools to have budgets and to be funded from both municipal and state revenues. In 1994 a first attempt was made to introduce per capita funding of general education, though a genuine per capita formula was only implemented in 1998. This was relatively simple as it contained 6 and later 8 coefficients related to municipal characteristics. As the school population continued to decline so did class and school sizes in rural areas, leading to complaints that rural schools were not sufficiently protected by the funding regime. Consequently, in 2008, the formula was drastically revised and its per capita element was disapplied to small schools in small rural municipalities which were funded instead on the number of classes they were deemed to need. The timeline for key developments in the Estonian school system is shown in Table 3.1.

As the chapter will demonstrate, Estonia provides an interesting case-study of how political pressures for maintaining small rural schools can weaken the efficiency incentives of a school funding formula. Section 3.2 of this chapter gives the historical background to the Estonian general education system. The design and implementation of the funding formula are examined in sections 3.3 and 3.4. Section 3.3.3 describes the development and evolution of school funding formula from 1994 to 2008. The municipal funding of schools is discussed in section 3.4.1, focusing on the school funding formula developed by Tallinn in section 3.4.2. Sections 3.5.1, 3.5.2 and 3.5.3 respectively assess the impact of the previous formula (1998-2007) and new formula on efficiency, equity and transparency and accountability, while section 3.6 concludes with key findings.

Table 3.1. Summary of Key Events in Estonian General Education: 1989 to 2008

1989	Local-self government re-established and local democratic elections held. Over 240 municipalities created. Counties stayed as deconcentrated units of central government ministries.
1991	Estonia left the Union of Soviet Socialist Republics (USSR) and returned to its pre World War II status as an independent state.
1993	First Basic Schools and Upper Secondary Schools Act assigned responsibility for basic and upper secondary education (not vocational) to municipalities and provided for schools being funded from municipal and state budgets. State budget covers teaching costs and the municipal contribution other costs.
1994-97	A rough and ready per student division of each county's education budgets passed on to municipal schools
1998	A genuine per student (per capita) funding formula introduced, initially with 6 weights for different types of municipality differentiated by urban/rural, size and island location. Funding continued to be channeled to counties which directly funded schools in the traditional way.
2001	Ministry of Finance began to pay state education grant directly to municipalities which now felt full force of per capita funding.
2003	State grant extended to cover extra-curricular activities
2005	Capital expenditure allocations included in the state grant for education.
2007	Grant for workbooks included
2008	A new, more complex funding formula introduced after four years deliberation. Per student allocation based on a calculation of teaching costs; small schools in municipalities with fewer than 1600 students protected by additional allocations so that they are funded to organize smaller classes than assumed for the standard per student amount.

3.2. Background

The costs of school provision in Estonia in the last two decades were heavily influenced by two structural features of the population. The first was the drastic decline in the number of school children which has imposed severe adjustment problems for the school network. The school age population peaked at 218,000 in 1997/98, falling 25 percent by 2006/7.[4] Another important feature of Estonia is that only 69 percent of the population is ethnic Estonian. Russians[5] represent 26 percent, and a large number of non-Estonian ethnic groups make up the remaining five percent (Estonian Ministry of Foreign Affairs 2006). The main language of instruction in a municipal school is decided by the local council.[6] The requirement to provide teaching in minority languages (mainly Russian) leads to smaller school and classes and hence higher per pupil costs than if only a single language of instruction were used.

The Estonian education system (reviewed by OECD (2001)) provides 9 years of compulsory eduction, starting at the age of 7, with grades 10 to 12 being optional. There are three types of public schools: primary schools catering to grades 1 to 6, basic schools for grades 1 to 9 and secondary schools, some of which are called gymnasiums, educating pupils from grades 1 to 12. In 2006 there were 85 primary schools, 264 basic schools and 236 secondary schools. Vocational schools also educate students in grades 10 to 12; their funding, however, is not considered in this chapter. There is a small private sector of around 30 schools, which has been functioning since independence. The BSUSS Act specifies that education provision by municipalities includes day time schooling, evening adult classes and distance education. General education for grades 1 to 12–including vocational–must be provided free of charge.

Since independence there has been a series of curriculum reforms. The latest version of the national curriculum began implementation in 2002. Current curriculum reform includes the gradual introduction of more subjects in grades 10 to 12 taught in Estonian in Russian medium schools[7] so as to better prepare ethnic Russian students for entry into the labor market and higher education in Estonia. A further reform was a new state-wide system of external assessment. Pupils are assessed at the end of grade 9 in three subjects. Two must be the mother tongue and mathematics, which are externally assessed. At the end of grade 12 there is a further national assessment in at least five subjects. The only compulsory subject since 2007 is the mother tongue: at least three of the subjects must be national examinations and the other two can be either school or national exams. Results in the national examinations are used for selecting students for entry into higher education institutions.

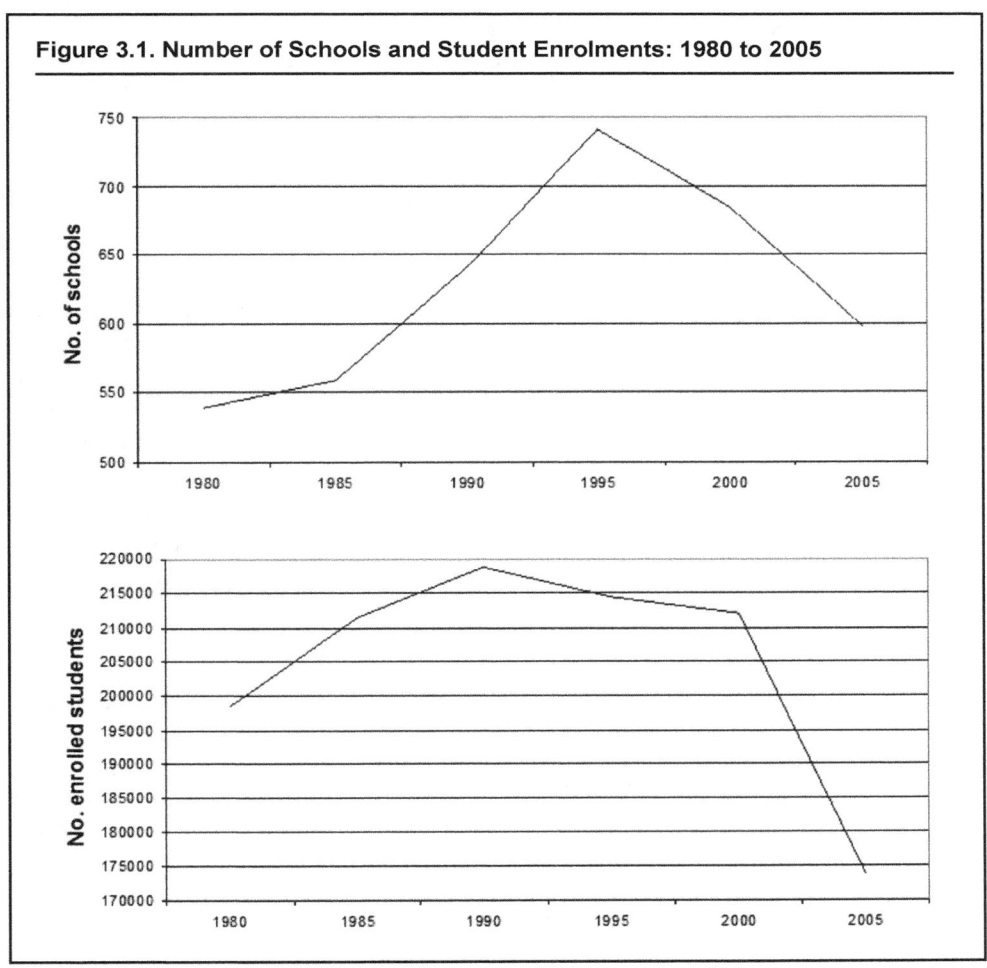

Figure 3.1. Number of Schools and Student Enrolments: 1980 to 2005

Source: National Statistical Office.

Since 1993/4 the most general education is provided in municipality administered schools. Exceptions are a a small group of 64 state' schools, half of which were special schools, under which remained under central government control, which also administers most of the vocational schools.[8] A municipality applies for an education license to the Ministry of Education and Research (MER) in order to establish a school, which has to conform to the national curriculum and be at least of minimum size as specified in the Act. The municipality defines a catchment area for each school for grades 1 to 9, though not all schools have catchment areas. Parents can choose an out-of-catchment school for their child if there is a vacant slot. Entry at grade 1 to schools that are perceived by parents to be of high quality and that do not have catchment areas is competitive since these schools can select students by oral or written examination. The BSUSS Act states that local governments shall allow children with special needs to attend their catchment area school, and if the local school cannot provide for their needs they have the right to attend the nearest suitable school.

On acquiring their responsibilities for education, the new municipalities were keen to open schools, which they were able to do with little capital expenditure by bringing empty pre-World War II school buildings back into use. The rise in the number of schools in the 1990s compared with falling student numbers is shown in Figure 3.1. Given the relative ease of opening small schools in old school buildings, the growth in schools was concentrated in primary schools, which increased from 149 to 190 from 1991 to 1993 and consist of grades 1 to 6.

3.3. The Design of the Funding Formula

3.3.1. The Per Student Funding Formula for General Education

The financing of general education has also undergone considerable reform, in particular the introduction of a per student grant for education for municipalities. This section of the chapter outlines the introduction of the national per student funding formula, examines the formula which used from 1998 to 2007 and then its replacement in 2008. This change represents a move away from per student funding as the new formula ensures that schools in small municipalities are funded a sufficient amount to cover the teaching costs of the number of classes that according to the formula they need. The number of classes needed according to the formula depends on the number of students in a grade and on the maximum permitted class size, which the government in 2008 reduced to 24 pupils in grades 1 to 9. A major reason for changing the formula was to make it easier for municipalities to afford the maintenance of small rural basic schools.

3.3.2. Introduction to Formula Funding

To finance the local services for which they are responsible, municipalities—local governments—receive a share of state income tax, have their own local taxes and in addition receive grants from the state. The requirement for the state to provide grants to owners of schools—both municipal and private—toward defraying the costs of educational provision was set out in the BSUSS Act passed in 1993. Chapter 8 of the Act states that:

1. a school shall have its own budget and may have its own bank account;
2. the school budget revenue comprises allocations from the municipality budget and the state budget, revenue from foundations, donations and income received from extracurricular activities provided for in the statutes of the school;

3. the expenses of a municipal school shall be covered by the municipality as the owner;
4. grants for education, based on the number of students, shall be allocated to local governments from the state budget each year in accordance with the State Budget Act in order to cover expenses related to the remuneration of teachers, related social taxes, in-service training of teachers of municipal schools and the purchase of textbooks;[9]
5. the draft budget of a municipal school shall be approved by the Board of Trustees of the municipal school and by the local government council.

Private schools are also entitled to the same per student current funding as the municipal schools in the municipality in which they are located. This is regulated under the Private Schools Act.

The BSUSS Act therefore required a fundamental change in how the newly assigned municipal schools were to be funded. Under the soviet system, the Ministry of Education channeled both revenue and capital funding for education to the 15 non-elected regional governments, known as counties. The counties then distributed revenue funding to schools using a set of norms for calculating how many teachers were required to teach a given number of students in a grade as determined by regulations regarding the number of lessons per subject per grade in the national curriculum. Further norms were used to allocate the school's complementary staff posts (i.e. a range of posts from directors, laboratory assistants to cleaners) depending on the number of classes or number of students within specified ranges. Per student funding was intended to replace the 'soviet era system of norms' for the determination of funding to support municipal education spending.

The government in power in 1993 was led by politicians of a neo-liberal persuasion, to whom per student funding of general education appealed for a number of reasons. It wanted to promote competition both between public schools and between public schools and private schools, whose growth would be encouraged by a per student state subsidy. There was, in addition, a desire to promote internal efficiency by inducing municipalities to reduce the number of schools, which had burgeoned since 1991, despite a stable or sharply decreasing–from 1998 onward–number of students of compulsory school age. From a peak of 218,000 in 1998, student numbers had plummeted to around 174,000 in 2005–a 20 percent reduction. As most of the newly opened schools were primary and basic schools, these types of school were particularly severely affected–numbers of children in grade 1 fell from 22,000 in 1995 to just over 12,000 in 2004 at which level it stabilized, though total enrolment will continue to decline till at least 2011. Thus, the fact that student numbers would continue to decline was, and remains, a vital consideration in designing the method of school funding.

The first attempt at per student funding was made in 1994.[10] In order to allocate the state budget contribution to general education, the Ministry of Education and Research (MER) took the total budget for general education for each county, which was still determined historically as in Soviet times, and divided it by the number of students in the county to derive the per student amount per county. Thus, there were 15 per student amounts–one for each county. MER channeled the money to the counties, which continued to distribute resources to schools using the Soviet era norms. This system was, of course, only per student in name as nothing had really changed.

In 1995 a new minister of education decided that a genuine per student funding system should be devised. A working group of around eight people, consisting of officials from the Ministries of Education and Research (MER) and Finance (MoF), and municipal representatives, was set up to work out a formula, which was considered by a bigger steering group of around 60 representing counties, municipalities, the teacher unions and school level representatives. After much discussion, a formula was devised for implementation in 1997 but due to a change in government the formula was not implemented until September 1998. The 1998 formula had six coefficients of differing value, which depended on whether the municipality was urban or rural and also on its size. Later two more coefficients were added.

The coefficients were derived from analyzing the actual expenditures of municipalities and not from an activity-led costing model of schools (Abu-Duhou 1999), which determines what schools of different sizes need to spend on teaching and non-teaching staff and other non-staff items. In part, this was because of the desire to abandon 'old-thinking' and move away from Soviet era norms. It was also simpler to base the formula on actual per student costs of municipalities and the ratios of these unit costs when comparing different types of local governments. The formula was designed so that a municipality with a coefficient of 1 could fund the teaching costs of a student-teacher ratio of 15. Until 2000, the funding went from MER to the education departments of the counties, rather than directly to municipalities. Each county received the total allocations by formula for the municipalities within its territory and continued in the main to distribute this funding to the schools using the Soviet era norms for working out teaching costs. However, since 2001 MoF has sent the funding directly to the municipalities, who at this point became fully exposed to the link between student numbers and funding and took full responsibility for determining their schools' budgets, constrained by the need to meet their legal obligations.

The municipal grant for education is not a general purpose grant–it must be spent on education. Central government makes explicit which types of expenditures the grant for general education is intended to support. Initially, the formula allocated money for teacher salaries—including social taxes—and textbooks. In 2003 small grants for academic subjects and extracurricular activities were added. A per student allocation for capital expenditure—investments—was introduced in 2005, and in 2007 a grant for workbooks was included as well. In addition, municipalities received a contribution from the state budget for providing school lunches as required by law for students in grades 1 to 9. Municipalities are expected to pay for school operational costs and non-teaching staff entirely out of their own budgets. Apart from the subsidy for the ingredients of school lunches, municipalities are not obliged to spend the sub-grants, into which total education grant is subdivided, in exactly the same amounts as they are calculated by the formula for distribution purposes.

The amounts allocated for each type of sub-grant within the general education grant for municipal and private schools are shown in Table 3.2. State schools are not funded by the formula but by MER from its own budget. These schools are not considered in this chapter, as they are not funded by formula: nor is the grant for providing school lunches included in Table 3.2. A small part of the state grant to municipalities for general education is not allocated by formula. A small percentage is held back, which represented two and a half percent in 2007. Municipalities can apply for additional funding in the course of the financial year. They need to make their case with respect to defined criteria

Table 3.2 General Education Grant: 2003 to 2007

General Education Grant ('000s Estonian kroons*)	2003	2004	2005	2006	2007
TOTAL	1,727,120	1,917,620	2,378,129	2,468,088	2,854,522
Distributed	1,658,068	1,891,999	2,333,844	2,401,598	2,781,928
- Regular per student funding	1,514,405	1,712,407	1,881,031	1,928,242	2,193,720
- Students with special educational needs per student funding	82,993	104,952	138,963	171,415	216,825
- Textbooks**	53,250	51,220	49,001	46,512	46,708
- Workbooks**					57,098
Counseling Committees***		8,000	8,000	6,000	6,000
Cultural and sports events for young people up to age 26		8,000	8,000	8,000	8,000
Kindergarten teacher in-service training	7,420	7,420	8,437	11,080	13,105
- Investments	0	0	240,412	230,348	240,471
Reserves	69,052	25,621	44,285	66,490	72,594
Per student for regular general education students					
Salaries funding per student	7,805	9,171	10,547	11,390	13,670
Textbook funding per student	265	265	265	265	282
Workbook funding per student	0	0	0	0	458
Investments per student	0	0	1,270	1,270	1,385
Number of students in local government and private schools					
Number of students including evening classes, prisons and distance education	202,549	194,973	186,737	177,071	167,171

Source: Ministry of Finance.
* Henceforth, we will refer to this currency as EEK. In June 2007 the exchange rate was 1.56 EEK to 1 Euro. Inflation in Estonia has been as follows in recent years: 4 percent in 2000, 5.7 percent in 2001, 3.5 percent in 2002, 1.3 percent in 2003, 3.1 percent in 2004, 4.1 percent in 2005, 4.4 percent in 2006, and 6.6 percent in 2007 (International Monetary Fund, 2010).
** The textbook allocation is less than the workbook allocation because textbooks are for a number of years (up to 10) and workbooks are issued annually to each student.
*** Counseling Committees determine the educational programs for students with special needs and hear parents' requests to delay start of compulsory education.

and can only apply if the number of students has increased by at least 12, the number of classes has increased and they show evidence of why the additional funding is needed. Municipalities can also apply for special grants for reorganizing their school network, for example if a school is closed and the municipality has to pay compensation to teachers.

3.3.3. The Funding Formula for General Education, 1998-2007

The formula now described was in operation from 1998 to 2007.[11] As can be seen from Table 3.2, the major allocation was for regular students in day schools. The per student amount for these students in 2007 was 13,670 EEK for teacher salaries, 282 EEK for textbooks, 458 EEK for workbooks and 1,385 EEK for investment–capital expenditures. These amounts were not differentiated by grade of student. However, different coefficients were applied to these per student amounts depending on the size of the municipality. The value of these coefficients is shown in Table 3.3. These coefficients were applied to grants to support teacher salaries for regular day-time and part-time students.

Table 3.3. Per Student Coefficients in the Funding Formula in 2007

Municipality criteria	Coefficient
Cities with over 5,000 pupils	0.89
Cities with 701-5000 pupils	0.9
Rural municipalities with over 700 pupils	1.0
Local governments with 501- 700 pupils	1.0
Local governments` with 351–500 pupils	1.1
Local governments with 251–350 pupils	1.2
Local governments with 181–250 pupils	1.3
Local governments with 121–180 pupils	1.4
Local governments with under 120 pupils	1.5
Weights for schools on islands (these are added to the municipal weight)	
Prangli, Ruhnu and Vormsi islands	1.2
Kihnu island	0.7

Source: Ministry of Finance.

There were additional allocations for other types of students than those attending regular day classes. The categories and numbers of students in these categories are shown in Table 3.4. Just over 4 percent of students come within the various categories of special needs for funding purposes. Various types of special needs students were distinguished with different coefficients. In order to qualify for additional funding for special needs a student must have a medical examination and receive a medical certificate.

Table 3.4. Number of Students by Category, 2006

Regular day classes	153,925
Special needs	6,467
Distance and evening	6,401
Prison	378
TOTAL	167,171

Source: Ministry of Finance.

The various weights in the formula for the different categories of student are shown in Table 3.5. In calculating the allocation for a municipality, the number of regular daytime students was multiplied by the per student amount and the number of evening and distance students by 0.8 times the per student amount. Each amount was then weighted by the appropriate municipal coefficient to obtain the total funding received for these categories of student. The allocations for students in special classes and for students who receive various forms of special provision (as indicated in Table 3.5) are obtained by multiplying the number of students in each category by the weight for that category and then multiplying by the per student amount for a regular student. In other words, the special needs weights were multiplicative. All municipalities received the same per student allocations for these categories of special needs students as the municipal weights were not applied to these allocations.

Table 3.5. Additional Factors in the Per Student Funding Formula

Special factors	2003	2004	2005	2006	2007
Distance learning or evening courses	0.8	0.8	0.8	0.8	0.8
Prison education	1.6	1.6	1.6	1.6	1.6
Special classes					
Supplementary learning class (with minor mental disorders)	1.9	1.9	2.2	2.2	2.2
Classes for children with severe and profound learning disabilities	3.5	3.5	3.8	3.8	3.8
Students with behavioral problems (including minor mental disorders)	1.6	1.6	2.2	2.2	2.2
Children with speech impairments, sensory and physical disabilities	2.3	2.3	2.6	2.6	2.6
Sanatorium school	1.2	1.2	1.2	1.2	1.2
Opportunity class (learning difficulties)	1.3	1.3	1.4	1.4	1.4
Students with various types of special provision					
Remedial classes	0.2	0.2	0.2	0.2	0.2
Home teaching	4.4	4.4	4	4	4
Psychiatry	1.3	1.3	1.3	1.3	1.3
Hospitals	0.6	0.6	0.6	0.6	0.6
Language integration				0.2	0.2
Students learning a simplified curriculum in regular classes	0	0	0	1.2	1.2
Students learning the curriculum for those with moderate or severe learning difficulties in regular classes	0	0	0	2.8	2.8

Source: Ministry of Finance.

The textbook allocation was calculated as the number of day-time, evening course and prison students times the per student allocation for textbooks. Workbooks were allocated per student for day-time students in grades 1 to 9. The municipal coefficients were not applied to textbooks and workbooks. In the Setumaa region three small local governments received in addition to the grant determined by their municipal coefficient a 20 percent addition to the grant for teacher salaries, textbooks and workbooks. Local governments also received a compensation grant for having amalgamated with another local government in previous years, but there were few in this category.

MoF shows how the grant is split into allocations for:

- salaries and teaching aids–including in-service teacher training–calculated using the above formula;
- investments (allocated per student);
- academic subjects, which are additional unweighted per student allocations;
- events and extracurricular activities, which are also an unweighted per student amount.

The types of grant allocated within the general education grant are shown in Table 3.6. General education grant in 2005 financed 36 percent of municipal spending on education, with municipalities funding 64 percent of the total, according to National Statistical Office.

Table 3.6. Grants for General Education to Municipalities by Type of Grant, 2007

Type of grant	Amount (EEK '000s)	Percentage of total grant
Salaries and teaching aids	2,514,352	0.881
Investments	240,471	0.084
Kindergarten teachers education (not part of general education)	13,105	0.005
Academic subjects section	6,000	0.002
Co-events	8,000	0.003
Total distributed	2,781,928	0.975
Reserve	72,594	0.025
Total General Education Grant	2,854,522	1.000

Source: Ministry of Finance.

Box 3.1. The Funding of Private Schools in Estonia

Private schools, which are regulated under the Private Schools Act, are funded by the state using the same set of coefficients as the municipality in which they are located. The municipality receives the money and passes it on to private schools. Municipalities can choose to fund private schools additionally for their operating costs. Strict criteria concerning adherence to the national curriculum are not applied and all private schools receive state funding. Private schools are free to set their level of fees but cannot change them by more than 10 percent a year. Private schools are mainly small (average size was 137 in 2006) and relatively few in number (31 in 2006), recruiting just under 3 percent of students. Private schools are varied in type and mission and so it is not possible to generalize about such schools. The Rocca al Mare school, in Tallinn, provides one example of how the state grant enables private schools to be established and continue in existence. This school, which is run as a non-profit and operates at a loss, is owned by a group of 18 people interested in promoting high quality education to build a future elite in Estonia who will contribute to the nation. As all private schools, Rocca al Mare receives its state funding via the municipality in which it is located. It receives the same per student current funding as Tallinn does from the state, which supports its teaching costs. Until 2007 Tallinn was the only municipality not allocating state capital grants to private schools. Rocca al Mare charges fees, which vary from 21,000 EEK per year for the early grades to 27,000 EEK for grades 10 to 12. Students from low-income families are subsidized. The school has found it difficult to increase fees in line with rising prices and teacher salaries in the state sector, partly because of the legal restriction on annual fee increases. It now pays about 30 percent more to teachers than the Tallinn municipality, but it initially paid 100 percent more. The school is over-subscribed and hence able to select by ability.

3.3.4. Determining the Size and Distribution of the Grant for General Education

Decisions about both the distribution of funding (the formula) and the amount to be distributed emerge from negotiations between MER, MoF and the two associations representing the municipalities, the Association of Estonian Cities and the Association of Municipalities of Estonia–for rural local governments. As already mentioned, the formula was the outcome of a joint working group and consultations with stakeholders. The annual negotiations focus more on the determination of the overall amount, as the coefficients in the formula have remained stable and have only been added to and not changed. The new 2008 formula was devised by a working group which began its deliberations in 2003. This marks a significant change in funding policy as the new formula is designed to ensure that smaller municipalities receive sufficient funding to cover the teaching costs of the number of classes it is deemed that each school in a municipality needs to organize, given the number of students per grade. A draft proposal for the revised formula was published and meetings took place around the country to discuss it. It was evident that this participation process is well-embedded, as municipal mayors and school directors spoken to were well informed about the proposal. The new formula is discussed further below. Here the focus is on how the annual amount available for distribution is determined.

In Estonia, local governments are relatively strongly placed vis-à-vis central governments. These are invariably coalition governments and change quite frequently: consequently ministers of education do not stay in office for prolonged periods. The two municipal associations send four representatives each to the Local Government Co-operation Assembly, which organizes how the municipalities negotiate with the government. Thus, the rural areas, though representing 30 percent of the population, have 50 percent of the votes in this Assembly. Its purpose is to present a united local government front to central government, so that it cannot exploit any conflicts of interest between cities and the countryside. In fact, there appears to be little urban resentment over high subsidies for rural education. This may well reflect the relatively recent emigration from the countryside of most urban dwellers and the close connections between urban and rural areas in a small, compact country. The budget negotiations between local and central government are formalized: an annual protocol setting out the positions of both parties and areas of agreement is signed as part of the state budgetary process.

Naturally, a major concern for local governments is affording the cost of teacher salaries. As stipulated in the BSUSS Act of 2000,[12] teacher salaries are determined in a two-stage process–a basic minimum set nationally and rates at or above the national basic level, which are set by each municipality. The basic salaries of the four grades of teacher are determined at the national level by negotiations between central government ministries, including MER, and by representatives from local governments and registered teacher associations. Basic salaries are not increased every year, there being a noticeable tendency for increases to occur in election years. Local governments have to pay teachers their basic salary but can decide locally on additional amounts. Municipalities reach agreement on local pay with local union representatives. MER puts its budget proposals to MoF for approval prior to the agreement on any annual increase in teacher basic pay, so that any increases are agreed in light of the amount available in the state budget. However, there is no fixed link between increases in teacher basic pay and the increase in the grant total, which is a cause for complaint by municipalities. For example, in 2007, teacher basic salary increased 18 percent, while the total grant increased by 15.7 percent[13] on average, though some municipalities got considerably less than this increase. Once MoF has announced what the education grant total will be, MER determines the per student unweighted allocation by dividing the total amount available for the salary fund and the other elements of the grant by the number of student units. Thus, budget determination is essentially top-down: it depends on what central government decides can be afforded, given other demands on the public purse and the government's macroeconomic policies, which currently aim at a steady reduction in income tax rates. It is not determined bottom-up by a calculation of what it costs to run schools. Municipalities fund the difference between the amount that the central government provides and the amount schools are able to persuade their municipality that they need.

Total education spending was 14.8 percent of public expenditure in 2005, which was higher than the EU 25 average of 10.8 (European Commission 2005). However, the proportion of GDP is relatively low by EU 25 standards. Estonia's spending on general education declined from 3 percent in 2003 to 2.4 percent in 2006 due largely to the rapid rate of growth in GDP of over 20 percent in these four years.

3.3.5. The 2008 Funding Formula[14]

In response to dissatisfaction with the 1998-2007 formula as no longer being suited to current circumstances, MER and MoF worked for four years with stakeholder groups on a substantive revision to the funding formula. The length of time the revisions were under discussion reflects the difficulty of reaching agreement between the stakeholders and the changing coalition of parties in central government about an alternative formula. The funding formula working group included representatives from both associations of rural and city municipalities as well as from MER and MoF. The proposals were consulted extensively and knowledge of the proposals was widespread among school directors and municipal leaders interviewed. The changes are not universally liked since the 2008 formula treats municipalities that do not have small schools less favorably than the previous formula.

The 2008 formula was introduced as a solution to perceived problems with the previous formula. Some complained that the previous formula was not sufficiently sensitive to the expenditure needs of some municipalities and schools because the weights in the formula, which were based mainly on the size municipalities, did not take into account differences in per student costs due to differences in the actual size of schools and in the distribution of pupils between schools and between grades within the schools. Municipalities also objected that the same amount was allocated for pupils of all ages, although older students cost more to teach as they have more class periods a week. Municipalities who have more schools for a given number of students than others complained that their higher per student costs were not taken into account. Another complaint was that the number of students in a class may be too small to generate sufficient state funding to cover the costs of the teacher time required by the national curriculum. A class may be formed in grade 1 with a sufficient number of pupils to generate funding to cover their teaching costs but if the number of pupils declines over time teaching costs for the class remain the same though the funding has declined. As the government was about to reduce the legal maximum class size from 36 to 24 for grades 1 to 9 (already implemented for grades 1-6 in 2007 and implemented for grades 7-9 in 2008/9) the problem of having class sizes below 24 because the actual number of students in a grade is not in even multiples of 24 became more pressing.[15]

A particular crucial concern in Estonia is that per student funding has put too much pressure on the financial viability of small schools during a period of marked demographic decline. There is a great desire in rural areas to preserve even very small rural schools. It is feared that if the village school closes, people will leave the village and the population loss will reduce municipal revenues. Despite concerns of some educationalists about the quality of education in small rural schools, they remain popular with many rural parents. Several of the political parties support the maintenance of small schools, but this requires a different kind of funding formula.

The 2008 formula favors municipalites that have 1,600 or less students in either of the major language categories—Estonian and Russian. These municipalites are funded according to the number of classes that the formula assumes each school in the municipality needs to organize, given the number of pupils in each grade, treating Estonian and Russian medium pupils separately if they are taught in sepereate classes. The municipalites with more than 1600 students in a language medium are funded per student for these students. Thus, a municipality that has 2000 Estonian students and 500 Russian students is funded per student for Estonians and according to the teaching costs of the assumed number of Russian classes needed in its schools. The municipalities and the schools are free to organize a different number of classes but funding remains based on the assumed number of classes needed, not on the actual number created. By determing the number of classes needed in relation to the number of pupils in each grade, the government has made explicit the minimum size of school it considers should be maintained, while municipalities can sustain even smaller schools if they choose to allocate additional funds to support teaching costs. The new funding formula is now explained in more detail.

The new funding methodology splits the education grant into two parts for the purposes of working out the per student amount allocated:

1. an allocation for the basic minimum costs of teaching and the other resources that the state grant is intended to support (textbooks, workbooks, investments and other items); these basic costs depend on the regulations, such as the number of weekly subject lessons students must receive, the number of lessons a week a teacher on a full time salary must teach, teacher basic salaries, maximum class size as well as on the normative class sizes and additional lessons per class assumed by the formula;
2. a further allocation in addition to allocation (1) above, which is intended for local governments to use according to their own choices for education spending; this is about 10 percent of the total and is derived from the amount left over from the total grant for education when the aggregate amount for part 1 for all municipalities is subtracted. However, this further 'free' allocation is included in the per student amount for each grade range and is not a separate allocation to the municipality.

3.3.5.1. CALCULATION OF PER STUDENT TEACHING COSTS

How teaching costs per student for each of the four grade ranges are calculated is shown in Table 3.7. Column 1 gives the total number of lessons per week that the three grades of students must be taught in each of the four stages. This is divided by 21 hours (the assumed average number of lessons per week taught by a full time teacher[16]) to arrive at the number of teachers needed for each stage (column 2). To arive at total teaching costs (given in column 3) the number of teachers needed (column 2) is multiplied by the cost of a teacher. This is assumed to be the basic salary of a regular teacher[17] (83 percent are in this or the lower junior teacher category) including unemployment insurance and other labor taxes paid by employers (33.3%) as well as 3 percent to cover in-service training.[18] The per student amount is shown in column 4, which is column 3 divided by the number of students assumed to define a small class. This is 17 students for stages I to III and 21 students for stage IV. Thus, the formula generates enough money to cover the costs of a class of 17 students in grades 1 to 9 and for class of 21 in grades 10 to 12. The last column shows the ratio of the per student allocations relative to the allocation for stage IV.

Table 3.7. Calculation of Per Student Funding Amount

Stage	Total number of compulsory lessons a week (col. 1)	Number of teachers needed* (col. 2)	Total cost of teachers** (col. 3)	Per student amount*** (col. 4)	Ratio of per student funding (col. 5)
I (grades 1-3)	68	3.2	533,505	10,461	0.80
II (grades 4-5)	83	4.0	651,190	12,768	0.98
III (grades 6-9)	96	4.6	753,183	14,768	1.13
IV (grades 10-12)	105	5.0	823,794	13,076	1.00

* Calculated as the amount in column 1 divided by 21.
** Calculated as the amount in column 2 multiplied by the gross basic teacher salary.
*** Calculated as the amount in column 3 divided by 17 for grades 1-9 and divided by 21 for grades 10-12.

The per student amounts in column 4 are enhanced by a percentage which is for part 2–the 'free' allocation. The part 2 percentage varies from year to year depending on the total amount of education grant left over after all basic cost allocations to municipalities have been subtracted. In 2008 this was 9.5 percent. Therefore, in 2008 the per student amounts for basic teaching cost were:

- stage I   11,455 EEK
- stage II   13,982 EEK
- stage III   16,172 EEK
- stage IV   14,319 EEK.

A small class is defined to be 17 students for stages I to III and 21 students for stage IV. Maximum class size is now regulated at 24 for stages I, II and stage III. It was still 36 for stage IV in 2009 but it was intended to bring this down to 24 in the future. The regulations also stipulate that for certain subjects classes of above 17 (21 for stage IV) are split into smaller teaching groups. The number of such split classes increases with the stage of schooling as the curriculum becomes more specialised—as shown in Table 3.8 (lessons per week for full classes). The last column of Table 3.8 shows the minimum number of students per class needed in order to generate sufficient funds to pay for the number of weekly lessons needed by a full class. It is still possible for a school with a class of 18 to afford to split the class for some subjects since teachers can be required to teach up to 24 lessons a week.

Table 3.8. Minimum Number of Students Needed to Bring in Sufficient Funds to Pay for Teaching Costs

	Lessons per week		Minimum number of students needed (21 lessons per teacher)	
	Small classes	Full classes	Small classes	Full classes
I (grades 1-3)	68	72	16	17
II (grades 4-5)	83	104	16	20
III (grades 6-9)	96	127	16	21
IV (grades 10-12)	105	150	20	28

Schools in municipalities which have 1600 or fewer students in either of the major language categories—Estonian and Russian medium schools—are funded according to the assumed number of classes so long as the grade has 33 or fewer students. This requires funding a sufficient number of 'empty places' so that the teaching costs of a class which is below either small size (17) or full size (24) can be met. The funding of 'empty places' is for grades I to III only. The cut-off points in terms of class size at which additional funding for empty places is provided is shown in Table 3.9. The crucial ranges for additional 'empty places' funding are:

- less than 17 students per grade—if there are seven or more students per grade in stages I and II or more than 10 per grade in stage III the formula funds as if there are 17 students;
- for 18 to 23 students, the formula funds as if there are 24 students (to provide the teaching costs of split classes);
- between 25 and 26 students the formula funds per student as it is assumed maximum class size can be exceeded by two students;
- 27 to 33 students the school is assumed to have to form two classes and so is funded as if it had 34 students in two classes of 17 and so it can afford to run two classes of between 13 and 16 students.
- when a grade has 34 or more students it is funded per student (for up to 50 students it is assumed to have two classes between 17 and 25 and from 51 onwards it can afford two classes of 17 or more).

Table 3.9. Additional Funding in Stages I to III for Small and Under-sized Full Classes

Number of students per grade	1-16	17	18-23	24-26	27-33	34-35	36 to 47
No. of assumed classes formed	1 small	1 small	1 full	1 full	2 small	2 small	2 full
Funding	P +A	P	P+A	P	P+A	P	P

P = per student funding; A = additional allocation

If the primary grades (stages I and II) have less than seven students it is assumed by the formula that two or three grades will be combined to form a single class and each combined class will be funded as if it had 17 students. The number of empty places that are funded is limited by a cut-off point which is that the amount of per student funding received for the school cannot be more than three times the base per student amount. Therefore, a school would receive funding for the assumed number of pupils plus empty places shown in Table 3.10. With only 1 student per grade the school would be made up to 17 students (an additional 16), but as it can only be funded for up to three times the per student amount, the number of empty places funded can only be two, therefore 17 is reduced by 14 to give three funded students per grade. The cut-off thus applies to grades with five or fewer students. Hence, with one student per grade a primary school could afford to run 1 mixed grade class for grades 1 to 6 as it is funded for 18 students. As schools are only allowed to mix grades 1 to 4 and 3 to 6 this would not be viable. However, a primary school with two students per grade would be funded as if it had six students for each two students and could therefore afford to run two mixed grade classes as it is funded as if it had 36 students when it has 12.

The new formula is deliberately calibrated so that it favors schools with primary grades in smaller municipalities. The funding of small classes for stage III is less generous. As already noted, at least 10 students per grade are required before the numbers are made up to 17 by funding empty places. There is no additional empty place funding for grades with less than 10 students in grade III (i.e 30 students in grades 7-9) and insufficient students in the lower grades for the school to be judged 'resiliant'.[19] Stage IV gets no additional funding for small classes.

Table 3.10. Additional Funding for Grades 1 to 6 with Fewer than 7 Students

Number of students in one grade	Financed places in grades I-II			
	Per Student	Additional	Cut	TOTAL
1	1	16	-14	3
2	2	15	-11	6
3	3	14	-8	9
4	4	13	-5	12
5	5	12	-2	15
6	6	11	0	17

Source: Ministry of Finance.

When Estonian medium students (which for funding purposes includes other foreign language mediums such as English and Finnish) and Russian medium students in the same school are taught separately, the additional funding allocations for 'empty places' are calculated separately. Evening class and distance students (who attend grades 10 to 12) are funded at 0.8 of the full per student rate. Private schools must have a least 10 students on average per grade to receive additional funding for non-Estonian language studuents.

Additional amounts for special educational needs (SEN) students are determined by the smaller class size in which they are taught as prescribed by regulations. The assumed maximum class sizes for SEN students are 7, 12 and 16 depending on the type of SEN. So if there are 14 SEN students for whom the maximum class size is 7, two classes are formed and funded as if there were 17 students in each (i.e. for 20 extra places). Mixed grade SEN classes can be formed across any grades. There are also students in regular classes who are funded as regular students but are studying a modified curriculum. If studying the modified curriculum such a student is funded for two additional lessons a week and if studying the curriculum for moderate learning difficulties or receiving home tuition they get funded for 4 extra lessons. Also each SEN class is funded for an additional lesson per week. If there are fewer than 5 SEN students then a class is not funded and any SEN student is funded for one extra lesson a week. The additional lessons funded for SEN students, described above, and for other factors are shown in Table 3.11.

3.3.5.2. Form Teacher and Management Staff Costs

Form teachers are in charge of a class and are funded additionally at 10 percent of teacher basic pay. The assumed number of form teachers is the same as the number of notional classes the school is funded for. The number of school director and deputy posts

Table 3.11. Funding for Additional Lessons and for Enhanced Costs

Criteria for the allocation of the costs of additional lessons	Number of lessons per week
Special classes	1
Simplified curriculum	2
Curriculum for students with moderate or severe learning disabilities	4
Home teaching	4
Composite classes extra	2
Small basic school extra	2
Students in prisons	2
New-immigrant students	4
Estonian in Russian speaking classes	1
Language integration students (20% of salaries funding)	
Regionally important school (20% of salaries funding)	

Source: Ministry of Finance.

depends on the calculated number of classes as shown in Table 3.12. Municipalities need not follow these allocations. A full time director or deputy post is funded at 1.4 times teacher basic pay, which is school director minimum pay. In small schools the school director teaches (e.g. 20 hours a week if there is just 1 class, 15 if there are 2, etc.) and even in large schools directors usually teach about 5 lessons a week. As can be seen from Table 3.12, only when the number of pupils exceeds 74 is the school funded for one full time post of school director. With 600 or more students a school is funded for 3 management posts. The formula therefore allocates the number of management posts multiplied by minimum school director salary.

Table 3.12. Allocation for School Directors and Deputies

Number of students	Number of classes	Posts
1- 74	1	0.10
	2-3	0.25
	4	0.5
75-99		1.00
100-199		1.50
200-349		2.00
350-599		2.50
600 plus		3.00

Source: Ministry of Finance.

3.3.5.3. REGIONALLY IMPORTANT SCHOOLS

These are schools which are allocated additional funding because of their local importance in providing access to education in sparsely populated or isolated areas. The funding is to compensate teachers who cannot be given sufficient teaching to work a full load and cannot obtain part time work at a second school because these are too far for daily travel. All schools on islands qualify as regionally important schools. Schools also qualify as regional schools if they have 10-30 students in stage III with the nearest alternative school with stage III classes more than 30 km distant by a metalled road.[20] Currently there are no schools in this cateogory. Regionally important schools are funded additionally for small classes but if situated on small islands they are funded 20 percent more per student than the standard rate and their funding is not capped at three times the basic per student amount.

3.3.5.4. Split Site Schools

Schools that have a single management but are on two or more sites at least 10 km apart for grade 1 and II funding and 30 km apart for grade III funding can, if the municipality requests this, have their funding allocation calculated as if the sites were separate schools.

3.3.5.5. Adjustment Funding

To prevent large year-to-year reductions in a school's funding there are provisions for dampening reductions in funding taking one year with the next. The adjustment funding is triggered when a school's annual increase in salary grant is less than the average national increase. If this is the case then:

- if the calculated number of classes is less than that in the previous year, per student funding compared to the previous year is increased by at least half the average increase in the state education grant;
- if the calculated number of classes is not lower than last year, then the smaller of the following is allocated:
  - the previous year's grant for teacher salaries is increased by half the national rate of growth;
  - the salary grant the school would have received according to the previous year's formula (i.e. if the formula has changed).

The adjustment funding was due to operate for three years (2008 to 2010) and was estimated to cost around 14 million EEK a year.

3.3.5.6. Textbooks, Workbooks and Capital Funding

As in the current formula there is a per student grant for textbooks (282 EEK per student) and workbooks (458 EEK per student). The investment grant is now allocated at 21,900 EEK per class and 438 EEK per student.[21] Evening and distance students do not count for workbooks and are weighted 0.8 for textbooks and per student investment grant. Counselling committee costs are funded for each municipality at 50 EEK pre student and for each youth in the municipality aged up to 26 there is 80 EEK for cultural and sports events.[22]

3.3.5.7. Amalgamations

In the year after amalgamation, an amalgamated municipality receives a compensation grant for 3 years.

3.3.5.8. Reserves

The 2008 formula requires a smaller reserve fund than the previous formula because it funds for the number of classes schools need to create and the per student allocation is tied directly to teacher basic pay. Therefore municipalities are fully funded for teacher pay increases and for keeping the number of classes unchanged during the year if student numbers decline. Under the 2008 formula if the number of SEN students changes or the number of classes needed changes from one year to the next the grant will be adjusted. Reserves are therefore needed only for paying compensation to teachers who are made redundant.

3.3.5.9. OVERALL ALLOCATION OF STATE EDUCATION GRANT

The overall allocation of the state budget to the sub-categories of grant is shown in Table 3.13. Grants to support salary costs make up 88 percent of the total education grant; of this, 69 percent is for the basic teaching costs of stages I to IV. Of the amount allocated for salary costs, 91 percent is allocated per student and 9 percent is for additional allocations to enable schools to pay for the teaching costs of the calculated number of classes in stages I to III for which 'empty places' are funded.

Table 3.13. Allocation of State Education Grant to Sub-categories of Grant, 2008

Purpose of the allocation	Per student	Additional	Total	Proportion
Stages I and II	915,110	97,882	1,012,993	0.31
Stage III	699,116	46,307	745,423	0.23
Stage IV	473,859	0	473,859	0.15
Language integration schools	9381	0	9,381	0.003
Form teachers addition	124,481	0	124,481	0.04
SEN: stages I-IV	52,469	42,757	95,226	0.03
SEN: Form teachers addition	5,791	0	5,791	0.002
Distance and evening classes	78,933	0	78,933	0.02
Form teachers addition (evening and distance classes)	3,807	0	3,807	0.001
Students with special needs	0	71,744	71,744	0.02
Management costs	205,405	0	205,405	0.06
Regionally important schools	0	1,905	1,905	0.001
For teaching Estonian in Russian speaking classes			9368	0.003
Expert teachers			18,612	0.006
Hospital and prison			3,941	0.002
Amalgamation			5,602	0.002
Compensation for implementing the new formula			10,323	0.003
Total Salaries	**2,568,351**	**260,595**	**2,876,794**	**0.88**
Textbooks			44,645	0.014
Other teaching aids (textbooks etc)			54,865	0.02
Investment grant			250,813	0.08
Cultural and sporting events			11,089	0.003
Counseling committees			7,919	0.002
Kindergarten teacher in-service training			13,173	0.004
Total funds available in state budget			3,274,417	1.00

Source: Ministry of Finance.

3.3.5.10. SUMMARY: COMPARISON OF OLD AND NEW FORMULAE

From an efficiency perspective a per student formula, which takes no account of the number of schools within a municipality or of the number of classes within schools, is desirable since it encourages municipalities to rationalize their school network and schools to organize efficiently-sized classes. However, to be horizontally equitable[23] a school funding formula should reflect differences in municipal costs per student that are due to structural factors beyond the control of the municipality. So, for example, if two municipalities with the same number of students each have three schools, but municipality A is sparsely populated and has three villages 2 hours to travel time apart while municipality B is quite densely populated and could operate with one school, then the formula should allocate more funding to municipality A according to its population density and poor road communications. The 1998-2007 funding formula did not contain indicators of population density or of travel times but relied only on municipal student numbers and city/rural/island distinction for differentiating per student allocations to reflect differences in structural costs.

The 2008 formula is derived from an activity-led model (Abu-Duhou 1999) of the costs of teaching and learning and therefore makes it easier for municipalities to fund their schools from the state budget for teaching and materials costs, so long as the municipality applies the costing model on which the funding formula is based. The 2008 formula provides funding for the calculated teaching costs of classes of assumed size, dependent on required lessons per week and an assumed average teaching load. It adjusts for variations in these costs by grade range. Because the formula is activity-led, any changes in government policy which affect teaching costs, such as the prescribed numbers of lessons per week or increases in teacher basic salaries, are directly mirrored in the grant allocations. The 2008 formula reflects a government commitment to reduce maximum class size to 24 and sustain small schools with less than 34 students per grade in stages I, II and III but not in upper secondary grades. There is a deliberate bias to provide additional funding for schools with very few students in the primary grades when the number of students in either language medium in the municipality is below 1600. A primary school with as few as 2 students per grade (12 in all) is funded to run 2 mixed grade classes. The 2008 formula also also explicitly funds minority language classes which the previous formula did not. Muncipalities with fewer than 1600 Russian students and small numbers of these students per grade receive sufficient funding for organizing mixed classes of 3 grades with as few as 6 Russian medium students. The previous formula funded just on the number of students regardless of lanuage medium.

Greater financial stability is provided to municipalities through the adjustment factor. As the allocation per student per stage exceeds the basic costs of teaching provision, there is built in flexibility for municipalities to spend this premium on additional expenditures not included in the activity-led model such as smaller teaching groups, more lessons per week or higher teacher salaries. While there is no requirement for a municipality to fund schools according to the MER/MoF funding model (apart from adhering to legal norms) the formula designers expected that municipalities will base their funding of their schools on it. The implications of the 2008 formula for equity and efficiency are discussed in the sections below on these issues.

3.4. The Implementation of the Funding Formula

3.4.1. Funding of General Education by Municipalities

As central government education grant to support current spending is meant to cover only teaching costs, textbooks and workbooks, municipalities are expected to fund as a minimum the operational expenses of schools, that is non-teaching staff and non-staff costs. As can be seen from Figure 3.2, all municipalities spent in excess of their grant for education. Rural municipalities tended to spend slightly more on education relative to the state grant than urban ones, and this was particularly pronounced for the richest group of rural municipalities. The range in the proportion of education expenditure financed by the state grant was also wider for rural municipalities, especially for the poor group. For the median municipality, education expenditures made up about half of its total spending on local services, though, as can be seen from Figure 3.3, there was a considerable range in this proportion. Rich rural municipalities tended to devote a lower proportion of their total spending to education.

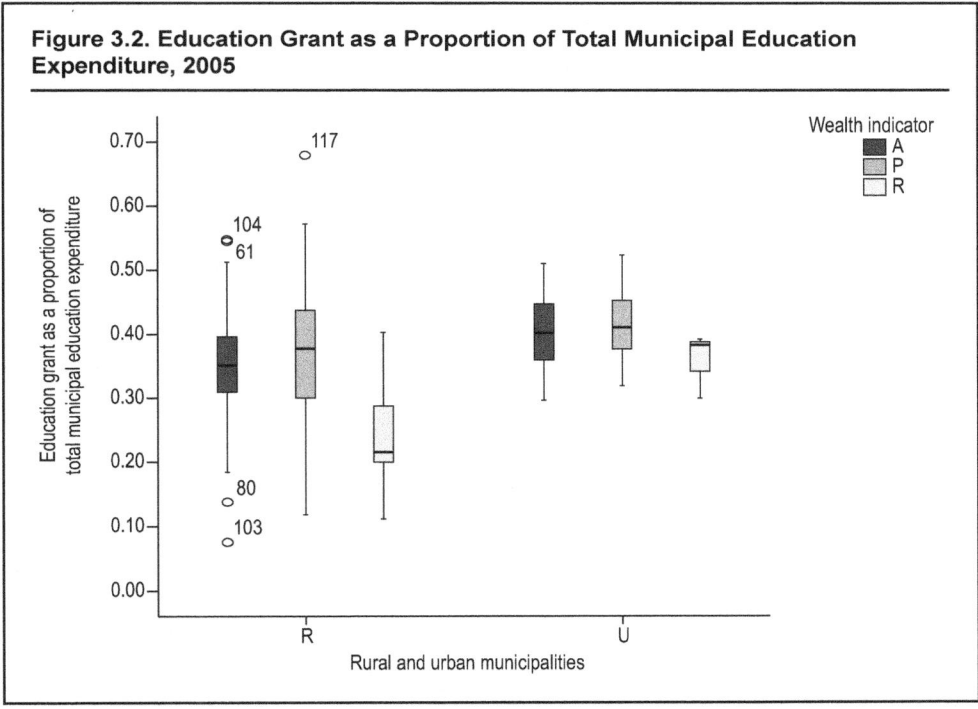

Source: National Statistical Office (http://pub.stat.ee/px-web.2001/Dialog/Saveshow.asp)
Note: Urban and rural municipalities are split into three income groups (from left to right: average (A), rich (R) and poor (P)) following the classification made by National Statistical Office, which is based on tax revenue per capita. In 2005, tax revenue per capita was 4,100 EEK or less for poor municipalities, 4,101 to 6,000 EEK for average municipalities and above 6,000 EEK for rich ones. The number of urban municipalities was P=18, A= 17 and R = 3: the number of rural municipalities was P= 104, A= 75 and R = 17.

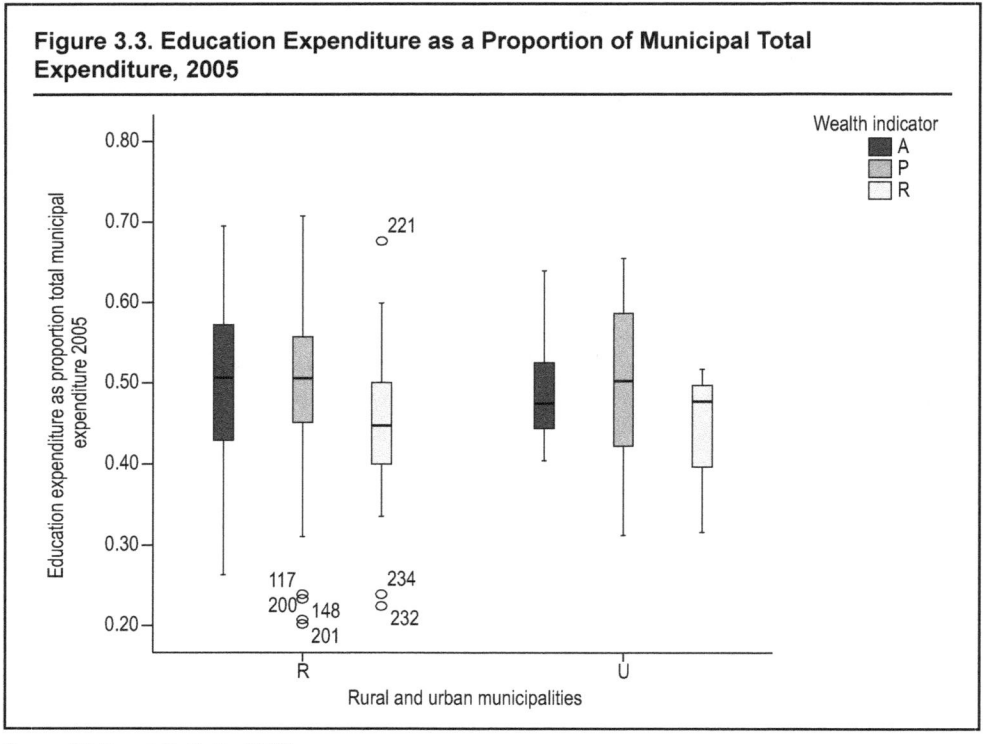

Figure 3.3. Education Expenditure as a Proportion of Municipal Total Expenditure, 2005

Source: National Statistical Office.

Estonian municipalities as a whole obtained almost sixty percent of their revenues from shares of local taxes, fees, charges and other own sources of revenue. About forty percent came from various forms of state grants, of which the education grant represented roughly 19 percent of revenues. Municipal sources of revenue are shown in Figure 3.4. Not surprisingly, municipalities differed greatly in their tax raising capacity. While the average tax revenue per inhabitant in 2005 was 4,482 EEK per annum, the maximum was 18,600 EEK and the minimum 1,480 EEK (National Statistical Office). There is an equalization fund, which allocates additional tax revenue to all municipalities except the richest (24 in 2005). The amount and distribution of the equalization fund is negotiated with central govern-

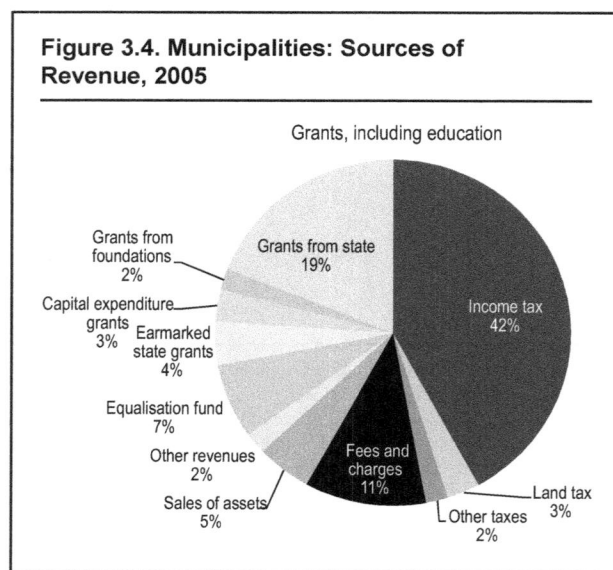

Figure 3.4. Municipalities: Sources of Revenue, 2005

Source: Association of Municipalities of Estonia.

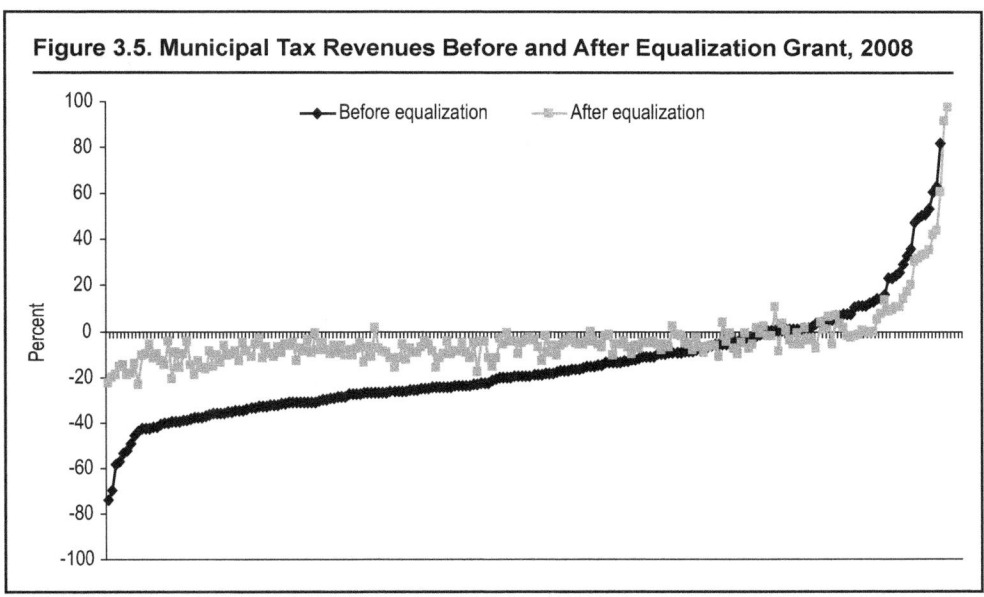

Source: Ministry of Finance.

ment each year and takes into account an estimate of the municipal need to spend as well as their tax revenues. Municipalities are equalized up to 90 percent of the difference between the costs of meeting their estimated need to spend and their revenues. Affluent municipalities remain with revenues that exceed their estimated need to spend. The redistributive effect of the equalization fund is shown in Figure 3.5. Tax collection was reported to be effective, with central government collecting tax revenues and distributing them to local governments.

Although central government grant is intended to cover teaching costs, many municipalities add more money to teacher salary costs, which enables them to run smaller classes and/or pay teachers more than allowed for by the formula. In deciding how much to spend on schools local governments are constrained by a number of regulated standards set by central government. These are:

- all children attending municipal schools must be provided with free education in grades 1-12;
- the number of periods a week (of 45-50 minutes) that students must be taught the subjects of the national curriculum: subjects are specified and the number of periods defined for the four groups of 3 contiguous grades (1-3; 4-6; 7-9 and 10-12) as shown in Table 16 below;
- maximum class size: this is 24 for grades 1 to 9;
- teachers are required to teach 18-24 periods a week for a full-time salary, which gives municipalities some flexibility;
- teachers must be paid the basic salary for their grade, which is determined nationally;
- employees who are not qualified teachers must be paid a national basic wage;
- MER regulations on non-class-room teacher posts that schools should have dependent on their size (these are not strictly enforced if municipalities or schools cannot afford particular posts).

Municipalities are able to determine the closure and amalgamation of schools. However, municipalities are reluctant to close uneconomic schools mainly it is said because of parental opposition rather than objections from teachers, given that there is a teacher shortage, particularly in rural areas. Another constraint is the difficult legal process of dismissing teachers.

Information on how municipalities finance general education was collected from four municipalities, which are listed in Table 3.14.[24] Out of the four, only Mustvee, a small town in rural western Estonia on the shores of Lake Peipsi, was poor, having tax revenues per capita of only half the national average. In contrast, Viimsi, situated on the coast near Tallinn with some industry and an expanding population moving into new housing and commuting to Tallinn, is one the wealthiest municipalities. Rae also benefits from its location in a rapidly developing part of Estonia around Tallinn. However, the stabilization fund adds as much as its tax revenues to Mustvee's total revenues and is zero for the other three municipalities. After other grants, including that for education and income from sales of services, Mustvee's total revenue per capita was 14 percent higher than the national average in 2005.

Municipalities have considerable flexibility in making resourcing decisions about their schools. They have the power to establish, reorganize and close schools. They also have some discretion in determining the number and types of non- teaching posts at their schools. As already noted, municipalities determine local policies for pay above the statutory basic amount. They can also fund additional optional subjects and extra-curricular activities. These so-called 'hobby classes' are very popular in Estonia and schools

Table 3.14. Case-Study Municipalities: Descriptive Statistics

	Tallinn	Rae *vald*	Viimsi *vald*	Mustvee *linn*
Total tax revenues in 2005	2,558,333	61,805	129,022	4,404
Total revenues (2005) (in '000s)	4,710,784	126,987	162,295	21,510
Number of inhabitants in 2005	398, 921	8,045	10,771	1,765
Tax revenues per capita in 2005	6,413	7,682	11,979	2,495
Total revenues per capita (2005)	11,809	15,785	15,068	12,187
Tax revenues per inhabitant as a percentage of the state average (2005)	125%	150%	234%	49.0%
Total revenues per inhabitant as a percentage of the state average (2005)	110%	148%	141%	114%
Number of students in municipal schools (grades 1—12) (2007)	44,916	966	1355	385
Number of schools (2007)	75	3	3	2
Percentage of municipal budget spent on education (2007) (These figures were provided in interviews and include all spending on education, including pre-school and capital expenditure)	43%	55%	38%	50%

Source: Source of 2005 data is National Statistical Office.
Note 1: *vald* indicates rural and *linn* a town municipality.
Note 2: Tallinn has 8 primary; 10 basic and 57 secondary (grades 1-12) schools.

are generally expected to provide them, except for the few still operating two shifts a day. Parents can exercise choice in educating their child in a school run by another municipality. There is cross charging: the municipality where the child is educated charges the municipality where the child resides, though invoices for school charges are not always paid.

Municipalities are free to decide how to allocate funding to their own schools and to private schools in their terrain.[25] By law, schools are required to have a budget, even when the scope of budget management is relatively limited because the staff budget is determined by agreement with the mayor as to how many staff are employed at the school. In all the municipalities visited there were close relations between the school and the mayor's office. The three small municipalities negotiated individual budgets with each of their schools. School directors submitted a budget plan with request for funding: the budget was negotiated with the mayor and finally approved by the council of elected representatives. Tallinn funds its schools by its own formula, agreed with school directors, which is discussed in greater detail below. In all the municipalities, including Tallinn, financial administration of schools is centralized. Schools financial transactions are operated by the municipality treasury and schools do not receive cash or have their own commercial bank accounts for state and municipal funding. Large schools are likely to employ a bursar or a deputy director responsible for business matters and will manage the school accounts using the municipal treasury.

3.4.2. Municipal Per Student Funding of Schools: The Case of Tallinn

As most municipalities have few schools, sometimes with quite different cost structures, a funding formula is not suited to them. Tallinn, being a large municipality, with 75 of its own schools and 12 private schools, has developed separate formulae, one for allocating central government grant to schools and the other for distributing money from the city budget. The city's contribution to school budgets and its formulae for allocating both municipal and state funding to schools is agreed with representatives of Tallinn Union of School Directors. The city budget formula is set out in Table 3.15, using an example of a school with 600 students. Schools with fewer than 501 students get an additional weighting per student: from 401 to 500 the weighting is 1.1; from 301 to 400 students 1.2 and for 300 students or less the weighting is 1.5. Ultimately, if a small school cannot manage on its allocation it has to be reorganized or closed.

The formula for allocating the state budget to the schools closely follows state guidelines. The allocation is weighted by grade depending on the number of lessons specified in the national curriculum for each grade range of students and on maximum class size. These calculations can be seen in Table 3.16. The numbers of lessons per week for the grades in each stage are summed: for example, stage 1 requires 73 lessons in all. The next column in Table 3.16 shows the number of teachers required to teach 1 class per grade in each stage. This is derived by dividing the lessons per week by the number of lessons teachers are assumed to work for a full time salary. In Estonia this is between 18 and 24 lessons. Tallinn assumes that teachers teach per week from 22 lessons for the youngest grades to 20 for the highest grades. To arrive at a weight for each stage for teaching, the number of lessons per week required for one class in each of the 12 grades is totaled—this is 445 lessons or an average of 111 lessons per stage. Then the actual number of lessons required for each stage is divided by 111 to obtain the stage's relative weighting. These

Table 3.15. Tallinn City: Formula for Determining the Part of the Municipal Budget Allocation that Goes to Schools, 2007

Example for calculation purposes
Number of students: 600   Area of school: 6,000 sq m

Direct calculation	Unit	Kroons per unit	No. of units	Total
Heating	Squared meters	51	600	306,000
Electricity	Squared meters	28	600	168,000
Water	Students	132	6,000	79,200
Maintenance	Squared meters	20	600	120,000
Current repairs	Squared meters	23	600	138,000
Security	Squared meters	8	600	48,000
Cleaner	Position	47,988	8	383,904
Repair man	Position	71,982	2	143,964
Sanitary worker	Position	47,988	1	47,988
Guard	Position	47,988	2.5	127,968
Management costs				
Deputy principal (business manager)	Position	159,960	1	159,960
Secretary	Position	95,976	1	95,976
Training	Students	14	6,000	8,400
Support services				
After school teacher	Position	111,972	1	111,972
Speech therapist	Position	111,972	1	111,972
Psychologist	Position	111,972	1	111,972
Co-ordinator- hobby clubs	Position	111,972	1	111,972
Co-ordinator (activities)	Position	111,972	1	111,972
Librarian	Position	103,974	1	103,974
Lab assistant	Position	47,988	1	47,988
ICT specialist	Position	103,974	1	103,974
Social worker	Position	103,974	1	103,974
Events	Students	25	6,000	15,000
Rent	Squared meters	8	600	4,800
Learning resources				
Reference books	Students	28	6,000	16,800
Teaching materials	Students	67	6,000	40,200
Equipment	Students	137	6,000	82,200
ICT hard and software	Students	81	6,000	48,600
Other expenses				
Reception costs	Students	2	6,000	1,200
Medical examinations	Students	3	6,000	1,800
Information	Students	2	6,000	1,200
Transport	Students	12	6,000	7,200
TOTAL				**2,966,130**

Source: Tallinn City Education Department
Note: The budget is allocated in two parts, the first from the start of the financial year in January to August and the second from September, adjusted for the number of pupils in the new school year.

Table 3.16. Tallinn City: Method of Allocating State Budget for Teaching

Stage I	Grade	Lessons per week	No. of teachers required
	1	20	0.93
	2	24	1.07
	3	29	1.30
	Total	73	3.30
Stage II	4	30	1.36
	5	34	1.52
	6	40	1.82
	Total	104	4.70
Stage III	7	41	1.84
	8	42	1.93
	9	44	1.98
	Total	127	5.75
Stage IV	10	47	2.35
	11	47	2.35
	12	47	2.35
	Total	141	7.05

Total lessons per week for all grades = 445
Average lessons per week per stage = 111
Divide each stage's total lessons by the average to get its weighting for lessons per week.

Stage	Weight
Stage I	0.66
Stage II	0.93
Stage III	1.14
Stage IV	1.27

Adjust weights for class size & lessons in split classes

	Class size	Adjusted weight	Allocation in EEK (weight times EEK 12,166.3)
Stage I	24	0.71	8,580
Stage II	26	0.92	11,210
Stage III	26	1.13	13,710
Stage IV	32	1.15	14,020

Source: Tallinn City Education Department.
Note: The figures in the table are rounded up whereas Tallinn uses figures to more decimal places. Consequently there are some minor discrepancies.

weights vary from 0.66 in stage 1 to 1.27 for stage 4. An adjustment to these weights is then made to allow for differences in assumed class size. These were in 2007, 24 for stage I, 26 for stages II and III and 32 students per class at stage IV. (At stage IV the number of lessons has been increased to allow for splitting larger classes for certain subjects, such as sport and languages.) The weights arrived at are 0.71, 0.92, 1.13 and 1.15 respectively. These weights are then used to multiply Tallinn's per student allocation from the state budget for teaching. This was 12166.3 EEK per student, which is arrived at by multiplying the cash allocation for 1 notional student, of 13670 EEK by Tallinn's weight, which is the lowest of all municipalities at 0.89. Tallinn then adds the unweighted amounts per student in the state budget for textbooks, teaching aids and workbooks.

Tallinn Education Department is clear that the purpose of funding schools by formula is to provide school directors with a lump sum budget, which they should manage efficiently. The department does not favor cost-based budget determination because it gives school directors little incentive to be efficient. The influence of Tallinn's funding system on promoting an efficient allocation to and within schools is examined in the next section on assessing efficiency.

3.5. Assessment of Outcomes

3.5.1. Efficiency

The assessment of the influence of the per student funding system on the effiiciency of schools is examined in three parts. First key indicators are considered: these are the numbers of schools, size of schools and student-teacher ratios at the system level over the period 1992 to 2006 or 2007. The second aspect considered is the policies of municipalities with respect to making their school systems more efficient. The evidence is drawn from the four case-study municipalities. The third aspect is an assessment of how the management of resources at the school level has been affected by the per student funding system and what kind of incentives for improved efficiency in the internal allocation and use of resources have been introduced.

3.5.1.1. System-Level Efficiency Indicators

Any assessment of the influence on per student funding on the internal efficiency of the school system must take into account the difficulties of maintaining an efficient network in the face of the decline in student numbers. Total students fell by 25 percent from 1998 to 2006. As the effect of the falling birth rate worked its way through the school age population, the decline in student numbers was much more severe in the early grades, as can be seen in Figure 3.6. Enrolment in the upper secondary grades actually rose due to increased participation in post-compulsory education by a student cohort too old to be affected by the great dip in birth rates. Thus, the need for adjustment has been much more pressing initially in primary grades.

As already noted, the post-independence creation of many small local governments caused the number of schools to burgeon. The introduction of a strong per student funding system in 1998 was intended to rectify this situation by putting financial pressure on local governments to reduce per student costs, where these proved too high to afford. How the school system has responded is shown by examining changes in the number of schools and in their distribution by size. The number of primary, basic and gymnasium schools is shown in Table 3.17 for four years between 1992 and 2006, together with the proportion of each type of school. The total number of public schools rose from 1992 to 1998 but has since declined by 139 schools or by 19 percent. This compares with a decline in total student enrolment between 1998 and 2006 of 25 percent. The number of primary schools fell somewhat more as basic schools and secondary schools have increased as a proportion of total schools from 75 percent to 85.4 percent. This is what would be expected given the larger decline in the lower grades and the initial spurt in the creation of primary schools by the newly founded municipalities.

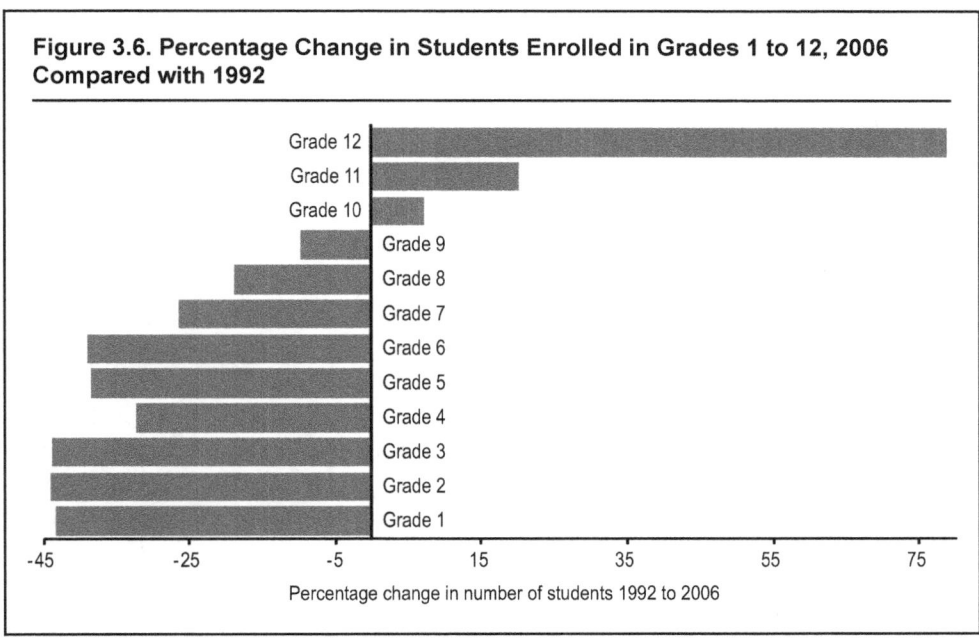

Figure 3.6. Percentage Change in Students Enrolled in Grades 1 to 12, 2006 Compared with 1992

Source: Ministry of Education and Research.

Table 3.17. Number of Schools, by Type: 1992-2006*

Number of schools	1992	1998	2002	2006
Primary (grades 1-3)	22 (3.2)	11 (1.5)	7 (1.1)	14 (2.4)
Primary (grades 1-4)	62 (9.0)	96 (13.3)	58 (9.1)	27 (4.6)
Primary (grades 1-6)	88 (12.8)	72 (9.9)	52 (8.2)	44 (7.5)
Basic (grades 1-9)	284 (41.2)	309 (42.7)	279 (43.9)	264 (45.1)
Upper secondary (grades 1-12)	233 (33.8)	236 (32.6)	240 (37.7)	236 (40.3)
Private schools		29	32	31
Total public schools	689	724	636	585

Source: Ministry of Education and Research
Note: Proportions of each type of school on total number of schools is shown in parenthesis.
* A historical review—all the way from 1981—of the evolution in the number of schools by type is offered in Table A2, in the Annex.

As the number of schools has declined, though less rapidly than the number of students, schools have tended to become smaller, as can be seen from Table 3.18. Although the very smallest category (less than 50 students) has fallen as a percentage of all public schools, the proportion in category 51–100 has increased and that in category 101–300 fallen, while the percentage of large schools (over 1,000) has halved. Taking all schools together, the system has succeeded quite well in the face of demographic decline in preventing the distribution of schools from skewing even more towards smaller schools. Nevertheless, per student costs in Estonia are burdened by the relatively large number of small schools: in 2006, 40 percent had 100 or fewer students. Considering only basic schools, which have 9 grades, 54 percent enroll 100 or less students, which means that their average class size is 11 or less, unless they organize mixed-grade classes.

Table 3.18. Distribution of Public Schools by Size Categories: 1992 to 2006 (Percentage of Total)

Size category	1992	1998	2002	2006
Less than 50 students	22.1	18.9	17.1	17.9
51-100 students	15.8	16.7	13.8	21.9
101-300 students	29.2	32.5	34.3	27.2
301-600 students	13.6	12.1	14.2	15.9
601-1,000 students	13.5	13.4	14.8	14.7
Over 1,000 students	5.8	6.4	5.8	2.4

Source: Ministry of Education and Research

Average class size for the years 2000 to 2004, for which data were available from the National Statistical Office, has declined in all but the highest grades as can be seen from Table 3.19, reflecting the greater demographic decline in the number of younger pupils and increased participation of older grades. The figures refer to the number of students in the main class into which students are organized: larger classes are split into two teaching groups for specified subjects, therefore the average size of teaching groups is smaller than the classes given in Table 3.19.

Table 3.19. Average Class Size in Estonian Public Schools: 2000-2004

Year	Grades 1-3	Grades 4-6	Grades 7-9	Grades 10-12
2000	21.3	23.2	23.5	26.1
2001	20.8	22.8	23.6	26.3
2002	20.1	21.9	23.5	26.3
2003	19.5	21.1	23.3	26.3
2004	19.3	20.1	22.8	26.4

Source: National Statistical Office.

The available data on the number of teachers only gives the total number for the years 1990 to 2006 without distinguishing full and part-time teachers: there are no data on full time equivalent (FTE) teachers. The ratio of students to the total number of teachers is shown in Table 3.20. This indicates a continual fall in the student-teacher ratio, which is consistent with the qualitative opinions expressed by those interviewed and is in line with expected trends, given the sharp decline in student numbers. However, this way of calculating this indicator, using total teachers rather than total FTE teachers, is not a good indicator of changes in the efficiency of teacher deployment, as it does not take into account any changes in the average number of lessons per week worked by teachers. The student-teacher ratio calculated this way could fall but at the same time the average number of lessons a week taught per FTE teacher could rise thus preventing a decline in the efficiency of deploying teachers. A pupil to full time equivalent teacher ratio would be a much better indicator of changes in the efficiency in the deployment of teachers, but these data were not available.

Thus, one can conclude from the national data on school numbers that the per student funding system has promoted efficiency to some extent by exerting pressure on municipalities to close schools. Also the number of teachers in the system has been reduced from a peak of 18,000 in 1998 to around 15,800 in 2006, though this was not sufficient to prevent a fall in the student-teacher ratio. However, it should be noted that the data are not strictly comparable, as data on the number of teachers are available from 1990 to 2000 on the National Statistical Office website, while MER could provide data on the number of teachers in 2006 only.

Table 3.20. Student-Teacher Ratio in Estonian Public Schools: 1990-2006

1990	1995	1996	1997	1998	1999	2000	2006
12.9	13.3	13.0	13.2	13.2	12.0	11.8	11.1

Sources: National Statistical Office 1990 to 2000, MER for 2006

3.5.1.2. Municipal Management of Their School Network

Of the four municipalities visted, Tallinn had the most explicit drive to improve the efficiency of its school network. In Tallinn funding schools via a formula has exposed schools which are too small to be financially viable. In the face of a 32 percent decline in student numbers between 1998 and 2007, the number of schools fell from 80 in 1994 to 75 in 2007, though the number had increased to 84 in 2002. The number of small schools has also been reduced as a percentage of the total, as can be seen from Table 3.21. The percentage of schools with fewer than 100 students has declined from 12.6 percent in 1998 to 9.4 percent in 2007, while the percentage of schools with 300 to 1000 students has risen. However, the number of schools with over 1000 pupils fell quite considerably between 1994 and 1998. According to data provided by Tallinn, the capacity of its schools–if full–has fallen from 99,000 students in 1998 to 67,000 in 2007. Given that the number of students is just over 40,000, there is still considerable over-capacity and the education department is continuing to seek school closures.

Though the school network in Talllinn has become more efficient in terms of the size distribution of schools, the number of teachers has risen at a time when student numbers have declined. According to the Tallinn Education Department, the number of FTE teachers rose from 1277 in 1994 to 1866 in 2007, implying a reduction in the student-teacher ratio from 44 to 28.[26] A major reason for this reduction in the student-teacher ratio is that in 1994 teachers taught up to 36 lessons per week, where as 10 years later it had been reduced to 20-24 per week. Another reason is that the average size of classes

Table 3.21. Tallinn City: Distribution of Schools by Size (Percentage of Total), Selected Years

	1994	1998	2002	2007
1-20 students	1.3	1.3	1.2	0.0
21-50 students	3.8	3.8	3.6	2.7
51-100 students	6.3	7.5	6.0	6.7
101-300 students	13.8	16.3	16.7	13.3
301-600 students	17.5	18.8	22.6	24.0
601-1,000 students	37.5	45.0	42.9	45.3
Over 1,000 students	20.0	7.5	7.1	8.0

Source: Tallinn City Education Department.

declined from 40 in 1994 to 25 in 2007. There are also more extracurricular activities provided outside the formal lesson time, which have increased in number as space in schools was freed up due to abandoning double shift schooling. In Tallinn's case the reduction in the student-teacher ratio and average class size cannot be said to indicate a deterioration in efficiency, given how high these were in the mid 1990s and that their reduction should have improved the quality of education.

The three small municipalities were much more reluctant to reduce the number of schools. Only Rae had closed a school by amalgamating a basic school with 37 pupils into a 720 student secondary school, housed in an attractive new building. The decision to close the basic school was made a few years earlier when its numbers had fallen to 75. There was a lot of parental opposition, which has receded with their experience of the alternative school. School transport is funded by the municipality, which provides a school bus service running several times a day.

Viimsi has three schools, a secondary school of 1,174 students in a newly opened state-of-the-art building, a basic school of 176 students and another basic school on Prangli Island (18 km from the mainland) with 11 students and 6 full time equivalent teachers. The municipality asserts that it will maintain Prangli school even if it has only one pupil. The population in the mainland part of Viimsi is growing and the large secondary school is already at full capacity.

Mustvee operates two secondary schools, which are only half a kilometer apart, for just 385 students. Two schools exist because about half of Mustvee's population is Russian, descended from the migration of Old Believers in the 17th century. Both gymnasiums have long traditions stretching back to the nineteenth century and have good inter-school relations. At present,[27] closing either of the schools is not contemplated because of the political opposition this would arouse, though in pure cost terms, as can be seen from Table 3.22, this would be justified, particularly as in the younger grades the students from both schools could be accommodated in one class. Around Mustvee are several villages with very small primary and basic schools. Some parents from these villages prefer to send their children to the Mustvee schools and travel by bus is not difficult. The mayor commented that these villages cling on to their schools for emotional reasons. The three rural municipalities illustrate the widespread resistance to closing small schools in villages.

Table 3.22. Tallinn City: Classes and Students in the Two *Gymnasium* Schools, 2007

Grade	Estonian Gymnasium	Russian Gymnasium
Grade 1	9	7
Grade 2	12	14
Grade 3	9	17
Grade 4	14	15
Grade 5	18	28
Grade 6	20	24
Grade 7	13	22
Grade 8	16	25
Grade 9	19	19
Grade 10	16	18
Grade 11	14	7
Grade 12	18	22

Source: Mustvee municipality.

3.5.13. Municipal Management of School Resources

Tallinn's formula funding regime is intended to promote internal efficiency within schools by "placing demands on school directors that they find the most economical way of running their school" (Tallinn Director of Education Services). The other three municipalities fund their schools by agreeing a budget for each school which will pay for the number of classes the municipality agrees to fund and hence the consequent teacher hours required by MER regulations, with additional teaching time funded at the municipality's discretion. The school budgets include funding for non-classroom based staff, utlities, maintenance and learning materials. Viimsi requires each school to produce a development plan to support its budget proposals. Both Rae and Viimsi have great differences in expenditure per student in their schools because of differences in their size. This is particularly marked in Viimsi where Prangli school's (11 students) recurrent costs per student were 173,000 EEK in 2007 compared 46,000 EEK at Viimsi secondary school (1,174 pupils). While Viimsi secondary school teaching allocation per student are roughly the same as the per student state grant, the municipality funds higher teaching costs at the other two schools from its own revenues.

Viimsi puts pressure on school directors to manage their budgets efficiently by giving them the annual budget as a control total within which the school director must manage. Once agreed, the school director has to manage the schools' expenditures within the control total. The other two municipalities practiced traditional input-based budget allocation and reimbursed expenditures. Apart from their ability to influence the annual budget settlement, these school directors' subsequent discretion was limited to certain non-staff items, such as learning materials.

All four municipalities have centralised accounting systems. While the schools have individual budgets, the financial transactions are administered by the municipality. This saves on the costs of employing personnel with accounting skills at school level, which would not be an efficient use of resources for small schools. Tallinn has recently centralised its school accounting, eliminating the different accounting systems used by schools in favor of a single accounting software package. Schools never handle cash. The two school directors interviewed considered the system worked well, for example invoices are paid in a day. This compared favorably with the previous arrangement when the school had to order cash some time in advance before being able to order and pay for goods and services. The interview evidence indicates that the municipalities operate an efficient accounting system for schools. In part this reflects the early adoption of computerized accounting in the Estonian public sector.

The four municipalities have spent considerable sums in recent years on refurbishing school buildings. The schools visited were quite well-maintained, while some had received lavish renovation (e.g. two had an olympic standard swimmming pool) and two schools had been relocated in new buildings. As central government limits municipal borrowing to 60 percent of their annual revenues, municipalities have to find other sources of capital funding. Rae sold municipal assets such as land to invest in a new building for its largest school, Juri Gymnasium. Viimsi, being short of its own land, devised a public finance initative scheme to fund a new building for Viimsi secondary school. The municipality set up a private company, which could borrow on the capital market, to build the school.[28] Now that the school has been built, the company rents the building to the school and charges for its services in operating the building. The efficiency of this arrangement is questionable. The school director can no longer directly manage the school building. The quality of cleaning is poor and the school director can do little to improve it. The annual building operation cost (including rent) per student is 21,000 EEK or 46 percent of the school budget, which is extremely high.

3.5.1.4. THE RELATIONSHIP BETWEEN RESOURCE MANAGEMENT AND LEARNING OUTCOMES

The line of accountability between responsibility for providing schools with resources and accountability for the quality of learning outcomes in the Estonian education system is blurred by the joint responsibility of MER and municipalities for funding schools and by the remaining role of the county education department in inspecting and evaluating schools. MER regulates educational standards through legislation specifying the state national curriculum content and teaching times. Maximum class sizes are also specified. There are national tests at grades 3, 6, 9 and 12, but only the results of tests at grades 9 and 12 are publicly available. They are published at school level by the press for the best 100 schools. The county education departments used to inspect schools by observing lessons and testing students in grades 3 and 6 and making comparisons with national averages. This inspection regime has been recently replaced by school self-evaluation in which schools evaluate their processes. The education departments provide schools with training for self-evaluation as well as professional development and consultancy advice for teachers and schools. Three percent of the state grant for teacher salaries should be spent on teacher professional development and county education department inspectors can put pressure on municipalities if they think insufficient is being spent on training or learning materials.

There is some debate as to whether county education departments still have a useful function. For a large municipality, like Tallinn, the value of a parallel organization with responsibility for school quality is questioned. However, small municipalities do not have the resources to employ staff for monitoring and promoting school quality. Tallinn has an explicit education strategy in which the main priorities are managing the education network so as to provide every child with a place according to their needs and abilities, and improving the learning environment and the quality of management. Tallinn has promoted and funded ICT in schools, including the e-school which provides parents with detailed information about their child's school and the child's progress. Tallinn also uses a system of performance related pay for school directors who are evaluated annually on their management of staff, finances, student learning and behavior, and external relations. Evidence examined includes student drop out and test results.

Currently, there is lack of data on which to assess the comparative quality of schools in value added terms. As far as has been ascertained, no value added analysis of the grade 9 and 12 test results or of PISA 2006 scores was available at the time of writing. The lack of such data makes it particularly difficult to make any judgement of the influence of per student funding on students' learning outcomes. Some experts express concern that per student funding, by rewarding schools which recruit well, contributes to increased differences in educational attainment between schools as parents become more competitive in their attempts to secure a place for their child at an elite school. Because secondary schools recruit pupils from grade 1, pressures on children to secure selection to a high performing school can start very young in areas where parents have choice of school. Some parents compete to secure places at those kindergartens which focus on preparing children for selection tests to elite schools at seven years old. Competition for school places at an early age is due to the pre-independence structure of the school system: post-communist pressures for individual economic success in the labor market and per student funding of schools have further accentuated it. However, changing the structure of the school system to eliminate all-age schools (even in urban areas) is not on the political agenda, despite the reported concerns of educationists about the undesirable effects of such selection, especially on children who fail to get selected for 'elite' schools.

> **Box 3.2. Per Student Funding: Efficiency Effects on Private Schools in Estonia**
>
> The funding formula has encouraged the development of private schools, though at 30 or so, taking 3 percent of students. This is still a small sector. This has provided a greater range of schools since the private schools are quite varied in character. They are not all expensive and exclusive schools for rich parents. There are a few international schools (these teach in English for both ex-patriate children as well as local children whose parents wish them to acquire fluency in English) and others, like Rocca al Mare, founded to promote specific educational values. Others cater for children with special needs. An interesting development is that some have been set up to fill a market niche for students who have attended secondary schools for grades 10-12 but failed to qualify for higher education and also failed to gain vocational qualifications by opting for the academic stream.

3.5.1.5. THE MANAGEMENT OF RESOURCES WITHIN THE SCHOOL

Having now considered efficiency issues at the national and municipal level, the next and last level to examine is the school. To what extent does the funding system promote efficient management of resources within schools? Evidence from nine schools visited in the four municipalities is drawn upon in considering how budgetary allocations are made within schools, focusing on determining the numbers and pay of teachers and non-teaching staff and on non-staff expenditures.

Municipalities and schools have some freedom with respect to teacher pay. There is no longer any differentiation of teacher pay by experience, as in soviet times. Salaries are differentiated according to four grades of teacher. Schools can assess teacher suitability for the first three grades. For the highest grade a teacher must take courses and present a portfolio and application to the National Examinations and Qualifications Center. Teachers must be paid the basic national salary for their grade. Municipalities can decide on their own salary rates in excess of the national basic rate. Viimsi, for example, has decided to pay 10-15 percent more than Tallinn in order to attract teachers. It also pays different salary rates at its three schools. Teachers in Viimsi secondary school get paid more as they teach larger classes. Teachers at the island school receive 20 percent more as this is mandated at state level. There is also variability in the number of lessons a week a teacher is required to teach for a full time salary of between 18 to 24 lessons a week. This provides some flexibility for schools with a tight budget to require more lessons per week or for schools which can afford it to award teachers by requiring fewer lessons per week.

The amount of grant allocated by the formula is designed to be sufficient so that in most schools there is money left over in the state funded part of the budget after basic salaries have been paid which is used for additional payments to teachers. The school director has the main say in determining the criteria for the bonuses, which varied amongst the schools visited. All awarded teachers for extra work, such as overtime, being a form teacher or organizing after-school activities. Viimsi secondary school had a clear performance related pay policy. Teachers have an annual performance review with their head of subject who proposes individual teacher weights for the bonus payment. Performance is judged largely in terms of activities for students. Only two out 100 teachers do not get a bonus because they not performing well. Interestingly, paying more to teachers in shortage subjects is not done as it would upset other teachers. At Viimsi secondary school the amount each teacher earns is not transparent and is not normally known by other teachers. Juri Gymnasium in Rae uses a similar system and takes account of how a teacher's students performed in examinations. At Lagedi school in Rae, salary is negotiated between the school director and the teacher according to the school director's assessment of the teacher's value to the school and how much she can afford to pay. Other schools had a more traditional approach. The City Russian gymnasium in Tallinn paid all teachers the same annual bonus (about 60 percent of the monthly salary). Not surprisingly, small schools had a communal approach based on assumed equality rather than individual desert. Puunsi School in Viimsi paid all teachers the same annual bonus. Here, the school director was concerned that performance related pay would not be transparent. Prangli Island school also paid all teachers the same percentage bonus.

In Tallinn, as school budgets are allocated by formula, school directors can determine the number of teachers and teaching hours employed at their school, subject to national curriculum regulations and terms and conditions of teacher employment. In the other municipalities the staffing establishment is agreed with the municipality as part of the annual budget negotiations.

School directors in Tallinn have to plan their expenditures constrained by the amount in the school budget determined by the formula. Except for emergencies, there are no additional amounts that can be negotiated from the municipality. The two Tallinn gymnasiums visited concentrated their planning efforts on the municipal part of the budget. According to the Tallinn school directors, the state funded part of the budget required little effort to plan as its expenditure is largely determined by the number of

Table 3.23. Tallinn City: Distribution of General Education Expenditure by Category, Selected Years

	1994	1998	2002	2007
Teachers	43	39	50	49
Non-teaching staff	17	20	23	21
Total non-staff recurrent	40	41	30	30
Teaching materials	3	4	4	3
Food	8	5	9	10
Utilities	25	21	13	12
Maintenance and repairs	4	5	1	2
Other	0	5	1	1
IT	0	0	2	1
Total recurrent	100	100	100	100
Capital expenditure as percentage of recurrent plus capital expenditure	6	24	2	11

Source: Tallinn City Education Department.

teachers that can be afforded from the state part of the budget. The municipal part of the budget is planned by first estimating all unavoidable expenditures and out of the remainder the school director decides how much is available to pay the technical and administrative staff as well as for learning resources.

Municipalities fund non-teaching staff from their own revenues. This term is used to cover all staff who are not classroom-based teachers, and includes school directors, deputies, educational psychologists and speech therapists as well as clerical staff and cleaners. The state makes a contribution to the salaries of school directors and deputies, but not other non-teaching staff categories. The MER has regulations, issued in 1999, specifying in some considerable detail, similar to the soviet era staffing norms, the non-teaching staff posts schools should have depending on school type and size (MER, 1999). Municipalities need to take account of these norms when determining their school budgets, as can be seen in Tallinn's funding formula in Table 3.15. When schools are small the municipality will fund a post, such as psychologist or speech therapist to cover several schools, or expect a large school to share staff services with smaller schools. School directors have some discretion in the employment of non-teaching staff. For example the diretor of a Russian gymnasium in Tallinn had been forced by a falling budget allocation due to decling students numbers to fire one of the 3 cloakroom attendants. He stated that the use of cleaners had become more efficient since the introduction of funding by formula. The MER was not able to provide data on the number of non-teaching staff employed at schools over time. Tallinn did provide such data, which show a steady increase from 387 in 1994 to 735 in 2007. This is due to schols employing new kinds of staff, in particular IT support staff and more security guards. Thus, there is little evidence that per student funding has been able to improve efficiency in the use of non-teaching staff apart from in some instances economising on cleaning staff.

One indicator of inefficiency in resource utilization at school level is a high proportion of recurrent expenditure on staff compared to the OECD average of around 19 percent.[29] Transition states were often characterized by a very high proportion of expenditure on gross wage costs as during a period of reduced funding for education staff posts were protected at the expense of non-staff expenditures, in particular buildings maintenance and learning materials. Of course, economic recovery and higher education spending can correct this tendency. Per student funding, if accompanied by greater school autonomy over budgeting, is also expected to promote some re-allocation of resources if schools no longer need to adhere to regulations on staffing norms and can over time shift spending from salaries to non-staff expenditures. MER was not able to provide data at national level on the distribution of education expenditure between different economic categories. However, Tallinn was able to do this for selected years from 1994 to 2007. As shown in Table 3.23 the proportion of expenditure on staff in 1994 was relatively low at 60 percent and has increased to 70 percent over the period to 2007. The fall in the percentage of expenditure that is for non-staff items is largely due to the fall in expenditure on utilities from 25 percent to 12 percent. The increase in the percentage spent on staff could be explained by increased flexibility in pay rates now that municipalities can set their own salaries, though teachers are still regarded as relatively lowly paid.

3.5.1.6. COMPARISON OF 1998-2007 AND 2008 FORMULAE

Comparing the efficiency incentives signaled by the previoius and the revised formulae is not easy as it is too early to tell how municipalities will react to the 2008 formula. The designers of the 2008 formula consider that it creates better efficiency incentives than the previous one because, being activity-led, it makes explicit the minimum number of pupils in each stage of schooling that central government funds for teaching costs. The previous top-down, purely per student formula did not inform municipalities about the relationship between numbers of students per grade and teaching costs and did not give clear signals about the size of grades below which the municipality would have to fund teaching costs above those financed from the state grant. At the time of writing (2008) it is too early to know whether municipalities will respond to the new formula by improving internal efficiency through more school closures and by creating larger classes. The 2008 formula shifted resources towards urban municipalities as they received an 18.2 percent increase in state education grant compared to 11.6 percent extra for rural municipalities.[30] The designers of the revised formula think that it has better efficiency incentives than the previous one because it informs municipalities which schools have teaching costs that exceed those funded by state grant. It was estimated that around 20 percent of schools with stage IV and III students have teaching costs which exceed those assumed in the 2008 formula. It is also argued that municipalities will not wish to run schools with stage I and II grades with less than 6 students per grade as such schools would have to operate with classes combing 3 grades unless the municipality provided additional funding. In the MoF view, parents and municipalities faced with the alternative of mixed-grade small classes or amalgamating schools and transporting children to a school with single grade classes will prefer the latter except where travel times are too long.

Given the lack of experience with the 2008 funding formula at the time of writing, the two formulae can only be compared in terms of the efficiency incentives they signal. The formula operating from 1998 to 2007 provided good efficiency incentives for municipalities because it was purely per student, apart from the weights which created different per student amounts dependent on the number of students in a municipality. Therefore, municipalities were given incentives to reduce unit costs through amalgamating or closing schools and increasing class size (up to the maximum size). The absence of any difference in the weights for students in different grade ranges to reflect differences in costs due to numbers of lessons per week was weakness of this formula as it penalized municipalities with a higher than average proportion of students in grades III and IV which have higher per student teaching costs. The 2008 formula has rectified this problem.

In contrast, the 2008 formula is per student only for those municipalities with more than 1600 Estonian or Russian students. For smaller municipalities the funding received depends the number schools run by the municipality as well as on the number of students and how they are distributed between schools. This blunts the incentive to close schools. For example a municipality with 20 students per grade in stage I (60 students in all) would get a state grant for teaching costs of 1,159,842 EEK if the students are enrolled in two schools (assuming 10 students per grade in each school) and 682,260 EEK if the students are enrolled in 1 school.[31] The 2008 formula creates discontinuities in funding per student at key transition points when the number of students in a grade increase by one and triggers off additional funding for an extra class. This is illustrated in in Figure 3.7, which shows the amount the new formula allocates per student for a school in relation to the number of students per grade, assuming for simplicity the same number of students per grade in each grade. There are ranges of student numbers over which an

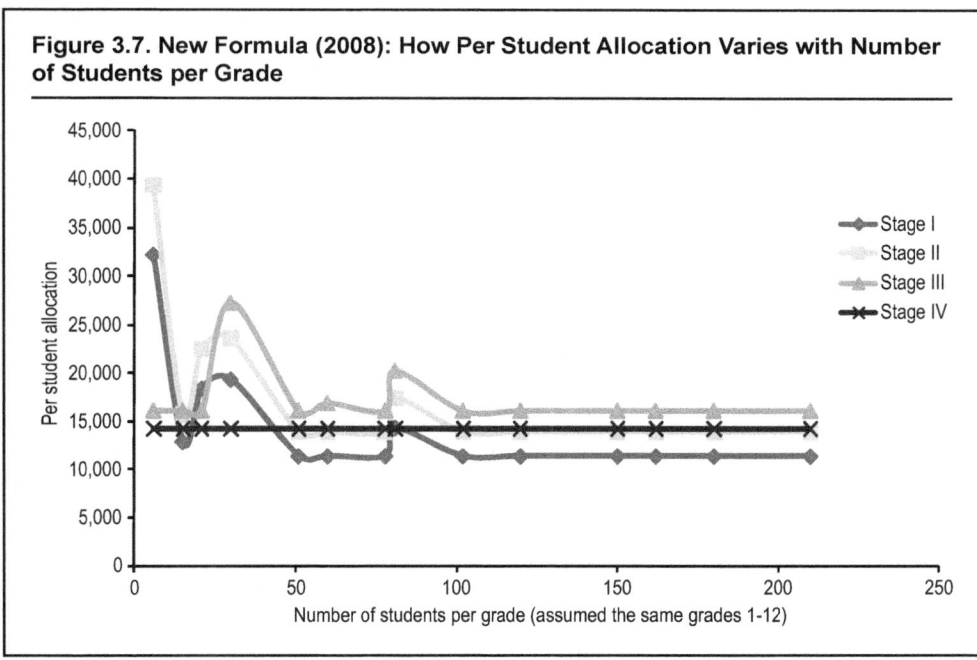

Figure 3.7. New Formula (2008): How Per Student Allocation Varies with Number of Students per Grade

additional student results in lower funding per student. Thus, the new formula has an element of moral hazard as it creates incentives for school directors and municipalities to organize students in stages I to III into grades in such a way as to maximise the funding per student.

3.5.1.7. SUMMARY: EFFECTS OF THE FUNDING FORMULA ON EFFICIENCY

The per student funding formula in Estonia was initially designed to encourage municipalities to operate more efficient school networks. The fall in the number of schools nationally and the reduction in the percentage of the smallest schools at a time of demographic decline indicates that the formula did contribute to preventing a decline in efficiency in relation to these indicators. However, as far as can be ascertained from the data, the student-teacher ratio has fallen over the last 10 years and, at around 11, is relatively low by OECD standards.

Considerable political opposition to putting pressure on municipalities to close small schools, especially for grades 1-6 or even 7-9, has emerged. With increasing affluence and a gradual migration to urban and suburban areas, the desire to preserve even very small rural schools for social reasons has strengthened. The pressure to sustain small rural schools is reflected in the revised 2008 funding formula which enables primary schools with as few as two students per grade to be financially viable, with mixed grade teaching.[32] By agreeing to adopt the new formula the government has made explicit its views on what is a financially viable school size, assuming the formula's class organization model. The new formula has the merit of making explicit central government policy towards school rationalization and focusing on sustaining small primary schools in villages, while funding older grades less generously for low numbers of students in the older grades. The policy expresses an explicit choice that favors the perceived social benefits of preserving small village schools near children's homes at the cost of internal efficiency.

The effect of per student funding on promoting efficiency in the utilization of resources within schools is dependent on how the municipality allocates budgets to school and holds school directors accountable. In the case of Tallinn, which uses its own funding formula, this encourages school directors to manage their schools' resources efficiently. Tallinn reinforces the incentives of allocating a control total for school directors to manage by including financial management in the criteria for assessing school director performance. Smaller municipalities negotiate budgets directly with school directors and in doing so make judgements about how resources should be used. All schools have their own budgets, so school directors have to pay some attention to how the funds are spent, especially for non-staff items.

An interesting feature of local school management in Estonia is the extent to which municipalities determine teacher salaries above the state basic pay rate. This flexibility extends to schools, so that different schools within the same municipality and teachers within the same school can receive different rates of pay, based on a number of criteria, including individual performance. This contributes to the area variation in teacher salaries and to how much they differ from average salaries in other occupations, as shown in Figure 3.8. From an economics perspective the usual assumption is that enabling salaries better to reflect market valuations and individual performance is allocatively efficient. Such flexibility does, however, raise questions about equity, when municipalities differ in their revenues per resident and hence in their ability to fund a given level of educational provision.

As the Estonian political system values self-determination by municipalities, this places considerable limitations on central government powers to require efficiency from local governments. A municipality is free to decide to spend money on maintaining costly small schools or on lavish new school premises and is held accountable for such expenditures by the local electorate. The small size of most municipalities should

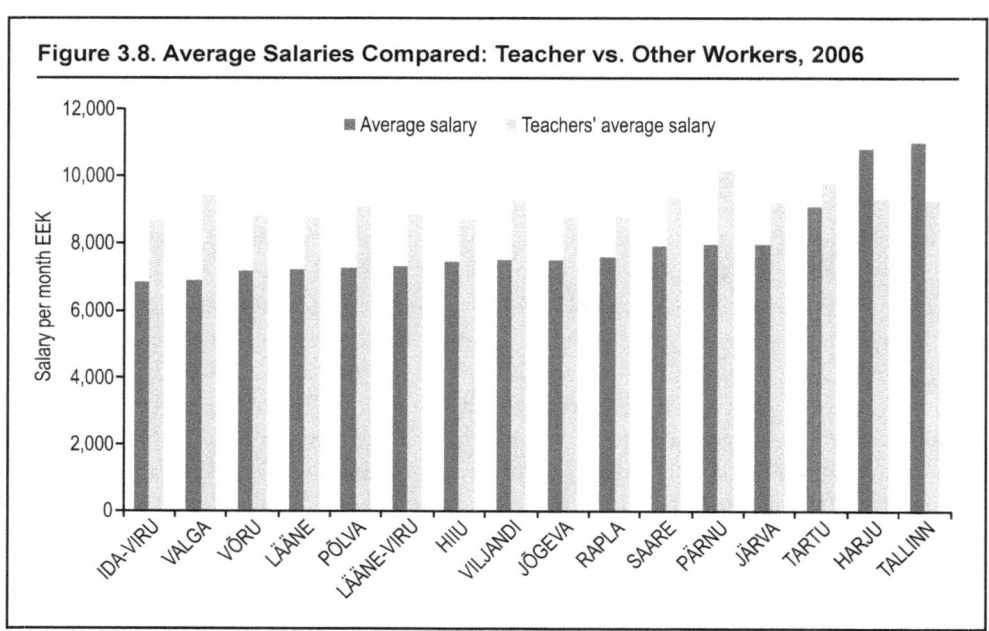

Figure 3.8. Average Salaries Compared: Teacher vs. Other Workers, 2006

Source: Ministry of Finance.

make it easier for local people to have greater involvement in local democratic decision making and be better informed about it than in large local government jurisdictions. Resource allocations that are internally efficient using narrow criteria of cost per student for a given quality of education, may well be different from those that are selected by collective local preference for a wider range of social objectives. Given the value placed on the freedom of local governments to determine their own priorities and the relative weakness of central governments formed from coalitions of parties, the absence of a strong drive from central government to improve the internal efficiency of the education system is understandable, especially in a period when the total demand of the schooling system on the public purse has been declining due to the falling number of children and rising public revenues.

Overall, the relative efficiency of the Estonian education system, as far as can be judged by international comparisons of expenditure per student relative to GDP per capita and the results in the PISA 2006, is high. Estonia scored significantly above the OECD average in maths, reading and science—where it came fifth. The proportion of high scoring students in science was high and that of low scoring students small. This good performance was acheived with a expenditure only slightly higher than the OECD average. Estonian lower secondary student expenditure as a ratio of GDP per capita was 0.25 in 2004 compared to the OECD average of 0.23.[33]

3.5.2. Equity

In assessing the per student funding system in relation to equity, vertical and horizontal equity are considered.

3.5.2.1. VERTICAL EQUITY

Vertical equity refers to the unequal treatment of unequals (Monk 1990). Here two dimensions of inequality are considered: differences in students' learning needs as defined by indicators of 'special need' and differences in municipal ability to pay for educational provision. The latter consideration is about equity in the distribution of the fiscal burden on residents.

The funding formula addresses vertical equity in relation to differences in learning ability by including a number of additional indicators for students with special educational needs. The categories and additional weights for funding for special needs are shown in Table 4 above. From this it can be seen that children with special needs are mainly educated in separate classes, units or schools and the muncipilaties are funded on a per student basis for children attending these forms of provision. Home-teaching has a particularly high weight of 4 to 4.4 reflecting the one-to-one teacher student ratio. From 2006 the previous formula included allocations for pupils with special educational needs in regular classes. The 2008 formula continued with the same categories and weights. The main problem with special educational needs funding commented on by teachers and school directors is not the inadequacy of the weights but the fact that parents are very reluctant for their child to be identified as having special needs. There is a medical process of certification which requires parental agreement. Parents are reported to fear that their child will be stigmatised by such a label and refuse to co-operate with the certification process. Consequently, children whom teachers perceive as having special needs and requiring additional provision do not obtain additional funding, leaving schools to cope with any ensuing problems due to lack of funding for appropriate provision.[34] Clearly, this is an issue that can only be tackled by a fundamental change in both the substance and image of special education, which a funding formula can at best support but cannot influence by itself. The 2008 formula, by providing some additional funding over and above the amount notionally required to fund each municipal schools according to the MoF/MER formula, enables local governments to use some of this 'spare' funding to give schools additional resources to support any students whom schools identify as having special needs but who are not officially categorized as such.

As education funding is a shared responsibility between central and local governments, municipal tax revenues, as well as education grant, affect their ability to resource their schools. The distribution of tax revenue per student is shown in Figure 3.9. Just under 80 percent of municipalities have between 20,000 to 60,000 EEK tax revenue per year per student. Neither the previous nor the 2008 education grant formula include any element to offset inequality in the distribution of local government tax revenues per student. Fiscal equalization is undertaken by a separate general grant. which, as already noted, equalizes 90 percent of the difference between average tax revenues and the assumed costs of the municipality's responsibilities.[35]

Using data from National Statistical Office on individual municipal tax revenues and expenditures plus data from the MoF on education grants, education spending per student and financial contribution per resident to education are compared for 6 groups of municipalities in Table 3.24. On average for the groups of municipalities, expenditure per student is similar in urban municipalities. The richest group of urban municipalities spends slightly more per student than the other two groups of urban municipalities and this is funded by a small additional contribution per resident. The rural municipalities spend considerably more per student, reflecting their smaller class and school sizes. Rich

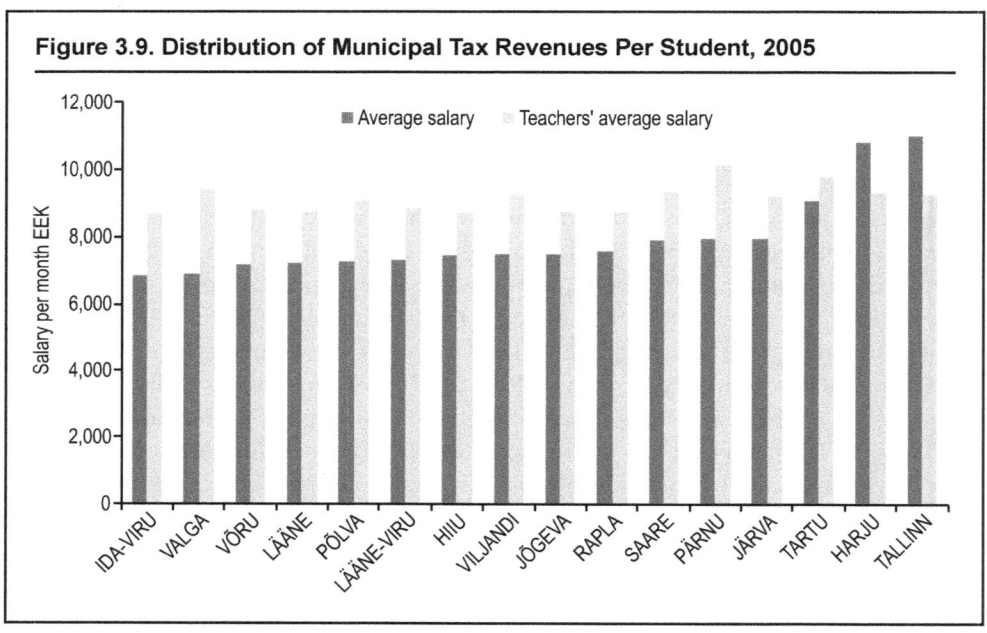

Figure 3.9. Distribution of Municipal Tax Revenues Per Student, 2005

Source: Ministry of Finance.
Note: Tax revenue is in thousands of EEK. Five municipalities with 100,000–380,000 EEK tax revenues per student are omitted from the histogram.

rural municipalities, however, spent on average over 50 percent more per student than less well-off rural municipalities, for which their residents contributed a third more per student. The fact that, on average, residents in poor and average income urban and rural municipalities contributed similar amounts per head to education spending suggests that the funding system for local governments does achieve equity in the distribution of the funding burden for local residents. However, about a quarter of municipalities contributed over 10,000 EEK per resident to education and the highest contributors were to be found amongst rural municipalities. Just a few poor and average income municipalities were contributing over 15,000 EEK per resident. An examination of the data indicates that these municipalities were maintaining one or two very small basic schools (grades 1 to 9). For example, Ruhnu with 101 inhabitants, contributed 24,000 EEK per inhabitant to run a 13 pupil basic school. Two other municipalities contributing over 20,000 EEK per inhabitant (Haanja and Vaivara) ran very small separate Estonian and Russian medium basic schools.

Table 3.24. Municipalities' Education Expenditure Per Student and Fiscal Burden on Residents, 2005

Municipality by type	Number of municipalities	Educational expenditure per student (EEK)	Municipality contribution to education per resident (EEK) Average (minimum, maximum)
Urban: poor	18	28,400	8,700 (6,050 to 12,550)
Urban: average	17	30,880	8,900 (6,850 to 10,730)
Urban: rich	3	32,530	10,600 (9,870 to 11,130)
Rural: poor	104	48,930	8,700 (5,650 to 20,320)
Rural: average	75	48,340	9,200 (6,250 to 27,43)
Rural: rich	17	73,130	12,800 (7,500 to 24,230)

Source: National Statistical Office website.
Note: The classification of municipalities follows that used by National Statistical Office.

3.5.2.2. Horizontal Equity

The criterion of horizontal equity for the distribution of expenditure is that students who have equivalent needs should be funded the same amount. The definition hinges on how 'equivalent needs' are defined. As students with special learning needs are considered under the criterion of vertical equity, horizontal equity is considered here with respect to 'regular students' ie those without special educational needs. Equivalence must also take account of structural cost differences. Only differences in expenditure per student which are due to differences in the structural costs of providing education in the local government area are consistent with horizontal equity.[36] The achievement of horizontal equity in educational expenditure per student nationally is incompatible with the political objective of local self-determination of spending levels on education (and other services) when localities have differing preferences for both the amount of pubic spending compared to private spending and different preferences for the distribution of public spending between the various local services. In these circumstances, the criterion of horizontal equity with respect to the funding systems is that local governments have sufficient local taxes and central government grants to be able to provide an equivalent common national standard of education for all students (excluding those deemed to need additional spending because of their learning needs), taking into account structural cost differences. If local governments decide to spend less or more than the amount needed to provide the national standard in their area, then so long as they can afford the standard, the central government financial equalization system is horizontally equitable, even though the school financing may not be. The problem with applying the criterion of horizontal equity to the school funding system is that a judgement must be made as to what each local government needs to spend in order to achieve a common equivalent national standard. This judgement must be informed by good data on the structural costs of a defined standard of educational provision in different localities. It was not possible within the limitations of this study to collect data at this level of detail and precision for Estonian municipalities.

The data on education expenditure per student from National Statistical Office indicate in Table 3.24 that this is higher for the more affluent municipalities, especially for rich rural ones. Using these data, a further examination of the relationship between education spending per student and local government affluence was undertaken. Expenditure per student was regressed on education grant per student, tax revenue per resident and some variables that are likely to associated with structural costs—population density, and size of municipality in terms of student numbers and area. Separate regressions were run for urban and rural municipalities. As shown in Table 3.25, both tax revenue per resident and education grant per student were positively related to expenditure per student. The number of students exerted a downward influence on expenditure per student, as economies of scale would lead one to expect. However, a large number of inhabitants was associated with higher spending per student. Area and population density were not significant and were therefore omitted in the regressions reported in Table 3.25.

Table 3.25. Determinants of Education Expenditure Per Student, by Type of Municipality, 2005

Independent Variables	Unstandardized Coefficients	t statistic	P-value
Regression for Urban Municipalities (values are in '000 EEK)			
(Constant)	21,520*	2.31	0.029
Education grant per student (2005)	1.87*	5.24	0.000
Tax revenue per resident	1.765*	2.45	0.021
Log of total number of students in 2005 (natural)	-2976*	-2.98	0.006
Number of inhabitants in 2005	0.024	1.58	0.127
Regression for Rural Municipalities			
(Constant)	130,179*	5.74	0.00
Education grant per student (2005)	1.16*	2.42	0.016
Tax revenue per resident	1.43*	2.35	0.020
Log of total number of students in 2005 (natural)	-24,504*	-7.39	0.000
Number of inhabitants in 2005	8.66*	7.65	0.000

Dependent variable: Education Expenditure Per Student, 2005.
Urban: adjusted R squared = 0.708. Number of cases = 30.
Rural: adjusted R squared = 0.531. Number of cases = 185.
Note 1:* indicates statistical significance at 99%.
Note 2: Some municipalities were excluded because of missing values.

The positive association between higher per capita tax revenues and education spending per student within both the urban and rural groups of authorities, indicates that even after for controlling for education grant, the school finance system overall was not horizontally equitable in 2005: the amount spent on a student's education, taking account of whether the municipality was urban or rural, depended on local income levels (as indicated by tax revenues per capita).

In making a judgment about horizontal equity it is also useful to examine school budgets in the case-study municipalities, as these differ considerably in wealth. In terms of tax revenue per student in 2005, Viimsi ranked 8th out of 220 municipalities, Rae ranked 25th, Tallinn 47th, while Mustvee was one of the poorest, at rank 217. As can be seen from Table 3.26, expenditure per student by school differed markedly. Prangli's extremely high expenditure is related to its very small size. Mustsvee's two schools are relatively small, while Viimsi and Juri and the two Tallinn gymnasiums are of more than minimum efficient size. Despite Mustvee's schools being smaller less was spent per student than in Viimsi and Juri secondary schools.[37] However, Prangli aside, the personnel costs per student were quite similar in the three rural municipalities, ranging from 23,457 to 19,575 EEK. Tallinn schools had the lowest per student personnel costs. Those for Tallinn Russian gymnasium were just 48 percent of those at Juri. There are even greater differences in expenditure per student in non-staff costs per student where the lowest is 12 percent of the highest. These school budget comparisons indicate that the main difference in spending between rich and poor rural municipalities is in operating costs. There is also a considerable difference between Tallinn where costs are low per student and the richer rural municipal larger schools. Municipalities have to fund non-staff costs largely out of their own budget whereas a much lower proportion of personnel costs come out of the municipal budget. Viimsi, as a rich municipality, was particularly lavish in the proportion of total expenditure on operational costs: at 50 percent this was well above the OECD average of 20 percent. The proportion was lower for the poor rural municipality, even though its schools are small, compared to the two richer municipalities. A school director in Mustvee pointed out that the school did not employ a psychologist or social worker or offer optional subjects, were short of foreign language teachers apart from English and lacked sufficient textbooks. When capital expenditure is included, costs per student were more equal as Mustvee spent a significant amount per student in 2007 on renovating old school buildings.

While Mustvee funds its two gymnasiums roughly equally, there is quite a disparity in per student expenditure between the two gymnasiums visited in Tallinn. The higher cost Gymnasium 21, has more teachers on the highest grade but it also spends considerably more on ICT and on the running costs for its building. This has been recently renovated by the municipality to a very high standard with an olympic standard swimming pool, splendid atrium and specialist teaching rooms, while the Russian gymnasium is still in an unrenovated building. School 21 earns a good income from letting its facilities which enables it to spend more on non-staff items than the Russian gymnasium.

Further disparities in spending per student might be observed if spending out of the schools' trustee funds could be compared. Schools can raise their own revenues from sponsorships and from 'voluntary' contributions from parents. It is to be expected that an 'elite' gymnasium, such as School 21 with a large proprotion of middle class parents, is in a better position than most schools to raise additional funds.[38] Thus, differences

Table 3.26. Comparison of Per Student Expenditure in 7 Schools in 4 Municipalities, 2007

	Prangli*	Viimsi*	Juri**	Mustvee Russian***	Mustvee Estonian***	School 21****	Russian Gymnasium****
Tax revenue per student ranking of municipality (from 221)	8	8	25	217	217	47	47
Number of students enrolled in school	11	1174	720	210	175	1,278	845
Personnel costs per student	85,782	19,575	23,457	20,668	20,225	12,452	11,372
Percent funded by municipality	59	32	47	26	26	NA	NA
Non-staff costs per student	86,028	25,076	9,961	5,973	7,411	5,146	2,949
Percent funded by municipality	98	96	92	84	87	NA	NA
Percent of non-staff costs in total current costs	50	54	30	24	29	29.2	20.6
Total recurrent cost per student excluding food	171,810	44,652	33,021	24,736	25,767	17,598	14,321
Percent funded by municipality	79	68	60	35	38	NA	NA
Total cost per student including capital	173,633	46,250	NA	40,927	43,921	19,805	16,351
Percent funded by municipality	78	66	NA	60	55	NA	NA

Source: Mustvee, Rae, Tallinn and Viimsi Municipalities.
* Viimsi Municipality.
** Rae Municipality.
*** Mustvee Municipality.
**** Tallinn Municipality.
Note 1: Per student amounts are in EEK. The budgets for the individual schools are provided in the Annex (Table A3.1 through Table A3.6). These present the state and municipal budgets of the schools separately.
Note 2: NA indicates data were not available.

in both municipal wealth and parental income result in differences in expenditure per student both between municipalities and between schools in the same municipality that are not due to structural cost differences. Some schools are able to pay teachers higher salaries to attract better staff and spend more on learning resources and school facilities.

3.5.2.3. COMPARISON OF PREVIOUS AND 2008 FORMULA

Neither the previous nor the 2008 formula take into account differences in municipal own revenues per resident. However, the 2008 formula reduces the fiscal burden on residents in rural municipalities that were making a relatively high contribution from own revenues per inhabitant to maintaining a high cost school network and in this sense is more equitable. Every municipality is funded equally for having schools of equivalent size with the same numbers of students per grade. For this reason that advocates of the 2008 formula argue that it is more equitable than the previous formula. However, the 2008 formula, like the previous one, takes no account of whether a high cost school network is forced upon a municipality by high structural costs per student such that costs could not be reduced by school closures or is due to local choice to maintain a costly school network for other social benefits. An alternative interpretation of equity is that a school funding formula should take account of structural cost differences between municipalities not actual cost differences based on existing school networks.

Box 3.3. A Look at the Effects of the Financing Reform on Quality: Equality of Outcomes in Estonia

Though more is spent on rural schools, due to their lower student-teacher ratios and higher per student operational costs, it is doubtful that those with poorer physical facilities and greater difficulty in recruiting teachers for specialist subjects in the older grades can provide as good a quality of education as would a larger school which could afford better facilities for the same amount of expenditure per student. At the time the data were collected for this chapter no evidence on the relative performance of students in different school locations, controlling for student socio-economic background was found. However, in the OECD's analysis of PISA 2006 (OECD 2007) Estonia also performs well in terms of equity, with a relatively low variance in its test scores, low between school variance in science performance and a relatively small proportion of the variance in students' science scores being explained by social, educational and cultural index of students' home background.

Table 3.27. Estonian National Test: 2006 Results (Average Student Marks)

Types of school	Subject and grade examined		
	Grade 9 Estonian language	Grade 12 math	Grade 12 Estonian language
Schools without catchment areas	80.82	63.7	67.68
Schools in county centers	70.98	53.25	60.14
Schools in big cities	70.44	50.82	57.07
Schools in rural areas and small cities	67.72	49.21	53.63
Adult education centers	66.16	29.2	42.09
Vocational Schools	Not applicable	17.04	35.34

Source: National Statistical Office.
Note 1: Schools without catchment areas are able to select pupils by ability.
Note 2: Marks for compulsory subjects shown.

Objective measures of externally moderated examination results in grades 9 and 12 are now available but data to control for the characteristics of students and schools that determine attainment are not yet collected systematically. Only raw examination data presented at the level of school groups were obtained and are shown in Table 3.27. The highest marks in national tests in compulsory subjects are obtained by schools that do not have catchment areas. These are secondary schools, which can select students by ability. Vocational and adult education center students do least well: (Vocational schools recruit less able students, and adult centers cater for second-chancers, who left school without exam passes). For basic and secondary schools, the worst performing are rural and small city schools, though the difference is very small between these and large city schools. However, the latter's student intake is likely not to include the most able students who have elected to attend selective schools without catchment areas. As the data do not correct for family background, we do not know whether children in rural and small town schools are on average from families of lower socio-economic status. Only if this explanation for the poorer results of rural and small town schools can be ruled out and the difference is statistically significant, could we conclude that these schools produce lower educational outcomes, as one might expect because of their small size, location, poorer non-staff resourcing and difficulty in recruiting teachers.

3.5.2.4. Summary: Effects of the Funding Formula on Equity

The 1998-2007 funding formula was equitable in a number of respects. It provided additional weightings for students with special educational needs, which were generally accepted as appropriate reflections of relative costs, as these are mainly determined by smaller class sizes. The failure of these weightings to apply to all students who need additional resources is due not to the formula itself but to problems of identifying special needs students because of the social stigma attached to this categorization.

Though the previous formula did not take account of differences in municipal tax raising capacity, municipalities are brought up to 90 of the difference between their estimated costs and tax revenues through a state equalization grant. This degree of equalization still does not provide a level playing field, given the evidence above that per student spending in municipalities is positively associated with tax revenues per capita

The previous formula took into account differences in the need to spend in a fairly crude way—apart from an island category, it used municipal school population size as predictors of differences in municipal structural costs. The reliance on these simple weightings is the main criticism voiced about the previous formula. It was quite widely perceived as unfair because it was claimed that some municipalities received more than they needed while others received less. However, in my view, this line of criticism usually assumes that the existing school structure in a local government determines its need to spend. So if two municipalities have roughly the same number of students in a similar sized area with similar transport links, and one municipality has one school and the other three, the latter is deemed to 'need' more per student than the former. It is this line of criticism of the previous formula that has motivated the design of the 2008 formula which interprets equity as meaning equivalent funding for municipalities for their existing number and size of schools.

Even though the municipal weights in the previous formula were fairly crude predictors of differences in municipal structural costs, the comparison of urban and rural municipal expenditure per student and municipal contribution to education spending per resident, indicate that on average urban and rural inhabitants' fiscal burden was roughly the same for average and poor municipalities, though there were some notable exceptions, with a few poor and average income municipalities having very high budget contributions to education per inhabitant. However, spending per student and contribution per resident were highest in the richest group of municipalities. So, while the fiscal burden did not appear to be inequitable for most municipalities, the evidence suggests horizontal inequity for students, since richer municipalities tend to spend more per student, particularly on non-staff items, for which there is a very small element of state funding. Comparisons of budgets for seven schools show considerable differences in expenditure per student that cannot be attributed to structural cost differences alone.

3.5.3. Transparency and Accountability

In examining transparency and accountability in the Estonian school finance system, first central govenment will be considered and then the financial flows followed to municipal level and finally to school level.

In terms of transparency a strong feature of the 1998- 2007 funding formula was its simplicity, with just 8 weights for different municipalities of different size and two for islands. The stability over time of the weights in the formula also aided transparency.

The previous formula was first developed by a working party with representatives from the major stakeholders (the two local government associations and school director association as well as MER and MoF) and was accurately known by all those interviewed in 2007. The development of the replacement formula was overseen by a representative working group of around 30 stakeholders. Consultative meetings of local government representatives and school directors were held where the proposals were discussed. Interviewees were all aware of these proposals and knowledgeable about the main features of the new formula.

Information about the flow of funds for education from central government to municipalities has changed as the method of transmission has changed. Before 2001 these funds were transferred by the MER to counties for disbursement to municipalities, and since then grants for education have been transferred to individual municipalities by the MoF. The amount of education grant each municipality receives is published on the MoF website. It was stated by some interviewees that the transparency of education expenditure had declined since the MoF took over the transfer of education grant directly to municipalities. According to MOF officers, this perception may be because the control methods of soviet times, when unspent money at local level was returned to the Ministry of Finance have been abandoned as a result of decentralization. Since municipalities are free to determine their own spending, detailed information on municipal budget lines no longer flows back and forth between counties and municipalities.

The calculation of each municipality's state grant for education by the previous formula was quite simple whereas the 2008 formula is very complex. While the general principle, that schools are funded so as to be able to afford the number of classes central government considers they need given the numbers of students in the different grade ranges, is relatively easy to grasp, the calculations of the amount of funding each municipality is entitled to are complex. The defintion of two kinds of classes—'small' and 'full'—is more complex than assuming one class size per education stage. Additional complexity is created by the amendment of per student funding to include additional lessons per week dependent on class size and additional funding to make up student numbers when either small classes or full classes have fewer students than needed to generate sufficient funding to cover teaching costs.

At municipal level there is a reasonable degree of transparency. As the law requires every school to have a budget, the amount spent on each school is publicly available information, though not widely published. Each municipality issues each of its schools with an annual budget, which is adjusted in September at the start of the new year. These budgets are approved by the municipal council. In small municipalities with only a few schools, the council should have intimate knowledge of the schools' budgets. The municipality holds the school director accountable for the management of the school budget. This is a major responsibility for a school director in Tallinn, which issues each school with a global budget to manage: the school director must provide the resources needed within the control total. In two other case-study municipalities, which base budgets on cost estimates, the municipality practices hands-on management of the budget. All the municipalities have centralised financial administration, which greatly restricts the scope for improper use of the school budget by schol personnel. School directors need to seek municipal approval if they wish to switch money from one budget line to another.

All the school directors interviewed stated that they presented the budget plan for the forthcoming year to the School Board for discussion and approval. School Boards were set up in the late 1990s. Their membership mainly consists of parents, with one or two municipal representatives or an ex-student. Boards at the schools visited varied between 7 to 10 members. School Boards are advisory and so do not have legal responsibilities for managing the budget. In the main, School Boards do not monitor the budget through the financial year, though they do usually receive a financial report on the spending of the budget at the end of the year.

Thus, the quality of financial control and management depends on the competence and financial probity of the municipality. One potential weakness in accountability at local level is that the school director is appointed by the municipality. These appointments can be politically motivated, as the political party in control of the local council may prefer to appoint a party member or sympathizer. School directors, as they are not state employees, can be members of the municipal council. It is therefore quite possible for school resourcing decisions at local level to be captured by particular interests.

Municipalities' accounts and financial procedures are subject to external audit. The Ministry of Finance does not check municipal expenditure—this is done by the state audit office. The presumption of a decentralized political system is that municipalities are free to make their own decisions and are therefore not subject to central government scrutiny, even for moneys provided by central government. The municipalities make annual financial returns to the MoF of their budget outturns, which contain details of the functional and economic categories of municipal education expenditure, though there may be some inconsistency in classification so that social expenditures, as on school food programs, are included as education spending. However, the MoF does not publish detailed data on municipal budget outturns on its website. The Estonian Statistics Office does publish data on municipal expenditures by service categories and by economic categories, but all education expenditure is included in a single category. It is not possible to separate out spending by stage of schooling or by national curriculum teaching and extra curricular activities.

Transparency and accountabilty in the school finance system present, therefore, a somewhat mixed picture. The transparency of the formula was good, though less so since 2008 due to the more complex formula. However, there are thorough consultation processes for agreeing the formula. School budgets are transparent at local level and, provided the municipality is competent and upright, school directors are held accountable for those areas of school budget expenditure that are within their discretion. Apart from standard auditing, little appears to be done to hold municipalities accountable for the expenditure of public money on schooling, as it is assumed that municipalities are not, apart from rare instances, engaged in fraudulent practices.[39]

3.6. Conclusions

In Estonia, the prime motivation for introducing per student funding to general education was political decentralization, which had led to the creation of numerous small municipalities. It is acknowledged that many municipalities are too small to be efficient administrative units for education; however they are valued as vital organs for local self-determination. The funding of general education was changed to a form of per student funding soon after independence. The opportunity was also taken to encourage the development of private schools, through providing them with at least the state per student funding allocation. A few years later, in 1998, the purely per student formula was introduced in order to improve the efficiency of the school network which had declined post independence as the recently formed municipalities re-opened pre-war schools. The higher per student costs of rural municipality and island schools was reflected in per student weights according to the size of the municipality in terms of student numbers and island locations. A revised formula which better protects small schools in smaller municipalities was introduced in 2008.

For a funding formula to operate smoothly, schools must be provided with sufficient funding for them to pay for the resources they must employ in order to comply with the regulations that govern the provision of education. Unless the formula can deliver exactly the amount a school needs to pay for the inputs it is required to provide for each student, the authorities that manage schools need some flexibility to ensure that schools are adequately funded. Therefore, in designing a formula, a balance has to be struck between regulatory constraints and permitted flexibilities. In Estonia, the main regulatory constraints faced by municipalities in discharging their duty to provide general education and the main flexibilities are listed in Table 3.28. The main constraint of per student funding is that municipalities have to operate within the budget constraint of the grant allocated by formula, whereas in an input-based funding system local units

Table 3.28. Constraints and Flexibilities in the Estonian School Funding System

CONSTRAINTS	FLEXIBLE ELEMENTS
The annual total grant from central government to municipalities for general education is fixed. The formula allocates a fixed amount to each municipality which is intended to cover the costs of teaching, in-service training, textbooks and workbooks and contribute to investment.	The previous formula kept back 2.5 percent of the total grant which was as a reserve to which municipalities could apply for additional funds according to MoF criteria. Municipalities are expected to finance non-teaching staff and operational costs of schools and can provide additional funding for teaching costs from their own resources.
Municipalities must provide compulsory free education in grades 1 to 9 and free education in grades 10-12, and must provide private schools with at least the state grant per student.	
National curriculum; specifies hours that each subject must be taught to students over a three year grade range (i.e. grades 1-3, 4-6, 7-9 and 10-12).	The municipality can fund additional teaching hours for split classes, optional subjects and extra-curricular activities.
Class size: the maximum is 24 in grades 1-9 and 36 in grades 10-12.	There is no limit to minimum class size–this is determined by municipalities.
Teachers are required to teach between 18 and 24 periods a week for a full time salary.	
Teachers must be paid the basic nationally determined salary for their grade. Staff who are not qualified teachers must be paid the national basic rate as a minimum.	Municipalities can pay more than the basic salary to teachers and other staff. Schools in the same municipality can pay different rates above basic pay.
Only qualified teachers can be employed to teach.	Teachers who are not qualified in a subject may still teach it.
The MER specifies norms for non-classroom teachers and non-teaching staff schools should employ according to type and size.	Municipalities can organize shared staff between schools.
Existing network of schools: in rural areas with good communications there are more schools than needed if the system were created from scratch.	The municipality can decide to close schools.
Health and safety regulations.	

are funded in relation to the inputs they already have in place and in accordance with past spending levels. There are sufficient flexibilities in the Estonian system, for the formula funding system to function smoothly (by this is meant that there are few instances of schools being unable to pay for necessary inputs). The budget constraint imposed by the state grant is eased by the ability of municipalities to use their own revenues and apply for additional funding from central reserves. The 2008 formula has further eased the funding constraint for small municipalities with small schools and classes.

The 1998-2007 pure per student formula provided a countervailing force to the growing inefficiency of the school system due to falling student numbers: it exerted pressure on municipalities to close small schools so preventing a greater decline in efficiency than would otherwise have occurred. Political will to use per student funding as an instrument for promoting school efficiency waned given economic growth more buoyant public revenues and strong rural opposition to the closure of village schools. The 2008 formula has weaker efficiency incentives than its predecessor as it reflects a preference for the perceived social benefits of preserving village primary and basic schools over the alternative use of the resources, such as creating larger and better resourced schools in rural areas to which students are bussed. The 2008 formula ensures that municipalities with less than 1600 Estonian or Russian medium students can afford the teaching costs of the number of classes within existing schools that the formula assumes tare needed, given the values of key determinants of school costs. The 2008 formula is a decisive move away from pure per student funding though not from funding schools by formula.

The legislative requirement that all schools have a budget should be a strong factor in promoting efficiency in the allocation and management of schools' resources by making school costs and their allocation to different inputs transparent. School budgets provide directors with the means to improve school efficiency, if they are able to avail themselves of it. All the school directors interviewed were actively involved in managing their school budgets, though the extent of this varied with the degree of budget delegation practiced by the municipality. As Estonians value local self-determination, there is a widely prevailing view that municipalities should be able to operate a high cost schools system if they so choose, as do many of the rich municipalities as well as some small rural ones. However Tallinn, which accounts for a quarter of Estonia's school population, does strive to achieve an efficient sized school network and promotes the efficient management of resources within schools by operating its own school funding formula. Overall, the PISA 2006 results taken in conjunction with international comparisons of education spending per student as a proportion of per capita GDP indicate that Estonian education at lower secondary level is comparatively efficient, despite the burden of financing high cost small schools.

At the time it was devised, the 1998-2007 funding formula was supported as an equitable method of allocating state education grant between the local governments in a decentralized system. The municipal weights in relation to numbers of students were selected as a simple and transparent way of reflecting average cost differences between municipalities in relation to their size. The fiscal burden on residents, in terms of the municipal contribution to education spending per resident in 2005, was on average very similar between urban and rural municipalities of poor and average tax revenues per inhabitant, indicating that the local government financing system overall was equitable for tax payers, though there were exceptions—a few poor municipalities with very high educational contributions per inhabitant. Analysis of data for 2005 shows that the school financing system in Estonia was horizontally inequitable, as students in more affluent municipalities had more spent on them per capita. The 2008 formula is unlikely to change these spending patterns, though it will make it less burdensome for poor and average income municipalities to maintain small schools. Both the previous and 2008 formulae contain no equity enhancing element for allocating additional funding to areas with lower income or more socially disadvantaged residents. Fiscal equalization grants bring municipalities up to 90 percent of the difference between estimated costs and tax revenues, but this still leaves a considerable disparity in revenues between the majority of municipalities and the high income municipalities. Differences in expenditure per student are illustrated in the budgets of individual schools which were examined for this study. Even if fiscal equalization succeeded in creating a level financial playing field for local governments, a political system which prizes local self determination for spending on public services will be nationally horizontally inequitable in the provision of specific local services when local preferences for spending on these services differ.

The assessment with respect to transparency and accountability is mixed. The previous funding formula was simple and hence transparent. In contrast, the 2008 formula is much more complex. As schools are legally required to have a budget, the allocation of resources to schools is transparent at local level and, given the small size of many municipalities, involves direct negotiation between school directors and mayors and is approved by the council. Tallinn has a transparent funding formula. Municipalities appear to operate efficient financial administration systems, which are centralized and computerized. As it is left to municipalities to determine how they utilize public funds, the MoF and MER take little interest in how municipalities spend education funding. Consequently, despite the existence of data on school budget outturns, there are no national level data on the amount spent on different types of educational resources or on different types of schools or grade ranges of students.

The recent history of school funding formula in Estonia well illustrates that school funding mechanisms cannot address all objectives equally: trade-offs have to be made between equity in its various interpretations, internal efficiency, transparency and external social benefits derived from specific types of schools. In replacing the previous formula the Estonian government has chosen to give greater priority to a particular variant of equity and to the perceived social benefits of preserving village schools at the cost of weaker efficiency incentives for the smaller municipalities and a more complex and less transparent formula.

References

Abu-Duhou, I. (1999). Issues in funding basic allocations per pupil by grade level: activity led funding. In K. Ross and R. Levačić, (Eds.) *Needs Based Resource Allocation in Education via Formula Funding of Schools*. Paris: International Institute of Educational Planning.

Estonian Ministry of Foreign Affairs (2006). 'Estonia Today: Population by Nationality: Fact Sheet'. Tallinn: Press and Information Department, Estonian Ministry of Foreign Affairs www.vm.ee accessed 10.12.2007.

Estonian State Chancellery (1993). *Basic Schools and Upper Secondary Schools Act*: www.legaltext.ee/text/en/X30049K9.htm (accessed 12.12.2007).

European Commission (2005). *Key Data on Education in Europe 2005*. Brussels: European Commission.
International Monetary Fund. (2010). *International Finance Statistics and Data Files*.
Monk, D. (1990). *Educational Finance: An Economic Approach*. New York: McGraw-Hill.
OECD (2001). *Reviews of National Policies for Education: Estonia*. Paris: OECD.
OECD (2007). PISA 2006: *Science Competencies for Tomorrow's World Vol 1*. Paris: OECD.
Põllumäe, S. (2002). "Rethinking the Sub-municipal Level of Local Government." Tallinn University of Educational Sciences, Department of Government Summer School "Public Management Reform" unpan1.un.org/intradoc/groups/public/documents/NISPAcee/UNPAN007842.pdf (accessed 14.12.2007).

Annex A. Additional Statistics

Table A1. Calculation of State Grant for Funding a School in a Municipality with Less Than 1600 Students in Each Language Medium, according to the 2008 formula

Grade	Number of students			
	Estonian Regular	Russian Regular	Estonian SEN	Estonian Evening
grade 1	5	2		
grade 2	5	1		
grade 3	10	2	2	
grade 4	20	1		
grade 5	27	2		
grade 6	35	2	2	
grade 7	7			
grade 8	50			
grade 9	60		3	
grade 10	10			20
grade 11	20			30
grade 12	30			30
SEN: Extended				
SEN: Simplified curriculum	5			
SEN: Moderate or severe			2	
Home teaching	1			
Total students	279	10	7	80

CALCULATION OF GRANT ALLOCATION FOR THE SCHOOL

Per student funding for regular classes

	No. students	Per student Amount (EEK)	Allocation (EEK)
Stage I	25	11,455	286,375
Stage II	87	13,982	1,216,434
Stage III	117	16,172	1,892,124
Stage IV	60	14,319	859,140
TOTAL	289		4,254,073

Funding for empty spaces (regular students)

Estonian	No. empty places	How calculated	Allocation (EEK)
Stage I	14	for grades 1+2 (17-10=7) and 3 (17-10=7), total 7+7=14	160,370
Stage II	11	for grades 4 (24-20) and 5 (34-27)	153,802
Stage III	10	for grade 7 (17-7)	161,720
Russian			
Stage I	12	for classes 1+2+3 (17-5)	137,460
Stage II	12	for classes 4+5+6 (17-5)	167,784
Cut to limit to 3 times per student amount	-4	(5 in Stage I*3 -17)*11,455 + (5 in Stage II*3-17)*13982	-50,874
TOTAL			**730,262**

1. Extra lessons for combined classes

	No. extra lessons	Criteria for extra lessons	Amount per lesson (EEK)	Allocation (EEK)
Estonian	4	2 grades in mixed classes	7,846	31,384
Russian	12	6 grades in mixed classes	7,846	94,152
Small basic school	2		7,846	15,692
TOTAL				141,228

2. SEN students

Stage	No. students	Per student amount	Allocation (EEK)
Stage I	2	11,455	22,910
Stage II	2	13,982	27,964
Stage III	3	16,172	48,516
TOTAL	7		99,390
For empty places	No. of empty places	Amount per place (EEK)	Allocation (EEK)
Stages I-III	10	16,172	161,720
Lessons for SEN classes	No. of classes	Amount per class (EEK)	Allocation (EEK)
	1	7,846	7,846

3. SEN curriculum

Curriculum Type	No. students	No. lessons per student	Amount per lesson (EEK)	Allocation (EEK)
Simplified	5	2	7,846	78,460
Moderate	2	4	7,846	62,768
Home tuition	1	4	7,846	31,384
TOTAL	8			172,612

4. Distance learning and evening classes

No. students	Per student amount (EEK)	Allocation (EEK)
80	11,455.2	916,416

5. Form teachers' addition

	No. classes	Amount per class	Allocation (EEK)
Regular classes			
Estonian			
Stage I+II	7	15,996	111,972
Stage III	7	15,996	111,972
Stage IV	3	15,996	47,988
Russian			
Stage I	1	15,996	15,996
Stage II	1	15,996	15,996
SEN class	1	15,996	15,996
Evening & distance	3	15,996	47,988
TOTAL	23		367,908

6. Extra Estonian lesson for Russian speaking classes

No. classes	No lessons per class	Amount per lesson (EEK)	Allocation (EEK)
1	2	7,846	15,692

7. Management costs

Number of students	No. posts	Management post salary	Allocation (EEK)
376	2.5	230,662	576,655

TOTAL GRANT FOR SALARIES			7,443,802

GRANTS FOR NON-SALARY EXPENDITURES

Type of non-salary expenditure	No. eligible students	Amount per student/class (EEK)	Allocation (EEK)
Textbooks	360	282	101,520
Workbooks	236	458	108,088
Investment grant per student	360	438	15,768
Investment grant	22.4 classes	21,900	490,560
TOTAL GRANT FOR THE SCHOOL (EEK)			8,301,650

Table A2. Numbers of schools in Estonia, 1981 to 2006

	Primary grades 1-6	Basic grades 1-9	Secondary grades 1-12	Special	Total
1981	72	237	189	43	541
1983	74	233	197	45	549
1985	81	232	204	42	559
1987	85	241	206	43	575
1989	100	246	216	44	606
1991	149	251	225	41	666
1993	190	259	228	47	742
1994	197	265	229	50	741
1995	196	269	228	49	742
1996	191	270	229	49	739
1997	182	268	232	48	730
1998	177	268	231	46	722
1999	169	256	236	45	706
2000	153	247	237	48	685
2001	130	242	236	46	654
2002	113	239	236	48	636
2003	106	236	235	48	625
2004	96	227	234	46	603
2005	91	225	236	46	598
2006	85	264	236	na	585

Source: Interview with A. Kommer (Tallinn University), Mimeo Estonia for data 1981−1989, National Statistical Office for data 1990−2005, MER for data for 2006.

Table A3.1. Budget of Prangli Basic School (2007)

Code	Item	Municipal budget	State budget	Total budget	% total current budget ex. food	Total current (ex. food) per student
50	**Personnel**	**559,427**	**384,175**	**943,602**	**49.9**	**85,782**
5002	Salaries	411,000	279,000	690,000	36.5	62,727
505	Social and other taxes	148,427	105,175	253,602	13.4	23,055
	Operating costs	**930,503**	**15,804**	**946,307**	**50.1**	**86,028**
5500	Administration	38,000		38,000	2.0	3,455
5503	Business trips	0	0	0	0.0	0
5504	Staff training	22,500	5,000	27,500	1.5	2,500
5511	Utilities	715,853		715,853	37.9	65,078
5512	Other buildings costs				0.0	0
5513	Vehicles	10,000		10,000	0.5	909
5514	ICT	48,000		48,000	2.5	4,364
5515	Furniture and equipment	57,000		57,000	3.0	5,182
5522	Medical and hygiene goods	3,200		3,200	0.2	291
5523	Art materials	3,600		3,600	0.2	327
5524	Textbooks and teaching aids	16,000	8,140	24,140	1.3	2,195
5525	Extracurricular materials	12,000	2,664	14,664	0.8	1,333
5532	Special clothes	1,000		1,000	0.1	91
5539	Other equipment	2,350		2,350	0.1	214
5540	Transport costs	1,000		1,000	0.1	91
4134	Subsidies for school food	0	20,059	20,059	1.1	1,824
15	Acquisition & repair of assets	0	0	0	0.0	0
	Total (excluding capital)	1,489,930	420,038	1,909,968	101.1	173,633
	Total (excluding capital & food)	**1,489,930**	**399,979**	**1,889,909**	**100.0**	**171,810**
	Total including capital	1,489,930	420,038	1,909,968	101.1	173,633
	Number of students	11				

Table A3.2. Budget of Viimsi Secondary School (2007)

Code	Item	Municipal budget	State budget	Total budget	% total current budget ex. food	Total current (ex. food) per student
50	**Personnel**	**7,339,312**	**15,642,077**	**22,981,389**	**43.84**	**19,575**
5002	Salaries	5,475,853	11,417,530	16,893,383	32.23	14,390
505	Social and other taxes	1,863,459	4,224,548	6,088,007	11.61	5,186
	Operating costs	28,243,509	1,196,175	29,439,684	56.16	25,076
5500	Administration	473,679		473,679	0.90	403
5503	Business trips	48,000		48,000	0.09	41
5504	Staff training	120,000	340,000	460,000	0.88	392
5511	Utilities	25,009,488		25,009,488	47.71	21,303
5512	Other buildings costs	303,200		303,200	0.58	258
5513	Vehicles	155,000		155,000	0.30	132
5514	ICT	1,127,112		1,127,112	2.15	960
5515	Furniture and equipment	245,000		245,000	0.47	209
5522	Medical and hygiene goods	175,000		175,000	0.33	149
5523	Art materials	80,000		80,000	0.15	68
5524	Textbooks and teaching aids	250,000	745,626	995,626	1.90	848
5525	Extracurricular materials	20,000	110,549	130,549	0.25	111
5532	Special clothes	100,000		100,000	0.19	85
5539	Other equipment	5,030		5,030	0.01	4
5540	Transport costs	132,000		132,000	0.25	112
4134	Subsidies for school food	0	1,676,381	1,676,381	3.20	1,428
15	Acquisition & repair of assets	0	200,000	200,000	0.38	170
	Total (excluding capital)	35,582,821	18,514,633	54,097,454	103.20	46,080
	Total (excluding capital & food)	35,582,821	16,838,252	52,421,073	100.00	44,652
	Total including capital	35,582,821	18,714,633	54,297,454	103.58	46,250
	Number of students	1,174				

Table A3.3. Budget of Juri Gymnasium School (2007)

Code	Item	State budget	Municipal budget	Total Budget	% total current budget ex. food	Total current (ex. food) per student
50	**Personnel**	**8,928,956**	**7,960,040**	**16,888,996**	**70.2**	**23,457**
5002	Salaries	6,698,392	5,776,720[N1]	12,475,112	51.8	17,327
506	Social taxes	2,230,564		2,230,564	9.3	3,098
55	**Operating costs**	**582,224**	**6,590,027**	**7,172,251**	**29.8**	**9,961**
5500	Administration		595,576	595,576	2.5	827
5503	Business trips		4,200	4,200	0.0	6
5504	Staff training	121,424	155,500	276,924	1.2	385
5511	Utilities		2,581,078	2,581,078	10.7	3,585
5512	Other buildings costs					
5513	Vehicles		33,000	33,000	0.1	46
5514	ICT		386,000	386,000	1.6	536
5515	Furniture and equipment		554,335	554,335	2.3	770
5521	Food supplies		286,369	286,369	1.2	398
5522	Medical and hygiene goods		36,645	36,645	0.2	51
5523	Art materials		1,189	1,189	0.01	2
5524	Textbooks and teaching aids	460,800	868,347	1,329,147	5.5	1,846
5525	Extracurricular materials		126,900	126,900	0.5	176
5539	Other equipment		16,100	16,100	0.1	22
5540	Transport costs		944,788	944,788	3.9	1,312
15	Acquisition and repair of assets	Data not supplied				
	Total excluding capital	9,511,180	14,549,478	24,061,247	100.0	33,418
	Total excluding capital & food	9,511,180	14,263,698	23,774,878		33,021
					Number of students	**720**

N1. Social taxes were not reported separately from salaries in the municipal part of the budget.

Table A3.4. Budget of Mustvee Russian Gymnasium School (2007)

Code	Expenditure category	Municipal budget	State budget	Total budget	% total current budget ex. food	Total current (ex. food) per student
50	Personnel	1,143,300	3,196,950	4,340,250	0.78	20,668
5002	Salaries	857,715	2,398,300	3,256,015	0.59	15,505
506	Social taxes	285,585	798,650	1,084,235	0.20	5,163
55	**Operating costs**	**1,048,900**	**205,500**	**1,254,400**	**0.29**	**5,973**
5500	Administration	85,000		85,000	0.02	405
5503	Business trips	4,500		4,500	0.001	21
5504	Staff training		71,950	71,950	0.01	343
5511	Utilities	431,900		431,900	0.10	2,057
5513	Vehicles	30,000		30,000	0.01	143
5514	ICT	20,000		20,000	0.004	95
5515	Furniture and equipment	55,000		55,000	0.05	262
5521	Food	400,000		400,000	0.07	1,905
5522	Medical and hygiene goods	3,000		3,000	0.001	14
5523	Books for library	3,500		3,500	0.001	17
5524	Textbooks and teaching aids	6,000	133,550	139,550	0.03	665
5525	Extracurricular materials	10,000		10,000	0.78	48
1510	Renovations (from Mustvee)	3,000,000		3,000,000	0.58	13,571
	Total (excluding capital)	2,192,200	3,402,450	5,594,650	1.08	26,641
	Total (excl food & capital)	**1,792,200**	**3,402,450**	**5,194,650**	**1.00**	**24,736**
	Total including renovations	5,192,200	3,402,450	8,594,650	1.65	40,927
					Number of students	210

Table A3.5. Budget of Mustvee Estonian Gymnasium School (2007)

Code	Expenditure category	Municipal budget	State budget	Total budget	% total current budget ex. food	Total current (ex. food) per student
50	Personnel	926,600	2,612,700	3,539,300	0.78	20,225
5002	Salaries	695,115	1,960,000	2,655,115	0.59	15,172
506	Social taxes	231,485	652,700	884,185	0.20	5052
55	**Operating costs**	**231,485**	**652,700**	**1,296,950**	**0.29**	**7411**
5500	Administration	1,129,100	167,850	78,000	0.02	446
5503	Business trips	78,000		5,000	0.001	29
5504	Staff training	5,000		58,400	0.01	334
5511	Utilities	432,600	58,400	432,600	0.10	2472
5513	Vehicles	30,000		30,000	0.01	171
5514	ICT	19,000		19,000	0.004	109
5515	Furniture and equipment	215,000		215,000	0.05	1229
5521	Food	327,000		327,000	0.07	1869
5522	Medical and hygiene goods	3,000		3,000	0.001	17
5523	Books for library	3,500		3,500	0.001	20
5524	Textbooks and teaching aids	6,000	109,450	115,450	0.03	660
5525	Extracurricular materials	10,000		10,000	0.002	57
1510	Renovations (from Mustvee)	2,150,000	700,000	2,850,000		
	Total (excluding capital)	2,055,700	2,780,550	4,836,250	1.00	27,636
	Total (excl food & capital)	**1,728,700**	**2,780,550**	**4,509,250**	**0.93**	**25,767**
	Total including renovations	4,205,700	3,480,550	7,686,250	1.59	43,921
					Number of students	175

Table A3.6. Budgets of Tallinn's Gymnasium Schools: School 21 and Russian Gymnasium (2007)

Tallinn code	Expenditure item	Gymnasium School 21			Russian City Gymnasium		
		Total Budget	% total budget (exc. food and capital)	Total current budget per student	Total Budget	% total budget (exc. food and capital)	Total current budget per student
50021000	Management grade salary	515,900	2.4	404	442,800	3.9	524
50021100	Additional pay	18,000	0.1	14		0.0	0
50021300	Management bonus	5,000	0.0	4	7,100	0.1	8
50021400	management holiday pay	105,700	0.5	83	90,000	0.8	107
50024000	Top grade teacher pay	1,192,729	5.6	933	503,100	4.4	595
50024100	top grade additional pay	23,000	0.1	18	9,000	0.1	11
5024300	Top grade bonuses	16,000	0.1	13		0.0	0
50024400	top grade holiday pay	165,171	0.8	129	70,100	0.6	83
50025000	Grade 3 teacher pay	856,600	4.0	670	592,900	5.2	702
50025100	Level 3 additional pay	18,000	0.1	14	15,000	0.1	18
50025300	Level 3 bonus	13,100	0.1	10	30,000	0.3	36
50025400	Level 3 holiday pay	77,900	0.4	61	53,900	0.5	64
50025500	Level 3 misc pay	2,000	0.0	2		0.0	0
50026000	Main grade pay	6,102,300	28.7	4775	3,488,000	30.4	4,128
50026100	Main grade additional pay	432,491	2.0	338	231,000	2.0	273
50026300	Performance pay	0	0.0	0	4,956	0.0	6
50026400	holiday pay	1,697,000	8.0	1328	975,400	8.5	1,154
50028000	Non teachers (workers) basic pay	547,600	2.6	428	579,700	5.1	686
50028100	Non-teacher additional pay	81,800	0.4	64	55,000	0.5	65
50028300	Non-teacher bonuses	17,700	0.1	14	15,000	0.1	18
50028400	Non-teacher holiday pay	40,100	0.2	31	47,100	0.4	56
50028500	Non-teacher misc pay	5,000	0.0	4		0.0	0
50028700	Non-teacher staff	5,400	0.0	4		0.0	0
	Total salaries	11,938,491	56.1	9342	7,210,056	62.9	8,533

		Gymnasium School 21			Russian City Gymnasium		
Tallinn code	Expenditure item	Total Budget	% total budget (exc. food and capital)	Total current budget per student	Total Budget	% total budget (exc. food and capital)	Total current budget per student
50600000	Social taxes	3,939,815	18.5	3083	2,377,700	20.7	2,814
50604000	Unemployment insurance	35,694	0.2	28	21,700	0.2	26
	Gross salaries	**15,914,000**	**74.8**	**12452**	**9,609,456**	**83.8**	**11,372**
55000000	Office goods	33,100	0.2	26	25,400	0.2	30
55000100	Printing	12,700	0.1	10	8,500	0.1	10
55001000	Communications	33,900	0.2	27	33,700	0.3	40
55001100	Post	1,600	0.0	1		0.0	0
55004000	Legal costs	4,200	0.0	3	5,900	0.1	7
55006000	Info and PR services	5,900	0.0	5	7,650	0.1	9
55030200	Business trips	9,069	0.0	7		0.0	0
55030400	Paervarahad	3,898	0.0	3		0.0	0
55040000	Training	278,900	1.3	218	187,300	1.6	222
55110000	Energy	766,100	3.6	599	237,300	2.1	281
55110100	Electricity	593,200	2.8	464	122,600	1.1	145
55110200	Water and sewerage	339,000	1.6	265	55,100	0.5	65
55110300	Repairs	200,000	0.9	156	12,711	0.1	15
55110400	Cleaning	614,700	2.9	481	67,800	0.6	80
55110500	Security	67,800	0.3	53	90,800	0.8	107
55110600	Refurbishment	101,700	0.5	80	99,200	0.9	117
55110800	Rent	13,600	0.1	11	16,155	0.1	19
55130800	Hire of vehicles	21,000	0.1	16	12,000	0.1	14
55140000	ICT	458,000	2.2	358		0.0	0
55146000	IT repairs	25,400	0.1	20	25,400	0.2	30
55148000	ICT communications	16,900	0.1	13	9,500	0.1	11
55150000	Inventory	92,600	0.4	72		0.0	0
55150010	Other	33,900	0.2	27	2,150	0.0	3
55156000	Repairs & maintenance	21,200	0.1	17	26,000	0.2	31
55211000	Catering	1,213,500	5.7	950	636,700	5.6	753
55223000	Medical items		0.0	0	76,300	0.7	90
55240000	textbooks	259,100	1.2	203	171,700	1.5	203
55242000	Workbooks	324,800	1.5	254	170,500	1.5	202

		Gymnasium School 21			Russian City Gymnasium		
Tallinn code	Expenditure item	Total Budget	% total budget (exc. food and capital)	Total current budget per student	Total Budget	% total budget (exc. food and capital)	Total current budget per student
55244000	Other study materials	110,200	0.5	86	50,900	0.4	60
55250000	Extracurricular materials	21,300	0.1	17	16,900	0.1	20
55252000	Special clothes	55,000	0.3	43	50	0.0	0
55252000	Events and exhibitions	12,900	0.1	10	18,600	0.2	22
60100000	VAT	831,133	3.9	650	304,700	2.7	361
	Total non staff	6,576,300	30.9	5,146	2,491,516	21.7	2,949
61000000	Depreciation	2,820,000	13.3	2,207	1,716,000	15.0	2,031
Number of students		1,278			845		
Total (excluding capital)		22,490,300	105.7	17,598	12,100,972	105.6	14,321
Total (excluding capital and food)		21,276,800	100.0	16,649	11,464,272	100.0	13,567
Total (including capital)		25,310,300	119.0	19,805	13,816,972	120.5	16,351

Annex B. List of People Interviewed for the Country Case Study

Tatjana Kiilo, Chief Expert, Foreign Relations Department, Ministry of Education and Research

Meelis Steinberg, Chief Specialist, State Budget Department, Ministry of Finance

Andrus Jõgi, Chief Specialist, Local Government Division, State Budget Department, Ministry of Finance

Teet Tiko, Head of School Network Bureau

Anneli Kommer, Tallinn University

Avo Veermäe, Head of General Secondary Education Division, Ministry of Education and Research in Tartu

Priit Laanoja, Analyst, Analysis Department, Ministry of Education and Research in Tartu

Director and inspectors, Tartu County Government

Mati Kepp, Mayor, Mustvee Municipality

School directors of Estonian and Russian Gymnasiums, Mustvee Municipality

Meelis Kond, Director of Education Services, Tallinn municipality

Andres Pajula Tallin, Head of the Education Department, Tallinn municipality

Liilia Oberg, Chief Expert, General Secondary Education Division, Tallinn municipality

Sigre Rõuk, Senior Specialist, International Relations, Tallinn municipality

School directors and deputy directors of Russian City Gymnasium and Gynmasium 21, Tallinn Municipality

Urmas Arumäe, Mayor, Viimsi Municipality

Endel Lepik, Vice Mayor, Viimsi Municipality

Kadi Bruus, Head of Education and Youth Department, Viimsi Municipality

School directors of Viimsi Secondary School, Püűunsi Basic School and Prangli Basic School, Viimsi Municipality

Raivo Uukkivi, Mayor, Rae Municipality

Enn Mänd, Vice Mayor, Rae Municipality

Tiit Keerma, Head Accountant, Rae Municipality

School directors of Juri Gymnasium and Lagedi Basic School, Rae Municipality

Rien Rebane, Director, *Rocca al Mare* Private School

Tiit Kirss, Advisor, Association of Municipalities of Estonia

Jüri Võigemast, Managing Director, Association of Municipalities of Estonia

Toomas Kruusimägi, School Director, Tallinn English College and chairman of School Directors' Association (Koolijuhtide Ühendus)

Notes

1. I would like to thank Tatjana Kiilo, of the International Relations Department of the Ministry of Education and Research, for organizing my study visit to Estonia from May 28 through June 8 of 2007. I would also like to thank Andrus Jõgi, of the Local Government Financial Management Department of the Ministry of Finance, for his unstinting assistance with information on funding formulae. I would finally like to thank everyone with whom I discussed education and who gave so generously of their time to explain the Estonian school funding system to me and show me around their schools. They are too many to name here and are listed in the appendix. All mistakes, errors of interpretation and judgments made are my responsibility.
2. "The Local Self-government Foundation Act adopted on November 10, 1989, re-established the basis for the local government system in Estonia. A month later, on December 10, 1989, the first democratic post-war municipal elections were held. From 1989 to 1993 the first tier of the Estonian local government consisted of rural communities, boroughs, and towns; the second—of counties. In December 1990 the Parliament established the Principles of local government. When the Constitution was adopted in June 1992, 90% of Estonia's 249 rural municipalities, boroughs, and towns were granted the status of self-governments. In May 1993 the State Assembly approved the creation of the one-level local government system and on June 2, 1993 adopted the Local Self-government Organization Act. On September 28, 1994, the State Assembly ratified in full the European Charter of Local Self Government." Excerpt from Põllumäe, S. (2002).
3. The BSUSS Act has been modified several times–the last being in 2005.
4. From data supplied by Ministry of Education and Research.
5. The majority of Russians originate from those who emigrated to work in new factories in Estonia after WWII, but there is also a long-established Russian emigré community of 'Old Believers' who moved to Estonia in the 17th century to escape religious persecution.
6. The language of instruction is that is used in 60 percent of teaching.
7. Schools which use Russian as the main language of instruction and which serve the Russian community.
8. Consequently vocational schools are not funded by the national formula examined in this chapter.
9. Section 6 of chapter 8 states that the expenses of a state school (i.e. one owned by MER) shall be covered by the annual State Budget Act in the amount prescribed for state schools within the budget of MER.
10. Information on the history of the formula is from an interview with Ms. Anneli Kommer, Head of Planning at MER in the period 1994-2002. Any errors are my responsibility.
11. The visit to Estonia to collect data took place in June 2007. I was updated on developments with respect to the 2008 formula by email correspondence with Andrus Jõgi.
12. The BSUSS Act is periodically revised.
13. Interview at MER.
14. I am indebted to Andrus Jõgi for this section, as he wrote a detailed explanation for it, which I have paraphrased, and unstintingly responded to my many queries. Any mistakes are my responsibility.
15. This issue can be illustrated by an example. Assume a per capita funding formula allocates sufficient money to fund the teachers for a class of 25 pupils. However the school has some grades in which there are 20 pupils and others in which there are 30. So it can organize classes of 20, for which it receives insufficient money, and offset these costs by having other grades with classes of 30 and use the spare pupil funding for five students to top up the teaching costs of the classes of 20. But if the maximum permitted class size is say, 28, then the school cannot have classes of 29 or more and would have to split them but it does not receive enough money in the formula for organizing classes of 15.
16. Teachers are required to teach between 18 and 24 lessons per week for a full time salary. The average of 21 hours is assumed for the formula.
17. There are four categories of teachers: junior teacher, teacher, senior teacher and expert teacher.
18. For the 2008 formula the basic teacher salary for the purposes of the formula is taken to be 10,000 EEK per month. This multiplied by 12 to get the annual salary, then by 1.333 to add in social fund contributions and then by 1.03 to include the costs of in-service teacher training. The total costs of a teacher in 2008 is 164, 759 EEK per year.

19. Additional funding in stage III is not granted if the number of students in grades 7-9 is less than 30 and in there are less than the following numbers of students: less than 36 in grades 1-3, 35 in grades 2-4, 34 in grades 3-5, 33 in grades 4-6, 32 in grades 5-7, 31 in grades 6-8.
20. The presence of gravel roads merits a coefficient of 1.2.
21. There is no investment grant for students in prisons.
22. Table A1 presents an example of how the new formula calculates the grant for a school in a municipality with less than 1,600 students in both the Estonian and Russian language mediums. The total state grant for the municipality consists of the sum of the grants worked out for each of its schools. As already noted, a municipality does not need to allocate to each school exactly the amount that the formula calculates.
23. Horizontal equity is defined as the equal treatment of equals and vertical equity as the unequal treatment of unequals (Monk 1990). The main problem with operationalizing the concept of horizontal equity is defining equals. It is standard to regard students in the same grade range and who have no special needs (i.e. 'regular students') as equals. Horizontal equity requires that such students receive the same per capita funding. The specification of equals requires further refinement when costs per student vary for structural reasons—that is factors beyond the control of the education authority, such as regional cost differences and geographic factors that make it infeasible to educate all 'regular' students in schools of minimum efficient size. Thus, for horizontal equity expenditure per student in each grade range (e.g. primary and lower secondary grade ranges) should be the same throughout the country, with any differences in expenditure per student being due only to difference in structural costs.
24. The municipalities were selected to include a poor small municipality (Mustvee) and a wealthy rural municipality (Viimsi) plus Tallinn. Rae was also visited as it was accessible from Tallinn.
25. Under the current (2007) formula the municipality could determine the allocation of state funding to private schools. The new formula will allocate the same amount to private and public schools, which have the same number of students per grade range.
26. The total number of teachers rose from 3,757 in 1994 to 5,490 in 2007, not only due to the reduction in lesson hours a teacher has to teach for a full time salary but also due to a considerable increase in the number of part-time teachers, of which there were only a few in 1994.
27. It is important to remind the reader that this chapter was finalized in 2008. Therefore, the situation refers to the prevailing conditions back then.
28. The legality of this arrangement was being investigated.
29. This percentage is reported in OECD (2006) Education at a Glance (and earlier editions).
30. Communication from MoF February 2008.
31. This assumes the same cash amounts per student as in given in Table 6.
32. With 2 students per grade the state grant would fund as if there were 18 pupils. One mixed age class for grades 1 to 6 could be afforded. As it is not permitted to mix so many grades the municipality would have to provide additional funding to run 2 classes. The formula designers think that fewer than 7 students per class in grades 1 to 6 is unlikely.
33. A simple regression of the PISA average score for maths, reading and science in 2006 on expenditure per lower secondary student as a proportion of GDP per capita for 33 countries indicated that the PISA score for Estonia is 20 points higher than would be predicted from the estimated coefficients and that this difference is statistically significant.
34. This point was made by some of the school directors and teachers interviewed.
35. From interview with Association of Estonian Cities.
36. In general structural cost differences are defined as those that are due to factors that the local government cannot control, such as small school and class size due to low population density, poor transport communications, climate and the divergence of the prices of local educational inputs from the national average.
37. Mustvee had recently experienced financial difficulties due to subsidizing communal water and heating, which it has now ceased doing. Thus, it chose to spend on these services rather than spend more on education.
38. A parent commented that the school made quite substantial requests for parental contributions.
39. Estonia ranked 24th out of 163 countries in the Transparency International Corruption Index 2006 (www.transparency.org/news_room/in_focus/2006/cpi_2006/cpi_table accessed December 20th, 2007). This is the highest of any ex-communist country.

CHAPTER 4

School Vouchers in Georgia: Implementation of a Simple Idea in a Complex Environment

Jan Herczyński[1]
Sergo Durglishvili

4.1. Introduction

The *rose revolution* of 2003 has brought to power in Tbilisi the strong reformist government of President Saakashvili. The government has been undertaking a series of far reaching reforms in many sectors of public life, trying to make up for the sluggish pace of reforms under the previous administration of Shevardnadze. The reforms in all sectors had been driven by liberal principles and the desire to grant more autonomy and freedom to most institutions. In education, the key beneficiary of the reforms was the school itself. Freed from the control and monitoring of corrupt local governments, and instead subordinated to the local community of parents, the autonomous school was given the right to decide, in the interest of the students and teachers alike, on key questions of budget and management.

The financing of autonomous schools had to come directly from the central Government to the schools, by-passing the local governments to avoid re-emergence of the previous system inherited from the Soviet times. The chosen financing system were the *vouchers*, which allocate the funds to each school proportionally to the enrollment (with some exceptions based on school location, see below). The voucher systems have many theoretical proponents, but few practical implementations. Georgia, alongside neighboring Armenia though in a completely different manner (see respective chapter on Armenian experience), made a bold if somewhat risky step to introduce an untried financing system. This brave step was part of wider radical overhaul of the country's administrative and institutional structures and very much in line with the hopes and promises of the rose revolution of 2003 (see Table 4.1).

The present chapter provides a sympathetic yet critical review of the voucher system in Georgia. It focuses on some key shortcomings of the system in the belief that only analysis of actual problems and difficulties may contribute to long term success of innovative and brave policy initiative. We review a number of thoughtful early decisions taken by Georgian reformers, such as network consolidation prior to education finance reform[2] and the avoidance of piloting phase (see also the timeline below). We point out, however, that serious changes need to be implemented to reduce the widespread phenomenon of *deficit schools* and the significant inequities inherent in the current system, if the vouchers are to become a stable financing system of schools.

The structure of the chapter is as follows.[3] In section 4.2, we discuss the background to the introduction of vouchers, in particular the preparatory work conducted by the Ministry of Education. The design and implementation of the voucher system is discussed in sections 4.3 and 4.4. An important implementation issue is how the Ministry treats the so—called deficit schools. The outcomes of the reforms are assessed in section 4.4. Section 4.5 assesses the outcomes of the financing reform along the domains of efficiency, equity, and transparency/accountability, but also touching on other important key areas like the reaction of stakeholders to the new system, and issues related to school autonomy and school competition. We conclude in section 4.6 with a brief review of main challenges facing the school voucher system in Georgia.

Table 4.1. Timeline of Key Events Related to the Education Finance Reform

Year	Key event related to per student financing reform in education
2003	Rose revolution open possibility of wide ranging reforms in Georgia
2005	Introduction of new data collection system in Georgian education
	Major school network consolidation
	Preparation of voucher system under Ilya Chavchavadze Project
	Ministry of Education becomes responsible for financing schools
	Ministry of Education obtains 30% increase of education spending in the national budget
2006	Introduction of the voucher system in Georgia
	Dissolution of local governments' education offices
	Increased institutional and budgetary autonomy of schools
	Creation of Education Support Centers to assist autonomous schools

4.2. Background

One of the main distinctive marks of the current reforms is a consistent and well publicized fight against corruption. Given the recent history of corruption at all levels within public institutions in Georgia, this approach has proved to be quite challenging.

Education finance was not immune to corrupt practices.[4] Two of the key challenges were the lack of transparency and the weak budgetary discipline, which characterized the inherited system of Soviet style local governments at the *rayon* and oblast levels. An important feature of those institutions were double reporting lines, both to elected local officials and to higher level institutions such as the line ministry. Thus, in education, *rayon* offices reported both to the local council, elected by voters, and to the oblast-level representatives of the Ministry, appointed by the central government. Similarly, and perhaps even more significantly, the analogous double reporting of budget offices effectively destroyed the budgetary autonomy of local governments.[5] This confusing arrangement dissolved any individual responsibility for financial decision making. The funds for education were sent to the oblast and *rayons*, which then distributed them among schools, in an unclear and unsupervised manner. Often a telephone call was more important in determining funding than decisions of local councils agreed through a formal voting procedure. Melikidze (2003) does a review of corruption in the Georgian education system just before the beginning of the current reforms. On the basis of a large survey and many interviews, the author assesses that there are two main forms of corruption in Georgian schools. One is private payments to public schools, solicited by the school director from the parents for the general purpose of school maintenance. These are very common and confirmed by 65 percent of parents and by 59 percent of school directors surveyed. This situation is usually accepted as "normal" by all stakeholders, especially in view of the very low teacher salaries (and is very different, we need to add, from paying teachers to increase marks given to students). Moreover, the sums of money involved are not very large. The second and much more serious issue is the misappropriation of funds earmarked for schools at the local government level. As Melikidze (2003) correctly points out, this type of corruption happened in fact outside of the education system. Anecdotal evidence shows that in some instances, complete investment projects were recorded and accounted for in the city documents, without anything being in fact done in the school itself, and without the school director being aware of the process.

As a result, the first radical step undertaken by the Ministry of Education (MoE) was to agree with the Ministry of Finance (MoF) to take those funds away from the system of local governments and to entrust them back entirely to the MoE. With this move, the loss of funds on the way to schools was stopped and their financial situation improved remarkably, even without increasing the allocation at the national level.

It is important to note that this line of reform activities of the Ministry was entirely consistent with overall liberal policies of the new Georgian government, which was to minimize the role of local governments, especially in the area of public finance. The main motivation for this approach stemmed from the need to fight corruption. The government took away most local government responsibilities, including health, social protection, and transportation. Some functions were decentralized to the level of service providers, some were centralized, accompanied by a serious effort to privatize providers of social services and to create market mechanisms.[6] Therefore, it was natural for Georgia to do likewise in education and to introduce decentralization directly to the school level in the area of school finance, while centralizing other functions in the sector. For example, openings and closings of schools is a responsibility of MoE, and as we discuss below it is exercised to achieve optimization of school networks. The Ministry also has to formally approve employment levels in all schools, although the current policy is to approve all the proposals from the schools, on the assumption *your vouchers, your decisions*.

Thus, fighting corruption was the main motivation of reform-minded education Minister Aleksander Lomaia and his team, which were in line with the priorities of the government. The reforms introduced to Georgian education management and finance very clearly serve this purpose. The key elements of the reforms may be summarized as follows:

- *Enhanced school autonomy.* Schools became independent entities under public law, with their own bank accounts and a right to enter contracts. School facilities are the property of the Ministry, given to the schools for use free of charge.[7] Schools are accountable to local communities, represented by school boards (or board of trustees, as they are sometimes called in Georgia). School boards have assumed significant responsibilities in the activities of schools, including the selection of school directors and approval of the budget.

- *Enhanced budgetary autonomy.* Although as discussed above formally the Ministry still approves the employment levels (number of positions), their salaries are set by the school director, together with the salaries of administrative and technical staff. Interestingly, the director sets his own salary as well. The key requirements are to fit within the budget as formed by the vouchers, and to have the approval of the school boards. An interesting open question is what happens if the school board does not approve the budget; it seems that this type of dispute is not regulated in the law.
- *Dissolution of rayon education offices and removal of any influence of local governments in education.* Direct administrative control over schools was removed, with a number of prerogatives taken over by the Ministry.
- *Introduction of state exams for school director candidates.* For each school, the Ministry proposes between 2 and 3 candidates who have passed the exams, and the director is chosen by the school board. Among the candidates, those who best passed the exams–top 20 percent of successful applicants–can choose to which school they will apply, while others are sent to specific schools chosen at random by the Ministry.[8]
- *Introduction of a school accreditation process and a teacher licensing system to ensure that the decentralized education system conforms to required education standards.* School accreditation will be performed every 5 years and will be a required condition of continued school operation. There is no separate school inspection in Georgia,[9] so accreditation will be the key education quality control mechanism.
- *Introduction of a per student voucher system to finance individual schools, which began in January 2006.* This element of the reform is the main focus of the present chapter.

The Georgian use of the term *school vouchers* is fully justified. Typically, school vouchers are such education finance systems in which the lump sum budget of the school is set to be proportional to the number of students, see for example Swanson and King (1991). In other words, vouchers represent the simplest possible formula-based allocation to schools, without regard to special needs of different groups of students.[10] The Georgian scheme departs slightly from strict proportionality in that it uses three differentiated values of vouchers for city, rural and mountain schools.

Although the reforms have been undertaken very recently, there has already been significant research into their design and impact. Godfrey (2007) discusses the fiscal and demographic context of the education reform.[11] In particular, the author analyzes the effects on Georgian schools of the very low proportion of the Gross Domestic Product (GDP) devoted to education. Zurab Simonia, the chief expert of the Ilia Chavchavadze Project involved in the design and implementation of the voucher system, wrote a review of the design of the voucher system (Simonia, 2007), including the new design of teacher wages. Tsagareishvili (2007) performed a financial review of finances of the so called *deficit schools*–those where the voucher funding is insufficient. Shapiro et al. (2007) also provide an assessment of the recent reforms based mostly on stakeholder opinions using surveys and focus groups. We use some of their insights in different places of the chapter. Therefore, the present chapter focuses mostly on the specific issues of the voucher system.

4.2.1. Preparatory Work to Introduce Vouchers

Preparations for the introduction of a new managerial and financial system in general education in Georgia were conducted by MoE in cooperation with the World Bank(WB)-supported *Ilia Chavchavadze Project*.[12] This project was responsible for the design of key new reforms in Georgian education, including also school director examination, school accreditation, and new institutional structure of the Ministry. The project received support from outside experts– provided by the consulting company Research Triangle Institute (RTI).

Prior to the introduction of the vouchers, the Ministry made two very important simultaneous steps as preparation to the introduction of vouchers:

- Conducted a massive school network consolidation process, reducing the number of schools from 3,154 in 2004/05 to 2,215 in 2007/08 with the target number of 1,800 schools. The ability to perform such a wide process of closing small schools testifies to great political strength of the Ministry. Consolidation process is still continuing, although on a smaller scale.
- MoE sought and obtained a government decision for a significant increase in the overall education allocation of 30 percent. Again, obtaining approval from the MoF for such a large increase of funds for education shows that MoE is a very strong political player. Nevertheless, education spending at under 2 percent of GDP is extremely low and should be increased.[13]

Regarding the consolidation process, MoE conducted a sort of school mapping exercise, and introduced some criteria for network optimization, such as proximity to a large school (especially in the cities), unsustainable small schools with possibility to transport students to a larger school (especially availability of roads in the mountains and countryside), small initial schools (which were changed into affiliated schools subordinated to a larger full secondary institution). The target of 1,800 schools was established on the basis of this analysis. The Ministry also bought a number of buses to help transport children to consolidated schools.

Those two steps made the introduction of the voucher system much easier, since they had reduced the number of schools with insufficient funding levels. It is very important to stress here that the voucher system is not seen as a tool to identify weak schools and to close them, rather the closures of small schools is a tool to introduce transparent financing mechanism of vouchers.

To support the newly autonomous schools with their new functions, MoE created a system of Education Resource Centers (ERC), whose function is to provide schools with legal and pedagogical support, with accounting services, and with management support for school directors. However, the Centers have no managerial and control responsibilities over the schools, whose full autonomy they are obliged to respect. ERC also collect enrollment and other statistical information from the schools and perform legal inspection of school activities. The design of ERC responsibilities was prepared by *Ilia Chavchavadze Project*, while USAID Georgia Educational Decentralization and Accreditation (GEDA) project assisted in their implementation[14] (through logistic support, initial and on the job training, provision of manuals and training materials, as well as support in rehabilitation of the premises and equipping the Centers).

We now focus on the process of consolidation of school networks in Georgia and illustrate it with actual school data.[15] The decrease of school numbers is shown in Table 4.2, with the last column providing the rate of decrease for each school size between 2004/05 and 2007/08:

Table 4.2. Number of Schools, by School Size

School size category	2004/05	2005/06	2006/07	2007/08	% change between 2004/05 and 2007/08
Below 20 students	638	71	92	59	90.8%
From 21 to 40 students	227	150	160	127	44.1%
From 41 to 60 students	225	214	215	193	14.2%
From 61 to 100 students	402	413	385	328	18.4%
From 101 to 200 students	715	740	720	622	13.0%
From 201 to 500 students	616	641	613	555	9.9%
Above 501 students	331	341	343	331	0.0%
Total	3,154	2,570	2,528	2,215	29.8%
Annual reduction in the number of schools		584	42	313	
		18.5%	1.6%	12.4%	

We note a significant effort to optimize school networks between the school years 2004/05 and 2005/06, with an almost 20 percent decrease in the number of schools. This reduction is most pronounced for the smaller-size schools, with a 90 percent decrease in schools with less than 20 students and a 44 percent downsizing in the number of schools with 20 to 40 students. An increase in the number of schools with larger student numbers shows the direction of consolidation, with students moving to larger consolidated schools. In the following year, 2006-07, network optimization was not as pronounced, but in the school year 2007/08 a second wave of consolidation occurred, with nearly 13% of schools closed. It is important to note, though, that network optimization was carried out under conditions of stable student population, as Table 4.3 shows.

Table 4.3. Number of Students, by School Size

School size category	2004/05	2005/06	2006/07	% change between 2004/05 and 2006/07
Below 20	6,741	970	991	85.3%
From 21-60	6,513	4,529	4,913	24.6%
From 61-80	11,466	10,721	10,935	4.6%
From 81-100	32,231	33,121	31,000	3.8%
From 101-200	102,625	107,158	104,173	-1.5%
From 201-500	194,095	201,561	190,611	1.8%
Above 501	274,576	282,770	281,123	-2.4%
Total	628,247	640,830	623,746	0.7%

Again, we see a large decline in the smaller school categories. It is worth noting that despite an overall declining trend of student numbers in Georgia, an increase was recorded in the school year 2005/06. We recall that 2005/06 was the first year of the voucher system and at least two processes intervened:

- Because of the importance of student numbers, a new improved data collection system—or Education Management Information System (EMIS)—was introduced in October 2005 as part of the WB funded project,[16]
- Schools had suddenly found an incentive to try to ensure more complete enrollment and to reduce student drop out.

Nevertheless, the calculations in Godfrey (2007) indicate that this was an isolated case and that the overall student population will decline in the coming years. Indeed, he assesses that between 2006 and 2010 the school age population (7-18 years old) will shrink from 689 thousand to 572 thousand.

Table 4.4 shows that the stability of the number of students together with the consolidation of school network in the school year 2005/06 led to a significant increase in the average school size.

Table 4.4. Change in the Average Size of Schools

	2004/05	2005/06	2006/07
Average school size	199.2	249.4	246.7
Increase compared to 2004/05		25.2%	23.9%

We see that the slow pace of network optimization in 2005/06 reversed the trend somewhat. However, the number of teachers[17] was increasing in both years, altogether by about 10 percent, despite the slight decrease of the student numbers between 2004/05 and 2006/07. As Table 4.5 shows, the highest increase was for schools between 201 and 500 students:

Table 4.5. Number of Teachers, by School Size

School size category	2004/05	2005/06	2006/07	% change between 2004/05 and 2006/07
Below 20 students	1,760	559	778	-55.8%
From 21 to 40 students	1,998	1,914	2,010	0.6%
From 41 to 60 students	2,879	3,288	3,325	15.5%
From 61 to 100 students	6,687	7,419	7,055	5.5%
From 101 to 200 students	14,373	17,179	16,513	14.9%
From 201 to 500 students	19,915	23,072	25,967	30.4%
Above 501 students	24,203	23,524	23,858	-1.4%
Total	**71,815**	**76,955**	**79,506**	**10.7%**

This had a negative impact on the student-teacher ratio,[18] as reported in Table 4.6:

Table 4.6. Student-Teacher Ratio, by School Size

School size category	2004/05	2005/06	2006/07
Below 20 students	3.8	1.7	1.3
From 21 to 40 students	3.3	2.4	2.4
From 41 to 60 students	4.0	3.3	3.3
From 61 to 100 students	4.8	4.5	4.4
From 101 to 200 students	7.1	6.2	6.3
From 201 to 500 students	9.7	8.7	7.3
Above 501 students	11.3	12.0	11.8
Total	**8.7**	**8.3**	**7.8**

The data in Table 4.5 may be misleading, as they refer to the physical teachers employed in the schools, and not just to their full-time equivalent. This artificially deflates the student-teacher ratio (STR). Indeed, as Table 4.7 shows, many teachers in Georgian schools work below the weekly teaching load of 18 hours (20 hours for initial education):[19]

Table 4.7. Average Number of Teaching Hours per Week per Teacher, by School Size

School size category	2004/05	2005/06	2006/07
Below 20 students	15.2	13.4	13.1
From 21 to 40 students	14.0	13.0	12.4
From 41 to 60 students	13.9	14.6	12.9
From 61 to 100 students	13.4	13.9	12.6
From 101 to 200 students	13.0	13.9	12.8
From 201 to 500 students	12.0	13.1	9.9
Above 501 students	12.0	14.4	13.0
Total	**12.5**	**13.8**	**11.9**

The increase of average number of lessons in the school year 2005/06 is difficult to explain and reflects either certain disorder in schools following massive consolidation effort or possible data errors. The first interpretation is supported by the observation that an increase is recorded in larger schools, those that had accepted students from closed small schools. It is possible that initially the larger schools had difficulties in using the teachers efficiently. Note nevertheless that, on average, a Georgian teacher works at about 66 percent of a full-time position. In order to assess full-time equivalent (FTE) teacher number, we need to review the number of weekly teaching hours and divide them by 18 (in our estimates we disregard the higher teaching load for initial education). We obtain the following Table 4.8:

Table 4.8. FTE Teachers, by School Size

School size category	2004/05	2005/06	2006/07
Below 20 students	1,483	416	566
From 21 to 40 students	1,549	1,384	1,385
From 41 to 60 students	2,229	2,660	2,387
From 61 to 100 students	4,981	5,723	4,938
From 101 to 200 students	10,383	13,306	11,715
From 201 to 500 students	13,312	16,729	14,306
Above 501 students	16,089	18,759	17,213
Total	**50,027**	**58,976**	**52,511**

As noted already in Table 4.7, the increase in 2005/06 is not easy to explain. Nevertheless, we see that the number of FTE teachers is also increasing, although at a slower rate than all types of teachers. Accordingly, the ratio of students to FTE teachers is also decreasing, though somewhat slower than the STR, as Table 4.9 shows:

Table 4.9. Students per FTE Teacher, by School Size

School size category	2004/05	2005/06	2006/07
Below 20 students	4.5	2.3	1.8
From 21 to 40 students	4.2	3.3	3.5
From 41 to 60 students	5.1	4.0	4.6
From 61 to 100 students	6.5	5.8	6.3
From 101 to 200 students	9.9	8.1	8.9
From 201 to 500 students	14.6	12.0	13.3
Above 501 students	17.1	15.1	16.3
Total	**12.6**	**10.9**	**11.9**

We observe that despite major consolidation efforts, most Georgian schools still have very low internal efficiency. Indeed, having a full-time equivalent teacher for about four students (as is the case with schools under 60 students) represents a very inefficient use of teacher resources. While for social and political reasons it may be necessary to maintain small isolated schools, the Ministry should introduce efficiency measures such as joint classes, multi-grade teaching, and improvement of teacher skills so that they are able to teach at least two subjects.

Interestingly, it seems that major effort of network optimization in 2005 led to fewer schools with significantly less efficient internal structure of teacher employment. This may indicate that the consolidation process was somewhat formal: all students and all staff of the small (closed) schools were transferred to the larger (consolidated) schools, without an improvement of efficiency. In other words, consolidation was an unprepared, somewhat rushed and ineffective process. However, in the following year the schools were able to adapt to the new situation, and in all school size categories except the smallest one the STR improved.

Finally, we note that network optimization was slightly more successful in bringing efficiency in employment of administration (excluding technical staff), as Table 4.10 shows:[20]

Table 4.10. Administration Staff, by School Size

School size category	2004/05	2005/06	2006/07
Below 20 students	403	133	177
From 21 to 40 students	298	309	353
From 41 to 60 students	422	542	558
From 61 to 100 students	1,063	1,243	1,133
From 101 to 200 students	2,438	2,666	2,446
From 201 to 500 students	2,796	2,792	2,462
Above 501 students	1,948	1,873	1,727
Total	**9,368**	**9,558**	**8,856**

Between 2004/05 and 2006/07, overall administration employment indeed decreased somewhat, however slower than the decrease of school numbers (year 2005/06 seems anomalous). Growth of administration staff in middle sized schools may reflect the policy of transferring administration staff, together with students, from closed schools to larger schools. The following Table 4.11 provides average number of administrative staff per school:

Table 4.11. Administration Staff per School, by School Size

School size category	2004/05	2005/06	2006/07
Below 20 students	0.6	1.9	1.9
From 21 to 40 students	1.3	2.1	2.2
From 41 to 60 students	1.9	2.5	2.6
From 61 to 100 students	2.6	3.0	2.9
From 101 to 200 students	3.4	3.6	3.4
From 201 to 500 students	4.5	4.4	4.0
Above 501 students	5.9	5.5	5.0
Total	**3.0**	**3.7**	**3.5**

It seems that administrative staff in large schools is not really sufficient to adequately service large student populations, with 5 administrator per over 800 students (compare Table 4.4 and Table 4.11). Nevertheless, from the efficiency point of view we note, again, that large scale network optimization in 2005 led to a decrease of efficiency, especially for small schools (probably this is due to the choice of small schools that were closed down[21]). In 2006 the trend was partially reversed.

4.3. The Design of the Funding Formula

4.3.1. The Design of the Voucher System

The Ministry needed a new financing system, which would ensure transparency, promote school autonomy, and lead towards more efficient use of financial resources. This meant that the required financial system would need to be very simple and easy to understand by all education stakeholders. Moreover, the funds were to be transferred directly to the school bank accounts, and not passed through *rayons* as before the reform. Clearly, the ministry wanted to allocate the funds to schools not on the basis of employment (as was historically the case, since the dominant element of the school budget are the salaries), but on the basis of enrollment, to implement the principle that *money follows the student*.

The Ministry also wanted to ensure education equity, and the simplest and most radical form of equity is making sure that for each student school receive the same amount of funding. This principle cannot be implemented in such a crude way, because there are many rural and mountain schools with extremely small classes in comparison with the cities. Providing them with the same level of funding on a per student basis would send them immediately into deficit. So the financing system had to take them into account.

The demand of simplicity and the need for equity dictated the choice of the school vouchers. In order to make sure that rural and mountain schools were not unfairly treated, three voucher values were introduced, for the cities, for rural areas and for mountains. As part of the World Bank-financed Ilya Chavchavadze Project, a voucher formula was devised in 2005 and implemented starting in January 2006, as part of the school year 2005/06. Thus, the current 2006/07 year is only the second year of operation of the system. Zurab Simonia, the main expert involved in this work, provides a review in Simonia (2007).

It is worth noting here that the Ministry did not see it necessary to introduce a pilot phase to test the voucher system prior to national implementation. This is unlike many World Bank-supported education projects, which include piloting of the formula before its full-scale implementation. Sometimes a number of independent simultaneous pilots has been organized, as in Tajikistan. Such pilots may be useful as learning exercises for new budgeting and managerial procedures, of course. This however requires their very careful preparations, so that for example the new powers of school boards are really transferred in pilot schools, while outside of the pilot the previous budget laws still operate. In practice the design of such good pilot project is very difficult, which means that sometimes they turn into formal exercises with little value both to the affected schools and to the monitoring agency.

It seems that two reasons lay behind the policy decision of Georgian reformers not to begin with a pilot. One reason is the specific Georgian motivation for education finance reform, which as we discussed earlier was related to corrupt practices of local governments formerly managing the schools. A pilot phase would have prolonged those practices in schools left outside of the pilot–most schools in the country–and postponed introducing better control over the use of education funds, to the detriment of the education process. A more fundamental second reason is that it is not at all clear what an allocation formula pilot would test. Indeed, if the question is whether the formula allocates enough funds for different types, locations, and sizes of schools, then simulations performed by the Ministry (for all the schools in the country, of course) would provide a much better understanding of who are the winners and losers under different possible formulas, without endangering the education process. Such simulations were indeed conducted by Zurab Simonia.

Another issue that we need to raise before we discuss in detail the Georgian system of school vouchers relates to systematic financial transfers from the Ministry to schools beyond the vouchers. The first transfer is a monthly allocation to schools, for which the vouchers are not enough. These schools are called *deficit schools* and their appearance is a major symptom that the voucher system is not very effective. We discuss deficit schools in more detail in the following section.

Apart from these funds for deficit schools, there are two types of transfers, called *supplements*. One type of supplement concerns additional support to schools in conflict zones (Abkhazia, South Ossetia). Those are either schools operating in very difficult conditions of reduced safety, or the schools for migrant populations. The second type of supplement is administered to provide funds to cover salary increases introduced by the government, such as an additional bonus for all the teachers to cover the increase of electricity and heating costs. The allocation of these supplements to schools is performed proportionally to the number of teachers and not proportionally to the number of students (as is the case with vouchers). The reason for this is that it is rather difficult to finance those specific allowances for teachers through adjustment of the value of the voucher. Thus, teachers receive 50 Georgian *Laris* (GEL) per year for gas and another 50 GEL for electricity price increases. Teachers also receive 120 GEL per year for a social program (health insurance). The supplements, of course, are inconsistent with the pure principle of per student financing. It is assumed that over time those supplements will be integrated into the voucher scheme.

Using vouchers means that the funds that the school receives from the central government[22] are proportional to the number of students. The voucher is used to cover the whole school budget, including teacher and non-teacher salaries, and school maintenance. However, capital expenditures were not included, as investment remained the responsibility of the central government.

On the basis of actual expenditures in schools it was assessed that 220 GEL is sufficient to cover teaching and maintenance expenditures of city schools (in conditions of 2005), however it is not enough for rural and mountain schools. Indeed, per student costs in small schools with small classes are relatively higher than per student costs in large city schools. The analysis of Ilia Chavchavadze Project experts led to the identification of three groups of schools that would receive different values of the voucher: for city schools, for schools in towns and villages (rural schools), and for mountain schools (schools located above 800 m. above the sea level). On the basis of the actual average class sizes for these three groups of schools the following ratios between the vouchers were adopted: rural (town and village) voucher at the level of 150 percent of the city voucher, mountain voucher at the level of 180 percent of the city voucher (see Simonia, 2007). The initial proposals to differentiate the vouchers also on the basis of education level were rejected after discussions with the Ministry of Finance.

Table 4.12 below provides the changing values of the vouchers (in 2007 there were two changes):

Table 4.12. Values of the Vouchers in Successive Years

Type of voucher	2005/06	2006/07	2007/08 (since October 2007)	2007/08 (since December 2007)
City voucher	220	235	250	300
Rural voucher	330	350	350	420
Mountain voucher	396	425	425	510

Table 4.13 now expresses those values as percentage of the city voucher:

Table 4.13. Values of the Vouchers in Successive Years as Percentage of City Voucher

Type of voucher	2005/06	2006/07	2007/08 (since October 2007)	2007/08 (since December 2007)
City voucher	100%	100%	100%	100%
Rural voucher	150%	149%	140%	140%
Mountain voucher	180%	181%	170%	170%

We note that initially in 2007 the relative values of the vouchers did not change (small changes are due to the desire to keep round values of the vouchers, e.g. 350 GEL rather than 352.5 GEL for rural voucher). In September 2007 the city vouchers were increased because the city schools had problems affording the heating costs. However, rural and mountain vouchers stayed unchanged, reducing their relative value to the city voucher from 150 percent and 180 percent to 140 percent and 170 percent, respectively (see Table 4.13). In December 2007 a new higher teacher pay scale was introduced,[23] and all three vouchers were increased at the same rate (the relative values of the vouchers in Table 4.13 did not change). We thus see that the Ministry was able to use the voucher system to reflect changing financial priorities.

Table 4.14 provides the distribution of schools by size categories and voucher type in school years 2005/06, 2006/07 and 2007/08 (we do not provide the totals, as they are already given in Table 4.2).

We note that the overall number of schools declines, reflecting continuing network consolidation. However, the numbers of schools in smallest size categories increased somewhat between 2006 and 2007, probably reflecting the demographic decline (with fewer students, a school may pass from higher to lower size category). In the school year 2007/08 we notice a second wave of school consolidation, especially marked in the cities, where most small schools were closed.

Table 4.14. Number of Schools in 2006, 2007, 2008, by Size Category and Voucher Type

	Voucher type								
	City			Rural			Mountain		
School size category	2005/06	2006/07	2007/08	2005/06	2006/07	2007/08	2005/06	2006/07	2007/08
Below 20 students	24	21		14	25	18	33	45	41
From 21 to 40 students	26	28	4	53	58	50	71	74	73
From 41 to 60 students	40	31	7	93	91	85	81	94	101
From 61 to 100 students	63	63	10	184	172	167	166	150	151
From 101 to 200 students	141	128	36	383	379	384	216	213	202
From 201 to 500 students	214	203	158	363	350	341	64	60	56
Above 501 students	286	292	283	50	47	44	5	4	4
Total	794	766	498	1,140	1,122	1,089	636	640	628

As expected, small schools are predominantly located in the mountains and villages, while large schools are concentrated in the cities. Interestingly, however, there are both very small schools in the cities, and very large schools in the mountains. The consolidation in 2008 has decreased the number of the small city schools, which are the easiest to integrate with larger units. Of course, those schools have very few students and FTE teachers, as evidenced in Table 4.15 (recall that FTE teachers are obtained by dividing the total number of lessons by 18).

Table 4.15. Number of Students and FTE teachers in 2006/07, by School Size and Voucher Type

School size category	Students, by Voucher Type			FTE teachers, by Voucher Type		
	City	Rural	Mountain	City	Rural	Mountain
Below 20 students	201	273	517	200	115	252
From 21 to 40 students	888	1,774	2,251	154	520	712
From 41 to 60 students	1,508	4,616	4,811	284	950	1,154
From 61 to 100 students	5,126	14,000	11,874	833	2,091	2,014
From 101 to 200 students	18,588	55,939	29,646	2,216	5,965	3,534
From 201 to 500 students	69,072	104,294	17,245	4,580	8,281	1,446
Above 501 students	248,772	30,168	2,183	14,786	2,305	122
Total	344,155	211,064	68,527	23,052	20,226	9,233

In Table 4.15 we do not provide the totals for all voucher types, because they appear already in Table 4.3 (for students) and Table 4.8 (for FTE teachers). For the sake of completeness, we also provide data for non-teaching staff in Table 4.16, also without the total, which was already provided in Table 4.10.

Table 4.16. Number of Non-Teaching Staff in 2006/07, by School Size and Voucher Type

School size category	Voucher Type		
	City	Rural	Mountain
Below 20 students	54	41	82
From 21 to 40 students	73	119	161
From 41 to 60 students	84	207	267
From 61 to 100 students	218	458	457
From 101 to 200 students	450	1,261	735
From 201 to 500 students	762	1,440	260
Above 501 students	1,434	274	19
Total	3,075	3,800	1,981

Taking the FTE teachers in Table 4.15 together with administration staff in Table 4.16 we obtain the FTE staff. Together with the number of students this allows us to obtain ratio of students to FTE staff, in Table 4.17:

Table 4.17. Students per FTE Staff in 2006/07, by Size Category and Voucher Type

School size category	Voucher Type			All
	City	Rural	Mountain	
Below 20 students	0.8	1.8	1.6	1.3
From 21 to 40 students	3.9	2.8	2.6	2.8
From 41 to 60 students	4.1	4.0	3.4	3.7
From 61 to 100 students	4.9	5.5	4.8	5.1
From 101 to 200 students	7.0	7.7	6.9	7.4
From 201 to 500 students	12.9	10.7	10.1	11.4
Above 501 students	15.3	11.7	15.5	14.8
Total	**13.2**	**8.8**	**6.1**	**10.2**

We observe that, as expected, schools receiving rural vouchers have lower student-FTE staff ratios (SFTESR), and schools in the mountains even lower. In numbers, SFTESR in rural schools on average is 66 percent of SFTESR in the cities, while SFTESR in the mountain schools is only 46 percent of the city SFTESR. If this average would be used to propose relative values of the voucher, it would lead to the rural and mountain vouchers equal 149.9 percent and 215.5 percent of the city voucher respectively. Comparison with the Table 4.13 above reveals that relative values of rural vouchers are surprisingly similar to this, but the mountain vouchers are relatively too small. Indeed we see that the decision by the Ministry, to increase it in 2006/07 to 192 percent of the value of the city voucher from the lower value of 180 percent in 2005/06, was based on the correct assessment of the situation in those schools.

However, we also notice that the variation of SFTESR within city schools of different sizes is much larger than the variation among averages for school location. It is clear that there are many small schools, even located in the cities, where the voucher will not be enough.

Georgian vouchers represent a radically simplified financing system. In most cases of formula based financing of schools in advanced countries, the actual formulas are much more complex, and cannot be reduced to a few values of vouchers.[24] The simplicity of vouchers makes it easy to apply them in the absence of trustworthy education data,[25] but has the effect of creating many underfunded schools and a certain number of overfunded schools. The *deficit schools* are the subject of the following section.

4.4. The Implementation of the Funding Formula

In Georgian practice there is no clear definition or identification of so called *deficit schools*, that is of schools in which vouchers provide insufficient funding, but it is generally assumed that those are the schools where teacher salaries, calculated at minimum allowed level for all the teachers who have to be employed by the school, exceed the value of school revenues from the vouchers. Of course this means that the average class size in the school or, alternatively speaking, the student-teacher ratio is too low.

Deficit schools are a problem for MoE for the simple reason that it is the entity that is responsible for both school closings and for school financing. All the schools that operate in Georgia have a clear mandate from the Ministry to function, otherwise the Ministry would decide to close the school. If a school is maintained, for whatever reason, and if it finds itself in financial distress, it will appeal to the Ministry for additional funding, and the Ministry will find it difficult to refuse to give additional funds.[26]

In the current 2007/08 school year, according to the information provided by the Ministry, 724 schools out of a total of 2,333 general education schools in Georgia are deficit schools.[27] This is just over 31 percent. This number is steadily decreasing: a year earlier it was over 800 schools. However, deficit schools are typically very small schools and they enroll a small fraction of students, about 5 percent of the total student population. Every month, the deficit schools submit to the Ministry a request for additional funding. Those requests are reviewed by the Budget Department of the Ministry and individual decisions are taken regarding the level of additional funds. In practice, the Ministry uses teacher employment data as the main indicator of funding needs. The requests are almost always accepted, because the Ministry realizes that cutting down funding to below the salary level would lead schools into closures in the middle of the school year and would be catastrophic for the students. Thus, above about 186 million GEL allocated through vouchers, the Ministry allocates about 7.4 million GEL of additional funding for the deficit schools. This is under 4 percent of the total voucher pool.

We conduct two types of analysis of deficit schools. First, at the level of individual school, we assess what minimum student-teacher ratios are supported by city, rural, and mountain vouchers. This can be then compared with the tables above to see the magnitude of the problem, i.e. to assess to what extent the actual number of students per FTE staff is insufficient compared to the value of the voucher. The value of this approach is that it provides a good estimate of the number of deficit schools by location (city, rural, mountain). In the second approach, we disregard the location of the schools and directly assess the voucher deficit and to a certain degree also surplus for all the schools in Georgia, using the size categorization that was used in both previous sections.

We begin by stating the assumptions for our analysis. All the calculations for school year 2007-2008 are provided using the values of the vouchers and of the salaries as of September 2007. The minimum salary in Georgia was 115 GEL,[28] however for employees with higher education, like teachers, it is increased by 30 percent to 149 GEL. Further, we assume that at least 5 percent of the school budget is spent on non-salary costs (this includes material expenditures such as heating and electricity). This is rather low, and in many individual schools non-salary expenditures represent a much larger proportion of the total costs, maybe over 15 percent. But in small schools, which are our primary focus, this seems to be realistic. Thus, we assume that one FTE employee needs 157 GEL per month (this already includes 5 percent for maintenance), including the taxes and social contributions. This allows us to compare the value of the voucher and deduce the required minimum number of students per FTE staff.

Table 4.18. Minimum Number of Students per FTE Staff, by Voucher Type

Voucher Type	Total amount of the voucher per year (GEL)	Monthly value of the voucher (GEL)	Average Monthly FTE Staff salary (GEL)	Minimum SFTESR
City voucher	235	19.6	157	8.02
Rural voucher	350	29.2	157	5.38
Mountain voucher	452	37.7	157	4.17

Comparing Table 4.18 with Table 4.17 of students per FTE staff by school size category in the previous section, we see that city schools below 200 students, and rural and mountain schools below 60 students are likely to be in deficit. Taking into account Table 4.14 and Table 4.15, this creates a possible pool of 658 potential deficit schools, with about 40 thousand students, that is about 6.5 percent of total enrollment. This is rather close to the estimate reported by the Ministry reports for the school year 2007/08 (as we recall, 724 deficit schools, 5 percent enrollment).

Our second approach is to assess the overall deficit of the voucher funding, and also possibly the surplus funding. To this end we use the data files obtained for school years 2005/06 and 2006/07 from the Ministry, which include the size of the voucher.[29] We know from Table 4.14 that in each location category (cities, villages, mountains) there are schools in all size categories that we use for analysis: there are small schools in the cities and large schools in the mountains. In Table 4.19 provide the total transfers from vouchers received by the schools, broken by the school size, and we calculate the average value of the voucher for each size category.

Table 4.19. Average Value of Student Voucher, by Size Category (in GEL)

School size category	Voucher funding		Average voucher	
	2005/06	2006/07	2005/06	2006/07
Below 20 students	306,350	362,510	315.8	365.8
From 21 to 40 students	1,543,564	1,786,255	340.8	363.6
From 41 to 60 students	3,599,354	4,014,655	335.7	367.1
From 61 to 100 students	11,223,520	11,151,060	338.9	359.7
From 101 to 200 students	35,139,258	36,510,680	327.9	350.5
From 201 to 500 students	59,619,362	60,063,945	295.8	315.1
Above 501 students	66,294,954	69,947,995	234.4	248.8
Total	177,726,362	183,837,100	277.3	294.7

We note that, as expected, larger schools have in general lower average per student vouchers. This reflects the fact that in general rural and mountain schools are smaller than city schools. The relationship is not strictly monotonic, though, due to the actual distribution of schools (some small schools are located in the villages and also in the cities, see Table 4.14). We also note that in 2005/06 the average voucher was equal to 126 percent of the city voucher, and in 2006/07 to 125 percent of the city voucher, despite an increase in the relative value of the mountain voucher.

We now perform the key step in our simplified analysis, i.e. we assess the minimum required expenditures for schools of different size. We take the minimum monthly expenditure per FTE staff of 157 GEL, which as we have discussed above (see discussion preceding Table 4.18) includes salaries and maintenance. Actual FTE staff employed is assessed, as we did in the previous section (see Table 4.17), by taking the number of FTE teachers and adding the administration staff (Table 4.8 and Table 4.10). In Table 4.20, first two columns, we calculate the minimum required expenditures for the actually employed staff. We also calculate, in columns 3 and 5, what percentage of those minimum expenditures is covered by the actually received vouchers, using data from Table 4.19.

Table 4.20. Minimum Required Expenditures and Their Coverage by Vouchers, by School Size

School size category	Minimum expenditures		Voucher coverage	
	2005/06	2006/07	2005/06	2006/07
Below 20 students	1,033,688	1,399,498	29.6%	25.9%
From 21 to 40 students	3,189,874	3,274,706	48.4%	54.5%
From 41 to 60 students	6,032,516	5,549,319	59.7%	72.3%
From 61 to 100 students	13,123,724	11,437,848	85.5%	97.5%
From 101 to 200 students	30,090,827	26,679,881	116.8%	136.8%
From 201 to 500 students	36,777,815	31,591,538	162.1%	190.1%
Above 501 students	38,870,320	35,683,157	170.6%	196.0%
Total	129,118,764	115,615,946	137.6%	159.0%

We note that as expected, vouchers are insufficient for small schools and more than sufficient for minimum expenditures in large schools. Table 4.20 confirms our previous analysis that all schools under 60 students are likely to be in deficit. Note however that large schools receive almost twice the minimum expenditures levels. Moreover, the discrepancies between the treatment of small and large schools increase from 2006 to 2007.

Table 4.20 has important implications for horizontal equity, i.e. for the relative treatment of students attending different schools. We observe that the simple voucher system introduced in Georgia penalizes small schools and greatly rewards larger schools. Even if Georgia undertakes some measures to increase internal efficiency of small schools (see discussion following Table 4.9), the present voucher system may still lead to inequities and will probably require future monthly interventions to allow small schools to continue to operate.

Although the vouchers seriously underfund small schools, the additional funds required to enable them to function properly are not large, due to the very few students attending those schools. This point was already discussed using global data from the Ministry (see the beginning of the present section). The following Table 4.21 provides the additional funding required to meet the minimum expenditures levels, and also estimates what proportion of the voucher funding this amounts to.

Table 4.21. Required Funding above Voucher, by School Size

School size category	Additional funding required		% of voucher funding	
	2005/06	2006/07	2005/06	2006/07
Below 20 students	727,338	1,036,988	237.4%	286.1%
From 21 to 40 students	1,646,310	1,488,451	106.7%	83.3%
From 41 to 60 students	2,433,162	1,534,664	67.6%	38.2%
From 61 to 100 students	1,900,204	286,788	16.9%	2.6%
From 101 to 200 students	0	0	0.0%	0.0%
From 201 to 500 students	0	0	0.0%	0.0%
Above 501 students	0	0	0.0%	0.0%
Total	6,707,014	4,346,891	3.8%	2.4%

Our simplified analysis showed that the additional funding required maintaining deficit schools in operation were equal to just under 4 percent of the total voucher funding in 2005/06, and to 2.4 percent in 2006/07. This is slightly below the actual additional funding provided by the Ministry to deficit schools in 2007 (estimated by the Ministry to be about 7.4 million GEL).

An interesting analysis of deficit schools was performed, at the request of the Ministry, by Lasha Tsagareishvili (Tsagareishvili, 2007). The focus of this analysis was to assess what should be the values of vouchers for small schools to ensure sufficient funding. The baseline of the analysis was the actual funding the schools received, that is vouchers with all additional funds (monthly adjustments from the ministry). For schools under 20 students in the mountains, the proposed figure is 1,984 GEL, i.e. 4 times higher than the present value of the voucher. This corresponds very closely to the findings of Table 4.20, where vouchers are shown to cover less than 26 percent of minimum required expenditures levels (using a somewhat different methodology). However, Tsagareishvili stops short of suggesting an amendment to the voucher system, as his analysis is restricted to deficit schools only.

It is difficult to assess reliably how many schools and to what degree obtain excessive allocation through the present voucher system. Indeed, teacher salaries are very low, and the need for school investment in Georgian schools are so great that it seems certain that the country needs to invest more in its education. The education spending at the level of under 2 percent of GDP (see Simonia 2007) is unacceptably low, compared to OECD and Central European averages of about 5 percent of GDP. Nevertheless there are already reports that large city schools have quite enough money. Godfrey (2007) quotes an example of a large school in Tbilisi that has been able to use the voucher funding to change from two shifts to single shift and to improve teaching conditions, has attracted more students (from 1,200 to 1,700) without increasing teacher employment, and as a result increased teacher salaries by 60 percent. This seems to be an exception, however, because high teacher unemployment means that the job of school teacher is in high demand, even in Tbilisi, so most schools may just pay teachers the minimum salary allowed by law without risking complaints. In contrast, some directors of large Tbilisi schools have set their own salaries at a very high level, which requires only approval of the school board.[30]

4.5. Assessment of Outcomes

The education management reforms were introduced in Georgia only two years ago. There has been little time to fine tune all the relevant laws and regulations, and to improve managerial capacities at all levels in line with the new allocation of responsibilities. The present section briefly addresses some of the implementation issues connected to the new financing system in regards to the following areas:[31]

- Efficiency,
- Equity,
- Transparency/Accountability and auditing of schools,
- Other issues (Reaction of stakeholders to the new system, School autonomy, School competition)

4.5.1. Efficiency

This section analyzes whether the education system in Georgia improved its allocative efficiency upon the introduction of the voucher system. By allocative efficiency we mean the ability of the education finance system to allocate funds so that all schools (in case of direct allocation to schools) or all local governments (in case the grants are allocated to municipalities) receive more or less what they need. Here of course the relative (or minimum) needs of schools have to be carefully assessed. We can use the assessment of minimum needs on which our Table 4.20 was based. A different methodological approach based on per class allocation and on Table 4.23, provides an independent, different insight into efficiency issues.

Table 4.20 seems to imply that Georgian vouchers were a highly non-efficient approach to education finance. Small schools appear to be seriously underfunded, while large schools are seriously overfunded. Indeed, schools with less than 40 students receive about 50% of what they need as minimum, while schools with over 500 students receive almost twice as much as they need. Of course, the model of minimum needs on which the calculations are based is rather simple. Still, informal information gathered in Tbilisi did indicate that some large Tbilisi schools have too many funds. This may be due to the fact that there are many unemployed teachers seeking work, so there is no need for schools to significantly raise their salaries, even if they could afford to do this. The salaries of teachers remain depressingly low.

Interestingly, the schools with highest surplus are the large, well known, prestigious education institutions, whose students include the elite of the country. They often operate in shifts and have very large classes, due to huge demand from the parents and students. It is rather amazing that elite students attend overcrowded schools, often in afternoon shifts.

A second way to assess efficiency is to review from the point of view per class allocation, summarized in Table 4.23 (see below). We assume that the national per class allocation is an empirical benchmark, representing the funds which the national government is able and wishing to allocate to schools. We can compare this benchmark to per class allocation for different groups of schools and assess for which schools the allocation far exceeds the benchmark. We note that excessive, inefficient allocation is provided to large schools, especially to schools with over 200 students (20 percent excess) and over 500 students (30 percent excess). In the same way, on average, city schools receive 20 percent excess allocation. The allocation for very large city schools, i.e. schools with over 500 students, is also inefficient (20 percent excess). There are however some special cases, such as very large schools located in rural areas, with 45 percent excess allocation, and even more so in mountain areas (4 schools with 65 percent excess).

Even dismissing these specific cases, we note from Table 4.20 that the overall voucher funding is well above the minimum needs of all Georgian schools together (60% more in 2006/07). This puts the efficiency of the voucher system in a clear but somewhat dramatic perspective: while overall there are enough funds to satisfy minimum needs of all Georgian schools, the voucher system still maintains a large number of deficit schools, i.e. schools struggling to make ends meet. At the same time, Table 4.23 indicates that there are a number of schools, even in the mountains, which receive relatively very high allocation. There is no doubt that the voucher system needs to be modified in such a way as to ensure a far greater degree of allocative efficiency than is now provided.

4.5.2. Equity

The issue of education finance equity is particularly sensitive, because at the same time it directly affects the quality and adequacy of education provided to many vulnerable groups in society, and it is difficult to measure in an objective and non-controversial manner. This means that an assessment of the fairness of the system is necessarily based on uncertain and questionable methodologies. Hence any review of equity needs to include a clear description of the methodological approach employed.

The approach we employ in the present section is based on analyzing per class allocation. Indeed, it should be assumed that under a fair system per class allocation to different schools should be similar, because the main recurrent cost of schools is driven by the number of teachers, hence by the number of classes: a teacher salary does not depend on how many students attend his/her lessons. Therefore in what follows we compare per class allocation for schools receiving different vouchers.

We focus our analysis on the school year 2007/08. Table 4.14 provides the number of schools categorized according to the voucher type they receive and also by their school size. We use the same classification below. The first step is a review of the average class sizes (see Table 4.22).

Table 4.22. Average Class Size, by School Size and Voucher's School Location Categories

School size category	Voucher's School Location Categories			Total
	City	Rural	Mountain	
Under 20	—	2.1	2.0	2.0
Between 21 and 40	4.4	3.5	3.1	3.3
Between 41 and 60	5.0	5.3	4.7	4.9
Between 41 and 100	8.4	7.6	6.6	7.1
Between 101 and 200	12.3	12.7	10.3	11.8
Between 201 and 500	21.6	17.5	15.9	18.4
Above 500	26.0	20.9	19.7	25.3
Total	24.3	14.0	8.6	16.6

Now using the values of the vouchers, provided in Table 4.12, we can calculate the per class allocation for schools in each size category and by school location categories (city, rural, or mountain, see Table 4.23).

Table 4.23. Average Per Class Allocation, by School Size and Voucher's School Location Categories

School size category	Voucher's School Location Categories			Total
	City	Rural	Mountain	
Under 20	—	890	1,003	966
Between 21 and 40	1,306	1,463	1,598	1,538
Between 41 and 60	1,496	2,215	2,392	2,287
Between 41 and 100	2,518	3,185	3,373	3,258
Between 101 and 200	3,699	5,326	5,237	5,203
Between 201 and 500	6,494	7,331	8,085	7,184
Above 500	7,802	8,788	10,035	7,951
Total	7,304	5,864	4,406	6,068

Of course, per class allocation for the smallest schools is exceedingly small, but these are exactly the deficit schools which receive each month additional allocation beyond the vouchers. We note, however, that even when reviewed on average, per class allocation for city schools is 66 percent higher than the allocation for mountain schools and 25 percent higher than for rural schools. Thus the higher values of vouchers for rural and mountain schools are not sufficient to compensate, on average, the smaller class sizes. Overall, assuming that rural schools, with per class allocation close to the national average, are funded fairly, we have to conclude that significantly higher per class allocation for city schools and significantly lower allocation for mountain schools indicates deep seated inequity.

At the same time, however, we note that for large schools (schools with over 200 students), the situation is reversed. Focusing on schools between 200 and 500 students, we note that mountain schools have a per class allocation 24 percent higher than city schools and 11 percent higher than rural schools. Even more dramatic is the difference for schools above 500 students. This indicates that the division of schools into the three locations does not adequately correspond to the class sizes and creates additional inequities, with some mountain schools receiving between 35 percent and 65 percent above the national average for per class allocation.

Here we note that equity problems in Georgian education finance are at least partially caused by the main point of the reforms, namely by removal of local governments from the entire budget process of schools. Indeed, local governments presiding over a number of schools have the ability to fine tune allocation to individual schools to improve funding equity. The example of Lithuania (see chapter on Lithuania) shows that this fine-tuning may be very effective. Local governments would also be a far better—and stronger—partner for discussing deficit schools with the Ministry.

In conclusion, it seems that the original assessment of the voucher values was based on detailed analysis of average class sizes and average student-teacher ratios. Nevertheless, the division of all schools into just three categories is a very blunt policy instrument, and it is not surprising that changes in the relative values of the vouchers were not enough to keep pace with the evolution of the school system, such as network consolidation and demographic changes. Presently the equity of the education finance system in Georgia appears to need thorough reexamination.

4.5.3. Transparency and Accountability

4.5.3.1. TRANSPARENCY

The issue of *transparency* is a very subtle one. On the one hand there is no doubt that transparency of the financial flows has increased considerably, and that in particular the opportunities for corrupt practices was very much reduced. The financial flows are well regulated, and are under the scrutiny of a number of stakeholders, primarily school directors, school boards, and ERC. As Shapiro *et al.* (2007) underline, schools are receiving the funds without any delays and are able to pay their teachers also without delay.

At the same time, Shapiro *et al.* (2007) note that parents and teachers who are not members of the school board "are very poorly informed about school management and budgeting issues". There are no effective ways of sharing the essential information with the wider school community. This creates the dangers that when experienced school board members leave, the new ones will be less able to monitor school activities and control the school director. This risk increases because of the election system, which results in a renewal of the full composition of the school board every 3 years.[32]

An important element of transparency is the public availability of the school budgets for scrutiny and comparison by different stakeholders. There is no legal requirement for the school boards to publish school budgets, and no established procedure for this (outside of Tbilisi, Internet access among the parents in Georgia is not high). In theory, parents may approach school board members to ask about the financial details, but this is a good source of information only if the board members themselves have good understanding of budget issues.

Interestingly, both deficit schools and schools with surplus allocation have very little incentives to publish their budgets. Budgets of deficit schools are usually quite unrealistic, with planned expenditures (mainly teacher salaries) far in excess of planned revenues (vouchers). However, budgets of surplus schools are also somewhat shameful, because they would exhibit an opposite situation, in which planned expenditures are significantly smaller than planned revenues. Publication of these budgets would raise uncomfortable questions, such as how to use the surplus resources for the benefit of students and teachers, or indeed what the schools intend to do with their excess funds. Forcing all schools to publish their budgets, for example by notifying them to the respective local government, would be a good step towards increased transparency.

4.5.3.2. ACCOUNTABILITY AND AUDITING OF SCHOOLS

We discussed above the problem of capacities of school directors to manage school budgets. Similar capacity issues undermine the *role of the school boards*. The introduction of powerful school boards, with the right to nominate and dismiss a school director and to approve the budget was intended to increase school accountability with respect to the parents of students and introduce a measure of social control over schools, especially necessary after the local governments' role in education was severely curtailed. However, in many places school boards have proved unable to control and oversee the activities of the school director, to assess his leadership skills and to analyze the proposed school budget.

To a large extent, the boards rely on the school director for information, including budgetary data, information about the activities of the schools, assessment of teachers, and for proposals on what to do. For example, school boards may expect that the school director will undertake actions to attract more students and thus to improve financial situation of the school, or, alternatively, that the director will apply to the Ministry for additional funds. It is however very difficult for the board to decide on the course of action different from what the director suggests. Reliance on opinions from one person creates a passive and reactive attitude of board members. The board has no budget of its own, so it cannot procure an independent assessment of the school activities or of the school budget. Unless well-trained specialists are already members of the board, it has little choice but to accept the director's proposals without discussions. Excessive salaries of some directors of Tbilisi schools, discussed in section 4.4, have all been approved by their respective school boards.

The situation is not eased by lack of clarity and absence of exact procedures. The Ministry expects that autonomous school boards will establish their own procedures and schedules of activity as is most useful for their specific schools, but this is often difficult and the boards themselves are sometimes lost. In particular, it is usually the school director who may prepare and propose such procedures, but many directors will chose not to do this and some boards operate without written procedures. One of the most important of these procedures regards selection of school board members. As many parents have insufficient motivation to participate in the process (board membership is unpaid, of course), sometimes it is the school director who tries to identify and persuade some parents to "volunteer" for the position. This obviously weakens the control mechanisms foreseen by the reformers. Anecdotal evidence shows that in many schools the board simply approves all the proposals of the school director, assuming that she or he is best placed to take professional decisions.

The difficulties faced by the school boards in their efforts to assume an active role in the system were made obvious during the first round of national selection process for the school directors in 2007. Aware of the problems of choosing the "right" candidate, the Ministry organized a sort of "national tests" for candidates, awarding the certificates to all persons who passed the tests. The school boards were supposed to choose candidates from this pool of persons. More than half of all the positions of school directors were left vacant and former directors were asked to continue to manage the schools. There are many reasons for this failure, in part the boards were not prepared enough for the decision-making process, in part former directors refused to take the tests and the boards had asked "their" directors to continue to work, and in part some remote schools had no good candidates. A second round of selection had to be organized, and some changes in the law have become necessary.

Lack of certainty regarding the roles of different stakeholders includes also the Education Resource Centers (ERC). As the schools turn to them for guidance and suggestions in many specific areas, ERC find themselves overwhelmed and unable to provide sufficient support. Shapiro *et al.* (2007) conclude that "ERC are entrusted with too many tasks and their physical and human resources are insufficient". It seems unlikely that without some legal changes ERC will contribute to school accountability.

With weak accountability of schools, the main audit instrument available to the Ministry is the controls performed in schools by the General Inspection (a budget control institution). Due to personnel constraints, every year this may happen only in some selected schools. The typical situation therefore is for the Ministry to learn, either from the Education Resource Center or from parents, that a school violates a given budgetary rule, and to send a team of General Inspection to verify and punish the persons responsible for this mismanagement. However, these controls are usually restricted to the verification of budgetary misconduct (improper use of funds etc.) or to criminal activities. No systematic audit of schools aimed at improving their functioning exists in Georgia as of today.

There is no doubt that the introduction of proper accountability standards requires new skills and additional training of all stakeholders: school board members, teachers, school directors, and ERC staff.

4.5.4. Other Key Areas

4.5.4.1. Reaction of Stakeholders to the New System

There is no doubt that in general the reaction of Georgian population to the reforms initiated with the rose revolution was enthusiastic, and this includes the reaction to the reforms of school finance. The most positive reactions were apparent among the schools themselves, especially among the school directors. They liked the simplicity and clarity of the voucher system, and especially the fact that they knew in advance budget resources used to finance school activities. The lessening of corrupt practices in education management from local governments that came out as a result of the financing reforms is very much appreciated even today, many years after the reform started, as most school directors still remember corrupt practices under the former system.

Parents also accepted their increased role in the education system, especially as during initial years of the reform a number of training courses and support was directed towards improving the competencies of the school board members.

The creation of Education Resource Centers was greeted with great expectations by the schools. In sharp contrast to former education departments of local governments and to delegated offices of the Ministry, ERC were designed to support schools and to offer advice rather than to issue orders and instructions. The fact that ERC do not have access to education funding, and therefore have no temptation for corruption, rather paradoxically strengthened their position and created good will from the school directors.

The main opponents of the reforms, unsurprisingly, were the local governments. The new, democratically elected mayors were interested in the quality and activities of the schools, and faced pressure from parents, but had no legal grounds for interference. In particular, some relatively rich cities, especially the city of Tbilisi, felt constrained in their desire to support the schools, decide on the school network, and promote better teaching practices. Some education initiatives of local governments are now taking shape, but as mayors have limited influence over key decisions of schools, they are not keen on committing significant funds or embarking on significant long-term projects.

Over time, the initial positive reaction of the education stakeholders became overshadowed with new, less fortunate experiences. Deficit schools have become a permanent phenomenon of the system, dragging energy and resourcefulness away from strategic planning and adaptation to needs of parents and students. The need for monthly requests for additional funds from the Ministry reduces the autonomy of schools and weakens planning at the school level. The uncertainty regarding how much the school should request and on what grounds the allocation decisions are being made further diminishes incentives for good budgetary practice.

Some Education Resource Centers have shown initiative and have been working very closely with the schools to address new challenges and help them in their decision-making process. For example, some ERC have been able to effectively support schools in the budget process, by advising how the budget should look like, by discussing with school boards past budgets of schools and their execution, and by proposing some practical steps to improve budget planning. Other ERC, however, have become little more than an agency that only takes care of the transmission of Ministerial guidelines and collection of data from schools, which shows that the role of ERC is very difficult to fulfill in practice.

4.5.4.2. School Autonomy

The efforts to increase *school autonomy* were described in the introduction. Schools adopt their budgets, within the funding received, and need just an approval of the Ministry, which is always granted. In particular, they can set the salaries of all staff, although in practice the typical situation is that teachers receive the national minimum wage for their education level, plus bonuses awarded by the school directors (interestingly, even schools running impressive voucher surplus tend to pay their teachers minimum national salary, because with high teacher unemployment teachers are not likely to demand pay increases). Schools may receive funding from sources other than vouchers (donations, participation in projects), but this opportunity is mainly used in the cities: according to Shapiro *et al.* (2007), only 16 percent of mountain schools had an experience of applying for funds from non-budget sources (apart from vouchers or additional allocation from the Ministry).

However, Shapiro *et al.* (2007) also note that schools "are not yet ready to fully utilize the opportunities offered by a decentralized education system", mainly because of insufficient budgeting and planning skills. Over time, school directors are becoming more adept at managing their schools. However, constrained fiscal situation and frequent changes of the values of the vouchers and of basic teacher salaries make systematic planning extremely difficult. Development of proper planning and budgeting skills requires more stability.

An important barrier to school autonomy is the insufficient voucher funding (see section 4.4). Schools which are under deficit are in fact highly dependent on the monthly decisions of the Ministry in response to their budget requests. Thus remote Ministry officials may have more impact on the decisions of the school director than the school board.

In discussing the need for school autonomy, one must also consider some necessary limitations of that autonomy. For example, as school funding depends only on student numbers, some schools have lowered their requirements, especially regarding student marking (better marks without good reason), student discipline, and school attendance. The Ministry may respond to such problems by creating a proper independent school inspection. This is indeed being developed in Georgia, but the process is much delayed.

School autonomy is also diminished by the fact that parents may threaten the school director that unless some of their demands are met, they will move their children to a different school (this may happen only in large cities). Such a move, especially by a group of parents, may hit finances of the school quite painfully. Conflicting demands by parents, unless negotiated through the school board, present a real challenge to the school.

In practice, the reform has strengthened the position of the school director, who typically proposes the budget and the school plan for approval by the school board, and single-handedly negotiates additional allocations with the Ministry of Education. This is seen in part by excessive salaries some school directors in larger cities decide to allocate to themselves (see the previous section). At the same time, the position of directors of deficit schools has become very weak, as they are dependent upon monthly decisions of officials in the Ministry. The question of how this affected autonomy of schools as teaching institutions (pedagogical process) and as financial units (budgeting process) requires a more in-depth empirical review.

4.5.4.3. SCHOOL COMPETITION

Turning to *school competition*, we note that it is inherently built into the system in which decisions by students to choose schools have a direct and immediate impact on school budgets. There are already some cases of schools experiencing a rapid increase in enrollment (mostly in Tbilisi). This must come at the expense of some schools that lose students, of course. The expected sharp decline in the student population in the coming years will make this competition even harder. However, it is still unclear how strong this competition is and what forms it will take. Godfrey (2007) warns that schools may be unwilling to take in special needs students and students who find learning difficult, and suggests that a separate voucher for those students would be needed. Teachers and school directors interviewed by Shapiro *et al.* (2007) were talking about the *vicious circle*, in which schools in less competitive situations—poorer conditions of building and equipment and poorer student community served—may find themselves losing both students and funding, thus compromising quality, in turn, leading to further exodus of students to better schools. They would like to see some sort of safety nets for those schools provided, for example, by ERC. There seems to be a need to review voucher financing quite independent of the problem of deficit schools.

4.6. Conclusions

The reforms introduced in Georgian education have been relatively successful. The new radically simple system of voucher financing has been well prepared in terms of legal basis, and was introduced in a rather smooth manner. Despite some inefficiencies and inequities, a workable *modus operandi* was developed, which is still functional after a few years of operations. The first round of selection of new school directors was only partially satisfactory, but during the second round most positions were filled, in what certainly represents a completely new democratic experience for all the school directors, teachers, and the school boards. Most importantly, the reforms have cut the most difficult and corrupt practices in Georgian education, namely management by local governments operating under double reporting lines, and have introduced transparency and clarity to education finance.

Interestingly, although the desire to improve school effectiveness was one of the goals of the voucher system, the actual approach taken by the Ministry was different. Rather than waiting until the voucher system eliminated unviable schools, the Ministry made a very significant effort into the optimization of the school network as a condition for a smooth operation of the voucher system. This sequencing of reforms seems to have been the crucial decision of the reformers leading to early success. Even now the number of deficit schools is significant, but one can imagine that without prior network consolidation it would have been almost impossible to introduce vouchers. One can make a rough approximate calculation.[33] Table 4.20 indicates that schools under 100 students are most likely to be in deficit. Table 4.2 tells us that without any consolidation effort, in the conditions of 2004 we would have about 1,500 deficit schools (half of the total). Another important condition for the success of the voucher system was an increase in overall allocation. Since any formula based allocation system creates losers, an increase of the funding level is a good way to minimize their numbers and to reduce the stress put on them.

Despite clear success of the reforms, there are still a number of problems. About 30 percent of all Georgian schools receive in vouchers insufficient funds for basic operations, and every month submit requests for additional funds, which they always receive. At the same time, it seems that a fair number of large schools in the cities—and, as seen from Table 4.14, also a few in the villages and in the mountains—receive far more funds then they actually need for regular school operations. Those funds may be used to improve the education process and for own school investments (computers, school equipment etc.), of course, but this type of allocation cannot be considered optimal. The functioning of many deficit schools makes it very difficult if not impossible to impose budget discipline. Nevertheless, the appearance of the deficit schools provided the Ministry with a new insight into how Georgian schools are operating. As there are examples of schools with similar numbers of students, some of which are functioning well, and some which are in deficit, the voucher system has revealed inefficiencies of internal school operations, which up to now were hidden. At present, those inefficiencies are maintained by allocating the deficit schools additional funding every month. The Ministry has yet to develop a more strategic approach to deficit schools, and to devise ways of actually refusing additional support in cases when there are no compelling reasons to maintain the small schools, or when the internal school management is evidently inefficient.

Another difficulty is the increasing number of supplements to the vouchers that are being introduced by the Ministry. As discussed in section 4.2.1, some of those supplements are related to specific Government policies, such as maintenance of Georgian schools in areas of armed conflict, while others reflect recent Government initiatives to increase teacher salaries. While in each case the introduction of the supplement may be defended on policy grounds, altogether their influence is dangerous, because they undermine the simplicity and transparency of the voucher system. They also show that the voucher financing system is not yet sufficiently flexible to allow implementation of new education policies. This may be a reflection of the fact that the vouchers, being a very simple system, cannot adequately take into account structural cost differences among areas or among schools of different size and type. Thus, the challenge is to integrate the supplements into the voucher scheme itself. If the Ministry fails to achieve this, the risk is that in the future, with the necessary yearly adjustment to the voucher levels, the Ministry will also have to manage the adjustments to all the supplements. This threatens to become a cumbersome task.

Funding of schools on the basis of school vouchers creates the illusion that education finance equity has been automatically achieved. Our simple review of equity in terms of per class allocation reveals that very significant areas of inequity remain. These issues have to be addressed directly by the Ministry of Education, either through a reform of the voucher system itself, or through a reform of the management of education finance. The first approach may include a more subtle differentiation of the vouchers or an introduction of lump sum allocation to schools, alongside voucher allocation (see Herczyński 2008). The second approach may include returning to local governments some role in setting the school budgets.

Analysis of voucher allocation also reveals issues with allocative efficiency. This is demonstrated by the fact that while overall allocation is much higher than overall minimum needs of schools, there are still many schools whose allocation is below their minimum needs (see section 4.4).

It is also not clear how the school autonomy will be strengthened. With very little capacities for self management and no experience in running their own budgets, schools rely on ERC for support and guidance. There is a risk therefore that ERC will take over the functions of former *rayon* education offices. The planned introduction of strong school boards may prevent this, but certainly the challenges are serious.

Finally, there is as yet no experience on what effect the new financing system will have on school performance and more importantly on education quality. The Georgian Ministry of Education has yet to understand the system of incentives the voucher system is putting in place, and its positive and adverse effects. In recent years the tone of discussions of education reforms has changed.[34] Initial enthusiastic reactions have been replaced with more sober understanding that the system needs continued revision and improvement. Much stronger control over individual schools is considered necessary, especially in the budget sphere. Discussions regarding the number of positions in each school have become standard. Stronger school inspection has reduced the freedom to keep non-attending and non-progressing students enrolled in the school. This probably eroded school autonomy, but at the same time improved monitoring and reduced inefficiency. Due to much greater control over the schools, the allocation of additional funds (above the vouchers) should become more rational, leading to improvement of equity. Nothing comes without a cost, however: the system may become less transparent and much more complicated than it was. The laws regarding the training and the selection of school directors are also being reviewed and changed. The Ministry understands now that it needs to monitor the situation very closely and be ready to adapt the financing system to new challenges. Hopefully, this new phase of reforms of Georgian education will benefit good schools, schools focused on proper education and on preparation of students to life in a democratic society, but striking the correct balance between autonomy and control is never easy.

References

Godfrey, M. (2007); *Education Policy Note: Georgia*, processed text, World Bank

Herczyński, J. (2001); *The Financing of Georgian Education*, CASE Studies and Analyzes 240

Herczyński, J. (2005a); *The Needs of Georgian Ministry of Education and Sport: Education Finance and Education Resource Centers*, processed text, GEDA, Tbilisi

Herczyński, J. (2005b), *Short Term Problems of Education Finance in Georgia*, processed text, GEDA, Tbilisi

Herczyński, J. (2008), *Possible Modification of the Voucher System. Explanations and Instructions for Simulator 08*, processed text, OSI/LGI, Tbilisi

Melikidze, V. (2003), *Role of the Formal Decision Making in Emerging of the "New Corruption" in a School Education in Transitional Societies (Case of Georgia)*, Tbilisi

Ross, K. and Levačić, R. (1999); *Needs Based Resource Allocation via Formula Funding of Schools*, Paris: IIEP UNESCO

Shapiro, M. (team leader), Nakata, S., Chakhaia, L., Zhvania, E., Babunashvili, G., Pruidze, N. and Tskhomeldze, M. (2007); *Evaluation of the Ilia Chavchavadze Program in Reforming and Strengthening Georgia's Schools*, Padeco Co. Ltd.

Rekhviashvili, I. (2001); *Decentralization Experience and Reforms: Case Study on Georgia*, processed text, Tbilisi

Simonia, Z. (2007); *School Funding System in Georgia*, processed text, World Bank,

Swanson, A. and King, R. (1991), *School Finance. Its Economics and Politics*, New York: Longman

Tsagareishvili, Lasha (2007), *Voucher Funding for General Education Schools: Financial Analysis (Interim Report)*, Georgian Education Project Coordination Center

Notes

1. We have profited from many discussions with Georgian experts, but particular gratitude must be expressed to Archil Gagnidze, former Deputy Minister of Education, responsible for school finance, for openly discussing with us the problems facing Georgian reformers.
2. In many countries, reformers hope that per student financing system, by introducing strong financial incentives, will motivate network consolidation, but that hope rarely materializes, see for instance chapter on Lithuania.
3. Georgia was included in the scope of the project quite late so it was decided that the Georgian chapter will be more focused on a few specific issues. This explains why the present chapter is much shorter and provides less detail than other chapters, like those on Lithuania or Poland.
4. See Herczyński (2001) and Melikidze (2003) for a review of Georgian education finance prior to the current reforms.
5. In Soviet times, this system of double reporting lines did not lead to confusion despite its obvious inefficiency since the real power rested with the Party organizations, which created the third, and only functional, chain of command and control. When that chain disappeared, the dysfunctional administrative system immediately became prone to mismanagement and corruption. Among post-Soviet republics, Georgia was maybe exceptional only in the degree of this corruption. Interestingly, the State Audit was empowered to investigate only state and oblast level institutions, leaving the finances of local governments completely unaudited. See Herczyński (2001) for details.
6. Documented descriptions of the process of local government weakening since the 2003 revolution do not seem to be available. However, in an ironic summary of this situation, a Georgian official informally stated that "responsibilities of local governments in Georgia have been reduced to waste collection and preschools, but waste collection will be privatized soon". For a pre-revolution review of decentralization, see for example Rekhviashvili (2001).
7. However, only a few schools have registered with the notary because of the additional costs required–mainly for creating a current plan of school buildings. Moreover, any non-educational use of school property, such as renting the school, needs permission from both the MoE and MoF.
8. The first round of exams was held in April 2007, and by July school boards were supposed to select new directors. About 30 percent of school boards failed to select new school directors, partly due to a lack of qualified candidates. The second round of elections of school boards in October 2007 filled most of the vacant positions.
9. Lack of independent school inspections is another trait of post-Soviet education systems, which inherited this feature. Under the Soviet system, inspecting the schools and checking the work of

teachers was performed by the same institution that managed the schools–i.e. the *rayon* and oblast education offices.

10. See Ross and Levačić (1999).

11. Unfortunately, most of the data used by Godfrey are from before 2005, so these exclude the impact of current reforms.

12. The preparatory work is described in the report by Simonia (2007).

13. See Simonia (2007). The main effect of increase education spending will be an increase of teacher salaries and better and more motivated teaching workforce. Additionally, non-salary expenditures should also be increased.

14. See Herczyński (2005a).

15. This and the following tables are obtained from the data files on all schools in Georgia, received from the Ministry. The data file include the following information about each school: number of students, teachers, weekly teaching hours, administrative staff, for the school years indicated in the table. For school years 2005/06 and 2006/07 the data file also provides the value of the voucher allocated to the school. The data files were filled in by the schools with limited verification by the ministry, so care must be taken in interpreting them. All data with the exception of Table 4.2, Table 4.14 and tables in section 4.5 use data up until the school year 2006/07.

16. As noted in Herczyński (2005b), just prior to the introduction of vouchers the Ministry had highly unreliable data on student numbers, in particular for a number of schools no student data were available.

17. This is the physical number of teachers, see Table 4.8 and Table 4.9 for full-time equivalent teachers. The data used may require some additional verification.

18. Student-teacher ratio in Georgia is one of the lowest in the region, see Godfrey (2007).

19. The number of FTE teachers in Table 4.8 is an underestimate, because a number of schools recorded zero number of weekly teaching hours. We assume those are random data errors, and use the data for the full set of schools.

20. This finding is supported by Shapiro *et al.* (2007), who found that while consolidated and non consolidates schools had about the same student-teacher ratio, ratio of students to not teaching staff is significantly higher in consolidated schools. On the other hand, Godfrey (2007) observes that Georgia has relatively high share of non-teaching staff in school employment. Data reported in Table 4.10 may require additional verification.

21. Indeed, one can assume that it was easier to close schools with fewer number of staff, because the effort of relocating those staff to larger consolidated schools was much smaller. Thus, the small schools which remained may have had less efficient employment levels.

22. In principle the schools may receive funds from other sources as well, including from local governments, from parents, or donations from local or international donors, but those non-budget revenues of schools are not significant in the school budgets.

23. Minimum salary was increased from 115 GEL to 165 GEL, an increase not paralleled by the increase of the vouchers.

24. Typically, there are components for basic teaching program, for strong students (academically, in sport, or in arts), for weak students (requiring remedial teaching etc.), and for maintenance costs. See Ross and Levačić (1999).

25. If the implementation of EMIS, currently under development, is successful, it will become possible to move to more subtle financial instruments than vouchers.

26. The risk of appearance of deficit schools and the need of the Ministry to prepare to deal with them was identified in Herczyński (2005a). Also the Ministry knew that about 38 percent of schools with about 10 percent of students will become deficit schools, and set aside 5 percent reserve for them, Simonia (2007).

27. The total number of schools and students from different sources are different, maybe due to the inclusion or exclusion of private schools.

28. In December 2007 this was increased to 165 GEL, but we do not reflect this or the increase of the vouchers in our calculations below.

29. Those data files were used before, in the section on preparatory school consolidation. In the present section, we do not use data for the school year 2004/05, because the voucher system was introduced only in 2005/06.

30. There were unconfirmed rumors that some prestigious Tbilisi schools may have put surplus funds in foreign bank accounts. Some of the large schools have even approached the Ministry with a question what they can do with their surplus revenues. Of course, as the main focus of education reform in Georgia is school autonomy, the Ministry invariably tells the schools to decide for themselves.

31. Our brief review is based on experience of one of us (SD) as director of secondary school in Tbilisi, on a number of interviews conducted in the country, and on Shapiro (2007).

32. This approach contrasts with a staggered system, in which every year about one-third of the membership is elected.

33. The calculation is performed purely for illustration purposes.

34. The original version of the report was prepared in 2008. In 2010 the paper was reviewed and completed, without however fully reflecting the changes introduced into the system since then. The last paragraph is the only place in the report where we look at Georgian experience with this additional hindsight.

CHAPTER 5

Student Basket Reform in Lithuania: Fine-Tuning Central and Local Financing of Education

Jan Herczyński[1]

5.1. Introduction

Like all post-communist countries, Lithuania in the early 1990s faced the daunting task of not only introducing the necessary political reforms, leading to a democratic society based on the rule of law and on the market economy, but also of changing the whole structure of management and methods of financing of each and every sector of the economy. In education the two tasks were particularly difficult to reconcile. The movement toward democracy involved removing ideological constraints on schools and teachers, retraining of all teachers to help them move away from traditional teaching based on one acceptable truth, given to students to memorize and repeat uncritically, and toward education based on dialogue and asking questions. This required changing the curricula, introducing more open and flexible teaching programs, rewriting all the textbooks, changing teaching methodologies, overhauling teacher pre-service training and especially in-service training. Given the traditions of Soviet schools and the strong ideological control exercised over the pedagogical process, this was a serious effort.[2] No wonder therefore that changes in management and financing were initially considered secondary and were introduced only in 2002.

Historically in the Soviet Union, education was managed and financed by *rayons*, under close scrutiny of the oblast and controlled by central or republican ministries through a web of double reporting lines.[3] Usually school buildings belonged to the *rayons*, and schools were financed from *rayon* budgets. Local government reforms in Lithuania in 1990 had created democratic *rayon* administrations,[4] which cut the double reporting lines and replaced them with autonomous budgetary procedures. Yet, general schools, with their complete budgets, remained under local government authority. Until the introduction of education finance reforms in 2002 municipalities received negotiated transfers for education.

The specific Lithuanian solution, quite different from other financing arrangements in post communist countries, is called *the Student Basket*. The Student Basket is a per student amount, calculated according to a formula adjusted every year through a decision of the Cabinet of Ministers that is designed to cover the *teaching process*, which includes teacher salaries, school management, education support staff such as psychologists, textbooks, and some specific education functions.[5] Remaining school expenditures, including the salaries of maintenance staff, energy and transportation costs, are called *teaching environment* and are covered by school founders–typically, municipalities. This arrangement represents fragmentation of education finance, as the school budget is made up from various sources: specific grants from the central government, and money from local budgets or the budgets of other founders.

However, although such fragmentation is typical in post-communist countries, the Lithuanian solution is very specific. Indeed, many post-communist countries finance salaries from the central government budget and school maintenance costs from local budgets. Typically, the salaries funded by the central government include not only teachers, but all staff, including the maintenance employees. Similarly, school maintenance includes not only heating and technical upkeep of the building, but also teaching aids and equipment.[6] This rigid fragmentation prohibits flexible budgeting and makes natural trade-offs between salary and non-salary expenditures very difficult. In Lithuania, both the teaching process and teaching environment include salaries as well as some maintenance expenditures, so this is a more flexible financing arrangement.

A second very specific feature of the Lithuanian model of education finance is what the Student Basket defines. In principle, the grant for the Student Basket is calculated for each school, and transferred to the municipalities with detailed information on amounts to be received by each school.[7] In other words, the methodology of the Student Basket defines the teaching process part of the budget of every school in the country. In this respect, the Student Basket is close to a voucher system.[8] However, the municipality has the right to reallocate among the schools up to five percent of the Student Basket amount it receives for all its schools.[9] This allows the municipality to adjust detailed school budgets to the needs of individual institutions, and gives them more flexibility. Viewed from this perspective, the Student Basket resembles more the financing of education through transfers to local governments, which have the responsibility to define the budgets of individual schools.[10] The budgeting of the teaching environment is completely determined by the municipality and not governed by any national norms.

We thus see that in both division of the school budget responsibilities between the central and local level, and in the actual implementation of the principle *money follows students* Lithuania has adopted a specific, thoughtful solution. Moreover, the implementation was preceded by careful preparations (see Table 5.1 below).

Indeed, in 2000 the Ministry of Education and Science (MES) set up a working group tasked with designing the reforms of education finance.[11] The methodology for the calculation of the Student Basket was introduced on June 27, 2001, in the Government Resolution No. 785.[12] The annexes to this resolution include the detailed allocation methodology with all the weights and factors. However, the total pool of funds necessary to finance the full Student Basket was rather high, and the Ministry of Finance was reluctant to increase the funding levels immediately. The ensuing negotiations between the two ministries led to the adoption of a compromise solution, namely an agreed implementation schedule. Under that schedule, the Student Basket implementation proceeded in three stages, respectively, in 2002, 2003, and 2004 and later, during which the Student Basket amount reached the level defined in Resolution 785.[13] On December 14, 2001, the government adopted Resolution No. 1520,[14] implementing the Student Basket and setting forth the provisions for the financial reform in general education schools with the agreed compromise–in particular, including the modified Student Basket methodology. The Student Basket grants for all municipalities were also defined in the budget law of 2002. On the basis of this agreed schedule, the Student Basket reform started on January 1, 2002. This chapter tells the story of what happened next.

The structure of this chapter is as follows. Section 5.2 provides a short review of the Lithuanian education system and also discusses the goals of the education finance reform of 2002, as they were formulated by MES. Sections 5.3 and 5.4 present the design and implementation of the funding formula. The design of the Student Basket is described in section 5.3, where we provide the structure and values of the basic per student amount as they evolved over time,[15] and section 5.4 discusses the implementation of the reform. Section 5.5 assesses the effects of the financing reform on four types of outcomes: efficiency (section 5.5.1), equity (section 5.5.2), transparency/accountability (section 5.5.3) and other key areas (section 5.5.4). Section 5.6 presents a series of concluding remarks summarizing the key aspects of the reform.

Table 5.1. Timeline of Key Events Related to the Education Finance Reform

Year	Event
2000	MES sets up a Working Group on education finance reform
2001	Publication of Government Resolution 785 with Student Basket methodology (June 27)
	Approval of Government Resolution 1520 introducing Student Basket (December 14)
	State budget law for 2002 includes Student basket allocations to municipalities
2002	Start of the reform (January 1)
2003	Comprehensive audit of Student Basket system carried out by State Audit and Accounting Office
	Reduction of reallocation threshold from 15 to 10 percent
2004	Reduction of reallocation threshold from 10 to 5 percent
	Introduction of *corrected coefficients* (see Table 5.19)
	Change of basic monthly salary amount from 105 Lt to 115 Lt (May 1)
	Change in the Education Law stipulating that no savings from the Student Basket grant may be used for other purposes other than the teaching process
	Change in the Education Law demanding that all municipalities adopt school network consolidation strategies
2005	Increase of teacher salary coefficients by 9.5 percent (September 1)
	Introduction of coefficient for pedagogical and psychological services in the Student Basket
2006	Change from partially additive to multiplicative structure of the formula for the main Student Basket amount
	Introduction of coefficient for cognitive development of students in the Student Basket
2007	Introduction of coefficients for vocational guidance and for libraries in the Student Basket

5.2. Background

Even today the structure of the education system in Lithuania still very closely resembles the Soviet model of general secondary schools, common in many post-Soviet republics. Yet, a move toward new types of schools can already be seen, especially in the cities. Essentially, the general secondary school includes grades from 1 to 10, with possible extension into grades 11 and 12, but only education till the age of 16 is obligatory (as most students begin their school at the age of 7, effectively this means that 10 years of schooling are obligatory). The graduates of grade 10 may either continue in general education (grades 11 to 12) or vocational schools. Moreover, some schools have only initial classes (grades 1 to 4), some only basic classes (grades 1 to 10), some full secondary (grades 1 to 12) and some only upper classes (grades 5 to 8 or 5 to 12). This means that within one single format there are many different institutional arrangements. The schools offering education in grades 1 through 4 we call *initial schools*, not primary schools as would typically be the case, to stress that also *basic schools* (grades 1 through 10) are primary.

The new types of schools are gymnasia, or accredited schools. In order to become a gymnasium, the school needs typically to go through a three-year long process of preparation, improvement of teacher qualifications and must obtain marked improvements in student test results. In other words, the movement toward the gymnasium model is an instrument of improving education quality, and it is assumed that over time all schools will become gymnasia, although MES does not impose any deadlines for this process. Gymnasium teachers of grades 11 and 12 receive a permanent 10 percent increase of their salaries, although the teaching program is the same. Again, the structure of gymnasiums varies among schools, like the structure of secondary schools. Some gymnasiums, especially in rural areas, offer education from grade 1 to 12, while some city gymnasiums only from grade 9 to 12. An interesting case is Vilnius, which tries to push the change of the school network by introducing the new school types. Thus, they attempt to introduce gymnasiums from grade 9 to 12, and lower secondary schools from grade 5 to 8 as separate schools. This may represent a local effort to divide the inherited 12-year long school into separate institutions for different levels of education. Although this is in line with general directives of MES, which are recommended but not obligatory, many parents resist because they prefer to have their children attend the same school throughout their education, to avoid the difficulties that arise when the child moves to a new school, and because they are used to this system. Moreover, schools and teachers resist as well because they are afraid that those changes will weaken their job security. So it is a slow process, in which the choice of strategy and all the difficult decisions are left to the municipalities.

Table 5.2 and Table 5.3 display the number of public schools and their students, in successive school years by school type:[16]

Table 5.2. Students by School Type: 2000 to 2005

	2000/2001	2003/2004	2004/2005	2005/2006
Initial	38,592	33,373	24,593	23,093
Basic	66,952	119,935	120,445	117,390
Secondary	389,768	315,817	302,338	279,794
Gymnasium	68,501	74,727	75,179	81,286
All	563,813	543,852	522,555	501,563

Table 5.3. Schools by School Type: 2000 to 2005

	2000/2001	2003/2004	2004/2005	2005/2006
Initial	808	448	198	114
Basic	578	644	613	604
Secondary	624	476	468	441
Gymnasium	80	91	92	107
All	2,090	1,659	1,371	1,266

There was a gradual decline of the student numbers, which seems to be rather uniform across the school types except for the gymnasium, except that between 2000/2001 and 2003/2004 there was a significant shift of about 50 thousand students away from general secondary schools (1-12) to basic schools (1-8). This shift is better examined when we look at the number of schools in the same school years, by school type:

Between 2000 and 2003 there was a remarkable decrease in the number of initial schools (grades 1-4) and of full secondary schools. However, the number of basic schools increased. It seems that in this period two consolidation processes were taking place: closures of many small initial schools, and reclassification of many secondary schools into basic schools. The latter process also has the character of consolidation because it can be likened to the consolidation of teaching in grades 9 to 12. Presumably, those highest grades were moved from smaller secondary schools, which became basic schools, and transferred to larger secondary schools. As a result, the number of full secondary schools fell, and the number of basic schools increased.

Table 5.2 and Table 5.3 also show the slow but clear progress of introducing new types of schools–that is gymnasia. Moreover, it seems that the rate of growth of gymnasia is increasing.

Instruction in Lithuania is provided in three languages, Lithuanian, Russian, and Polish (there are few students in one school learning in Belarusian, whom we ignore below). The distribution of the students learning in different languages is provided in Table 5.4:[17] As is seen there, while in two years the overall number of students declined by five percent, the number of students learning in Russian and Polish decreased by 15 percent and 11 percent respectively.

Table 5.4. Students by Instruction Language, Selected School Years

Instruction language	2004/2005		2006/2007		Decrease
	Students	%	Students	%	
Lithuanian	491,495	91.3%	470,528	92.1%	4.3%
Russian	27,155	5.0%	23,190	4.5%	14.6%
Polish	19,507	3.6%	17,321	3.4%	11.2%
Total	538,157	100.0%	511,039	100.0%	5.0%

The institution responsible for the school budget and for the school facilities is called the school founder. For the state schools MES, counties,[18] and municipalities are the founders, as presented in Table 5.5.

Table 5.5. Founders by Type of School

Founder	Types of schools
MES	Vocational schools, a few central level schools
County	Schools in prisons, in hospitals, in sanatoriums, full program artistic and sport schools, special schools
Municipality	General education schools (initial, basic, secondary, gymnasium)

The law allows for the creation of private schools, but there are still very few of them. For example in Vilnius there are only 12 private schools teaching about 2,100 students.

The responsibilities of the founder in the system are defined in the Education Law. They have influence on the choice of the school director because they have two representatives in the 5-person selection commission, which is created ad hoc whenever needed. The other three representatives are nominated by MES, by the county, and by the school council (the last person may be either teacher or parent).

Founders are responsible for the school network. In particular municipalities decide whether to consolidate schools or change the status of the school. Municipalities also finance student transportation, leaving its organization to schools. The legal obligation is to transport the students who live farther than three kilometers from the nearest school, to that nearest school free of charge. This can be either through public or private transport, or using transportation owned by schools, which include the newly acquired so called *yellow buses* that typically are Mercedes vans with carrying capacity of 12 to 19 and are provided by the government.[19] Table 5.6 provides a breakdown of transported students by transportation type in the school year 2006/2007.[20]

Table 5.6. Students by Transportation Mode

Type of transportation	Students	%
Public	61,195	62.4%
Private	9,243	9.4%
School vehicles	7,547	7.7%
Yellow busses	14,842	15.1%
Other (incl. parents)	5,259	5.4%
All	98,086	100.0%

Interestingly, although the municipalities are obliged to provide transport to the nearest school only, about 9,500 students are transported to a school that is not the nearest. This may be due to instruction language or to specific parental preferences.

5.2.1. Policy Objectives

In 2000 and 2001 a working group was set up by MES with the goal of assessing the inherited system of education finance in Lithuania, identifying the main problems, and proposing reform measures. The report of the Working Group was the basis for the introduction and further adjustment of the Student Basket system. Additionally, important parts of the report were used in the Government Resolution 785 of June 27, 2001[21]—including the general methodology of calculating the Student Basket. That document listed the main problems of the previous financing system:

1. Education spending varied greatly in different regions or municipalities, although the Education Standards for pupil achievement were the same.
2. The network of schools of general education was not at its optimum; hence the funds were used inefficiently.
3. The largest share of funding was spent on running the schools and paying salaries to teachers, while the part for modernization of the teaching process or for purchase of teaching aids was in decline every year.
4. Student transportation issues had grown in importance because of school network reform. The number of students living at considerable distance from school was increasing. Parents were afraid to send their children to a school fur-

ther away from home, and this hindered efforts to use more education funds for education improvement. When students lived in one municipality but attended a school in another, the two municipalities could not agree on who should be paying for transportation of the students in question.

5. When distributing funds for implementing the teaching plans for a certain academic year among general education schools the money was allocated per number of class sets, not per number of students. This situation led to the funding of a large number of vacancies in classes. Schools were not motivated to seek new students because if they did they would usually not receive additional funding for the education costs of those students. Municipalities tried to limit formation of new sets of classes because even if only a few students are added funding must be allocated as per full class set.[22]
6. When students transferred from one institution of education to another, especially when the two are subordinate to different founders, the budget of the new institution of education was not supplemented to cover the real costs of educating the new students. This caused dissatisfaction among those schools in great demand, particularly those in cities, and hindered free movement of students among schools. Urban municipalities incurred losses.
7. Schools had neither independence in planning their spending nor incentives to use the allocated funds efficiently and economically.[23]
8. Non-governmental schools of general education received less funding from the State and municipal budgets for providing education at the national standard than State and municipal general education schools of the same type.

Accordingly, the goals of the new system were defined as follows:[24]

1. Through more efficient use of education funds, to improve the quality of education services and to provide the public with access to such education services as would meet their needs.
2. To optimize the network of general education schools and to ensure equal opportunities to rural and urban students regarding access to quality education.
3. To create conditions for the network of non-governmental general education schools to develop.
4. To reduce the number of children who do not attend school.
5. To strengthen the financial independence of schools.
6. To create a transparent education funding arrangement.
7. To provide students and their parents with a choice of schools and to ensure necessary conditions for exercising this choice.
8. To increase the responsibility of education managers at all levels to ensure that when shaping education policy, all implementation decisions are supported with the necessary financial resources.

Following the end of communism all the countries in the region, including Lithuania, allowed the establishment of non-public schools—usually referred to as *non-governmental* schools—to a large extent as a reaction to previously mandated uniformity and ideological control over schools. The key motivation was to allow local initiatives and pedagogical innovation. The same rationale stood behind the introduction of choice on textbooks, for example. At the same time, it was expected that diversity and competition among school types would lead to more choice and better quality. However in Lithuania the growth of non-public schools was slow in part because of high tuition fees. To help the non-public schools, MES included them in the Student Basket system.

The following results were expected from the proper functioning of the Student Basket:

1. Education funds would be distributed according to uniform principles and would be used more efficiently.
2. It is likely that the quality of education services would improve even without an increase in funding, purely through inter-school competition that is encouraged by this system.
3. The number of children who do not attend school would decline because schools would be motivated to keep existing students and attract new students.
4. The school community would know what amount of funds to expect each year, hence it would be able to plan and manage its activities economically.
5. The network of non-governmental schools would expand.
6. The school network would acquire a form that would better accommodate the needs of students and parents and guarantee implementation of the 'National standards' of education.

As with all complex reform projects, there were many goals of the introduction of the Student Basket in Lithuania, all of which were linked and complementary to each other, but not all of which are clearly stated. Thus, for example, the wording of the first expected result above suggests, but does not express unequivocally, a desire to achieve horizontal equity in education. Thus, identification of key goals of the reforms is to some degree a matter of interpretation. Three main areas of expected results may be identified as follows:

1. Quality:
   Improvement of quality and ensuring complete attendance in schools were the primary goal of the reform. Improved quality of education was foreseen to be the result of better efficiency (leaving more funds for the education process) and of competition among schools with a real choice (so that schools would improve their education standards to attract students). Introduction of non-governmental schools would also strengthen competition and introduce more diversity, leading to better quality. Finally, by motivating schools to increase their enrollment and to draw in more students, MES hoped to obtain more relevant education and a reduction of dropouts.

2. Efficiency:
   Efficiency would be mainly improved through consolidation of school networks, and through better management at the school level due to increased responsibilities and autonomy of schools. It is also assumed that competition among schools would motivate the schools to more efficient use of resources, to better serve the teaching needs of students and thus to attract them.

3. Autonomy:
   Autonomy of schools would increase due to their financial independence and to strengthened responsibilities and positions of schools directors. Stability of

funding provided by the Student Basket system will allow schools to better plan their activities and achieve better efficiency. School autonomy is the prerequisite for school competition, and is therefore seen in Lithuania as an important tool toward better education.

In order to review how Lithuania tried to achieve those objectives and to assess the success of this effort, we have to review first the design of the Student Basket and understand how it was implemented in practice. Each of them is presented sequentially in the next section.

5.3. The Design of the Funding Formula

Our discussion of the Student Basket is divided into three parts:

1. Legal framework within which the Student Basket was introduced, including the determination of what is included in the basket and what is excluded.
2. The place of the Student Basket within general public finances of Lithuania, including the growth of the pool of funds dedicated to the basket.
3. The formula for the Student Basket as it evolved over time (the detailed methodology is discussed in Annex A), including the internal structure of the basket.

5.3.1. Legal Framework

The introduction of the Student basket was preceded by very serious legislative preparation, including amendments to the Law on Education, Budget Law, as well as numerous government resolutions. In particular, the amended Law on Local Self Government,[25] article 5, divides all the functions of local governments into four categories:

1. Independent functions,
2. Assigned functions of limited independence,
3. Delegated functions by the state, financed through targeted grants from the central budget to local budgets.
4. Contractual functions.

Whether a specific function is an independent function, assigned function, or delegated function depends on sectoral legislation, not on general definitions in the Law on Local Self Government, which distinguishes them mainly through the financing mechanisms. Thus, independent functions are financed from local governments' own revenues (such as shared taxes, property tax, locally collected fees, etc.). Assigned functions are financed by grants received from the central budget. Delegated functions are financed by special grants.[26] There are 27 such grants for different functions delegated to local governments, from social protection to education. Contractual functions are typically when a municipality signs a contract with the central government to execute some investment project.

Specifically, education functions are also divided among those categories (arts. 6, 7, and 8):

1. Independent education functions: preschools[27]; additional education (involvement in after school activities and vocational training of children and youth); informal education of adults; provision of meals at preschools and general schools.

2. Assigned education functions: organization of general education for children, youth, and adults; organization of transportation to schools and to places of residence of pupils of rural schools of general education, who live far from schools; ensuring of education of children under 16 years of age who live within the territory of a municipality, at schools of general education or other schools within the education system;
3. Delegated education functions: administration of free-of-charge meal provision for pupils at schools established by a municipality and schools not belonging to the State which were established within the territory of a municipality, as well as administration of provision with pupil supplies for pupils from low-income families, who have declared the place of residence or reside within the territory of a municipality.

As the Law on Local Governments of 1994 was adopted long before the introduction of the Student Basket mechanism, it does not refer specifically to *teaching process* and *teaching environment*. However, they are specified in the amended Law on Education. The general division of costs between the teaching process and teaching environment is summarized in Table 5.7.

Table 5.7. Expenditures of Teaching Process and Teaching Environment

Budget Part	Expenditures Included
Teaching process	Teacher salaries, salaries of administration (directors, secretaries), salaries of professional and support staff (librarians, school pedagogues), teacher in-service training, textbooks for students, books for the school library, teaching aids (including computers and chalk), pedagogical and psychological services, student career guidance, cognitive development of students.[28]
Teaching environment	Salaries of maintenance staff (including cleaners, drivers, gardeners, cooks where applicable,[29] etc.), communal expenses (heating, water, electricity) communications (telephone, Internet access), materials necessary for the functioning of the schools (cleaning materials, paper), non-educational services, facility maintenance and small repairs, student transportation (including petrol for the school buses, bus repairs and spare parts, and salaries of bus drivers).

The *teaching process* is a delegated function, financed through a special grant called Student Basket (one of 27 special grants mentioned above). The organization and management of the *teaching environment* is an independent function, financed from revenues of the municipality (and all other founders of schools, for example owners of private schools).

Thus, the central budget is responsible for the teaching process in all the schools—public and private—and finances it through a special grant to local budgets in case of public schools, and to school owners for private schools. Every year the Budget Law states the amount of Student Basket transfer for each municipality. The founder, which in the case of general public schools is the municipality, is fully responsible for teaching environment.

The division of the school budget into the teaching process and teaching environment expresses a clear policy decision of the Ministry. MES is and wants to remain responsible for the content and quality of the pedagogical process, for improving teacher qualifications, for the learning options available to Lithuanian students, since the level of the Student Basket does not depend on the ownership of the school.[30] Moreover, this responsibility is exercised equally for all schools in Lithuania, both public and private. The responsibility of making sure that the school facilities are in good condition, for heating and cleaning the schools, for ensuring that all students are enrolled in schools (through maintenance of school network and through bussing) is fully decentralized to the founder (is an independent function). Thus, local governments have not been entrusted with any responsibility for the quality of education in the schools of which they are the founders, while MES intended not to be engaged in issues of networks.

The division of expenditures into teaching process and environment is not without its problems. For example, computers are generally recognized as forming part of the teaching process, while chairs and tables not. Hence the money from the Student Basket may be used for school computers, but not for school furniture. Similarly, some material expenditures such as chalk are included in the Student Basket, while other such as paper are not. The school provides textbooks, but the accompanying exercise books, which the students need for homework, have to be purchased by the parents, and thus, do not belong to either the teaching process or the teaching environment. Thus, in a number of ways this distinction is not clearly defined in the laws, and the schools and municipalities regularly phone MES to ask about what may and what may not be financed from the Student Basket.

Moreover, we may safely expect the boundaries to shift. For example, as provision of computers to schools of all types become plentiful and natural, then most likely computers and basic software will move to the teaching environment part of the school budget, together with responsibility for local networks and Internet access. However, provision of specialized education programs and content may still remain within the teaching process.

Similarly, as we shall see below, the initial decision not to involve the central level in the issues of local school networks had to be reversed in 2004, when MES realized that municipalities were very slow in school consolidation efforts. It introduced an obligation for all municipalities to adopt their own consolidation strategies, and has even been rewarding those local governments that made the largest consolidation steps by giving them preferential treatment in the allocation of school buses. This situation shows that the incentive for school consolidation from the per student financing system alone was not enough.

Nevertheless, the division between the teaching process and teaching environment, despite some controversies and occasional lack of clarity, seems to cause no major problems and serves Lithuanian education well. In its primary objective, which is to delineate the roles of the central government and municipalities, it created a stable system with closely aligned managerial and financial responsibilities.

The general principles of the new system of education finance based on the Student Basket were formulated in the Resolution 785 of June 27, 2001 of the Government of the Republic of Lithuania.[31] Annexes to Resolution 785 included key tables with Student Basket values and associated coefficients–especially the table of coefficients for calculation of reference students in its Annex 3, see Table 5.45. Since 2002 the formula has been amended each year with the adoption of new elements of the Student Basket and with other changes. These changes were mandated into law in successive amendments to Annex 3 of Resolution 785, passed every December of the following year.[32]

5.3.2. The Student Basket within General Public Finances of Lithuania

In order to understand the education finance system in Lithuania it is necessary to take a general look at how the funds of the Student Basket are positioned within public finance.

The place of the Student Basket as a special grant for delegated functions in overall expenditures of Lithuania is illustrated in Table 5.8. To avoid double counting, education expenditures are divided into three components: the Student Basket (SB) grant, other expenditures of the state budget on education (vocational education, universities), and other education expenditures of local governments (preschools, teaching environment).

Table 5.8. Education as Part of Lithuanian Public Finances (million Lt[33])

	2001	2002	2003	2004	2005	2006
GDP	48,585	51,971	56,804	62,587	71,200	81,991
State budget	6,975	10,012	10,816	12,653	14,822	17,998
LG budgets	n.a.	3,707	3,760	4,235	4,622	5,640
Education expenditures	2,949	3,169	3,266	3,642	3,919	4,470
of which:						
SB		1,003	1,022	1,113	1,165	1,296
other state education	1,025	1,158	1,210	1,343	1,475	1,686
other LG education	1,925	1,009	1,034	1,186	1,278	1,488

Although the Student Basket methodology included preschools starting in 2004 (see Table 5.45), the funds for preschools have not been included in the Student Basket grants listed above, as can be inferred since there is no serious growth in these grants in 2004. In 2006, Student Basket grant amounted to about 47 percent of all local education expenditures.

We review Table 5.8 by providing percentages. In Table 5.9, education in the state budget includes other state expenditures on education and Student Basket grant to municipalities (sent), while education in LG budgets includes other LG expenditures on education and Student Basket grants (received).

Table 5.9. Education as a Proportion of the GDP, Central, and Local Budgets

	2002	2003	2004	2005	2006
Education as % of GDP	6.1%	5.7%	5.8%	5.5%	5.5%
Education as % of republican budget	21.6%	20.6%	19.4%	17.8%	16.6%
Education as % of LG budget	54.3%	54.7%	54.3%	52.9%	49.4%

First we observe that Lithuania spends a very significant proportion of its GDP on education, which at over 5.5 percent is relatively high in the region. As Table 5.9 indicates, the share of education in both the state budget and in local budgets is slowly declining. This is the result of rapid economic growth (in real terms, expenditures on education are increasing). Moreover, about half of all budgets of local governments in Lithuania are spent on education. This share is certainly lower in the cities, which have many other expenditures, and certainly higher in rural *rayons*.

Another way to review Table 5.8 is to analyze the percentage distribution of education spending between the Student Basket grant, other state expenditures on education, and other LG expenditures on education provided in Table 5.10.

Table 5.10. Structure of Education Spending in Lithuania

	2002	2003	2004	2005	2006
Student Basket	31.6%	31.3%	30.5%	29.7%	29.0%
Other Republican	36.5%	37.1%	36.9%	37.6%	37.7%
Other Local Govts.	31.8%	31.6%	32.6%	32.6%	33.3%

We recall the content of the three components: the Student Basket includes teacher salaries and the teaching process, other state includes vocational and tertiary education, and other LG includes preschools and teaching environment. We can assume that preschools consume a significant part of the overall LG expenditures on education, maybe more than half of the total. This would mean that the Student Basket accounts for about 65 percent of school budgets, which is consistent with international experience–teacher salaries are the largest part of the school budget.

This overall picture is confirmed by the example of a budget of one of Lithuania's municipalities, namely Panevezis *rayon*, a rural municipality. We first present the revenues and expenditures of that municipality in 2006 (see Table 5.11 and Table 5.12 below).

Table 5.11. Revenues of Panevezis Budget, 2006

Source	Amount (Lt.)	Share	Including	Amount (Lt.)	Share
Taxes	30,137	42.0%	Personal income tax	27,371	38.2%
			Property tax	2,362	3.3%
			Taxes on services	404	0.6%
Grants	37,166	51.8%	Student basket	16,511	23.0%
			Other grants	20,655	28.8%
Other	4,421	6.2%	Other	4,421	6.2%
Total	71,724	100.0%	Total	71,724	100%

Table 5.12. Expenditures of Panevezis Budget, 2006

Sector	Total Expenditures (Lt.)	Share	Including	Expenditures (Lt.)	Share
Administration	21,372	30.4%	Administration	15,553	22.1%
			Financial Department	5,820	8.3%
Social sector	9,963	14.2%	Social Assistance	7,535	10.7%
			Child Care	914	1.3%
			Old Age Home	728	1.0%
			Communal Enterprise	786	1.1%
Culture	3,881	5.5%	Library	1,331	1.9%
			Cultural Center	2,550	3.6%
Education	35,004	49.8%	Pedagogical Center	163	0.2%
			Psychological Services	191	0.3%
			Pre-Schools	3,853	5.5%
			General Schools	29,384	41.8%
			Informal Education	751	1.1%
			Musical School	662	0.9%
Total	70,221	100.0%	Total	70,221	100.0%

We note from Table 5.11 that over half of revenues of Panevezis come from various types of grants from the central budget. This is typical of poorer local governments, whose own revenues are relatively modest and the budget relies on grants from the central government. According to the Lithuanian budget classification, revenues from shared personal income taxes include also equalization grants, amounting to 14.8 million Lt. Typically, however, equalization grants are not included in shared income taxes because they are allocated in a different way (i.e. on the basis of relative poverty and not on the basis of tax origin). It is more proper to treat those revenues as included in grants from the central budget, in which case the share of those grants in all revenues would increase to over 70 percent.

Comparison of Table 5.11 and Table 5.12 shows that in Panevezis the received Student Basket grant is about 47 percent of overall expenditure on education. This relationship is consistent with Table 5.9 (see comments following that table). There are separately reported expenditures on preschools in Panevezis, but they are extremely low. This may indicate that at least some preschool expenditures are reported together with the general secondary schools budgets. Such a situation might arise when a preschool forms a part of the general secondary school, implying that only stand-alone preschool budgets are reported in Table 5.12. Another important type of expenditure reported for general schools and coming from the budget of Panevezis (and not from Student Basket) is student transportation, including both the salaries of staff and the maintenance costs. School level budget data are needed to fully understand that somewhat puzzling relationship.

5.3.3. The Structure of the Student Basket

The Student Basket is the standard per student amount for the teaching process for a student of grades 5 to 8 in an urban general secondary school, with an assumed class size of 25.[34] Students in other schools or grades receive a higher or lower allocation, based on a table of allocation coefficients. We discuss the methodology for calculating the Student Basket and the table of allocation coefficients in Annex A, while Table 5.45 in Annex B provides a complete table of those coefficients for 2007. The evolving internal structure of the Student Basket, as well as its total value, is summarized in Table 5.13 which appears as Table 5.44 in Annex A (in current Lt):

Table 5.13. Structure of the Student Basket: 2002 to 2007

Elements of the Student Basket	2002	2003	2004	2005	2006	2007
Total Amount (Lt.)	1,521	1,538	1,654	1,753	1,942	2,333
Teacher Salaries	1,368	1,368	1,454	1,519	1,664	1,986
School Management	135.6	136.0	145.0	152.5	181.9	216.6
Teacher Qualifications	4.5	9.0	14.2	24.4	24.4	24.2
Textbooks	10.5	21.0	33.5	41.4	47.6	62.0
Teaching Materials	2.1	4.2	6.7	8.3	9.5	12.4
Pedagogical Psychological Services				7.2	10.9	13.1
Students Cognitive Development					3.7	7.3
Vocational Guidance						3.7
Libraries						7.3

It is important to understand that the division of the Student Basket into the specific elements, as seen in Table 5.13, is only indicative and not obligatory. This means that the schools are free to use the Student Basket funds allocating different proportions to various functions, which are included in the teaching process. Those budgeting decisions are taken by the municipalities, when they approve detailed school budgets (by budget line items), and when they decide on the reallocation of the Student Basket funds among the schools. As we shall see, municipalities may use this freedom to set their own education policy at the local level.

Because of the large number of small components of the Student Basket, not easily comparable, we will use a simpler breakdown: into teacher salaries, school management, and other educational functions. This breakdown is provided in Table 5.14.

Table 5.14. Simplified Structure of the Student Basket: 2002 to 2007

Elements of the Student Basket	2002	2003	2004	2005	2006	2007
Total Amount (Lt.)	1,521	1,538	1,654	1,753	1,942	2,333
Teacher Salaries	1,368	1,368	1,454	1,519	1,664	1,986
School Management	135.6	136.0	145.0	152.5	181.9	216.6
Other educational functions	17.1	34.2	54.4	81.3	96.2	130.1

The first issue that we need to discuss is the growth of the Student Basket amount. Over the period of six years the value of the Student Basket amount rose from 1,521 Lt to 2,333 Lt, a growth of 53.4 percent. That growth was not equal for each component: while salaries grew by 45 percent and administration by 60 percent, other education functions started from next to nothing and increased their value more than six fold.

It is also interesting to review the year-to-year growth. Table 5.15 provides the growth rate for each of the three components of the student Basket, as well as for the total, compared to the previous year:

Table 5.15. Yearly Rates of Growth of the Student Basket: 2002 to 2007

Elements of the Student Basket	2003	2004	2005	2006	2007
Total Student Basket	1.1%	7.5%	6.0%	10.8%	20.1%
Teacher salaries	0.0%	6.3%	4.5%	9.5%	19.4%
Administration	0.3%	6.7%	5.1%	19.3%	19.1%
Other education functions	100.0%	59.1%	49.4%	18.3%	35.3%

The doubling of other education functions in 2003 and growth by 60 percent in 2004 is a result of an agreed implementation schedule (see Annex A). We observe that the administration component grew more or less at the same rate as teacher salaries, except for 2006 when the appropriate coefficient was changed from 10 percent to 11 percent. Every year, the allocation for other education functions grew much more rapidly. It is also very interesting to note that the yearly growth rate of the total Student Basket amount was increasing every year, from 1.1 percent to over 20 percent. Finally note that each year the growth of the Student Basket is higher than inflation.[35]

The rapid growth of the allocation for other education functions means that over time internal structure of the Student Basket was changing. Table 5.16 shows the share of each of the three major components in the Student Basket over the years:

Table 5.16. Major Components of the Student Basket: 2002 to 2007

	2002	2003	2004	2005	2006	2007
Teacher salaries	90.0%	88.9%	87.9%	86.7%	85.7%	85.1%
School administration	8.9%	8.8%	8.8%	8.7%	9.4%	9.3%
Other education functions	1.1%	2.2%	3.3%	4.6%	5.0%	5.6%

We see that the allocation for other education functions was steadily increasing not only in absolute terms (compare with Table 5.15) but also as a share of the Student Basket from an initial 1.1 percent to 5.6 percent. Simultaneously, the share of teacher salaries decreased by the same 5 percentage points, from 90 percent down to 85 percent. This represents a consistent effort of MES to finance not just teaching, but an increasing range of educational services and functions.

5.3.4. The Allocation Formula for the Student Basket

The reference student, that is the student of grade 5 to 8 in an urban secondary school, is allocated the *factor* (or a weight) of 1, and the value of the Student Basket for him, provided in Table 5.13, is the basic Student Basket amount. We now discuss the amounts allocated to other students. For students of other schools or other grades the methodology calculates a set of allocation coefficients, which need to be multiplied by the basic Student Basket amount. Those allocation coefficients depend on two factors:

- normative size of the class, which is assumed for different schools based on their size and location;
- normative number of lessons a class receives, based on curriculum norms and depending on grade.

In general, and as seen in the methodology of the Student Basket discussed in Annex A, the allocation coefficient is inversely proportional to the normative class size, and proportional to the number of lessons.

For the purposes of defining normative class sizes, all rural schools are divided into four categories of sizes, which we call for simplicity XS (extra-small), S (small), M (medium-sized), and L (large) (no such naming convention is used in Lithuania). The larger the school, the larger the normative class size. Urban schools by definition belong to size category L. The division into size categories depends on the education level and on student enrollment, and is defined in Table 5.17. Normative class sizes, independent of the grades, are also indicated.

Table 5.17. Size Categories of Schools and Normative Class Size

Size category	Initial (1-4)	Basic (1-10)	Secondary (1-12)	Normative Class size
XS	up to 50	up to 130	—	10
S	51 to 80	131 to 300	up to 400	15
M	81 to 200	301 to 600	401 to 700	20
L	over 200	over 600	over 700	25

Table 5.18 provides the basic values of the allocation coefficients by size category and by grade level. We call those coefficients *initial* because they are later corrected for policy reasons (see Table 5.19 and Table 5.45). The different relative cost coefficients are

essentially proportional to the normative teaching loads for different grades and inversely proportional to normative class sizes.[36] The values are for 2007, but in fact they have not changed at all since 2002. In the complete Table 5.45, those coefficients appear in top lines in rows 1 to 5.

Table 5.18. Initial Allocation Coefficient by Size Category and Grade Level

Size category	Normative class size	Grade level			
		1 to 4	5 to 8	8 & 10	11 & 12
XS	10	1.7765	2.1201	2.4636	—
S	15	1.1924	1.4216	1.6504	1.8151
M	20	0.9005	1.0772	1.2440	1.3684
L	25	0.8208	1.0000	1.1913	1.3104

We note that for an urban school, which is always in the L category, a student attending grades 5 to 8 has an allocation coefficient equal to 1. This reflects the fact that such a student is a reference student in Student Basket calculations. As expected, as school size increases, the coefficients grow smaller, reflecting lower spending per student in larger classes. Similarly, as grade level increases, the coefficients increase, reflecting longer teaching time per week, and hence also more required teachers per class, based on curriculum norms.

Coefficients of Table 5.18 were applied in 2002 and 2003. Since then, an additional step was introduced, which consisted of correcting the coefficients, primarily by decreasing coefficients for size category SX by 10 percent, as mandated in Resolution No. 1617 of the Government of the Republic of Lithuania (December 16, 2003) titled *"Amendments of Resolution No. 785 of June 27, 2001"*.[37] Moreover, the coefficients for size category S were increased by one percent, and for M and L by two percent.[38] The corrected coefficients[39] are listed in Table 5.19.

Table 5.19 Corrected Allocation Coefficient, by Size Category and Grade Level

Size category	Normative class size	Grade level			
		1 to 4	5 to 8	8 & 10	11 & 12
XS	10	1.5989	1.9081	2.4636	—
S	15	1.2043	1.4358	1.6669	1.8336
M	20	0.9185	1.0936	1.2689	1.3958
L	25	0.9164	1.0150	1.2698	1.3366

The decrease of allocation coefficients for small schools seems to be a policy decision to motivate local governments to consolidate school networks, but partially breaks the logic of the Student Basket amount, which is a bottom-up calculation.

On the basis of Table 5.19, for each size category and each grade level, three allocation coefficients are defined:

1. Coefficients for regular schools (i.e. coefficients of Table 5.19).
2. Coefficients for minority schools (i.e. coefficients of Table 5.19 increased by 10 percent).

3. Coefficient for Vilnius schools and for mixed language schools[40] located in southeast Lithuania (i.e. coefficients from Table 5.19 increased by 21 percent).

In Table 5.45 in Annex B, allocation coefficients are listed one above the other, with the second and third one in parenthesis.

Finally, for each size category and each grade level, the allocation coefficients for schools with integrated teaching, with migrant students, and for schools providing instruction in many languages, the three coefficients listed above are increased by 35.6 percent. This factor was equal 10 percent originally in 2002 to 2003, was increased to 20 percent in 2005 and 2006, and again increased to 35.6 percent in 2007. The coefficients of Table 5.19 and the above considerations are summarized in Table 5.45 (lines 1 to 5).

In addition, there are special allocations for the following six types of schools. For each of these types we provide the general level of allocation, the normative class size, and quote the appropriate line number in Table 5.45:

- For school age youth who have difficulties attending regular schools (de-motivated or delinquent students), at about twice the funding level of standard students—class size 10, line 6,
- For adult education, at about the same level of funding as standard students—class size 20, line 7,
- For independent learning, that is learning at home for children who are too ill to attend school, at about twice the funding level of standard students—class size 10, line 8,
- For vocational schools, at the same funding level as standard students —class size 25, line 9,
- For special schools, at about twice the funding level of standard students—class size 10, line 10,
- For preschool students, at about 2/3 the funding level of standard students[41]—class size 10 to 20, line 11.

Multiplying the actual number of students in each category by those factors and summing for each school or for each municipality yields the number of reference ("weighted") students for that school or for an entire municipality. The value of the Student Basket grant for a municipality is obtained by multiplying the number of reference students in all its schools by basic Student Basket amount. The Student Basket grant for the municipality is defined for the fiscal year on the basis of enrollment numbers in September of the previous year.

The Student Basket model also includes the provision for the situation when a student leaves a school during the school year and moves to another school, possibly located in another municipality. From 2005, for each student relocating to another municipality, the municipality where he was originally enrolled[42] has an obligation to send appropriate funds to the receiving municipality.[43] The Student Basket methodology, in the regularly amended Resolution 785, defined a specific monthly amount that should *follow the student* in this case. In Table 5.45 this amount appears in line 12,[44] it depends only on grade level, and not on location of the school or its size. For students in grades 5 to 8 in 2007, the amount is 188 Lt per month, so the ten-month school year amount is 1,880 Lt or 2,256 Lt. for 12 months, which surprisingly is below the basic Student Basket amount of 2,333 Lt.[45]

Finally we note that although the formula discussed here calculates the amount of the Student Basket for each school, the funds are in fact transferred to the municipalities, which have the right to re-allocate a certain amount of that received transfer among their schools. That amount was initially 15 percent in 2002, was reduced to 10 percent in 2003 and 2004, and to 5 percent since 2005. We discuss this reallocation in the following section (see Table 5.26), but note here that this legal approach creates a significant margin for municipality decisions also within the Student Basket.

5.4. The Implementation of the Funding Formula

The implementation of the Student Basket in Lithuania began on January 1, 2002. As discussed in the previous section, the new system was introduced after serious legal preparations, and after an agreement has been reached with the Ministry of Finance regarding the implementation schedule (see Introduction) and the financing methods. The new special grant for the Student Basket was introduced into the budget law. It is an interesting fact that the new system was introduced without a pilot project testing the new solutions. Indeed, the value of such pilot projects in the case of education financing seems to be rather limited. Since the key problem of allocation is the budgetary constraint on the total pool of funds and the corresponding need to allocate as best as possible limited resources, the relevant questions can only be tested and resolved on a nationwide scale, and not through a pilot project.[46] Indeed, it seems that only more localized procedures can be subjected to reasonable piloting, such as budgetary autonomy of schools, but as we know from the previous section this was not part of the reform design.

Our discussion of the implementation of the student basket will focus on the following issues:

- Correctness of the application of the formulae,
- Practical application of the Student Basket to municipalities,
- Allocation of funds to individual schools.
- Budgetary autonomy of schools and the Student Basket.
- Equity of Student Basket allocation (schools and municipalities).

5.4.1. Correctness of the Application of the Formulae

As seen clearly from the discussion of section Table 5.19 and of Annex A, the Student Basket, while simple in theory, is arithmetically a rather complex system. It is not surprising that its practical implementation encountered initially some serious problem. The two key problems were the actual calculation of Student Basket grants to municipalities, and the legal uncertainties over the use of these funds.

In 2003, during the second year of implementation of the Student Basket, the State Audit and Accounting Office (*Audito ir Apskaitos Tarnyba* or AAT) conducted at the request of MES a comprehensive review of the new system (see AAT 2003),[47] and immediately focused on these two issues. The report of AAT was very critical of the implementation of the new system and concluded that achieving the policy goals of the reform was at risk.

The AAT report noticed that there were many problems with the actual calculation of the Student Basket for schools and municipalities, and that all municipalities received more funds than they should have been allocated by the methodology. For example, for the Jonava municipality the report noted that:

- The municipality should have received 15.91 million Lt according to the methodology,
- MES calculated wrongly 16.14 million Lt,
- The Ministry of Finance received a budget proposal of 16.18 million Lt,
- The 2002 Budget Law allocated 16.18 million Lt to Jonava in the form of the Student Basket grant,
- Of those funds received from the central government, Jonava used only 13.77 million Lt for the teaching process, used 0.82 million Lt of the Student Basket grant to cover old school debts, and used the remaining 1.59 million Lt to pay for the education environment and for other educational needs.

These errors in calculating the due amounts of the Student Basket grants meant that the allocation of the Student Basket per reference student[48] was not uniformly 1,521 Lt as the methodology required, but ranged from 1,523 Lt for Alytaus to 1,592 Lt for Kedainiai *rayon*. This means that for each municipality MES had actually provided more funds under the Student Basket system than they were entitled to, in the extreme case 4.7 percent more. The report concluded that there were too many mistakes in the actual application of the formula, and that insufficient control had been exercised over the actual allocation process. Interestingly, the report did not conclude that the formula itself was too complicated.

As a reaction to this criticism MES developed a computer program, which allows it as well as all municipalities to calculate effortlessly the allocation according to the Student Basket for each school. The computer program, of course, needs to be amended every year due to changes in the coefficients and in the basic Student Basket amount. The creation and distribution of that program solved the immediate problem of correct usage of the allocation formula (assuming of course that the program itself works correctly). It creates, however, a different danger, namely that the very complicated system of allocation of funds, especially one implemented in a computer program, will become too difficult and too inaccessible for policy discussion. With a computer program at hand, it is easy for the few experts to introduce every year new elements into the already complex and inaccessible calculations. This has been in fact happening,[49] and the level of understanding the formula among education stakeholders seems to be decreasing. MES officials and municipalities no longer need to actually look into the coefficients of the formula or understand the details of the calculations. A risk arises that a vital policy instrument may become the sole property of experts. Moreover, municipalities lose an independent means of checking whether the Student Basket allocation they receive is exactly what the legal regulations provide for.[50]

It is worth noting, nevertheless, that some municipalities undertake the effort to calculate on their own the size of the Student Basket grant they should receive. For example, the Sirvintai municipality has developed an Excel program, updated each year as new coefficients come into force, and uses it to verify the results of the program supplied by MES (there has been remarkable agreement so far between the two independent calculations). Sirvintai uses their program also to facilitate the allocation of Student Basket amounts among their schools.

The AAT report also noticed that the excess funds from the Student Basket, not used for the teaching process, were used to finance the teaching environment and repayment of school debts. Although this was in accordance with the Law on Education, it contradicted the goals of the reform and should be addressed because some municipalities were reducing their contributions to the teaching process by using the Student Basket funds for other education purposes. According to AAT estimates, about 4.7 percent of the Student Basket allocation was not used for the teaching process. That recommendation was indeed adopted by MES in the amendment of the Law on Education, and since 2004 any savings from the Student Basket may be used only for the teaching process.

Further criticism of AAT was that there were no criteria or methodologies for the reallocation of the Student Basket funds among the schools. It was recommended that such criteria should be defined by MES, so that all financial decisions would be based on a clear legal stipulation. However, MES did not issue such a methodology because it believes that different municipalities face many specific circumstances, and therefore the municipal governments should have the authority and autonomy to decide on the reallocation on their own. In this MES strongly defended the right of local governments to define and pursue their local education policies, which may and should be different in different counties and communities. Nevertheless, at least partially in reaction to AAT criticism, MES had reduced the margin of allowed reallocation from initial 15 percent to the current five percent, as discussed above.

The report also criticized the large differences in the per student allocation for municipalities, maintaining that one of the policy goals was to reduce the inequalities among different local governments in education finance (see the review of those differences in the following subsection). Again, this criticism was not accepted by MES, which had argued that some expenditure differences due to school organization and to teaching programs were justified, and has in fact maintained the main allocation coefficients unchanged.

The report of AAT and subsequent decisions by MES testify to healthy open policy dialogue in Lithuanian education. However, it is a pity that such a thorough review of the Student Basket was not repeated. In part this is needed because the Student Basket system has undergone major changes since 2003. However, the key issue is that MES has little independent assessment of the financing of schools. We will have the occasion to use below a later report by AAT on school network consolidation published in 2006.

5.4.2. Practical Functioning of the Student Basket in Municipalities

In the present subsection we take a look at the functioning of the Student Basket system at the municipality level. We first discuss the actual allocation of Student Basket grants to local governments, and then how they use of these funds.

Regarding the determination of Student Basket grants to municipalities, it is clear that because of the large number of allocation coefficients that were higher than 1 (see Table 5.45), the actual per student allocation to municipalities was likely to be higher than the Student Basket amount. This was indeed the case, as Table 5.20 shows for years 2003 to 2007.[51] We use the basic Student Basket amount (from Table 5.13), the national average per student allocation for the republic, the per student allocations for the municipality that received the lowest and the highest per student allocation, as well as their relation to the basic Student Basket amount.

Of course, the lowest per student allocation is for the cities because all their schools belong to size category L. Large cities of Kaunas, Šiaulis, and Panevėžis had the lowest per student allocation between 2003 and 2007. The group of rural *rayons* with highest per student allocation was also quite stable over the years, and included Alytaus, Panevėžis, Šalčininkųs, Neringas, and Vilnius *rayon*.[52] Interestingly, city Vilnius remained below the national average even in 2007, when it obtained the additional weight of 121 percent for its schools.

Table 5.20. Per Student Allocation to Municipalities 2003 to 2007

	2003	2004	2005	2006	2007
Basic SB amount (Lt.)	1,538	1,654	1,753	1,942	2,333
Per student allocation (Lt.)					
National Average	1,799	1,941	2,093	2,337	2,881
Smallest among Municipalities	1,584	1,714	1,840	2,052	2,498
Largest among Municipalities	2,380	2,520	2,721	3,039	3,719
Per student allocation as % of basic SB amount					
National Average	117.0%	117.3%	119.4%	120.3%	123.5%
Smallest among Municipalities	103.0%	103.6%	104.9%	105.7%	107.1%
Largest among Municipalities	154.8%	152.4%	155.2%	156.5%	159.4%

We note a rather interesting stability. The ratio of actual average per student allocation to the basic Student Basket amount is very slowly and not significantly increasing. This is probably a result of changes in policy coefficients, discussed in previous section, for example change of the coefficient for integrated teaching from 110 percent to 135.6 percent, or the introduction of a 121 percent coefficient for Vilnius and South-East Lithuania mixed schools.[53] Indeed, the national average per student allocation in terms of the Student Basket amount grows from 117 percent in 2003 to 124 percent in 2007. However, the main coefficients, based on nominal class sizes and on curriculum norms stayed constant, so the growth of the allocation compared to the Student Basket is very small (about seven percent). We conclude that the main driver of the increase of actual per student allocation was the increase of the basic Student Basket amount.

After allocation of the Student Basket grant to municipalities, the following adjustments need to be taken into account:

- Funds received by the municipality for students who have moved to the schools of that municipality from another one,
- Funds paid out to other municipalities for students who moved out of schools of that municipality,
- Funds added to the Student Basket grant for the teaching process from municipal budget,
- Unused funds returned to the central budget at the end of financial year.[54]

Table 5.21 shows that these adjustments have very small effect on the funds destined for education at the State level:[55]

Table 5.21. Student Basket Grant and Expenditures on Teaching Process (Thousands Lt.)

	2003	2004	2005	2006
Received SB grant	1,049,378	1,146,183	1,197,319	1,324,805
Received from other LG's			1,081	1,111
Paid out to other LG's			1,120	1,166
Contribution from own funds	436	3,138	2,251	3,859
Returned to central budget	115	83	181	296
Expenditures on teaching process	1,049,699	1,149,238	1,199,350	1,328,314

Of special interest are contributions to the teaching process from municipal revenues. They express the local community's commitment to support education, and have an impact beyond just financing. Thus, for example, whenever a municipality decided to contribute from its own revenues to education, it has a strong motivation to monitor the proper use of these funds for the greatest benefit of the voters. At the national level, municipal contributions are still very small, but the number of contributing municipalities is growing: from four in 2003, to 16 in 2003, and to 18 in 2005 and 2006. For an important minority of municipalities municipal contributions are significant. Table 5.21 shows the three largest contributors, ranked by their contributions expressed as a proportion of Student Basket grants received from the central budget:

Table 5.22. Municipalities That Contribute Most to the Teaching Process above the Student Basket Grant

	2003	2004	2005	2006
Largest contributor	Palangos m.	Neringos m.	Neringos m.	Neringos m.
Contribution as % of SB grant	3.4%	9.8%	18.8%	20.1%
Second largest contributor	Zarasų	Zarasų	Birštono m.	Birštono m.
Contribution as % of SB grant	3.1%	6.7%	8.2%	6.9%
Third largest contributor	Birštono m.	Palangos m.	Zarasų	Palangos m.
Contribution as % of SB grant	1.2%	6.3%	4.1%	4.4%

Table 5.22 is very important because it shows what is likely to be the trend in the future, namely that as the role of municipalities becomes more established, and as they feel more confident in their position as owners and managers of local school networks, they will be more likely to contribute significantly to their schools from their own resources. Another useful observation coming from Table 5.22 is that high contributors tend to be almost exclusively cities (indicated by "m." in their names).

Moving on to the use of Student Basket funds by Lithuanian municipalities, we recall from Table 5.13 that the basic Student Basket amount included the following nonsalary components:

Table 5.23. Non-Salary Elements of the Teaching Process: 2003 to 2006[56]

	2003	2004	2005	2006
Allocation in the SB grant (Lt. per student)				
Teacher professional development	9.0	14.2	24.4	24.4
Textbooks	21.0	33.5	41.4	47.6
Teaching aids	4.2	6.7	8.3	9.5
Pedagogical psychological services			7.2	10.9
Student cognitive development				3.7
Expenditures by municipalities (Lt. per student)				
Teacher professional development	3.1	5.2	10.5	18.9
Textbooks	22.0	32.8	40.3	47.4
Teaching aids	11.2	16.3	17.4	17.4
Pedagogical psychological services			6.8	13.8
Student cognitive development				3.3
Expenditures as percentage of allocation				
Teacher professional development	34.4%	36.6%	43.0%	77.5%
Textbooks	104.8%	97.9%	97.3%	99.6%
Teaching aids	266.7%	243.3%	210.1%	182.7%
Pedagogical psychological services			94.8%	126.6%
Student cognitive development				88.6%

When reviewing Table 5.23 it is important to note that allocation for specific elements of the Student Basket amount is only indicative for municipalities, not obligatory. Moreover, it is based on Table 5.13 and does not take into account further coefficients of Table 5.19 as summarized in Table 5.45.[57] Nevertheless it is very interesting to note that there are rather stable differences between the methodology of calculating the basic Student Basket amount and the actual expenditures. Municipalities tend to spend much less than foreseen on teacher professional development than stipulated in official MES documents, and much more on teaching aids. However, the discrepancies are reduced every year. We note that for teacher professional development, realization increases every year toward 100 percent from below, while for teaching materials it decreases every year toward the same 100 percent from above. This probably indicates the power of emphasizing the structure of the basic Student Basket, as amended Resolution 785 does every year: although the stated amounts are only indicative, over the years municipalities make an effort to conform to those guidelines and to minimize the discrepancies in planning the budgets of their schools.

A simpler way to look at Table 5.23 is to compare the total of the Student Basket allocation for non-salary functions with the total actual expenditures on the same functions (Table 5.24).

Table 5.24. Expenditures on Non-Salary Items in Student Basket Expenditures: 2003 to 2006

	2003	2004	2005	2006
Allocation for non-salary components	34.2	54.4	81.3	96.2
Expenditures for non-salary components	36.3	54.3	75.0	100.8
Percent difference	6.1%	-0.2%	-7.7%	4.8%

The first row expresses the preferences and policy choices of MES ("theory"), while the second row expresses the preferences and policy choices or inherited spending patterns of municipalities ("practice"). We see that MES was indeed able to implement to a very considerable degree its policies through the actions of independent local governments.

We conclude that in Lithuania the Student Basket was an effective tool to convince the municipalities, while giving them full freedom, to adapt their education spending to indicative values contained in the Student Basket structure. Nevertheless, precisely because of non-obligatory status of the Student Basket amounts, there is considerable regional variation in the way the funds are used.

Finally we discuss the movement of students among municipalities. In 2005, there were 7,154 students who moved to a school in different municipality, and in 2006 only 6,481. This decrease is interesting because it shows that there is some counter-incentive to changing schools. Indeed, if a large number of students leave the schools operated by a municipality, it is obliged to send to neighboring local governments appropriate funds (see section 5.3). This may cause budget problems because the expenditures on teachers will not change (movement of a few students will not affect the number of classes and lessons, but may affect the school budget). One may suspect therefore that the decrease of the number of students moving across municipal boundaries is due to some actions by municipalities to deter such movement, especially as it is unlikely that quality difference among schools could have changed much in one year. This problem may be illustrated with the example of city of Panevėžis and the rural Panevėžis *rayon*, whose area surrounds the city.[58] The seats of both municipalities are located in the city. Table 5.25 shows the number of incoming and outgoing students for the two municipalities:

Table 5.25. Incoming and Outgoing Students in Panevezis Municipalities

	Incoming	Outgoing	Balance
2005			
Panevėžio city	328	153	175
Panevėžio rayon	115	314	-199
2006			
Panevėžio city	264	156	108
Panevėžio rayon	122	239	-117

From discussions with local officials we know that most of students "lost" by Panezis *rayon* in either 2005 or 2006 went to Panevezis city schools. Therefore comparison of 2005 and 2006 indicates that over the course of one year Panevezis *rayon* schools managed to persuade about 75 students to return to *rayon* schools from the city schools (it remains an open question what were the persuasive arguments). Of course not all of those students are the same. We observe an overall trend rather than specific decisions taken by the students.

Discussions with Panevezis *rayon* officials indicated also that in some villages in the *rayon* two schools buses began to transport students to schools, one to the city school, and another one to the school owned by the *rayon*, but located close to the city itself. Clearly the city was trying to "steal" *rayon* students using their own transportation. It took some discussions between the two municipalities to resolve the problem and to ensure that only one school bus, owned by *rayon*, arrived in the village every morning and took the students to the *rayon* school. This example illustrates that the competition for students, if it appears in Panevezis, is not among the schools but rather among the municipalities, and that administrative decisions, not only the free choice of students, determine its outcomes.

A separate problem concerns the students who change school in the middle of the school year. The required movement of funds–line 12 of Table 5.45–in that case may cause disruption.

5.4.3. Allocation of Funds to Individual Schools

As discussed above, the Student Basket grant is calculated for each school separately, but allocated to the municipality as a lump sum. In general the municipalities are expected to fund the schools according to the Student Basket methodology, but within a prescribed limit of the total Student Basket grant received they can reallocate these funds among the schools. We recall that this limit was 15 percent in 2002, 10 percent in 2003 and 2004, and is five percent since 2005. This reallocation becomes thus an important instrument of realizing local education policy, and as such is very interesting for understanding the practical operations of the Lithuanian education finance system. In the present subsection, we first report on the degree of the reallocation, and then focus on the practices of local government regarding this issue. We do not discuss a separate though linked allocation problem the municipalities face, namely the allocation of funds for the teaching environment. This is a process left entirely to local governments, and no specific data are collected by MES.[59]

There are good reasons why the reallocation of Student Basket funds among schools happens. Typically, it is the large schools for which Student Basket funds are sufficient, and small schools for which they are insufficient. This happens because the allocation of funds is based, as discussed in the previous section, on the basis of normative, rather than actual, class sizes. Larger schools find it much easier to maintain actual class sizes at or above the normative level, so their Student Basket allocation may exceed the costs of the teaching process. If a small school has class sizes smaller than the normative, it will have problems financing the teaching process from its Student Basket allocation. But a small decrease of allocation for a large school translates into a relatively large increase for a small school. In other words, the cost of reallocation to large schools is small, but the benefit to small schools may be very large. Initially in 2002 and 2003 this variation was significant, and some small schools received up to 30 percent less or more than the Student Basket methodology had determined for them (see AAT 2003). As the Student Basket system stabilized, this variation diminished, and now typically a large school may receive a few per cent less than the Student Basket methodology would assess, while a small school up to 12 percent more.

Table 5.26 shows the degree of reallocation of Student Basket funds between 2003 and 2006 based on budget execution data.

Table 5.26. Reallocation of Student Basket Funds by Municipalities: 2003 to 2006

	2003	2004	2005	2006
Average reallocation	2.65%	2.51%	2.79%	2.08%
Municipalities with 0 reallocation	9	12	7	6
Municipalities with reallocation more than 5%	10	9	4	1
Highest reallocation	10.10%	9.89%	9.67%	8.03%
Municipality with highest reallocation	Raseinių	Raseinių	Biržų	Pasvalio
Second highest reallocation	10.00%	8.33%	9.23%	4.64%
Municipality with second highest reallocation	Šiaulių	Pasvalio	Pasvalio	Skuodo
Third highest reallocation	9.97%	8.09%	6.48%	4.56%
Municipality with third highest reallocation	Pasvalio	Skuodo	Skuodo	Vilniaus

We note that average reallocation varies between 2.1 percent and 2.8 percent, so is much lower that the current limit of five percent. In 2003 and 2004 the limit was 10 percent, and indeed a number of municipalities used fully this option. The decrease of the limit to five percent in 2005 caused them difficulties. Some, like Raiseniu, managed to keep their reallocation within the new limit, others struggled. For example Skuodo made an effort to decrease the level of reallocation, but managed to fit within the new limit only in 2006, while Pasvalio more or less continued the old approach. However, the number of municipalities that are above the limit is decreasing quickly.[60]

Interestingly, we see also that the number of municipalities that do not do any reallocation is decreasing. Those are the municipalities which apply the allocation exactly as received from MES, in other words which do not have their own vision and determination to assess the real needs of their schools and to decide, through their own local negotiation process, the budgets of their schools (with respect to the teaching process). More and more local governments take an active position with regards to the budgeting process. We may assume that Lithuanian municipalities are going through a learning experience, in which they become more self-confident in their budgetary and management control over their schools.

With this said, we now briefly discuss how local governments decide on the Student Basket part of school budgets, within the reallocation limits prescribed by law. This area is not regulated by any Ministerial directives. We have discussed earlier that despite the insistence of the State Audit and Accounting Office in its report AAT (2003) that MES issues such guidance, MES decided not to interfere in the local decision-making process.

When a Lithuanian municipality has to decide on the allocation of the Student Basket grant to individual schools, the typical problem is faces is to provide enough funds to small schools. This is done by reducing the allocation to large schools by a small percentage. As discussed above, this yields funds for a relatively high increase of the Student Basket for a small school.

However, some municipalities use more systematic approaches, based on policy considerations. We describe here the approach used in the Sirvintai municipality, a rural local government with many small schools.

The municipality allocates the funds for teacher salaries and for school administration on a needs basis, making sure that the funds do not exceed the budgets as calculated by the Student Basket methodology. In order to ensure this, they control the formation of classes, with the goal of achieving an average class size that is never smaller than normative class size for the appropriate size category of each school. This is done directly discussing the number of classes, without interfering in student enrollment in different schools. Then they review budget requests of schools, submitted by the school directors. The process they use is to first review and accept the requests of schools for funds for pedagogical and psychological services and for teaching aids. Finally, they allocate to schools the remaining funds proportionally to the number of students, and assign them for teacher professional development. Thus, the result of the budgeting process is not dissimilar to the pattern displayed in Table 5.23 for early years of Student Basket financing, in which funds for teacher professional development are much lower than for services provided directly to students.

This policy choice is motivated by the situation in Sirvintai schools. The teacher work force is largely old, often beyond retirement age, and major investment in their skills is not deemed necessary. Indeed, there is expectation that many will soon retire. However, because the population served by Sirvintai schools comes from small villages, and often from families with a low level of educational attainment, psychological and pedagogical services are an urgent priority.

Of course, urban municipalities face very different challenges. In particular, they have to invest more in their teachers to motivate them and to keep them from changing profession. Thus, the freedom to reallocate Student Basket funds allows municipalities to adapt their funding strategies to their specific needs and education priorities.

5.4.4. Budgetary Autonomy of Schools

Although managerial and budgetary autonomy of schools was identified as one of key policy goals of introducing the Student Basket in 2002, this is an area where the progress has been rather slow and very uneven. The amended Law on Education had foreseen that the municipality may decide either to grant the schools on its territory accounting independence, or to keep the accounting centralized at the municipal level. Some municipalities have used both models. We discuss centralized and decentralized accounting below.

In two key areas of budgetary autonomy and programmatic autonomy of the school, there is no difference between the two models. The schools cannot increase teacher salaries. Indeed, in either case the school director prepares a detailed budget proposal that is approved by the municipality council.[61] That approved budget broken down by detailed budget classifications is obligatory for the director, who may apply to municipal council for some adjustment of the budget (rebalance), if there is a need to move funds between budget lines or between quarters of the financial year.[62] Most often, this request will be granted, with one important exception: only in special cases will the director be allowed to move funds from the LG funded part of the budget (teaching environment) to the Student Basket funded part of the budget (teaching process).[63] This means that budgetary autonomy of the school is limited.

Similarly, there is very little programmatic autonomy of the schools, irrespective of whether they are autonomous or not. All schools have to follow the same curricula, and as discussed above even the accreditation as gymnasium, with its higher teacher salaries, does not change this. The schools have some limited freedom to choose additional extracurricular activities according to the needs of students. However, it is still impossible for Lithuanian schools to compete with each other by adopting different curricula or experimental pedagogical programs.

There is nevertheless a difference between the two models of accounting systems, and to review it we describe briefly the procedure that the school director has to go through when buying some piece of equipment or materials for his school (based on discussions with school directors):

- Centralized accounting (non-autonomous schools):
  After a decision to buy some equipment or materials is taken, the school director needs to visit the supplier (most often a shop or wholesaler in Vilnius[64]), obtain the document for ordering the supplies, visit the municipal office, have the order document approved and signed by city accountant, return to the supplier, order the purchase, and submit the invoices to the municipal authorities for execution.

- School based accounting (autonomous schools):
  After a decision to buy some equipment or materials is taken, the school accountant may issue an appropriate document certifying that funds for the purchase are available. With this document the director visits the supplier and buys the supplies. The number of visits to the capital is thus reduced from two to one.

We see that the non-autonomous schools have to follow some archaic accounting procedures inherited from the Soviet past, while autonomous schools have those procedures streamlined and rationalized. Even they, however, are severely limited in their pedagogical and budgetary autonomy.

5.4.5. Consolidation of the School Network

Consolidation of the school network was one of key policy goals of the reform and it was hoped that it would lead to improvement of life chances of students from rural schools (the two goals were stated together). We have seen in Table 5.3 the dramatic decrease in the number of small initial schools (teaching grades 1 through 4), from 808 in the school year 2000/2001 to just 114 in the school year 2005/2006. Table 5.27 below displays school sizes in the same period:

Table 5.27. Average School Sizes by School Type 2000 to 2005

	2000/2001	2003/2004	2004/2005	2005/2006
Initial	48	74	124	203
Basic	116	186	196	194
Secondary	625	663	646	634
Gymnasium	856	821	817	760
All	270	328	381	396

We see, indeed, that consolidation of initial schools led to a dramatic increase of their average size from under 50 to over 200. The same is true of the results consolidation of teaching at grades 9 to 12.[65] By reducing the number of full secondary schools, and transferring highest grades to larger secondary schools, the average size of both the remaining secondary schools, and of the new basic schools (formerly secondary) increased.

The difference between the two consolidation processes is also clear: while consolidation of teaching in grades 9 through 12 happened between 2000 and 2003 (unfortunately we don't have the data for the intervening school years) and achieved its goals, consolidation of initial schools was continuing for a number of years.

In reviewing Table 5.27 it is important to remember that school network consolidation was an important component of the Education Improvement Project, see World Bank (2007). With technical support of the project, MES developed guidelines for local school network consolidation strategies, and in 2004 mandated their adoption by Lithuanian municipalities. This was a key step for the Ministry, because initially it expected that the Student Basket reform will be sufficient to motivate municipalities to optimize their school networks. Out of 60 Lithuanian municipalities, 58 adopted network optimization strategies by 2006.

In 2006, State Audit and Accounting Office reviewed the effects of this decision in a number of municipalities (AAT 2006). Three municipalities were audited directly, and data was collected from 51 units. A number of issues were identified in the audit report. Auditors found that in many schools the number of students per class was still below the norms assumed in the Student Basket calculation methodology. In some places, the networks were consolidated but the municipality failed to provide obligatory free student transportation to schools (the parents had to organize it themselves). In the cities, significant number of student attended second shifts. Overall, only 30% of schools met all the pedagogical norms including school space, teaching equipment and similar. These findings suggest that perhaps the consolidation happened too quickly and the municipalities were not able to develop the necessary support services such as student transportation or improvements in school equipment. State Audit and Accounting Office suggested, very sensibly, that the Ministry should provide a yearly summary report of how school optimization strategies are implemented across the whole country.

Once again we need to say that public debate about education in Lithuania is greatly enhanced by reports of the State Audit and Accounting Office, especially through their critical review of how the reforms are implemented over time.

5.4.6. Equity of Allocation of Student Basket Funds to Schools and Municipalities

Equity of student finance must be understood of course not as absolute equity, with every student receiving the same per student amount, but as relative equity, taking into account different conditions of providing education in different schools. The main determinant of those conditions is of course class size. Small schools with small classes are of necessity more expensive per student than larger institutions. The second important determinant is the number of lessons per week, mandated by curriculum norms and dependent on the grade level.

Viewed from this perspective, the Lithuanian Student Basket system represents a serious attempt at taking into account both of these two key determinants of per student costs (see section 5.3). Namely, the main table of allocation coefficients is built precisely on the basis of class sizes and curricular norms. However, as Table 5.17 shows, the coefficients are based on normative, not actual class sizes. This has important implications, noted first by AAT (2003), and discussed below in some detail.

Figure 5.1 displays the Student Basket funds allocated for an initial school in 2007, for school sizes between 0 and 250 students. As we know from Table 5.17, for less than 50 students the school is in category XS, when the number of students is between 51 and 80 it is in category S, above 80 and below 200 in category M, and above 200 students in category L. When the category increases, the coefficient for the student decreases–we use the coefficients from Table 5.18. This creates three thresholds, at which the allocated Student Basket funds decrease even though the number of students goes up.

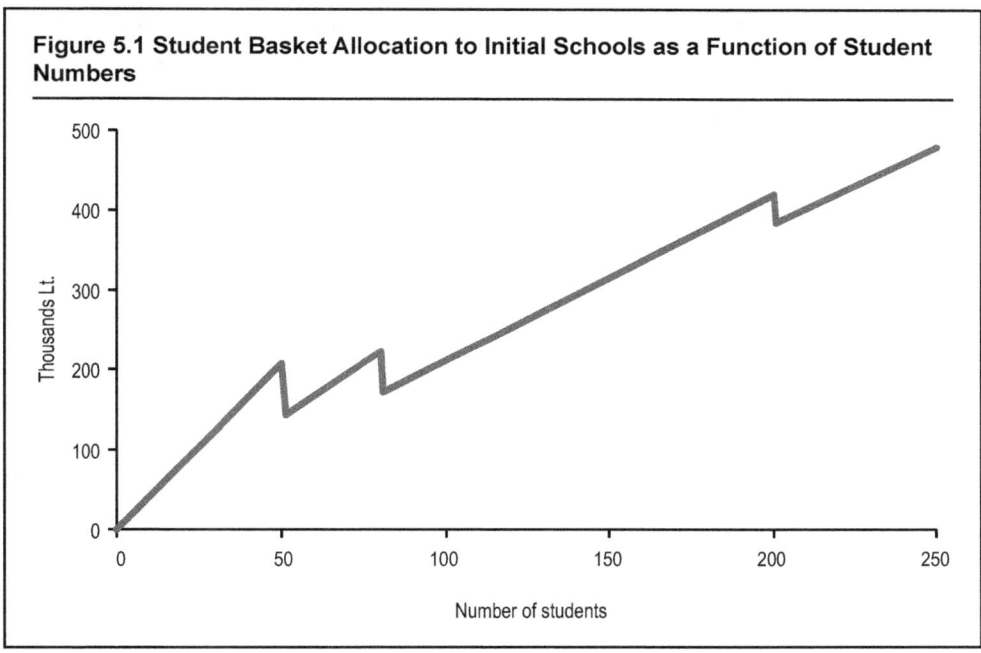

Figure 5.1 Student Basket Allocation to Initial Schools as a Function of Student Numbers

Table 5.28 shows details of the threshold points for initial schools.

Table 5.28. Allocation Thresholds for Initial Schools

	First threshold		Second threshold		Third threshold	
Number of students	50	51	80	81	200	201
Size category	XS	S	S	M	M	L
Coefficient per student	1.7765	1.1924	1.1924	0.9005	0.9005	0.8208
Amount per student (Lt)	4,145	2,782	2,782	2,101	2,101	1,915
Amount per school (000 Lt)	207	142	223	170	420	385
Decrease at threshold	31.5%		23.5%		8.4%	

The decrease of 31 percent when the number of students goes up by one is surely not a desirable feature of an allocation mechanism.

What is particularly troubling is that at the second threshold point the allocated Student Basket amount goes below the first threshold point, in other words that the line of 200 thousand Lt is crossed three times. Thus, three initial schools, with 48 (XS category), 72 (S category), and 95 (M category) students are allocated the same amount of 200,000

Lt. This is not an equitable allocation. Moreover, this represents a very serious disincentive to consolidation. Indeed, if a municipality has an initial school of 96 students and divides it into two schools of 48 students each, it will receive 200 thousand Lt more. Of course, local governments are not likely to do this because they will face increased maintenance costs, which they have to fully cover from their own revenues, but the disincentive remains. Analogous thresholds appear for basic and full secondary schools. Since the graph looks similar, we provide only two tables analogous to Table 5.28. As allocation coefficients for basic schools we use the average of coefficients for grades 1-4 and 5-8 in Table 5.18.[66] Again there are three threshold values, 130, 300, and 600 students, and Table 5.29 demonstrates the decrease of allocation at those thresholds.

Table 5.29. Allocation Thresholds for Basic Schools

	First threshold		Second threshold		Third threshold	
Number of students	130	131	300	301	600	601
Size category	XS	S	S	M	M	L
Coefficient per student	1.9483	1.3070	1.3070	0.9889	0.9889	0.9104
Amount per student (Lt)	4,545	3,049	3,049	2,307	2,307	2,124
Amount per school (000 Lt)	591	399	915	694	1,384	1,277
Decrease at threshold	32.4%		24.1%		7.8%	

For full secondary schools, we also use the simple averages of coefficients of Table 5.18.[67] In the present case there are only two thresholds, 400 and 700 students. Table 5.30 shows what happens at the thresholds.

Table 5.30. Allocation Thresholds for Full Secondary Schools

	First threshold		Second threshold	
Number of students	400	401	700	701
Size category	S	M	M	L
Coefficient per student	1.5199	1.1475	1.1475	1.0806
Amount per student (Lt)	3,546	2,677	2,677	2,521
Amount per school (000 Lt)	1,418	1,074	1,874	1,767
Decrease at threshold	24.3%		5.7%	

We note again that the decrease of Student Basket allocation of 32 percent or 24 percent due to an increase in the number of students by one is highly undesirable, and contradicts equity. It is also worth noting that this decrease of allocation at these thresholds appears always when the per student allocation amount depends on the size of the school, as opposed to some other characteristics, such as rural or mountain location, and cannot be corrected without some adjustment procedures that would violate the per student allocation approach.

Another way to understand the impact of coefficients in Table 5.18 is to view them on a per class spending. In Table 5.31 we translate those coefficients into per class allocations, by multiplying them by the basic Student Basket amount (2,333 Lt for 2007) and by the normative class size.

Table 5.31. Initial Per Class Allocation by Size Category and Grade Level

Size category	Normative class size	Grade level			
		1 to 4	5 to 8	9 & 10	11 & 12
XS	10	41,446	49,462	57,476	
S	15	41,728	49,749	57,756	63,519
M	20	42,017	50,262	58,045	63,850
L	25	47,873	58,325	69,483	76,429

The review of Table 5.31 provides interesting findings. For each grade level, initial per class allocation is largely independent of the class size, or there is a minimal monotonic increase of per class allocation as class size increases, except for the largest size category L, where it is higher by about 15 percent for grades 1 to 8 and by 20 percent for grades 9 to 12. Thus, the coefficients of Table 5.18 show a clear preference for larger class sizes. Maybe the explanation is that there are some pedagogical norms that make teaching of large classes more expensive. Such norms could include, for example, splitting of large classes into groups for some subjects. Another possibility is that large schools are better equipped with more expensive types of equipment, such as computers, which may lead to disproportionately higher per class teaching allocation. However, apart from the splitting of classes and the corresponding increase of teaching hours, teachers are not rewarded for teaching large classes (see Box 5.1).

The same process using the 'corrected coefficients' in Table 5.19 yields corrected per class allocation in Table 5.32:

Table 5.32. Corrected Per Class Allocation by Size Category and Grade Level

Size category	Normative class size	Grade level			
		1 to 4	5 to 8	9 & 10	11 & 12
XS	10	37,302	44,516	57,476	
S	15	42,144	50,246	58,333	64,167
M	20	42,857	51,027	59,207	65,128
L	25	53,449	59,200	74,061	77,957

As recalled from discussion of Table 5.19, the corrected coefficients for small classes, size category XS, are decreased by 10 percent (with the exception for grades 9 to 10). Therefore, Table 5.32 reveals the same allocation preference for large classes (size category L) as Table 5.31, strengthened by a decrease of allocation for smallest classes (size category XS). Per class allocation for grades 1 to 4 is illustrated in Figure 5.2.

The shape of the graph is governed by two policy decisions: to increase the allocation of largest class sizes for initial coefficients, and to decrease the allocation for smallest class sizes for corrected coefficients. The equity implications of this graph are clear and very important. Initial grades are precisely the education level with most similar per class teaching effort—i.e. typically one classroom, one teacher and very similar teaching aids. Moreover, splitting of classes for initial grades is very rare. Thus, the fact that classes in small schools receive only 70 percent of the allocation for large schools does not seem to be equitable.

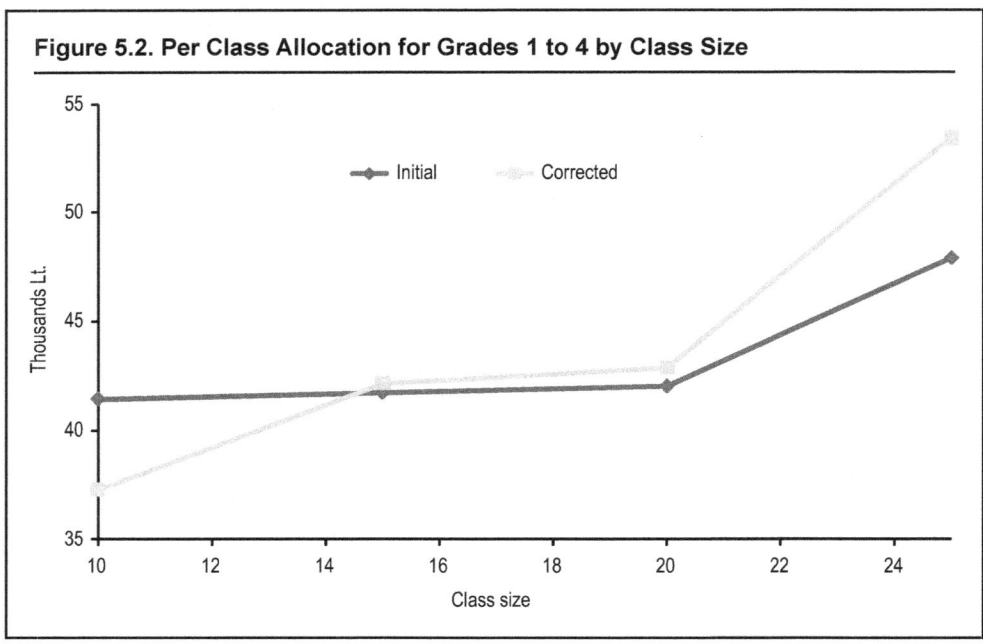

Figure 5.2. Per Class Allocation for Grades 1 to 4 by Class Size

Since schools have students attending all the grades, an assessment of the weighted average coefficients over grades taken from Table 5.19 is needed for a proper comparison with the actual allocation to municipalities. This is provided in Figure 5.3.

In Figure 5.3 we note that average corrected per class allocation for small class sizes is about 70 percent of the allocation for largest class sizes. The inequities have not been reduced when complete schools are considered. As we shall see below, the negative equity impact is softened in actual allocation, when the complete table of coefficients—Table 5.45—is taken into account.[68]

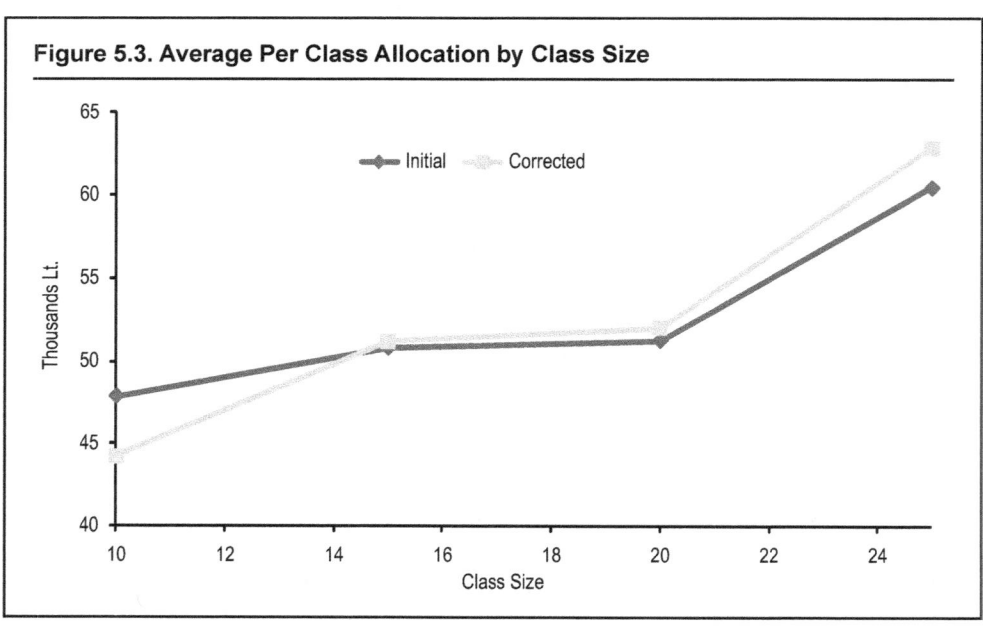

Figure 5.3. Average Per Class Allocation by Class Size

Of course, we have to remember that for small schools with small classes, the municipality can compensate relatively lower per class allocation from the Student Basket grant using its right to reallocate the funds among the schools. This, however, points once again crucial role of the municipalities, which may need to counteract some potentially negative effects of the Student Basket allocation system.

In view of the possibility of reallocation, a better measure of equity in actual budgeting process would be to measure the relationship between the actual allocation to schools and class sizes or student teacher ratio. Lacking those data for individual schools, we conclude the present subsection with a review of relationship between Student Basket allocation to municipalities and average class sizes in those municipalities. We use 2006 data.

In Figure 5.4, each Lithuanian municipality is represented by a dot, the X-axis indicates average class size, and the Y-axis indicates the actual Student Basket allocation per student, which we know to be equal to spending on the teaching process.

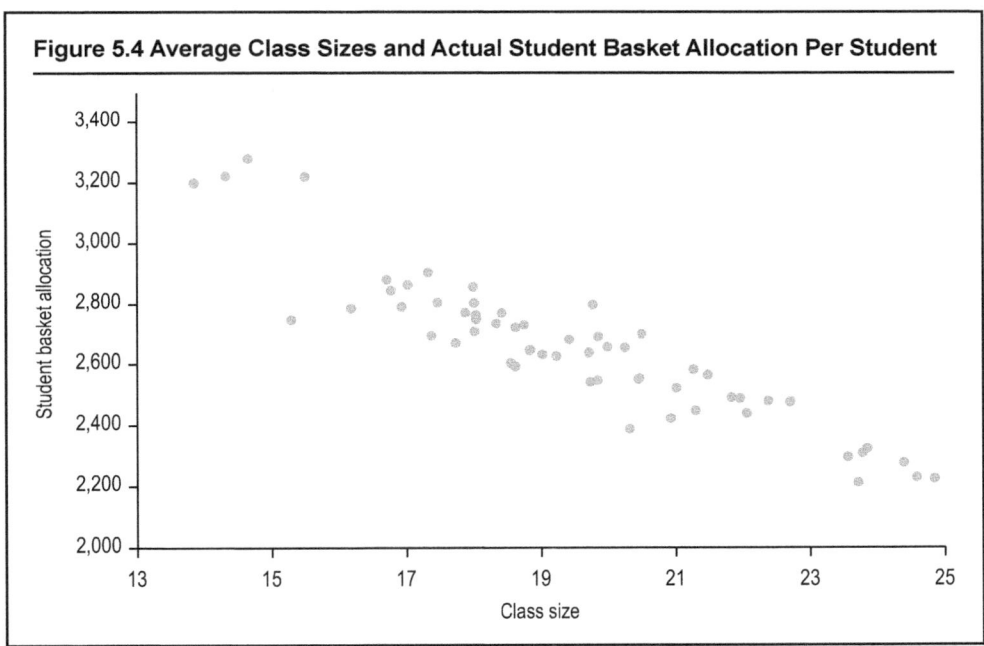

We stress that unlike the previous graph, the graph above represents actual allocations to municipalities. We note first, in Figure 5.4 above, that there is considerable variation of average class sizes among Lithuanian municipalities, ranging from below 14 to 25. Similarly, Student Basket grants per student vary considerably between 2200 and 3200 Lt.

We note a clear linear relationship between class sizes and per student allocation, although a number of the outliers–municipalities that are outside the main line in the graph–require further analysis. The Student Basket allocation per student decreases as average class size goes up. For municipalities with class sizes of 25 students, per student allocation is about 2,200 Lt, for average class sizes of 20 students it is about 2,700 Lt, and for average class sizes of 15 students it is about 3,200 Lt. Therefore, different per student allocation does not preclude a high degree of allocation equity of the Lithuanian Student Basket methodology. What we need to check is whether, on average, per class allocation is independent of class size. This is what we would expect from an equitable allocation[69] because it should be assumed that the cost of the teaching process for an average class in Lithuanian schools should be more or less the same, as it is governed by the same curriculum norms–unlike the costs of the teaching environment, which may vary due to other factors. Of course we cannot expect that they will be exactly constant because Student Basket finances some expenditure items that are not linked to class teaching, such as administration, textbooks, or psychological services, which are more related to the number of students. Moreover, we know from Figure 5.3 that allocation coefficients provide higher allocation to larger classes, in part to compensate for split teaching and more experienced teachers. Therefore, we may expect that per class expenditures should be slowly increasing with the average class size in a municipality.

In order to test this hypothesis, we provide a graph (Figure 5.5) comparing average class sizes and actual per class Student Basket allocation.

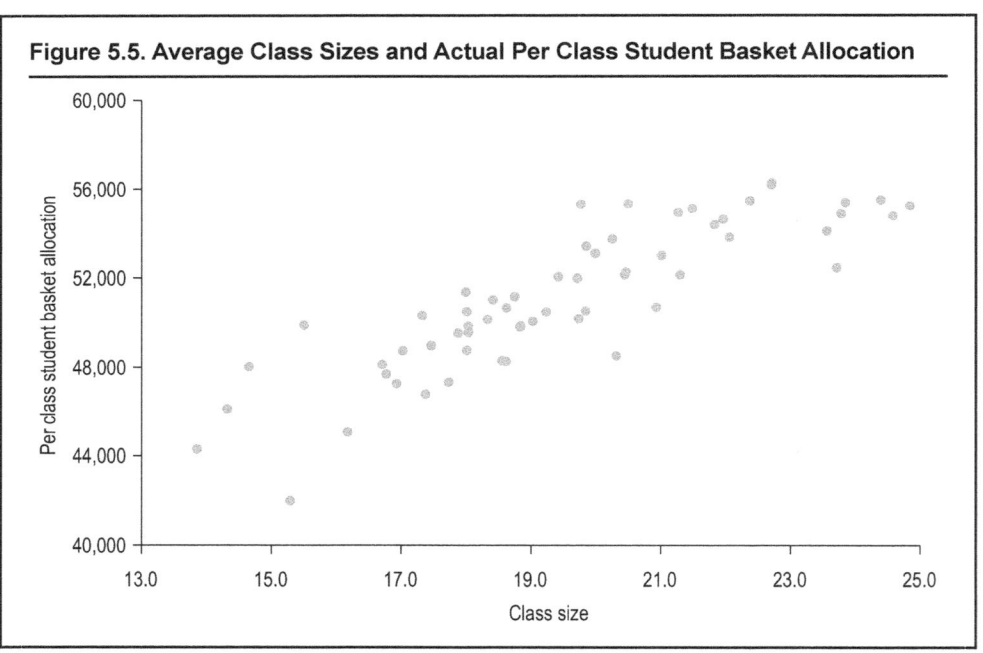

Figure 5.5. Average Class Sizes and Actual Per Class Student Basket Allocation

We observe that indeed, there is growth of per class Student Basket allocation, indeed probably higher than expected. This growth stops at the average class size of 20. For municipalities with higher class sizes, the per class Student Basket allocation remains constant.[70] Municipalities with smallest classes receive on average about 80 percent of per class allocation of municipalities with large average class size. It is interesting to compare Figure 5.5, showing actual per class allocation (using complete set of allocation coefficients) with Figure 5.3, showing normative per class allocation, based only on initial and corrected coefficients. The behavior is quite different, the main discrepancy being that in Figure 5.5 we do not observe an increase in per class allocation above the threshold of 20 students, so apparent in Figure 5.3. This may be due to the fact that Fig-

Box 5.1 Teacher Qualifications and Salaries in Lithuania

The salaries of all staff in the public sector in the Republic of Lithuania are calculated on the basis of salary coefficients. The salary coefficients are multiplied by a fixed salary amount, which occasionally is changed. Until the end of April 2004 this fixed salary amount was 105 Lt, it was then increased to 115 Lt. Effectively, this means that coinciding with EU accession salaries of all public servants in Lithuania were increased by 9.5 percent. However, the typical way of increasing the salary is by increasing the salary coefficients. For example, on September 1, 2005 MES raised salary coefficients of teachers and thus increased their salaries. This made it necessary to adapt the Student Basket value in September 2005, see Annex A.

The salary coefficients of Lithuanian teachers depend on their level of professional career. There are five levels of professional career: unaccredited, accredited, contractual, methodic, and expert. Teacher salaries depend on these levels as well as on the length of service and location of the school, but cannot be permanently increased by the school—only occasional bonuses are allowed. Table 5.33 shows the average salary coefficients for each level of professional career in 2002 and 2007.

Table 5.33 Salary Coefficients of Lithuanian Teachers, 2002 and 2007

Level	2002	2007	Increase
Not accredited	5.83	6.91	19%
Accredited	6.52	7.80	20%
Contract	7.76	8.66	12%
Methodic	8.70	9.38	8%
Expert	10.00	10.73	7%

It is interesting to note that between 2002 and 2007 the salary coefficients for unaccredited and accredited teachers rose much faster than the coefficients for methodic teachers and experts. As a result, the salary differential decreased: while in 2002 expert earned 72 percent more then a novice teacher, in 2008 he earned only 55 percent more.

Table 5.34 provides the distribution of teachers among the career levels in 2002 and in 2007: Putting aside the somewhat strange evolution of the distribution of teachers among career levels, we note that the above two tables allow us to estimate the weighted average salary coefficient of Lithuanian teachers, used in the calculation of the Student Basket. The average salary coefficient in 2002 was 7.6499, and in 2007 it is 8.444, a growth of 10 percent. Taking into account the growth of the fixed salary amount, we see that the average monthly salary of a Lithuanian teacher rose nominally from 803 Lt to 971 Lt, an increase of 21 percent.

Table 5.34 Distribution of Teachers by Career Level, 2002 and 2007

Level	2002	2007
Not accredited	5%	20%
Accredited	12%	5%
Contract	70%	53%
Methodic	12%	21%
Expert	1%	1%

ure 5.5 exhibits in fact an average over different schools in each municipality, and even in the municipalities with on average very large classes there are some schools with small classes too. This is also the reason, probably, why actual average per class allocations are lower than normative allocations of Figure 5.3. Of course, those can be only conjectures until a review of allocation for individual schools is undertaken.

However, taking those two graphs into consideration, it seems that the Student Basket funding system in its practical application is more equitable than corrected coefficients—Table 5.32 and Figure 5.3—seem to imply. Indeed, we may conclude that the system is equitable for municipalities, whose average class size is over 19 students. For rural municipalities with smaller class sizes, especially for those with average class below 16 students, the Student Basket system does not seem to provide sufficient financing on a per class basis.

5.5. Assessment of Outcomes

The outcomes of the implementation of the Student Basket in Lithuania should be looked at from two perspectives. On the one hand, it is important to analyze the impact of the reform on improvements in efficiency, equity and transparency, all of which to some degree are considered in the policy goals–and the expected results tied to them–stated at the beginning of the process. No less relevant is to review the other policy goals that are less tied to these four broad themes and to assess whether they have been achieved, and to what extent.

We begin by recalling from section 5.2.1 the six results that were expected by MES from the Student Basket reform:

1. Greater efficiency in the use of education funds through uniform principles of their allocation.
2. Improvement of education quality due to competition of schools for students.
3. Increased enrollment rates due to care of schools for their students.
4. Better planning and management of education resources due to their transparency and predictability.
5. Expansion of non-governmental schools and provision of choice of schools.
6. Improvement of school networks.

We need to add also two policy objectives (numbers 7 and 9), as listed in section 5.2.1, as well as two more general objectives (numbers 8 and 10) typically accompanying education finance reforms that are important for equity and transparency, respectively:

7. Equal opportunities to rural and urban students (goal 2 under section 5.2.1).
8. Equity of education finance (general objective).
9. Transparency of education finance (goal 6 under section 5.2.1).
10. Accountability of public finance in education sector (general objective).

We now discuss these 10 points with subsections on efficiency (point 1 and 6), equity (points 7 and 8) and transparency/accountability (points 4, 9 and 10), and then the other expected results (points 2, 3 and 5), which are either less directly related to these themes or practically not at all.

5.5.1. Efficiency

POINT 1: GREATER EFFICIENCY IN THE USE OF EDUCATION FUNDS

The best measure of efficiency is the student-teacher ratio, with the teachers estimated as FTE teachers (we separately discuss below consolidation of school networks). Table 5.35 provides a measure of the student-teacher ratio in Lithuanian schools. It includes teachers in all general education schools (including preschool groups in primary schools, special schools, schools for adults etc.) because of the limitations of the data.

Table 5.35 Student-Teacher Ratios in Lithuanian General Education Schools[71]

	2000/2001	2003/2004	2004/2005	2005/2006
Students	603,824	583,063	563,107	538,541
FTE teachers	49,007	47,930	46,642	43,372
STR	12.32	12.16	12.07	12.42

The student-teacher ratio reported in Table 5.35 is rather low, due to inclusion of many institutions with small classes (special schools, schools for adults, etc.). Nevertheless it is clear that student-teacher ratio is very stable and has not improved between 2000 and 2005.[72] However, this needs to be viewed in the context of overall decline of the student numbers, by about 10 percent in the period covered in Table 5.35. With decreasing student numbers, maintaining student-teacher ratio is a difficult challenge because reducing the number of teachers in parallel to the number of students faces two obstacles:

- Reduction of the number of teachers can only be achieved by a reduction of the number of classes (each class needs to receive full curriculum load), and will not be initiated by the decline of class size,
- Making teachers redundant is socially and politically difficult.

We conclude that the expectation of increasing school efficiency was not realistic, and that the goal of maintaining student-teacher ratio at a constant level was already ambitious enough. And indeed, this is the most that can be expected from a per student financing mechanism which, as in Lithuania, tries to mimic closely existing cost differentials. Municipalities had the motivation to keep employment levels in line with student numbers because this was needed to obtain sufficient funds for teacher salaries. However, the municipalities were less motivated to seek savings from the teaching process because they were not allowed to use those savings for the teaching environment. This is a demonstration how fragmentation of education finance, even in the thoughtful and relatively sophisticated version adopted in Lithuania, still remains an obstacle to efficiency.

POINT 6: IMPROVEMENT OF SCHOOL NETWORKS

Consolidation of school networks is the single most important efficiency gain which may be expected from per student financing system, since by closing small schools and by transporting students from villages to larger consolidated schools, the local education system achieves cost savings and at the same time improvement of education quality. The difficulty usually consists in reluctance or even opposition of parents to the closure of small schools located in their villages. Indeed, transition countries have seen many successful protests of parents against school closures.[73]

Within this context, experience of Lithuania has been remarkably successful. We have seen already in Table 5.3 the decrease in the number of small initial schools (teaching grades 1 through 4). Table 5.27 shows how in the same period average school sizes increased.

This experience must be seen in historical perspective. In section 5.4 we have described that the initial expectations of the reformers, namely that the introduction of the Student Basket will automatically lead to network optimization, were not fulfilled, and that in 2004 the Ministry introduced a legal obligation for municipalities to adopt local network optimization strategies (almost all of them did so). The report of State Audit and Accounting Office (AAT 2006) shows progress but noted many failings as well, the most important being that in some places the municipalities had consolidated their school networks without providing free transportation to schools to all affected students. This indicates a general need to assess the progress of network optimization together with a review of what happens to students of closed schools.

It is not possible to say whether the Student Basket system itself, without the obligation of adopting network consolidation strategies, would have led to the same far reaching improvement of school networks.[74] We can safely say that both incentives worked in the same direction. But more importantly, we see that the success of this policy goal of MES depended on the overall vision of education decentralization in Lithuania. Indeed, as we have stressed in many places, Lithuania entrusted very significant responsibilities to municipalities. When the Student Basket reform was implemented, it established a prepared local agent–namely the municipalities–to take the necessary decisions. With technical guidance from EIP project that agent was able to design local strategy and implement it cooperatively with school communities. Thus, we can certainly say that the Student Basket reform has contributed significantly to that process.

5.5.2. Equity

POINT 7: EQUAL OPPORTUNITIES TO RURAL AND URBAN STUDENTS

Assessment of equal opportunities of different social groups (rural versus urban, ethnic minority versus majority, special needs students versus mainstream, etc.) requires examining of the results of policy led activities over a long period of time, for example by monitoring access to tertiary university or even the level of earnings in adult life. This means it is premature now to make such an assessment (which also requires different tools and approaches than those adopted in the present chapter). In the absence of such an assessment, countries monitor access to secondary education, especially to gymnasia, completion rate of full secondary schools or entrance exams to universities. However, we do not have those data either, so we are unable to comment whether this expected outcome of the Student Basket reform was in fact achieved.

POINT 8: EQUITY OF STUDENT FINANCE

The whole final subsection of section 5.4 is devoted to the problems of allocative equity, so we summarize briefly the findings. For specific schools the allocation is not equitable because the Student Basket methodology creates specific thresholds, where an increase of student numbers in the school has the effect of lowering Student Basket allocation in some cases by more than 30 percent. However, this negative phenomenon may be countered through reallocation of funds within municipality. Indeed, Table 5.26 indicates that the number of municipalities, which do not use this policy instrument, is decreasing, although we cannot judge whether those actions are sufficient to counter the negative effects of the Student Basket mechanism revealed in Figure 5.1.

Therefore more relevant for equity is the problem of actual per student allocation *at the level of municipalities* rather than *at the level of schools*. We have found that in general, actual allocation for the teaching process to municipalities is quite equitable, at least for the municipalities that manage to operate schools with large average classes (over 19 students per class). This is seen in the linear relationship between the class sizes and actual per student allocation, making actual per class allocation more or less independent of the class size. At the same time, for municipalities with smaller classes, it seems that the Student Basket system provides significantly smaller allocations on a per class basis. For these rural municipalities the equity of the Student Basket system is probably not achieved.

Furthermore, as good data on the funding of the teaching environment are not available, it is impossible to assess how horizontally equitable this funding is. This criterion is a very important part of education finance, as it is related to school equipment and to overall conditions of teaching. The Student Basket system does not have any instruments to promote equity in this area.

5.5.3. Transparency and Accountability

POINT 4: BETTER PLANNING AND MANAGEMENT OF EDUCATION RESOURCES

The problem of planning and managing education resources needs to be considered on two levels: planning by the municipality and planning by the schools. The discussions with officials of Lithuanian municipalities indicate that they are increasingly involved in policy planning in the education sector. This is reflected, among others, by the fact that in 2006 58 out of 60 local governments have adopted local strategies for network consolidation (see comments on improvement of school networks below). Our discussion regarding contributions of municipalities to the Student Basket grant received by the central authorities (Table 5.21 and Table 5.22) shows that municipalities increasingly see themselves as responsible managers of their local school network. Finally, our discussion of reallocation of Student Basket funds among the schools (Table 5.26) indicates that attitude of Lithuanian municipalities to management of education resources is become more proactive. Predictability and relative transparency of the Student Basket funding helps the planning process considerably.

The situation seems to be less clear at the level of schools. As noted in section 5.4, budgetary autonomy of schools is still limited, and even rather simple reforms of accounting of school expenditures are proceeding slowly. It is therefore premature to assess financial planning and budgeting skills of school directors and their professional teams, although World Bank (2007) reports that that appropriate trainings and capacity building efforts are reaching many school directors. We conclude that one of key goals of education finance reforms, that is *strengthened financial independence of schools* (see section 5.2.1) still needs to be pursued.

POINT 9: TRANSPARENCY OF EDUCATION FINANCE

Transparency of education finance can be considered in terms of supply and demand. On the supply side, we may ask if the information regarding allocation and use of public funds in education is sufficient, timely, complete, and comprehensible to all interested parties. On the demand side, we may ask if various education stakeholders require, obtain, and use this information in their education related activities.

In both areas Lithuania used the Student Basket reform to make significant steps forward, yet in both areas much remains to be done. On the supply side, the information regarding the principles and details of financial allocation in education is publicly available. The rules of allocation change every year, of course, but always within the limits of the law, through amendments to government resolutions (see section 5.3). The changing allocation coefficients are discussed every year in the working group, with representatives of MES, Ministry of Finance, association of local governments, and experts. Once the working group agrees, their agreement becomes a part of the budget law, providing final official information to all municipalities about the funds they will receive in Student Basket grants for the following year.

However, not all the participants in those discussions understand the allocation formula and the consequences of incremental changes every year, so transparency on the demand side requires improvement. The growing complexity of the formula deters technical debate regarding its structure and assumptions. MES does not prepare and discuss with the stakeholders simulations of the formula for the municipalities and schools. Such simulations, with the ability to change parameters and assess the impact of any changes, would make the discussions more concrete and more substantive. Very few municipalities are able to conduct on their own the necessary calculations and check whether the funds allocated to them are indeed equal to what methodology prescribes. In fact all the main stakeholders, that is MES, Ministry of Finance, and the association of local governments,[75] use the same input provided by the same experts. In this way Lithuania loses a vital element of transparency, namely mutual checking and verification, opening the way to errors.[76]

At the municipal level, Lithuania also made progress compared to the pre-2002 period, when allocation of funds to schools was made solely on the number and teaching programs of classes. The introduction of Student Basket norms per school, based on the number of students, limited arbitrary decisions by local governments. Despite this progress, transparency is less pronounced than at the national level. Even if the municipality has a clear policy of financing the schools this is rarely published and openly discussed.[77] School budgets are known, but some school directors expressed complete lack of interest in the setting of the budget, assuming that it is the responsibility of the municipality to ensure that schools can operate effectively. For the school directors interviewed, the main information regarding the Student Basket amount assessed for their school by the methodology (in practice this means by the computer program supplied by MES, see section 5.4.1), is the extent to which the funds are sufficient or insufficient. It seems therefore that important policy incentives, included in the Student Basket structure (section 5.3) and understood by municipalities (section 5.4), are directed essentially to local governments.

POINT 10: ACCOUNTABILITY OF PUBLIC FINANCE IN THE EDUCATION SECTOR

The final discussion of the outcomes of the Student Basket financing system in Lithuania concerns its impact on accountability. Accountability is closely related to transparency, it means that once education stakeholders (parents, teachers, etc.) know how the funds were allocated or used by various agents (central or local authorities, schools), they can demand explanations and clarifications, and through a democratic process may influence future allocation or expenditure decisions. The required explanations will typically be arguments of what the agent tried to achieve, and what were the results obtained. In some special cases accountability may also include holding decision makers responsible for misuse of funds or for corruption.

The limited budgetary autonomy of schools means that financial accountability of school directors to education stakeholders is not an important issue. The main element of financial accountability of school directors is their obligation to the municipalities to maintain budget discipline.

Municipalities are responsible for important budgetary decisions in the sector, so holding them accountable is needed. However, it seems that the main process of holding them accountable is local elections. School communities are too weak and don't know enough about education finance to engage in serious discussions with municipal officials over the allocation and use of funds. The school councils exist at some schools, but their role in setting or monitoring the budgetary process is minimal.

Three institutions may hold MES accountable for their allocative decisions in pre-university education: Ministry of Finance, State Audit and Accounting Office, and the association of local governments. The primary focus of the Ministry of Finance is the proper use of funds and the budgetary discipline. It has no particular opinion or interest in the allocation issues of public funds for schools, although it remains very closely involved in the discussions regarding the evolution of the Student Basket.

The State Audit and Accounting Office is the national institution responsible for checking the correctness of activities of other public bodies, both in the sphere of finance and of policymaking. In the implementation process of Student Basket reforms, AAT has performed an invaluable function by providing a comprehensive early critical report of the Student Basket in 2003. However, it has not returned to those issues since then. The AAT point of view, even if at times rather strict (and not always accepted by MES, see discussions of section 5.4), is useful because unlike MES of Finance and the Association, it was not involved in the process of preparing the reform and drafting of Student Basket methodology. Therefore accountability will be much improved if the AAT would undertake more regular reviews of the functioning of the Student Basket.

This leaves us with the Association of Local Governments. In my view the Association has a unique role to play in monitoring education finance, in particular the Student Basket allocation methodology, to demand explanations and to propose amendments. Throughout the chapter we stressed the role and relevance of Lithuanian municipalities in education. They have become the most important education stakeholders besides MES. And in fact the association is very active in this area. However, due in part to the specific consensual nature of Lithuanian politics, these activities are performed more in closed-door discussions than in public reports and in the media. The Association has not developed yet its own capacities to analyze the Student Basket methodology and to review potential consequences of various amendments to it. Municipalities have benefited, of course, from Student Basket reforms and naturally support them. However, they are also more interested than anyone else to improve the system, to correct the mistakes, and to make it more transparent and predictable. They also are in the best position in the country to demand that MES explains clearly what it is doing.

5.5.4. Other Key Outcomes

POINT 2: IMPROVEMENT OF EDUCATION QUALITY

MES expected that education quality will improve due to increased competition among the schools. As the example of Panevezis municipalities shows, there is probably more competition among municipalities than among individual schools. In rural municipalities such as Sirvintai there is no competition among the schools at all. Vilnius city officials see competition in the fact that three well-known gymnasia have many more candidates than places, and have to conduct selective entrance examinations. However, this seems to be more the result of long established general opinion regarding relative quality of education in those schools, and not of specific activities, which the schools have undertaken recently. This degree of competition is not understood to be linked with the introduction of the Student Basket. Moreover, schools with decreasing numbers of students can rely on the municipality to reallocate some of the funds destined for larger schools. Incentive for schools to compete against each other contained in the Lithuanian Student Basket system is therefore rather weak.

Nevertheless, the Student Basket mechanism does include a strong pro-quality instrument, used effectively by MES, although not relying on competition. As discussed at length in Annex A and section 5.3, the Student Basket grants include a growing number of components for additional, quality-related, non-teaching elements of the pedagogical process. Most of them contribute to quality: textbooks, teaching aids, teacher professional development, pedagogical and psychological services, career guidance, or cognitive development of students. Table 5.24 shows that over time expenditures on these items became more prominent as a share of the Student Basket funding. Moreover, as discussed in section 5.4, the fact that the Student Basket methodology contains indicative amounts, which should be spent on those activities, has a practical impact, and over time municipalities have made an effort to conform to this guidance.

It is therefore not entirely surprising that World Bank (2007) has found some positive indication of improved education quality between 2002 and 2006. For example, the percentage of basic school 8th grade students attaining basic (and high) standards in Lithuanian, mathematics, science and social studies was measured (indicator 1). In 2002 this ranged from 53 percent for mathematics to 63 percent in science. In 2006 all those indicators were between two percent and four percent higher.

Of course, this result can't be entirely explained by the Student Basket reform, as the World Bank-funded Education Improvement Project had a specific component entirely dedicated to education quality. But it is certainly consistent with the use of the Student Basket to fund successively increasing number of education functions beyond teaching. In other words, when Lithuanian reformers understood that the new system did not stimulate competition among schools, they decided to use the Student Basket in a manner not initially planned, by adding new elements to stimulate spending on specific education functions. Even if the funds are very small on a per student basis (and compared with the full Student Basket amount), they are used for specific purposes, which have a direct positive impact on teaching quality.

POINT 3: INCREASED ENROLLMENT RATES

MES expected that schools would be motivated to seek out all children residing in their catchment areas who do not attend (early drop outs), and to try to convince their families to send them back to school. And indeed, the example of two municipalities of Panevezis (section 5.4) indicates that the interest of municipalities and schools in ensuring high enrollment translates into practical actions, which do bring results. If the municipality is interested and able to reduce the number of children on its territory who travel to a school located in a neighboring municipality by convincing them to attend local schools, presumably analogous effort may convince parents to cooperate with the schools in combating dropping out of school of their children.

The statistics on early dropouts are, however, notoriously inaccurate in all transition countries. Unfortunately, Lithuania did not participate in a recent cross-country study,[78] conducted by ESP/OSI in 2006, see ESP (2007). In its discussion of the results of EIP project, World Bank (2007) indicates that net enrollment rates for basic schools increased from 88 percent in 2002 to 96 percent in 2006. Again, to what extent this is due to efforts undertaken under EIP or to Student Basket funding reform is open to debate.

POINT 5: EXPANSION OF NON-GOVERNMENTAL SCHOOLS

By design, Student Basket is provided to all the schools irrespective of their founder. This means that public schools (funded by municipalities) and private schools benefit from the same level of financing of the teaching process under the Student Basket. Of course, this does not apply to teaching environment, which in private schools is financed from tuition fees of the students.

This relatively generous funding of private schools[79] was meant, in part, to encourage the creation of non-public schools, to provide greater diversity and greater competition. However, the results may be described as disappointing. Table 5.36 shows the growth of non-public schools in recent years:[80]

Table 5.36. Private Schools: 2000 to 2005

	2000/2001	2003/2004	2004/2005	2005/2006
Schools	17	16	17	19
Students	1,676	2,136	2,288	2,514

Since the overall student population in Lithuania numbers about half a million, private education in Lithuania still is not a significant presence.

5.6. Conclusions

The detailed review of Lithuanian Student Basket system, undertaken in the present study, allows us to formulate a number of conclusions. We divide them into three groups: comments regarding the implementation process, regarding the system design, and regarding the expected and unexpected results.

Implementation process:

1. There can be no doubt that much of the success of the Lithuanian education finance reform of 2002 is due to proper prior preparation. The preparations included not only a clear formulation of the problems MES faced at the time (i.e. 2001) and of policy goals to be achieved, but also the design of the system in terms of major policy choices (e.g. division of education finance into teaching process and teaching environment, per student amounts calculated

for each school, but allocated to municipalities with the right to reallocate), detailed design of the formulas, changes in budget laws and in the laws regulating the obligations of the municipalities. Those preparations created a group of knowledgeable experts who have been able to monitor the system and provide regular feedback, and allowed MES to manage the evolution of the system from year to year.

2. On the basis of the early preparations there was no need to introduce a pilot project in a selected part of the country, or test selected elements of the new system. Instead, MES relied on good monitoring procedures and on the experience acquired during the preparations to adjust the Student basket system as problems arose. The use of an early critical report by the State Audit and Accounting Office in 2003 was particularly important.

3. Nevertheless, there have been no public assessments of the Student Basket system undertaken since 2003. All the policy discussions are restricted to a group of experts and have not become a matter of public debate.[81] MES has not published publicly any assessment, either its own or prepared by independent consultants, of which goals of the reform were reached, which were not reached, and what it plans to do next. Such assessment may then invite needed public discussions, for example the association of local governments or teacher trade unions may have different perspectives on the achievements and problems of the reform.

4. The arithmetic complexity of the allocation formula had a clear negative impact on the implementation process. This is the case despite the fact that basic principles of the Student Basket system are simple and easy to explain and defend. These principles are, however, implemented in an excessively complicated and cumbersome manner, as the Student Basket coefficients of Table 5.45 clearly show. The number of people who understand the details of the Student Basket system and are aware of the possible consequences of various potential incremental changes is very small. Even the authors of the official audit have struggled with the complexities of the formulas. Consequently, the changes in the methodology of the Student Basket were not subject to policy discussions, and the system is becoming more and more complex every year.

5. The implementation process shows increasingly an active attitude of local governments toward the management and financing of their schools. There seems to be a learning phase of a few years that is necessary for local officials to get accustomed to new tasks, understand the different needs of their schools, and adopt some form of local education strategy. However, the Lithuanian experience shows that a real transfer of responsibilities, and not just a limited pilot, is necessary for this learning process to be effective.

System design:

1. The Lithuanian education finance system is a very interesting attempt to define a middle road between what is usually called decentralization to schools and decentralization to local governments.[82] However, it seems that municipalities become more assertive over time, and therefore that the future evolution of the system is likely to lead to more municipal involvement, financing, and responsibilities. The slow progress of increasing budgetary autonomy of schools is an

important indication. The key decisions taken by Lithuanian reformers, namely that it is municipalities that have the final responsibility for school networks–including school closures–and for setting the budgets of individual schools within some constraints, have defined the nature of education finance in Lithuania. This underlines the importance of early adoption, prior to the reform start, not only of publicly formulated policy goals, but also of a clear vision of future development of the system.

2. The prominent role of municipalities in education finance was not a foregone conclusion and was not adopted without opposition. Godfrey (2004) reports that many education stakeholders complained that the Student Basket system in Lithuania does not implement the principle *money follows student*, but a supposedly inferior version, *money follows student to municipality*. These stakeholders considered clarification of the position of municipalities, meaning reduction of their role, as a key challenge for MES. However, in our meetings and discussions with education stakeholders in 2007 no such sentiment was visible, and the present role of municipalities in education was not questioned. Moreover, the analysis in the preceding sections indicates that it would be impossible to reduce the role of municipalities without a major redesign of the system–and without losing some of its distinctive achievements.

3. MES knows very little about how the municipalities manage the maintenance of schools and finance material conditions for the pedagogical process. This is a result of the early decision to accept fragmentation of education finance into the teaching process–through the Student Basket–and the teaching environment–from revenues of school founders. By design, MES left the teaching environment as the sole responsibility of municipalities. Yet this precludes, at the same time, critical review of the functioning system and introduction of possible corrective measures. It seems that whatever the design of the management and financing system, MES should collect complete information on education finance, including all sources of funds (state budget, local budgets, parental contributions, etc.). It also seems very reasonable to provide MES with some instruments for addressing potential inequity in the area of teaching environment.

4. Interestingly, the Student Basket system has some paradoxical consequences resulting from using normative class size as the basis for allocation coefficients, with schools of quite different sizes receiving the same Student Basket allocation.[83] Those potentially serious consequences may not in practice harm the operations of the system precisely because municipalities have the right to reallocate a limited part of the Student Basket grant among schools. However, we have only limited data (e.g. Table 5.26) regarding this reallocation.

Results:

1. MES published the expected results of the reform of the financing system prior to the reform,[84] but never assessed whether they were achieved and to what degree. Clearly, such a review from the authors of the reform would be most interesting. In the current section we have provided an external review of whether the expected results were achieved. This analysis is summarized below.

2. The following expected results seem to have been achieved: quality improvement, increased enrollment rates, better planning and management of educa-

tion resources at the municipal level, and restructuring of school networks. We note, however, that quality improvements were not the result of increased competition among schools, as originally planned, but probably more related to specific non-teaching components of the Student Basket.[85] The World Bank-funded EIP project has also contributed to some of those achievements.

3. Regarding education finance equity, we have noticed that on the level of municipalities the equity of allocation for the teaching process has been largely achieved, at least for municipalities with sufficiently large average class sizes. However we do not know to what extent this has happened in the individual schools, and even more importantly we do not have the data on horizontal equity of the teaching environment–namely whether the expenditures on the teaching environment do not depend on the wealth of municipalities. Detailed assessment of horizontal equity requires more subtle analysis using more data on individual schools.[86]

4. Transparency of education finance needs to be considered on two levels. At the national level, it has been greatly improved through the adoption of public procedures and public formulas, accessible to all concerned. However, excessive complexity of the arithmetic approach adopted limits the practical impact of this transparency because despite simple basic principles, the actual formulas are too difficult to be a subject of wide public discussions. At the level of municipalities, however, there is very limited transparency and even the school directors have limited knowledge and understanding of the allocation system.

5. Public accountability of the education systems is notoriously underdeveloped in post communist countries, and Lithuania is no exception. Schools do not have to report how the funds they have been allocated have been used nor what results have been achieved. Municipalities do not adopt local education strategies that may be monitored and be used to judge whether local governments have reached their stated measurable goals. It is probably fair to state that development of necessary public democratic procedures in this area requires more time.

6. The following expected results seem not to have been achieved: increased efficiency of the education system, competition among schools, expansion of private education, budgetary autonomy of schools. Here the greatest hope of the reformers, namely that, through increased competition, schools would be forced to adopt more efficient plans and budgets, has not been realized. Indeed, as municipalities were very slow to consolidate their school networks, they had to be forced by the Ministry to adopt their network consolidation strategies, which over time stopped the decline of the student teacher ratio. However, given the demographic decline in the school age population, the maintenance of the student teacher ratio should be considered a major achievement.

7. It seems that the following unforeseen results have occurred: use of the Student Basket as a tool to improve education through financing new school functions, and significantly strengthened position and role of Lithuanian municipalities in education. The first of these shows that the Ministry was quickly able to begin to use the Student Basket system in a productive though unforeseen manner. The latter brings the hope that local school systems are in the hands of responsible and predictable owners, who will be able to use their new powers in the sector for the benefit of students and teachers.

References

AAT (*Audito ir Apskaitos Tarnyba*) (2003); *Ataskaitą Apie Igyvendinimo Mokinio Krepšelį (Report into the Implementation of the Student Basket)*, State Audit and Accounting Office, Vilnius.

AAT (*Audito ir Apskaitos Tarnyba*) (2006); *Ataskaitą Apie Mokyklų Tinklo Konsolidacija (Report into the Consolidation of the Local School Networks)*, State Audit and Accounting Office, Vilnius.

Bischoff C. (editor) (2009), *Public Money for Public Schools*, Local Government Initiative, Budapest.

ESP (2007); "*Monitoring School Dropouts,*" Education Support Program (ESP) of the Open Society Institute (OSI), Budapest, Hungary.

Godfrey, M. (2004);, "*Lithuania: Policy Note on Financing Education, with Particular Reference to Higher Education,*" Vilnius, Lithuania: Unpublished Manuscript.

Herczyński, J. (2002); "*Key Issues of Governance and Finance of Kyrgyz Education,*" CASE Studies and Analyzes 244, Warsaw.

Herczyński, J. (2004); "*Getting Ready for Take-Off? Current Issues of Education Decentralization in Romania*, processed text, CNFIPS, Bucharest.

ITC (2007); (ITC), "*MK Palyginimas 2002-2007, savivaldybiu mokykloms) (Comparison of the Student basket 2002-2007, municipal schools),*" Information Technology Center, Ministry of Education and Science, Vilnius, Lithuania.

LDS (2005); *Svietimas 2004 (Education 2004)*, Lithuanian Department of Statistics (LDS), Vilnius.

LDS (2006); *Svietimas 2005 (Education 2005)*, Lithuanian Department of Statistics (LDS), Vilnius.

LDS (2007a); *Bendrojo Lavinimo Mokyklos 2006/2007 (General Education Schools 2006/2007)*, Lithuanian Department of Statistics (LDS), Vilnius.

LDS (2007b); *Vartotojų kainų indeksų (Consumer Price Indices)*, Lithuanian Department of Statistics (LDS), Vilnius, available at http://www.stat.gov.lt/en/pages/view/?id=1370.

Levitas, T. and Herczyński, J. (2002); "Decentralization, Local Governments and Education Reform in Post-communist Poland," in K. Davey (ed.) *Balancing National and Local Responsibilities*, LGI Budapest, pp. 114-190

Lietuvos Bankas (2007); "Financial Stability Review 2006," Lietuvos Bankas (National Bank of Lithuania), Vilnius, Lithuania, available at http://www.lbank.lt/eng/publications/stability/fsa2006e.pdf.

MES (2006); *Education in Lithuania: Facts and Figures 2006*, Ministry of Education and Science (MES),Vilnius.

Plukas, V. (2006a), *Mokinio Krepselio Lesu Naudojimo Metodines Rekomendacijos (Student Basket, Methodological Review and Recommendations)*, processed text, Vilnius , Lithuania.

Plukas, V. (2006b), *Mokinio Krepselio Papildymai Ir Pakeitimai 2006 Ir 2007 (Change of Student Basket between 2006 and 2007)*, processed text, Vilnius.

Plikšnys, A. (2009), *Education Funding and Payment System Reforms in Lithuania*, in Plikšnys A., Kopnicka S., Hrynevych L. and Palicarski C. (2009), *Transparency in Education in Eastern Europe*, Institute for International Education and Planning. Paris: UNESCO.

World Bank (2007), *Implementation Completion and Results Report for Education Improvement Project, Lithuania*, Report No. ICR000091, Human Development Sector Unit, Europe and Central Asia Region. Washington, DC: The World Bank.

Annex A. Methodology of Student Basket

The basic Student Basket is calculated for a student of urban primary school, attending grades 5 to 8, in a large *normative* class of 25 students. We now describe in detail the assumptions and approach used from 2002 to 2007 (with the focus on the first and the last published methodology). The author of the calculations for MES since the introduction of the Student Basket in 2002 until now is Mr. Vytautas Plukas.

As discussed in Box 5.1, the salaries in Lithuania are calculated on the basis of salary coefficients and of the fixed salary amount. Therefore it is not surprising that also the calculation of the Student Basket is based on those salary coefficients.[87] For each year MES needs to propose a Student Basket coefficient K_{SB} and have it approved through a government resolution.

Table 5.37 summarizes the factors used in the calculation, together with their values between 2002 and 2007, beginning with the factors that had not changed in the intervening years. The symbol used is based on the convention used in 2007. We don't have the values or the formula for 2005.

Table 5.37. Value of Factors Used to Calculate the Basic Student Basket Amount

Factor	Symbol	Value 2002 to 2004	Value 2006	Value 2007	Character of the factor
Normative class size	N	25	25	25	Assumption
Weekly teaching load (contact hours)	P	18	18	18	Based on education legislation
Social contributions on salaries	K_{soc}	31%	31%	31%	Based on tax legislation
Share of teacher wages needed to support administration etc.	K_{adm}	10%	11%	11%	Assumption
Average teacher salary coefficient[88]	R	7.6	7.7	8.77	Empirical facts
Normative weekly number of hours a class in grade 5 to 8 needs	h	50	53.35	55.78	Based on curriculum norms, includes teaching split classes, since 2006 includes also non-teaching time
Number of days a teacher may use for in service development	K_{qual}	3	5	5	Based on education standards
Monthly fixed salary amount	Q	105 Lt[89]	115 Lt	115 Lt	Based on labor legislation

The main idea of the Student Basket calculation is simple: based on weekly hours per class and on weekly teaching load of teachers, we obtain how many FTE teachers are needed for next class. Multiplying this by the average salary coefficient of teachers, we obtain the salary coefficient necessary to teach one class. This will have to multiplied by Q (105 Lt or 115 Lt depending on the year) to obtain monthly take home salary, and by 12 months to obtain yearly salary per class. We need to divide this amount by the number of students, to obtain the salaries per student. We need to take into account also:

- Increase for teacher qualification, to cover the costs of necessary teacher replacement,
- An increase of 10 or 11 percent (depending on the year) to allow for administrative etc. costs of the school,
- 31 percent which go to social contribution,
- Add the elements of the Student Basket that are not related to teaching salaries.

In Lithuanian practice, as already mentioned above, the whole calculation is performed for the salary coefficient, and the multiplication by 12 x 115 Lt is done at the end. Accordingly, the non-teaching elements of the Student Basket are also provided in terms of salary coefficient. We thus need to calculate the Student Basket coefficient $K_{sb} = K_{teach} + K_{nont}$, a sum of the teaching Student Basket coefficient K_{teach} and non-teaching Student Basket coefficient K_{nont}. We discuss those calculations separately.

Teaching Student Basket Coefficient

The formula for 2002, defined in *Resolution No. 1520 of the Government of the Republic of Lithuania (December 14, 2001), titled "Approval of the Provisions for the Financial Reform of General Education, Vilnius,"* has the form:[90]

$$K_{teach} = \frac{h}{P} R \frac{1}{N} \left(1 + \frac{K_{qual}}{5*4*12} + K_{adm} + K_{soc} \right)$$

The expression in the brackets has four elements: the first is for teacher salaries, the second for teacher replacement,[91] the third for administration of the school, and the last one for social contributions. Taking into account that $K_{qual} = 3$, $K_{adm} = 0.1$, and $K_{soc} = 0.31$, we obtain:

$$K_{teach} = \frac{h}{P} R \frac{1}{N} * 1.4225$$

For the standard class, with values from Table 5.37 above, we obtain the value $K_{teach} = 1.2012$. However, in the original calculations of the student basket, a number of rounding procedures was employed,[92] of which the main was rounding of $h/P = 2.7778$ to 2.8, and as a result the value of the coefficient was $K_{teach} = 1.2040$ about 0.2 percent higher than the actual value.

However, as discussed in section 5.2, the introduction of the Student Basket was agreed in compromise with the Ministry of Finance, which wanted to begin with lower values and then stepwise increase the coefficient K_{teach} to its value as given by methodology. This agreement is contained in Government Resolution No. 1947 (December 11, 2002),[93] it was agreed to begin with the value $K_{teach} = 1.1971$ in 2002, $K_{teach} = 1.2006$ in 2003, and finally $K_{teach} = 1.2040$ in 2004 and beyond. Every year the coefficient increases by 0.00355.

The formula for 2006 and 2007 has a slightly different form, namely:[94]

$$K_{teach} = \frac{h}{P} R \frac{1}{N} \left(1 + \frac{K_{qual}}{5*4*12} \right) (1 + K_{adm})(1 + K_{soc})$$

The difference between the 2002 formula and the above is that now the factors for teacher replacement, overhead for administration, and social contributions enter the formula multiplicatively, not additively. From the methodological point of view, multiplicative structure seems more justified because the expenditures on teacher replacement and on administration are mainly salaries, so 31 percent social contribution applies to them as well, and not just to teacher salaries. This approach ,however, has the impact of increasing the coefficient.[95] Using the values from 2007, namely $K_{qual} = 5$, $K_{adm} = 0.11$ (with K_{soc} staying equal to 31 percent), we find:

$$K_{teach} = \frac{h}{P} R \frac{1}{N} * 1.4844$$

as is also obtained in Plukas (2006b). This means that since 2006 MES abandoned the previous practice of repeated rounding procedures.

For the standard class, using the values of parameters from Table 5.37, we obtain K_{teach} = 1.3552 for 2006 and K_{teach} = 1.6136 for 2007. This is significantly higher than the coefficient for 2002, more than 34 percent more, and the main source of the difference lies in the higher value of R, and in higher value of h, the normative weekly hours per class (see Table 5.37). We see that the increase of K_{teach} is in part driven by higher teacher salaries, and in part by increasing normative pedagogical effort of the schools.

In the year 2005, two values of K_{teach} were used: K_{teach} = 1.2112 from January until August, and K_{teach} = 1.2646 from September until December. This was due to an increase of teacher salaries through an increase of their salary coefficients, so K_{teach} had to be adjusted too. We can summarize the evolution of K_{teach} in Table 5.38.

Table 5.38. Teaching Student Basket Coefficient: 2002 to 2007

	2002	2003	2004	2005 I to VIII	2005 IX to XII	2006	2007
K_{teach}	1.1971	1.2006	1.2040	1.2112	1.2646	1.3552	1.6136

Between 2004 (when original methodology was fully applied) and 2007, the teaching Student Basket coefficient K_{teach} grew by 34 percent. This growth is due to three changes: increase of share for administration from 10 to 11 percent, increase of number of days for teacher replacement from three to five, and most importantly increase of average teacher salary coefficient R from 7.6 to 8.77.

For non-standard classes, i.e. for different grades with different values h of the number of hours per week, and for different size categories of schools with different normative class sizes N, we obtain different values of the relative student basket. Those values are in general, as seen from the formulas above, proportional to the number of weekly hours and inversely proportional to the normative class size.

Non-Teaching Student Basket Coefficient

The non-teaching Student Basket coefficient K_{nont} is defined as the sum of items responsible for specific non-teaching functions of the schools. Table 5.38 provides the values of coefficients for all those functions between 2002 and 2007, together with their sum (the symbols are provided for ease of reference):

Table 5.39. Non-Teaching Student Basket Coefficient: 2002 to 2007

Coefficient purpose	Symbol	2002	2003	2004	2005	2006	2007
Textbooks	TB	0.0083	0.0167	0.025	0.0300	0.0345	0.0449
Teaching aids	TA	0.0017	0.0033	0.005	0.0060	0.0069	0.0090
Pedag. psych. services	PPT				0.0052	0.0079	0.0095
Cognitive development	CD					0.0027	0.0053
Vocational guidance	VG						0.0027
Libraries	L						0.0053
Total non-teaching		0.01	0.02	0.03	0.041	0.0520	0.0767

It is worth posing and reviewing Table 5.39 in some detail. The first issue regards the first three years of operations of the Student Basket. The slow increase of the coefficients in the first three years was the agreed schedule of implementation of the student basket, described in section 5.2. The original methodology of the Student Basket stated the coefficients as applied in 2004.[96] The compromise stated in Resolution No. 1520 (December 14, 2001),[97] necessary to obtain the acceptance by the Ministry of Finance, was to apply 1/3 of the coefficient in 2002, 2/3 of the coefficient in 2003, and full coefficient since 2004. This agreement was fully carried out.

We note, however, that since then MES was using the Student Basket in a new way, namely was aiming to improve education by introducing the financing for new educational services. Of course this led to increase of the financing introduction of new coefficients. One new coefficient was introduced in 2005, for pedagogical and psychological services; another one in 2006, for cognitive development of students. In 2007 two new coefficients were introduced, namely for vocational guidance and for libraries. It is important to note that the latter in fact has salary implications, it was introduced to reflect 20 percent increase of salaries of librarians.[98] Moreover, each coefficient, once introduced, began to grow from year to year. Thus, after a slow beginning, and after accepting the limitations and slow introduction of the Student basket methodology, MES adopted a very active policy of modernizing Lithuanian education using the new financial mechanism.

Between 2004 (when original methodology was fully applied) and 2007, the non-teaching Student Basket coefficient K_{nont} grew by 156 percent, a significant achievement. This growth is due to increasing value of each coefficient, and to adding of new items.

Complete Student Basket Coefficient

We can now put the two parts of the Student Basket coefficient K_{SB} together and look at the evolution of the complete Student Basket amount. We need to take into account that in May 2004 the fixed salary amount was increased (see Box 5.1), so we need to break both 2004 and 2005 into two parts. Table 5.40 provides all the coefficients used (as listed above), K_{SB} as their sum, the monthly fixed salary amount Q, and the Student Basket amount, defined to be $K_{SB} * 12 * Q$.

Table 5.40. Complete Student Basket Coefficient: 2002 to 2007

Symbol teach K_{nont} SB	1.1971	1.2006	1.2040	1.2040	1.2112	1.2646	1.3552	1.6136
TB	0.0083	0.0167	0.025	0.025	0.03	0.03	0.0345	0.0449
TA	0.0017	0.0033	0.005	0.005	0.006	0.006	0.0069	0.0090
PPT					0.0052	0.0052	0.0079	0.0095
CD							0.0027	0.0053
VG								0.0027
L								0.0053
	1.2071	1.2206	1.2340	1.2340	1.2524	1.3058	1.4072	1.6903
Q	105	105	105	115	115	115	115	115
SB	1,521	1,538	1,555	1,703	1,728	1,802	1,942	2,333

Between the initial months of 2004 (when original methodology was fully applied) and 2007, the basic Student Basket amount grew by 50 percent. This growth can be decomposed into the growth of K_{SB} by 37 percent and the growth of Q by 9.5 percent.

We can also translate the coefficients into amounts in Lt and review the division of the Student basket amount into component parts, as is typically done in Lithuania. Before we do that, however, we need to pause and consider how it is possible to identify from the formulas above the amount of funds destined for administration and for teacher professional development (funds for replacement of teachers for absence in the school due to in-service training). This is not done easily, since those two components are deeply imbedded in the formulas for K_{teach}. It is, however, important from a policy point of view, since MES identifies teacher qualification component of the Student Basket and checks to what extent those funds were in fact used for that purpose.[99]

The simplest approach, which we will follow here, is as follows (see Table 5.41). We want to divide the teaching part of the Student Basket amount into components for teacher salaries, for teacher professional development and for administration. We do this is such a way that administration component will be exactly K_{adm}, and the teacher qualification component exactly $K_{qual}/(5*4*12)$, of the teacher salaries component.[100] The shares depend on the year, of course. We therefore assume that between 2002 and 2005, 10 percent of the teaching salaries was used for administration, and 1.25 percent for teacher professional development.[101] For 2006 and 2007, we have the shares of 11 percent for administration and 2.08 percent for teacher professional development.

Table 5.41. Stipulated Structure of the Student Basket: 2002 to 2007

SB component	2002	2003	2004 I to IV	2004 V to XII	2005 I to VIII	2005 IX to XII	2006	2007
Teacher salaries	1,356	1,360	1,364	1,494	1,502	1,569	1,654	1,969
Administration	135.6	136.0	136.4	149.4	150.2	156.9	181.9	216.6
Prof. development	16.9	17.0	17.0	18.7	18.8	19.6	34.5	41.0
Textboks	10.5	21.0	31.5	34.5	41.4	41.4	47.6	62.0
Teaching aids	2.1	4.2	6.3	6.9	8.3	8.3	9.5	12.4
Psycholog. etc.					7.2	7.2	10.9	13.1
Cognitive dev.							3.7	7.3
Career guidance								3.7
Libraries								7.3
SB	1,521	1,538	1,555	1,703	1,728	1,802	1,942	2,333

We note first that we have obtained, as assumed, that administration component is 10 percent (and later 11 percent) of the teacher salaries, and analogously that teacher professional development are 1.25 percent (and later 2.08 percent) of those salaries. As we shall see below, the assessment of amounts for teacher professional development obtained above are quite different from official data of MES (see Table 5.43).

Finally, we note that for comparative purposes it is necessary to obtain average values for the years 2004 and for 2005. We need to use weighted averages, of course, depending on the number of months specific coefficients were in force.[102] The results are provided in Table 5.42.

Table 5.42. Stipulated Structure of the Average Student Basket: 2002 to 2007

SB component	2002	2003	2004	2005	2006	2007
Teacher salaries	1,356	1,360	1,450	1,525	1,654	1,969
Administration	135.6	136.0	145.0	152.5	181.9	216.6
Prof. Development	16.9	17.0	18.1	19.1	34.5	41.0
Textbooks	10.5	21.0	33.5	41.4	47.6	62.0
Teaching aids	2.1	4.2	6.7	8.3	9.5	12.4
Psychologists etc.				7.2	10.9	13.1
Cognitive development					3.7	7.3
Career guidance						3.7
Libraries						7.3
SB	1,521	1,538	1,654	1,753	1,942	2,333

Those values can now be compared with the official Lithuanian estimates provided by the Information Technology Center (ITC) at MES, see ITC (2007). MES does not publish their estimates of teacher salaries or administration costs. All other amounts of Table 5.42 are the same as ITC (2007), with the exception of the allocation for teacher professional development. Indeed according to ITC (see also Pliksnis 2009) the allocations for teacher professional development were as follows:

Table 5.43. Official Lithuanian Allocation for Teacher Professional Development: 2002 to 2007

	2002	2003	2004	2005	2006	2007
Qualifications	4.5	9.0	14.2	24.4	24.4	24.23

It is difficult to reconcile the two estimates, and even less the decrease of allocation for teacher professional development in 2007. In one year (2005) official data are higher than our estimate, but in all other years they are lower (sometimes less than half of our estimates), which is also difficult to explain. We don't know the detailed methodology that ITC used to obtain their estimates. Nevertheless, and despite those methodological problems, in the chapter we use official Lithuanian estimates. The difference between our and ITC estimates is added to teacher salaries, this of course will somewhat destroy the relationship between the teacher salaries, administration, and professional development, on which our calculations were based. The result of those changes is reflected in Table 5.44, summarizing the evolution of the structure of Student Basket:

Table 5.44. Adjusted Structure of the Average Student Basket: 2002 to 2007

SB component	2002	2003	2004	2005	2006	2007
Teacher salaries	1,368	1,368	1,454	1,519	1,664	1,986
Administration	135.6	136.0	145.0	152.5	181.9	216.6
Prof. Development	4.5	9.0	14.2	24.4	24.4	24.2
Textbooks	10.5	21.0	33.5	41.4	47.6	62.0
Teaching aids	2.1	4.2	6.7	8.3	9.5	12.4
Psychologists etc.				7.2	10.9	13.1
Cognitive development					3.7	7.3
Career guidance						3.7
Libraries						7.3
SB	1,521	1,538	1,654	1,753	1,942	2,333

Data in Table 5.44, except for the first two rows, are exactly as reported in official estimates of MES ICT (2007).

Finally, we need to point out that although MES does not provide official estimates for administration component of the Student Basket, the State Audit and Accounting Office did. In fact, for 2002 the State Audit report AAT (2003) states that administration costs were 440 Lt, and assigned only 1,064 Lt for teacher salaries.[103] This means that administration costs would be about 41 percent of teacher salaries, in direct contradiction of the 10 percent assumed in Resolution No. 785 (June 27, 2001), cited on footnote 12 above. Therefore it seems safe to assume that AAT estimates are incorrect and not to use them in this chapter.

Annex B. Complete Table of Allocation Coefficients for Student Basket in 2007

The allocation of the funds for Student Basket is performed each year on the basis of the Resolution No. 1947 of the government,104 amended each year. The resolution describes briefly the methodology for calculating the Student Basket, as recalled in Annex A, however, the main part of the resolution consists of the table of all coefficients used in the allocation (unfortunately, it is only this Annex 3 which is amended every year). Below we provide the table of Annex 3, version for the fiscal year 2007. Since the table is rather complicated to read, we provide the following comments to clarify the meaning of different coefficients:

- Lines 1 to 11 represent allocation coefficients, which should be multiplied by the basic Student basket amount (2,333 Lt in 2007). The structure and meaning of those coefficients is described in section 5.3.
- In lines 1 to 11, in brackets are coefficients for national minority schools (first figure) and Vilnius city and Southeast Lithuanian mixes schools (second figure).
- Lines 12 represents coefficients for students migrating among schools located in different municipalities, they are allocated student per month and should be multiplied by basic salary amount (115 Lt in 2007, see Box 5.1).
- Line 13 represents coefficients for informal education, which are also allocated per student per month, and should also be multiplied by the basic salary amount.
- Lines 14 to 15 represent coefficients for non-teaching components of the Student Basket, they are allocated per student per year, and should be multiplied by 12 times the basic salary amount (1,380 Lt in 2007). Those lines are not used for allocation of funds, but are included in the table for information purposes.

Table 5.45. Coefficients for Allocation of Student Basket (From January 1, 2007)

Line #	School	Average number of students in the class to determine the coefficient	Grades 1–4		Grades 5–8		Grades 9-10 (years 1-2 gymnasium)		Grades 11–12 (years 3–4 gymnasium)	
			Regular student	Integrated, minority, migrant student, multi-language schools	Regular student	Integrated, minority, migrant student, multi-language schools	Regular student	Integrated, minority, migrant student, multi-language schools	Regular student	Integrated, minority, migrant student, multi-language schools
1	Settlement:	10	1.7765	2.4089	2.1201	2.8749	2.4636	3.3406	x	x
	initial school (1-4) (satellite), number of students to 50	10	1.5989 (1.7588) (1.9347)	2.1681 (2.3849) (2.6235)	x	x	x	x	x	x
	basic school (1-10) (satellite), number of students to 130	10	1.5989 (1.7588) (1.9347)	2.1681 (2.3849) (2.6235)	1.9081 (2.0989) (2.3088)	2.5874 (2.8461) (3.1307)	2.4636 (2.7100) (2.9810)	3.3406 (3.6748) (4.0422)	x	x
2	Settlement:	15	1.1924	1.6169	1.4216	1.9277	1.6504	2.2379	1.8151	2.4613
	initial school (1-4) (satellite), number of students from 51 to 80	15	1.2043 (1.3247) (1.4572)	1.6330 (1.7963) (1.9760)	x	x	x	x	x	x
	basic school (1-10), number of students from 131 to 300	15	1.2043 (1.3247) (1.4572)	1.6330 (1.7963) (1.4572)	1.4358 (1.5794) (1.7373)	1.9469 (2.1417) (2.3558)	1.6669 (1.8336) (2.0170)	2.2603 (2.4864) (2.7351)	x	x
	secondary school (1-12), gymnasium, number of students to 400	15	1.2043 (1.3247) (1.4572)	1.6330 (1.7963) (1.4572)	1.4358 (1.5794) (1.7373)	1.9469 (2.1417) (2.3558)	1.6669 (1.8336) (2.0170)	2.2603 (2.4864) (2.7350)	1.8336 (2.0170) (2.2187)	2.4864 (2.7351) (3.0085)
3	Settlement:	20	0.9005	1.2211	1.0722	1.4539	1.2440	1.6869	1.3684	1.8556
	initial school (1-4), number of students from 81 to 200	20	0.9185 (1.0104) (1.1114)	1.2455 (1.3701) (1.5071)	x	x	x	x	x	x
	basic school (1-10), number of students from 301 to 600	20	0.9185 (1.0104) (1.1114)	1.2455 (1.3701) (1.5071)	1.0936 (1.2030) (1.3233)	1.4829 (1.6312) (1.7943)	1.2689 (1.3958) (1.5354)	1.7206 (1.8927) (2.0820)	x	x
	secondary school (1-12), gymnasium, number of students from 401 to 700	20	0.9185 (1.0104) (1.1114)	1.2455 (1.3701) (1.5071)	1.0936 (1.2030) (1.3233)	1.4829 (1.6312) (1.7943)	1.2689 (1.3958) (1.5354)	1.7206 (1.8927) (2.0820)	1.3958 (1.5353) (1.6889)	1.8927 (2.0819) (2.2902)
4	Settlement:	22/25	1	1.0670 1.1130	1.0000	1.3560	1.1913	1.6154	1.3104	1.7769
	initial school (1-4), number of students above 200	20	0.9164 (1.8100) (1.1890)	1.2426 (1.3670) (1.5370)	x	x	x	x	x	x
	basic school (1-10), number of students above 600	25 (grades 1-4: 20)	0.9164 (1.8100) (1.1890)	1.2426 (1.3670) (1.5370)	1.2000 (1.1220) (1.2342)	1.3831 (1.5214) (1.6736)	1.2151 (1.3366) (1.4730)	1.6477 (1.8124) (1.9937)	x	x
	secondary school (1-12), gymnasium, number of students above 700	25 (grades 1-4: 22)	0.8372 (0,9209) (1.1300)	1.1352 (1.2487) (1.3736)	1.2000 (1.1220) (1.2342)	1.3831 (1.5214) (1.6736)	1.2151 (1.3366) (1.4730)	1.6477 (1.8124) (1.9937)	1.3366 (1.4730) (1.6173)	1.8124 (1.9937) (2.1930)
5	Rayon centers and cities:	22/25	1	1.6700 (1.1130)	1.0000	1.3560	1.1913	1.6154	1.3140	1.7769
	initial school (1-4)	20	0.9164 (1.8100) (1.1890)	1.2426 (1.3670) (1.5370)	x	x	x	x	x	x
	basic school (1-10)	25 (grades 1-4: 20)	0.9164 (1.8100) (1.1890)	1.2426 (1.3670) (1.3736)	1.1500 (1.1165) (1.2282)	1.3763 (1.5140) (1.6654)	1.2689 (1.3958) (1.5354)	1.7260 (1.8927) (2.8200)	x	x

Table 5.45 (continued)

Line #	School	Average number of students in the class to determine the coefficient	Grades 1–4 Regular student	Grades 1–4 Integrated, minority, migrant student, multi-language schools	Grades 5–8 Regular student	Grades 5–8 Integrated, minority, migrant student, multi-language schools	Grades 9-10 (years 1-2 gymnasium) Regular student	Grades 9-10 (years 1-2 gymnasium) Integrated, minority, migrant student, multi-language schools	Grades 11–12 (years 3–4 gymnasium) Regular student	Grades 11–12 (years 3–4 gymnasium) Integrated, minority, migrant student, multi-language schools
5	secondary school (1-12), gymnasium	25 (grades 1-4: 22)	0.8331 (0,9164) (1.8100)	1.1297 (1.2426) (1.3670)	1.1500 (1.1165) (1.2282)	1.3763 (1.5140) (1.6654)	1.2920 (1.3310) (1.4631)	1.6397 (1.8360) (1.9840)	1.3310 (1.4631) (1.6940)	1.8360 (1.9840) (2.1823)
	secondary school (11-12), gymnasium (3-4), with two parallel class	25	x	x	x	x	x	x	1.4631 (1.6940) (1.7730)	1.9840 (2.1823) (2.4600)
	gymnasium without general education	25	x	x	x	x	1.3310 (1.4631) (1.6940)	1.8360 (1.9840) (2.1823)	1.3310 (1.4631) (1.6940)	1.8360 (1.9840) (2.1823)
6	Classes for youth under 18, classes in sanatorium and hospitals	10	1.5989 (1.7588) (1.9347)	2.1681 (2.3849) (2.6234)	1.9810 (2.9890) (2.3880)	2.5874 (2.8461) (3.1370)	2.4636 (2.7100) (2.9810)	3.3460 (3.6748) (4.4220)	2.4636 (2.7100) (2.9810)	3.3460 (3.6748) (4.4220)
7	Adult general education classes, with instruction:	20	0.9005		1.7220		1.2440		1.3684	
	Consistent	20	0.6304	x	0,7505	x	0,8708	x	0,9579	x
	External	20	0.4503	x	0,5361	x	0,6220	x	0,6842	x
8	Independent learning (home instruction for more than half of subjects)	10	1.9542	x	2.3321	x	2.7100	x	2.9810	x
9	Vocational schools	25	x	x	x	x	1.1913 (1.3140)	1.6154	0.8220 (0.9042)	1.1146
10	Special schools, special needs classes:	10	1.7765	x	2.1201	x	2.4636*	x	2.7100	
	Special classes in regular schools	10	2.3095	x	2.7561	x	3.2027	x	3.5230	x
	Special class for deaf and blind students	10	2.7714		3.3073		3.8432		4.2276	
	Development classes	10	3.3026	x	3.9413	x	4.5799	x	x	x
		1-7	3.6329	x	4.3354	x	5.0379	x	x	x
11	Preschool groups:									
	Settlement initial school (1-4), number of students to 80, and basic school (1-10), number of students to 130	10	1.0479	1.4209	x	x	x	x	x	x
	Village schools and preschools	15	0.7815	1.0597	x	x	x	x	x	x
	Schools and preschools in cities which are district centers	20	0.5902	0,8003	x	x	x	x	x	x
	Special preschools	10	1.9245	x						
12	Payment for students who left municipal schools	K	1.4560		1.6368		1.9500		2.1449	
		Lt/st./m.	167		188		224		247	
13	Informal education	K	0.1296		0.0819		0.0955		0.1092	
		Lt/st./m.	14.90		9.42		10.98		12.56	
14	Textbooks	K	0.0449 (0.0494)							
		Lt/st./y.	61.96 (68.16)							
15	Teaching aids	K	0.0090							
		Lt/st./y.	12							
16	Teacher professional development	K	0.0177							
		Lt/st./y.	24.23							
17	Psychological pedagogical services	K	0.0095							
		Lt/st./y.	13.11							
18	Student cognitive development	K	0.0053							
		Lt/st./y.	7.31							
19	Vocational guidance	K	0.0027							
		Lt/st./y.	3.73							

Annex C. List of People Interviewed for the Country Case Study

Institution of the President of LR
Sigitas Šiupšinskas, Advisor to the President

Ministry of Finance:
Rimantas Večkys, Director of the Budget Department,
Daiva Kamarauskienė, Deputy Director of the Budget Department
Česlava Bareikienė, Head of the Municipal Budget Section

State Audit and Accounting Office:
Rita Švedienė, Deputy Director of 3rd Department
Rimantas Sanajevas, Deputy Director of 3rd Department
Jonas Izokaitis, Auditor of 5th Department

Ministry of Education
Arūnas Plikšnys, Director of the Department of General Education
Alvidas Dekaminavičius, Economics Department

Information Technology Center, Ministry of Education:
Irena Vainorienė, Director
Eduardas Daujotis, IT Expert
Ona Dzilbutė, Education Information Expert

Vytautas Plukas, Expert of the "Student basket"

Municipality of Panevėžio:
Povilas Žagunis, Mayor
Kęstutis Rimkus, Head of the Education Department,
Genovaitė Šarkiūnienė, Head of the Finance Department
Diana Kanišauskienė, Specialist of the Finance Department

Vilnius municipality:
Algimantas Šventickas, Director of Education and Culture Department
Teresė Blaževičienė, Deputy Head of Education Department
Danutė Dalinkevičienė, Specialist of Financing (Student Basket)

Municipality of Širvintu:
Kęstutis Pakalnis, Mayor
Monika Bilotienė, Head of Education Department
Danguolė Jakštienė, Accountant of Municipality

Paliūniškio Basic School:
Nijolė Sereikienė, School Director
Audronė Grigaliūnienė, Deputy School Director
Milda Stankuvienė, Accountant

Ramygalos' Gymnasium:
Agis Adašiūnas, School Director
Laima Černienė, Deputy School Director
Sandra Marozaitė, Deputy School Director
Regina Garuckienė, Accountant

Notes

1. Jonas Mickus was my guide to the complexities of Lithuanian education. I am truly grateful for his patience with my inquisitive questions and for his constant display of goodwill. Jonas provided all the documents and statistical data files I have used and also commented on early drafts of my report. I have both enjoyed meeting and profited from the discussions with three persons most crucially involved in the design and implementation of the Student Basket: Arunas Plikšnys from the Ministry of Education and Science, Rimantas Veckys from the Ministry of Finance, and Vytautas Plukas from the Antano Vienuolio gymnasium in Anyksciu *rayon*, which had designed the mathematical details of the Student Basket. A complete list of people interviewed for collecting evidence on this chapter can be found in Annex C.
2. This effort was aided in part by donor-funded projects, including the World Bank-funded Education Improvement Project.
3. Double reporting lines arise for example when a *rayon* education department reports both to the *rayon* council and to the oblast education department or directly to the Ministry of Education. Separate reporting lines, which disappeared in 1989, operated within the party apparatus. For an analysis in the context of education, see Herczyński (2002).
4. There are 60 autonomous and democratically elected municipalities in Lithuania. They are traditionally divided into cities and *rayons* (e.g. Vilnius *rayon* includes rural areas around the capital). However, the new municipalities created in the 2003 administrative reform have not been assigned the denomination of either "city" or "*rayon*". The sub-municipal level of *elderates*—there are about 500 of them—has no responsibilities for education.
5. See Table 5.7.
6. This is the case, among others, in Romania and Macedonia, see Bischoff (2009).
7. Because of the complexity of the formula and frequent errors in its calculation in the first years it was introduced, MES now sends to municipalities a computer program that calculates the allocation for each school–the program is a part of the student database. Some municipalities still calculate on their own what they should receive from the central government using an excel spreadsheet, but those calculations may still have occasional errors.
8. A voucher system assigns, through a national or regional level formula, the budget of each school (or a specific part of the budget of each school) proportionally to the number of students, with some variation possible on the per student amount. Among transition countries, Georgia has a radical voucher system with three values, which depend on the location of the school–city, rural or mountains.
9. The reallocation threshold was initially 15 percent.
10. An allocation formula to municipalities may be defined in such a way that it cannot be then applied to determine the budgets of individual schools. It may be based, for example, on some characteristics of the municipality, such as population density, as in Macedonia, see Bischoff (2009). Another barrier to using the national formula for municipalities to define school budgets is the use of buffers, as was the case for many years in Poland.
11. The history of the Student Basket is also told in Pliksnys (2009). Lithuania is similar to Poland and Estonia in that the MES introduced the per student financing system and did not rely on donor-funded Western experts.
12. Resolution No. 785 of the Government of the Republic of Lithuania (June 27, 2001), titled "Implementation of the General Education Financial Reform Measures".
13. See the reflection of this schedule in the Student Basket methodology, Annex A.
14. Resolution No. 1520 of the Government of the Republic of Lithuania (December 14, 2001), titled "Approval of the Provisions for the Financial Reform of General Education".
15. All values are provided in nominal values, without taking inflation into account. The Lithuanian Litas has been pegged to the Euro at the exchange rate 1 = 3.45528 Lt since 2002 (it was pegged to US dollar before). Inflation in Lithuania in recent years was as follows: 1.4 percent in 2000, 2.0 percent in 2001, -1.0 percent in 2002, -1.3 percent in 2003, 2.91 percent in 2004, 3.0 percent in 2005, 4.6 in 2006, see LDS (2007b), and over six percent in 2007, see Lietuvos Bankas (2007).

16. All tables in the report are based on data files provided by the Information Technology Center (ITC) of MES unless a specific source for statistical data is cited. Table 5.2 and Table 5.3 above are based on data from the Lithuanian Department of Statistics; see LDS (2005, 2006).
17. Data for the 2004/2005 school year is from MES (2006) and data for the 2006/2007 school year from LDS (2007a).
18. There are 10 counties in Lithuania. Those are administrative regions, with a county governor appointed by the central government. There is no elected local representation. Education department at the county level function as deconcentrated offices of MES, with school inspection as their main function.
19. See *Resolution No. 437 of the* Government of the Republic of Lithuania *(April 17, 2000), titled "Approval of the Program "Yellow buses" as the Mode of Transport Provision for Rural Schools."*
20. Data from Statistical Office (2007).
21. Cited on section 5.1 . See also Pliksnys (2009) for more details.
22. This reflects a conflict between the local governments, which tried to increase internal efficiency of the schools, and the schools, which wanted to avoid firing teachers despite decreasing student numbers.
23. Under the inherited system, if a school director decided to merge a few classes and reduce teacher employment, the funding of the school would be accordingly decreased, with no overall benefit for the school. Conversely, any new employment in the school would be compensated with additional funds for salaries. This created a serious disincentive to rationalize school resources.
24. We continue to quote from Resolution No. 785 of the Government of the Republic of Lithuania (June 27, 2001), titled *"Implementation of the General Education Financial Reform Measures"*. See section 5.1 above.
25. Issued on July 7, 1994, by the *Sejmas* of the Republic of Lithuania.
26. See article eight in the Law on Local Self-Government (July 7,1994) for details on this issue on special grants, which in Lithuanian terminology are categorical–conditional–grants that can be used only for the purpose indicated, and are akin to earmarks.
27. Preschools remained independent function until 2004, when they were included in Student Basket.
28. Cognitive development includes funds for visits to theater and museum, for educational excursions, for going to historical places, etc.
29. Most Lithuanian municipalities have outsourced provision of meals by turning their cooks and waiters into independent service providers and by introducing tenders and contract based services. Same is true of occasional school shops.
30. This reflects a clear policy decision of MES that the teaching process will be equally funded for schools owned by any founding institution. For non-public schools, Student Basket is transferred to school owner. In some transition countries the policy was to differentiate on the basis of ownership, for example in Poland from 1996 to 2002 non-public schools were funded at the level of 50 percent of their public counterparts (since 2003 the funding levels were equalized).
31. See section 5.1 above.
32. See resolutions of the Government of the Republic of Lithuania No.1947 (December 11, 2002) and No.1617 (December 16, 2003) both titled "Amendments of Resolution No.785 of June 27, 2001," but also Resolutions No. 1561 (December 3, 2004), titled "Basic Coefficient for the Student Basket in 2005 Amending Resolution No.785 of June 27, 2001," No. 1428, (December 28,2005) titled "Basic Coefficient for the Student Basket in 2006 Amending Resolution No.785 of June 27, 2001," and No. 1332, (December 22,2006) titled "Basic Coefficient for the Student Basket in 2007 Amending Resolution No.785 of June 27, 2001."
33. Recall from footnote 15 that we provide always nominal values.
34. See subsection 5.3.4 for a review of the legal basis on which the allocation methodology described below is based.
35. Compare footnote 15.
36. The derivation of those coefficients follows a bottom-up approach to defining the standard per student amount, so the proportionality and inverse proportionality are not exact.
37. See point 19 of the Attachment.

38. With the exception of grade level 9 and 10 for size category XS, of grade levels 1 to 4, and 8 and 9 for size category L, which may indicate arithmetical errors in moving from Table 5.18 to Table 5.19. However, three errors in a table of 15 coefficients seem to be many, and the size of those discrepancies is also significant (from 6 percent to 11 percent). MES should investigate this issue carefully.

39. Those *corrected coefficients* can be seen in Table 5.45 in rows 1 to 5, as the top coefficients in groups of three (without the parenthesis). We introduce here a specific terminology, not used in Lithuania, to distinguish initial (Table 5.18) and corrected (Table 5.19) coefficients to clarify the discussion (similarly to our classification of size categories).

40. Those are schools with more than one language of instruction.

41. Preschools were included in the Student Basket methodology in 2004, but are not included in Student Basket grants to municipalities.

42. This means, the municipality who is the founder of the school in which that student was enrolled in September of the previous year.

43. The reason for stating this monthly amount directly is clear: without such guidance, municipalities would at a loss at deciding how much money should be sent to another municipality when a student changes schools.

44. See Annex B.

45. See also Table 5.21 and discussion of Table 5.25.

46. Interestingly, the Lithuanian experience is here quite close to the Polish. For primary schools, although decentralization and corresponding financing reforms proceeded in stages, the per student allocation formula was introduced, without a pilot, only in 1996 when all municipalities obligatorily took over their primary schools. For secondary schools Poland introduced a pilot, so called *large cities project*, but it ended in problems and was discontinued, see Levitas and Herczyński (2002).

47. The present subsection is based on that report.

48. Reference student is a physical student multiplied by its allocation coefficient. A grade 5-8 student in an urban school has an allocation coefficient of 1, as discussed above, so is both a physical student and a reference student.

49. Annex A describes the changes in the calculation of the basic Student Basket amount, section 5.3 discuses changes in the overall formula.

50. Such independent verification of application of allocation formula is crucial in democratic countries. Moreover, it has many benefits for the education system as a whole. In Poland, for example, every year a number of local municipalities come to MES to claim their education grant is not enough, and discuss specific numbers with MES officials. Sometimes the differences are due to errors (of either side), sometimes to data inconsistencies, and the dialogue over the years has helped to improve data collection as well as mutual understanding.

51. We do not have the student numbers for 2002.

52. Here we refer to the rural *rayon* surrounding the capital city of Vilnius.

53. An alternative hypothesis would be that this reflects movement of students to schools with higher coefficients. However, this is not likely since in general there is migration to the cities, where the coefficients are lower.

54. Since the Student Basket is a special grant which can be used only for the teaching process, some municipalities fail to use of all it, but the sums returned to the central budget are very small, see Table 5.21.

55. In Table 5.21, the sixth row is the sum of first, second and fourth rows minus third and fifth row. The values in the second and third rows should in theory be the same, their difference points to some inaccuracies of budget reporting.

56. Strictly speaking funds for teacher professional development are meant for replacement teaching, so these may be considered salary. In Table 5.23 we limit ourselves to fiscal years 2003 to 2006, for which we have budget execution reports.

57. This is a common problem when different policy driven allocation coefficients are multiplied by each other. In this case, judging by the data in Table 5.20, we perhaps should multiply the per student allocation for non-salary components of the teaching process in 2006 by 1.203. We cannot do this because this ratio is different for different municipalities, and moreover because every year the

municipalities obtain the information regarding the values of the components of the basic Student Basket amount as stated in Table 5.19.

58. Such municipalities are called *doughnut municipalities* in Poland.

59. Overall expenditures of municipalities on the teaching process and the teaching environment are available from the yearly budget reports submitted to the Ministry of Finance. Those report do not discuss specific schools.

60. MES has not up to now taken any action against the municipalities which break the legal limitation.

61. Usually the preparation of budget documents requires support of the accountant. For autonomous school, this is the school accountant, and for non-autonomous schools this is the accountant from municipality.

62. The director may move the funds among months within a quarter.

63. The movement in the other direction is prohibited because special grants such as the Student Basket are categorical.

64. Lithuania is a small country and specialized school equipment will usually be available in Vilnius.

65. See discussion following Table 5.3.

66. This is equivalent to a simplifying assumption that the number of students in each of 8 grades is the same.

67. Again, this means we assume that the number of students in each grade from 1 to 12 is the same.

68. See discussion following Figure 5.5.

69. The measure of equity used here assumes that all existing schools should be financed irrespective of whether it is justified on internal efficiency grounds. Of course on the basis of the data used in the present report such an assumption cannot be verified.

70. Although outliers may require more attention from MES.

71. Table 5.35 is based on Lithuanian Department of Statistics LDS (2005), LDS (2006). Unfortunately, those sources do not provide breakdown of teachers by school type, so we cannot calculate the student-teacher ratio for different types as in Table 5.2 and Table 5.3.

72. This is in disagreement with the findings of World Bank (2007), which reports an increase of the student-teacher ratio between 2003 and 2007. In particular according to World Bank (2007), the student-teacher ratio in rural areas grew from 11.4 to 17.7. We cannot explain the reasons for this disagreement and stress that Table 5.35 is based on official data of Lithuanian Department of Statistics.

73. See for example Levitas and Herczyński (2002).

74. Poland in early 2000s saw far reaching consolidation efforts by local governments without guidance from MES and without an obligation to adopt local strategies.

75. All 60 Lithuanian municipalities belong to one such association.

76. Errors in the first two years of operations of the Student Basket were analyzed by AAT (2003). A few errors are present even in the 2007 table of allocation coefficients.

77. For an example, see the Sirvintai policy for reallocation discussed in section 5.3.

78. The study included Albania, Kazakhstan, Latvia, Mongolia, Slovakia, and Tajikistan.

79. It is worth pointing out that still private schools receive, on a per student basis, less from public resources (from state or municipal budgets) than public schools. In Poland, for instance, all primary and secondary non-public schools receive financial support equal to average per student spending on analogous schools in the same community. This is of course more generous to private schools than the Student Basket in Lithuania.

80. Based on LDS (2005), LDS (2006). Table 5.36 includes initial, basic, full secondary schools and gymnasia. There is also one private kindergarten and one private special school, not included.

81. This may be a result of the specific political culture of Lithuania, with a strong tendency for consensus and mutual agreement. However, this has the effect of preventing open formulation and discussion of opposing views.

82. See Herczyński (2004) for a review of those approaches, together with implications for education finance.

83. See the discussion of equity in Section 4.

84. See section 2 for details.
85. See discussion in section 5 for more details.
86. Horizontal equity in education is notoriously difficult to assess and is a much-debated subject.
87. Although they are no longer applied just to salaries, of course.
88. The average salary coefficients R of Lithuanian teachers in 2001 and in 2007 are calculated in Box 5.1. For an unclear reason 2007 Student Basket calculation uses the value 8.77 rather than 8.44 obtained in Box 5.1. This seriously inflates the value of the Student Basket for 2007.
89. As discussed in Box 5.1, the value of Q changed from 105 Lt to 115 Lt on May 1, 2004.
90. This equation does not appear in Resolution No. 785 of the Government of the Republic of Lithuania (June 27, 2001), titled *"Implementation of the General Education Financial Reform Measures,"* cited in section 5.1 above. It was obtained as a review of successive calculation steps provided in the methodology.
91. It is assumed that teachers work five days per week, four weeks per month, and 12 months per year, so the yearly replacement rate required in 2002 to 2004 was 3/(5*4*12)=0.0125 . However, as there is no replacement need during the summer, perhaps this coefficient can be calculated for 10 months only, giving the value of 0.015.
92. At most stages of the calculation, rounding to four decimal places was used.
93. Cited in full on footnote 32 above.
94. This equation appears in a somewhat disguised from in the supporting analytical document, Plukas (2006b) and was rewritten here for ease of comparison with the formula for the period 2002 to 2004.
95. Indeed, if in 2002 a multiplicative form were used, the value obtained would be K_{teach} = 1.2320, which is 2.6 percent higher.
96. See Resolution of the Government of Lithuania No.785, cited on footnote 12 above.
97. See full title of Resolution on footnote 14 above.
98. It would be much more consistent with the original methodology not to introduce this additional coefficient in K_{nont}, but to include it in the calculation of K_{teach}, for example by appropriately increasing the factor for administration to 11.5 percent or 12 percent.
99. This is not done, however, for the administration component. In other words, MES does not assess how much funds should be spent on administration, does not publish those estimates and does not monitor how much money was spent on education in practice. The stated share of funds for administration, that is 10 percent and 11 percent in different years, is used only in the calculations of the Student Basket.
100. Technically, this means we multiply the Student Basket teaching amount by $K_{adm}/(1 + K_{qual}/(5*4*12) + K_{adm})$ to obtain the administration component, and by $K_{qual}/(5*4*12)/(1 + K_{qual}/(5*4*12) + K_{adm})$ to obtain the teacher professional development component. The rest are then stipulated to be teacher salaries.
101. We assume that the values of allocation parameters in 2005 were the same as in 2004, and lower than in 2006.
102. This means that for year 2004, we take the values of the Student Basket for the period January to April with weight 1/3 and for the period May to December with weight 2/3. For 2005, the period from January to August has weight 2/3, and the period from September to December weight 1/3.
103. See AAT (2003), diagram 2. The same very high amounts for administration component are stated in Pliksnys (2009), which may indicate that MES was indirectly involved in their calculation.
104. Cited on footnote 32 above.

CHAPTER 6

Per Capita Financing of General Education in Poland: A Case Study

Rosalind Levačić[1]

6.1. Introduction

After the election of the first non-communist government in 1989, Poland underwent profound economic, political, and social changes in the 1990s. Among them was the decentralization of political power, seen by many as essential to breaking up the centralized communist state. In the communist period, several ministries had run different kinds of educational establishments from primary schools through to a large variety of vocational schools. In 1990 around 2500 democratically elected local governments, called *gminas*, were created and assigned a wide range of local social services, including pre-school and basic general education, for which they were assigned sources of tax revenues and grants (Jakubowski & Topinska 2006). Further administrative reforms in 1999 reduced the number of regional governments—*voivods*—from 46 to 16 and created a second tier of local government—*powiats* between *gminas* and *voivods*. Consequently, there exist in Poland three nested levels of regional and local government—groups of *gminas* are located within a single *powiat*, and each *powiat* is located in a *voivod*. The three levels have separate functions and are not hierarchically subordinate (Bury and Swianiewicz 2002).

Having decentralized the administration of education, the government needed to find a satisfactory method of supplementing the revenues of local governments (LGs) so that they had sufficient funding to operate their schools. Per capita (i.e. per student) funding was introduced as a more equitable and efficient way of financing LGs for discharging their educational responsibilities than the previous input-based system. It took a number of years from 1994 to 2000 to develop a genuine per capita funding system centred on a funding formula whose basic structure has remained unchanged since then. Political decentralization was the principal driving force behind the introduction of per capital funding rather than a main focus on increased efficiency or enhanced school quality. School financial reforms were accompanied by comprehensive reforms of all aspects of education. The school structure was changed, the curriculum reformed, new externally assessed assessments introduced and teachers' qualifications and pay structure altered.

This chapter focuses on the development of the per capita financing system in Poland from the early 1990s to 2007 and attempts to assess its effects on the Polish education system. Section 6.2 reviews the decentralization reforms, education reforms and the changes in the school finance system in the 1990s. It also examines the gradual evolution of per student funding up to 2000 when the current formula was introduced. Sections 6.3 and 6.4 revolve around the design and implementation of the funding formula. Section 6.3 explains the formula in detail, using its 2007 version as an example. It also outlines aspects of school management in Poland that affect school costs. Section 6.4 discusses the implementation of the formula in two local governments: an urban one (the city of Kwidzyn) and a rural one (the Czosnów rural *gmina*). Section 6.5 presents an assessment of the impact of the formula on three key domains: efficiency, equity, and transparency/accountability. Section 6.6 concludes with key findings.

6.2. Background

In both the communist and pre-World War II period, education in Poland had been centrally run. With the Act on Local Government, 1990, this began to change: *gminas* were assigned responsibility for kindergartens and primary schools. All *gminas* were required to take over kindergartens straight away but the devolution of primary schools was initially on a voluntary basis and was to due to be made compulsory in 1994. The 1991 Education Schools System Act did not initiate fundamental changes to the general education system, which came later, but it did establish advisory school councils, which are made up equally of elected parents, teachers, and students. It also included legal provisions for the establishment of private schools. The decentralization of primary education was further delayed. In 1993, Parliament, fearing *gminas* were not yet ready for these additional responsibilities, postponed the compulsory devolution of primary schools to *gminas* until 1996, though a *gmina* could take this on earlier if it wished (MEN 2001). Some cities in the mid 1990s also took over the running of secondary schools. By 1995–the year before *gminas* had to take responsibility for primary education–35 percent of primary schools had been voluntarily been transferred to *gminas* (Levitas and Herczyński 2002).

Gminas required adequate sources of revenues to undertake the major responsibilities of the local services assigned to them. The Law on *Gmina* Incomes (1990) guaranteed *gminas* a non-earmarked contribution from the state budget for recurrent expenditures on education. The Law on *Gmina* Incomes was changed in 1993 to guarantee *gminas* a grant for education of 6.6 percent of national budget revenues. As is detailed below, from 1994 onwards the National Ministry of Education (MEN) was required to develop a formula[2]—referred to in Poland as algorithm–for allocating a general purpose grant to *gminas* to contribute towards the costs of running schools. This was revised in 1996, with a major redesign in 2000. Thus, fundamental reforms in local government were intertwined with educational reforms and are difficult to summarize both briefly and clearly–the key events are listed in chronological order in Table 6.1.

The main reason for decentralizing general education to local governments (LGs) was to promote local democratic institutions and diffuse political power rather than to use decentralisation as an instrument for improving the quality of education (Jakubowski and Topinska, 2006:2). It was, however, hoped that local governments would be willing to invest more in school facilities than central government and would have the incentive to solve the problem that due to insufficient funding in the past many schools had accumulated debts due to unpaid social insurance contributions and utility bills. Decentralization of education was initially challenged by 'education centralizers', who wanted strong central control to push forward more fundamental reforms of the curriculum and

Table 6.1. Summary of Key Events in Polish General Education, 1989 to 2005

1989	Election of first non-communist post-war government. Fundamental political and economic changes.
1990	Around 2500 democratically elected *gminas* created.
1991	*Gminas* made responsible for pre-school education. School Education System Act: MEN must define core curriculum requirements; advisory school councils of elected parents, teachers and pupils established; private schools given legal basis. *Gminas* must take over primary schools by January 1, 1994.
1993/4	Compulsory *gmina* takeover of primary schools postponed to 1996: could be done voluntarily before then.
1996	Primary schools managed by *gminas*. First formula is created. *Gminas* were allocated a subvention for education from the state budget determined by a formula- protected *gminas* with declining student numbers.
1997/8	New government: major reforms in education. Curriculum reform: common core and minimum time allocations plus decentralization to school. National examinations to be devised.
1999	Reformed school structure. Primary (grades 1-6), *gimnazjums* (grades 7-9) run by *gminas*. *Liceums* (academic, grades 10-12) or vocational schools (grades 10-11) run by *powiats*. New local government structure: 16 *voivods* and 380 *powiats* (65 of these are cities).
2000	Major change to formula: included students in primary, lower and upper secondary establishments and related institutions in *gminas*, *powiats* and *voivods*. More strongly per student than before. Revised pay structure for teachers (4 grades of teacher): revised Teachers' Charter. MEN sets minimum pay for teacher qualification grades: school owner determines pay policy- supplementary pay.
2001/2	New structure fully in place for primary and *gimnazjum* schools.
2002	First national examinations at grades 6 and 9.
2005	External *matura* introduced nationally (*nowa matura:* for grade 12)

Source: Jakubowski and Topinska (2006); MEN (2001).

organization of education, and by unions—including Solidarity—who insisted on national terms and conditions favorable to teachers.

The decentralizers prevailed. Further political decentralization as well as major education reforms were instigated by the post-Solidarity government, which came to power in 1997. It wished to improve education by restructuring schools to raise standards, particularly in the lower secondary grades, and to encourage more young people to participate in upper secondary general education. The school structure inherited from communist times consisted of primary schools (*podstawowa*) for grades 1-8 followed by a secondary phase for grades 9-12 in a 4-year *liceum* for academically inclined students or in a vocational school offering 3-year courses. The reforms, commencing in 1999, reduced the primary phase to grades 1 to 6 and created a new lower secondary stage for grades 7 to 9 in a separate *gimnazjum* school. The government envisaged that the new *gimnazjums* would improve the quality of education, particularly in rural areas, as the schools would be of an efficient size and consequently better equipped and staffed than grades 7 and 8 had been in small rural primary schools. *Gminas* became responsible for both primary and *gimnazjum* schools. The structural changes to *gmina* schools, which took place between 1999/2000 and 2001/2, make it difficult to compare the numbers and sizes of schools before and after these reforms.

Compulsory education ceases at age 16 (grade 9) after which a young person is required to take some form of full time education or vocational training until the age of 18. After grade 9 students proceed to a three-year *liceum* (grades 10-12) or a two-year vocational school or to a profiled *liceum* offering both tracks. These institutions are run by the *powiats*. As well as being responsible for *liceums* and vocational schools, *powiats* run special schools and other educational institutions previously administered by the central government, such as sports and boarding facilities and centers providing education psychiatry services. *Gminas* and *powiats* were required to reorganize their schools to fit the new structure, but without any specific educational financial contribution from central government for the capital costs involved. Consequently, many rural *gminas* did not establish separate *gimnazjums* but run *gimnazjum* schools for grades 7 to 9 in the same building as a primary school.

Prior to decentralization, schools had been run locally by the deconcentrated units of the Ministry of National Education called *kuratoria*, each headed by a kurator or 'superintendant. The *kuratoria* both managed and financed schools and monitored quality. *Kuratoria* remained in existence stripped of some of their powers with respect to managing schools which had gone to local governments, but retaining responsibility for ensuring that each school is organized according to MEN regulations, in particular those concerning curriculum delivery and teacher qualifications. *Kuratoria* must approve the annual organizational plan of the school prepared by the school director, which is a major determinant of the resources the *gmina* or *powiat* must provide to the school. A local government cannot close a school without the *kuratorium*'s approval. *Kuratoria* also retained powers to inspect schools, though the form of this inspection has changed in recent years. In communist times, the *kuratoria* had been part of centrally run regional governments. As part of the new laws on education in 1991, MEN obtained control over *kuratoria*. However, the power to appoint *kuratoria* officials was returned to the *voivod*s a decade later.

Kuratoria had been in charge of setting the *matura* examination taken at the end of grade 12, which had consequently varied from area to area and there were no examinations in other grades. A major reform, vital for setting national standards and for the monitoring and evaluation of education quality, was the introduction of externally set and moderated national tests at the end of each level of schooling in grades 6, 9 and 12, the latter being the *nowa matura* required for entrance to higher education. These tests have been in place since 2002 with the *nowa matura* being fully implemented in 2005 (MEN 2001).

6.2.1. The Introduction of Per Student Funding: 1993 to 2000

The devolution of power over primary schools to *gminas* required the introduction of a new method of funding primary education from 1994 onwards. The Law on *Gmina* Finance (1993) required MEN to develop a formula for allocating a general purpose education grant, or subvention as it is referred to in Poland, to *gminas* as a contribution to financing their recurrent educational expenditures. It also provided for those non-public schools, which taught the national curriculum and employed qualified teachers, to be funded on a per student basis from the state budget.[3] MEN was faced with the problem of considerable differences in per student costs between rural and urban *gminas*. Costs in the former often being 3 or 4 times those in the latter. Furthermore, the much higher rural area costs were in many cases not due the *gmina* having to operate small schools due to sparse population or poor communications, but due to their preferences for keeping small schools open in areas where if the existing school were closed pupils could easily travel to a larger school (Levitas and Herczyński, 2002). Thus, MEN had to grapple with two conflicting objectives: creating a funding system that was more horizontally equitable and efficient on the one hand and, on the other, a system that was politically acceptable to teacher and rural interests. Funding *gminas* according to the number of teachers was ruled out not only because it would create poor efficiency incentives, but also because adequate data on the number of teachers was not available.

Initially, in 1994 the design of the formula ensured that per student allocations were higher for *gminas* with low student-teacher ratios. The initial weights for *gminas* were based on average class size.[4] Clearly this arrangement gave perverse efficiency incentives, which were removed in 1996 when the class size criterion was abandoned and rural *gminas* got a weight of 1.33 per student and small towns with fewer than 5000 residents a weight of 1.18. There was a further weight related to the proportion of teachers in the *gmina* in each of the pay categories. However, in practice for many *gminas* the formula did not allocate funds according to the number of students but was based on historic spending (Jakubowski & Topinska 2006, p.8). This situation came about because legislation specified that a *gmina* must not receive less than 100 percent or more than 110 percent of its inflation adjusted subvention in the previous year.[5] Consequently, in *gminas* where student numbers fell, as was often the case, expenditure per student could increase. "Despite appearances, the formula was not in fact allocating money on a per student basis, but on the basis of historical costs (Levitas and Herczyński, 2002:20).

A major reform of the formula was carried out in 2000. A precipitating factor was the need to include in the formula the funding of upper secondary schools in the newly created *powiats*. Redeveloping the formula to include *liceum*s, vocational schools and other educational institutions run by *powiats* (and it some cases *voivod*s) presented a number of difficulties. Vocational schools, which had been under the aegis of various ministries, offered many different courses and so had vastly different per student costs. Also, the *powiats* differed considerably in the non-school educational institutions they had inherited. In 1999, MEN began to fund *powiats* on a per student basis by distinguishing around 27 different vocational profiles and funding them according to historic unit costs. According to Levitas and Herczyński (2002), MEN was dissatisfied with per student funding based on historic costs because it did not want to perpetuate the existing network of vocational schools, many of which had very high costs and provided anachronistic training. A further problem was that the *powiats* lacked the volume of own revenues available to *gminas*, so that the subvention had to fund the bulk of upper secondary school costs as well as correct the imbalance of per student funding that favoured the primary sector. Another factor pushing MEN towards abandoning historic cost-based per student funding was pressure from some politicians and opinion makers for the introduction of an education voucher. At this time the Ministry of Finance was also pressing for vouchers to stop the rise in per student spending as student numbers declined and to promote competition between schools. The voucher was undesirable to MEN because a single value for the voucher would make many schools financially unviable, while differentiated vouchers were not feasible as no one knew how much vocational schools with specific profiles should cost and MEN did not want to pronounce on these costs itself. Levitas and Herczyński (2002), who were part of a team of external experts advising MEN on the 2000 revised formula, consider that per student funding was attractive to MEN because it fended off the voucher advocates, while making *gminas* and *powiats* responsible for deciding how much per student to spend in their different types of institution.

The formula introduced in 2000 was more genuinely per student than the previous one. It therefore 'had a tremendous impact on many *gminas* because it was no longer based on historical costs' (Jakubowksi and Topinska, 2002:6). A disparate set of ad hoc funding streams for upper secondary education was brought within a single formula for allocating subvention to all types of general education institutions owned by local governments and non-public bodies owning schools eligible for state funding. The 1998 Law on Local Government Revenues specified that 12.4 percent of national budget revenues was to be divided up between local governments for financing education. This percentage has changed over time. In the new formula, the per student allocations for urban primary schools and *liceums* were made equal, though subsequently a weight of 0.08 for post-primary students was introduced. The equalization of funding in favour of secondary schools in effect shifted funding towards *powiats*. A significant improvement in efficiency incentives for *powiats* was to replace 27 different per student allocations for different types of secondary schools by a weight of 1 for *liceums* and 1.15 for vocational and professional schools. Some specific kinds of professional/vocational school and non-school institutions and pupils with various types of special need had their own weights. The actual per user costs of non-school institutions were used to derive weights applied per user, thus encouraging *powiats* with more expensive provision to reduce costs while enabling those with below average costs to increase per student spending if they so chose. The additional weights for rural and small town *gminas* remained[6] but an additional per student allocation was given in relation to the number of students transported to school. This again gave an efficiency incentive for local governments to rationalize their school networks compared to the previous system, which had not funded school transport in the formula. In total there were 41 categories of student or user defined weights in the 2000 formula (some of the weights had the same value). The basic structure of the 2000 formula is still in place in 2007, though there are now 47 weights. These weights are additive and local governments are allocated funding according to the number of weighted student units.

A further substantial improvement in efficiency incentives in the 2000 formula was that local governments were no longer guaranteed at least last year's inflation adjusted allocation. This was replaced by an alternative buffer, which ensured that the allocation per student could not be cut or be increased above given levels. This meant that jurisdictions with declining student rolls could experience for the first time since 1996 a reduction year by year in total grant. This clearly put stronger pressure on such local governments to cut back on total spending and so slow down the increase in costs per student as numbers fell.

Since 2000 the weights for rural and small town *gminas* have tended to change annually, depending on the relative political influence of different *gmina* interests. Also, some of the categories of students selected for special weighting have changed. For example students transported to schools were dropped from the formula, more categories of special need have been distinguished and the weight for day students non-public schools increased to 1. A notable change was the removal of the buffer in 2004, so that local governments now feel the full effect of declining student numbers on their allocation. The formula has never included allocations for student expenditure or pre-school provision. Indeed, MEN has avoided being explicit about the types of current education expenditures that the subvention is intended to cover or contribute to (for example, a basic amount required for teacher salaries as in Estonia), which is a source of complaint among some LGs.

The formula was created with the involvement of local government stakeholders and is subject to annual revisions in the course of the negotiations in the Commission for Central and Local Governments between representatives of the local government associations, the Ministry of Finance (MoF), MEN and the *kuratoria*. The different local government associations represent rural *gminas*, metropolises, towns, large cities and *powiats*, cities and *voivods*. These associations have different interests to promote in these negotiations and do not present a united front. The Commission is concerned with both the size of the total subvention and the formula distributes it. MEN negotiates with MoF to reach agreement on teachers' salaries (negotiated with the Union of Polish Teachers (or ZNP, in its Polish acronym), the size of the subvention and some additional budget allocations for education. MEN and the local governments tend to unite in putting pressure on the MoF to increase the subvention, which is ultimately determined by the MoF subject to the agreement of the Council of Ministers. MEN and the local government associations negotiate about the various weights in the formula, which are not of much interest to the MoF. Since the PiS[7] led government took power in 2005 it was reported by observers that MEN no longer had clear policy guidelines to help it steer the negotiations and was mainly concerned with securing agreement between the LGs.

6.3. The Design of the Funding Formula

6.3.1. The Formula in 2007

The structure of the formula since its major re-design in 2000 has remained stable, with minor amendments, such as additional weights or changes in the value of a weight. The details of the formula are now explained using the 2007 version. For the purposes of calculating the total subvention it is divided into three parts, SOA, SOB and SOC, each with its own set of weights.

SOA is for funding the basic educational provision for children in grades 1 to 12, who attend primary (*podstawowa*), *gimnazjum* and upper secondary schools of various types and special schools. Kindergarten children from ages up to 6 are not included in the subvention. The schools that qualify for funding are not only local government schools but also non-public schools and private schools that have the status of public schools conditional on teaching the national curriculum and employing qualified teachers. SOB is a supplement for more costly forms of educational provision, which have various additional weights and are given below. SOC is an allocation for types of provisions outside regular teaching activities. It covers care and boarding costs and extracurricular provision. This includes special-needs kindergartens, centers for offenders, social therapy and boarding costs, as well as financial help for students.

Recurrent expenditures are supported by the subvention, not capital expenditures. The amount of the subvention, SO, that is allocated to local governments by the formula excludes 0.6 percent, which is retained by MEN as reserves and distributed according to approved applications from local governments.

Thus the total subvention is SO = SOA + SOB + SOC.

6.3.1.1. DEFINING THE FINANCIAL STANDARD

SO is the total amount available nationally for allocation to the local governments. It is predetermined by the MoF and Cabinet of Ministers. The financial standard, A, is the cash value of an unweighted student. It is derived by dividing SO by the total number of weighted student units, U_p, in the country as a whole. The number of student units depends not only on the actual number of students in the system, but also on the various weights attached to different types of student which are summed up to give U_p.[8] Thus the financial standard, $A = SO/U_p$.

The three parts of the subvention are calculated according to a particular set of student weights, as given below.

$$SOA = \sum_{i=1}^{N} SOA_i = \sum_{i}^{N}[A(U_{ri}D_i)]$$

where:
- N_i is the ith local government. (In total in 2007 there were N=2873 *gminas, powiats*, cities with the rights of *powiats* and *voivod*s.)
- U_{ri} is the weighted number of pupils enrolled in day schools and adult schools, owned by local government i or non-public schools entitled to the subvention in local government i's area;
- D_i is teacher salary index for local government i, which will be explained further below; its purpose is to correct for local government differences in the percentages of teachers in each of the four teacher grades as they have differentiated basic salaries.

The types of students included in U_{ri} and their weights are shown below. The data were supplied by the National Statistics Office (GUS) and more recently by MEN's Statistical Information System (SIO).

SOA includes:
a. students in public schools for children and youths and also in institutions for teacher development and for training social workers: coefficient is 1;
b. adult students in public schools and students in related teacher and social worker training institutions: coefficient is 0.7;
c. students in non-public schools for children and youths: coefficient is 1;
d. adult students in non-public schools: coefficient is 0.35.

The second part of the subvention is given below, where i = 1 to N is the same as for SOA.

$$SOB = \sum_{i=1}^{N} SOB_i = \sum_{i}^{N}[A(U_{ui}D_i)]$$

where:
- U_{ui} is the weighted number of students in local government i for which there are additional allocations because educational provision for these students is expected to cost more than the basic amounts allocated in part SOA.

There are 27 weights in this part of the formula, as listed below from P_1 to P_{27}.

- P_1 = 0.38 for primary and *gimnazjum* students in rural local governments and town with fewer than 5000 inhabitants

- $P_2 = 1.40$ for students with moderate learning difficulties
- $P_3 = 2.9$ for students who are blind or partially sighted, who are disabled or who have learning difficulties
- $P_4 = 3.6$ for students who are deaf or partially deaf, or with severe learning difficulties,
- $P_5 = 9.5$ for children and youths with very severe learning difficulties who attend special schools
- $P_6 = 0.8$ for handicapped students with motor problems who attend an integrated class in a mainstream school
- $P_7 = 0.08$ for students in post-primary schools
- $P_8 = 0.15$ for students in vocational schools
- $P_9 = 0.2$ for students who are from national minorities and local students who speak a regional dialect and need additional lessons in Polish
- $P_{10} = 1.50$ for the above students who receive additional lessons when there are fewer than 84 of such students in primary grades and fewer than 42 in *gimnazjum* and upper secondary grades. If P_{10} is received then P_9 is not included.
- $P_{11} = 0.2$ for students in sports classes
- $P_{12} = 1.00$ for students in master of sports classes
- $P_{13} = 1.00$ for students taking vocational course for the health professions
- $P_{14} = 1.01$ for students in music schools grade 1
- $P_{15} = 1.70$ for students in music schools grade 2
- $P_{16} = 2.01$ for students in general music schools grade 1
- $P_{17} = 3.36$ for students in general music schools grade 2
- $P_{18} = 0.92$ for students in art schools
- $P_{19} = 1.35$ for students in general fine art schools
- $P_{20} = 3.42$ for students in ballet schools
- $P_{21} = 1.00$ for students in teacher training schools
- $P_{22} = 1.00$ for students in various vocational schools for medical occupations
- $P_{23} = 1.84$ for primary and post-primary students, taking part in out of school classes organized in health institutes
- $P_{24} = 0.6$ catch up classes for students falling behind
- $P_{25} = 0.17$ for bilingual students
- $P_{26} = 0.04$ for students in *gimnazjums*
- $P_{27} = 3$ for students taking maritime and inland waterways vocational courses.

All the weights are additive. If a student belongs to more than one category the weights for that student are added. The weights are derived from estimates of the differences in the relative costs per student of the different types of provision. These relative cost differences have been studied by MEN's experts, recommendations made and debated in the Commission, which agreed to the weights. The number of weighted students in local government i is summed over the 27 categories and is expressed as:

$$U_{ui} = \sum_{k=1}^{k=27} P_k N_{ki}$$

where:
- P_k is the kth weight and N_{ki} is the number of students with weight k in local government i.

The third part of the subvention is shown below.

$$\text{SOC} = \sum_{i=1}^{N} SOC_i = \sum_{i}^{N} [A(U_{zi} D_i)]$$

where:
- U_{zi} is the weighted number of students in categories not included in SOA and SOB.

These categories include students with special needs, boarding students and extracurricular activities. There are 14 weights in this part of the formula, as listed below from P_{28} to P_{41}. All the weights are again additive.

- P_{28} = 4.00 for children who are deaf or partially deaf, blind or partially sighted, disabled, or who have severe learning difficulties and who attend special kindergartens and special kindergarten classes in primary schools
- P_{29} = 1.5 for children cared for in boarding schools
- P_{30} = 0.50 in addition to P29 if the students attend special schools
- P_{31} = 3.64 for boarding students in various artistic fields
- P_{32} = 2.00 for boarders in holiday homes
- P_{33} = 6.5 for boarders in special educational centers and centers for social therapy
- P_{34} = 11 for boarders in special care centers for young offenders
- P_{35} = 1.5 for children attending day care centers for social therapy
- P_{36} = 9.5 for boarders with severe learning problems in kindergarten classes in primary schools
- P_{37} = 0.02 for students who use school hostels based on number of places and months of occupancy
- P_{38} = 0.84 for children who need help with development in schools and centers
- P_{39} = 0.001 for students attending institutions providing out-of-school activities, based on number of students in the *gmina* schools
- P_{40} = 0.03 for institutions providing out-of-school activities related to the national curriculum based on number of students in the *powiat* schools
- P_{41} = 0.008 for institutions running out-of-school activities based on number of students in the *voivod* schools.

The weighted number of students in local government i for the SOC part of the subvention is:

$$U_{zi} = \sum_{k=28}^{k=41} P_k N_{ki}$$

where:
- N_{ki} is the number of each type of student with weight P_k.

The total number of student units, U_p, is therefore obtained by adding the weighted number of students in the three parts of the formula and adjusting this number by the teacher salary index, D_i, and summing this for all local governments, 1 to N.

$$U_p = \sum_{i=1}^{i=N} (U_{ri} + U_{ui} + U_{zi}) D_i$$

6.3.1.2. THE TEACHER SALARY INDEX

The teacher salary index is needed because there are four grades of teacher, each with a different basic salary. Consequently, expenditure on teacher salaries in each local government depends on the proportion of teachers in each grade as well as on the total number of teachers. The LG does not control the proportion of teachers in each grade, which consideration is used to justify the inclusion of this index in the formula. Each LG has its own index, D_i.

The four salary grades and the percentage of their salary in relation to the average salary base line established annually by law are:

- Novice teacher: 82%
- Contract teacher: 125%
- Nominated teacher: 175%
- Diploma teacher: 225%
- D_i is the index for correcting local governments according to the formula:

$$D_i = W_r + (1-W_r)W_{ai}$$

where:

- W_r is the index of expenses for goods and for salaries of administrators in local governments and its weight is 0.2;
- W_{ai} is the the index of the four grades of teacher.

The index of the four grades of teacher is made up of two parts. The first part is the weighted average of teacher salaries for the local government and the second part is an additional weight for rural local governments and for towns with less than 5000 inhabitants.

$$W_{ai} = \frac{P_{ks}W_{si} + P_{kk}W_{ki} + P_{km}W_{mi} + P_{kd}W_{di}}{P_{ks}W_{sk} + P_{kk}W_{kk} + P_{km}W_{mk} + P_{kd}W_{di}} \left(1 + R\left[\frac{L_{wi}}{L_i}\right]\right)$$

where:

- P_{ks} is the national average salary of novice teacher;
- P_{kk} is the national average salary of contract teacher;
- P_{km} is the national average salary of nominated teacher;
- P_{kd} is the national average salary of diploma teacher;
- W_{si} is the number of novice teachers employed in local government i schools;
- W_{ki} is the number of contract teachers employed in local government i schools;
- W_{mi} is the number of nominated teachers employed in local government i schools;
- W_{si} is the number of diploma teachers employed in local government i schools;
- W_{sk} is the number of novice teachers in the country as a whole;
- W_{kk} is the number of contract teachers in the country as a whole;
- W_{mk} is the number of nominated teachers in the country as a whole;
- W_{dk} is the number of diploma teachers in the country as a whole;
- $R = 0.12$ is an additional weight for the cost of teachers in rural *gminas* and towns with fewer than 5000 inhabitants; for the rest $R = 0$;

- L_{wi} is the total number of students in schools in rural areas or small towns with fewer than 5000 inhabitants in the LG area as reported by the National Statistics Office (GUS) for the base school year;
- L_i is the total number of students in schools the LG area as reported by GUS.

6.3.1.3. The Final Calculation of the Formula

The financial standard, A per unweighted student unit, is worked out by dividing the total subvention, SO, by the total number of student units in the country as a whole, U_p. Thus,

$$A = \frac{SO}{U_p}$$

For local government i the subvention is:

$$SO_i = SOA_i + SOB_i + SOC_i$$
$$SO_i = A(U_{ri} + U_{ui} + U_{zi})D_i$$

Thus each local government receives the financial standard per unweighted student unit, A, multiplied by the total number of weighted student units enrolled in its educational establishments, which is further weighted by D_i (the teacher salary index for LG_i). A reserve is kept back of 0.6 percent of the subvention for which LGs make a formal application against specified criteria to MEN whose decisions are presented to the Commission for agreement. This enables LGs, which have an unexpected increase in student numbers, to receive additional funding or if they have experienced some unforeseen emergency, which necessitates additional funding. The amounts allocated in total for the subvention and the financial standard, A, for the years 2001 to 2007 are shown in Table 6.2. Table 6.18 in the Annex gives more detail on how the education subvention was distributed between different types of school and student in 2000.

Table 6.2. Total Amount of Subvention for Education, 2000-2007

Year	Total Subvention (złoty)	Total subvention in 2007 prices (złoty)	Annual Growth in Total Subvention in 2007 prices (%)	Financial Standard: Per Student Amount in 2007 Prices (złoty)	Number of Students (thousands)
2000	19,367,363	—	—	2,299	7,477
2001	22,117,633	23,036,969	10.7%	2,447	7,357
2002	22,318,178	25,502,985	-1.1%	2,566	7,250
2003	24,321,215	25,219,541	9.0%	2,717	7,083
2004	25,082,854	27,482,973	-0.8%	2,873	6,961
2005	26,097,496	27,253,486	1.1%	2,925	6,773
2006	26,780,958	27,560,907	0.7%	3,071	6,518
2007	28,204,949	27,763,745	1.6%	3,199	6,264

Source: MEN.
Note: Nominal values have been adjusted to 2007 prices using the GDP deflator from World Data Bank http://databank.worldbank.org/ddp/html-jsp/QuickViewReport.jsp?

6.3.2. The Management of Schools in Poland

The subvention is not earmarked, so local governments can spend less than the subvention on education or add more from their own revenue sources. The revenue sources of *gminas* and *powiats* include a share of national personal and corporate income taxes, which are decided by law and can vary year by year.[10] In addition, *gminas* can collect local taxes from agriculture, real estate, vehicles and stamp duty. *Gminas* also obtain revenues from property, and charges for services. Property tax on average forms 15 to 17% of the *gminas*' revenues. Subventions in 2007 made up 36% of *gmina* revenues of which 24% was for education.

It is up to *gminas* and *powiats* to determine the amount they spend on education and how they allocate this to schools. In making these decisions local governments are constrained by several key regulations.

- The number of lessons per week that students must be taught the national curriculum: this is expressed as a given number of lessons per subject over a three grade range (1-3, 4-6, 7-9, and 10-12) and so provides some minor flexibility within each grade. In addition, local governments (LGs) can add extra hours for optional subjects and extra-curricular activities.
- Teachers are required to teach only 18 (45 minute) lessons per week—this is known as the *pensum*—and was enshrined in the Teachers' Charter in 1982.[11]
- Teacher salaries are set mainly according to criteria in the Teachers' Charter. This was revised in 2000 to create four levels of teacher: novice, contract, nominated and diploma, who receive respectively 82%, 125%, 175% and 225% of the basic pay for the profession, which is defined annually.[12] To reach nominated and diploma grades teachers must submit an application, to the *kuratoria* with a portfolio of evidence about their activities as teachers.[13] Most teachers who apply for the two higher grades are successful. The Teachers' Charter also contains provisions for additional payments for extra responsibilities, such as form tutoring, and 'motivation', which largely refers to undertaking extracurricular activities with students or participating in and contributing to professional development. A key point is that LGs have limited control over the teacher salaries they have to pay to teachers once they are on the payroll, since the LG has no say in teacher promotions to higher grades. LGs are required to set the bonuses for additional teacher pay so that on average in their schools teachers in each grade receive at least the basic salary for their grade (OECD 2006). LGs complain that they are required to pay for increases in teacher salary costs, in particular those which arose from promotions, which are not fully reflected in the education subvention.
- It is very difficult for LGs to dismiss surplus teachers: this can only be done when a school is closed and even then the LG has an obligation to redeploy teachers in another local school.[14] LGs can dismiss a teacher for incompetence if negatively evaluated by the school director, but these provisions are rarely used.
- A LG cannot close a school without the approval of the *kuratorium*, though the latter has no means to offer financial support to the LG.[15]

The areas of flexibility for LGs are that there are no maximum or minimum class sizes defined by MEN or nationally defined norms for non-teaching staff posts at schools. There is also a role for the LG in defining the criteria for teachers' additional pay, above the average for each grade in the LG's schools that must equal the salary norm set by MEN. However, LGs regard themselves are severely constrained in their ability to influence the number of teaching hours that schools employ. Regulations stipulate that for the start of the school year, the school director prepares an organizational plan which details the subject lessons and hours taught to each class and the teachers employed to provide these lessons. The *kuratorium*, not the LG, approves the plan. LGs have freedom in determining non-teaching staff positions, and expenditures on learning materials, school maintenance and student expenditure, subject to adhering to health and safety regulations.

6.3.2.1. Resolving Tensions between Demand for and Supply of School Funding

In Poland the tensions between the financial needs of schools and the available funding is resolved first in the Commission of Central and Local Governments, which tries to influence the total subvention the MoF sets and has a strong say on the formula and how it shares out the total cake. The final conflicts between the demand for and supply of resources are resolved by the *gminas* and *powiats*. *Gminas* either find additional resources on out of their own revenues or put pressure on schools to increase class size or close schools altogether. *Powiats* have fewer own resources and classes in *liceums* tend to be large. One *powiat* education director maintained that vocational schools are underfunded by the MEN formula with the result that he has had to close vocational courses. Consequently, more training is done within companies with schools providing general education courses to trainees.[16] The conflicts between local and central government over the volume and distribution of education funding are endemic in any system where central and local governments share responsibility, especially one where local governments are relatively strong compared to coalition based central governments, but these disagreements are generally accepted as natural in a plural, democratic society. The most pressing issue is the determination of teachers' pay and how it is funded. LGs like to argue that they cannot control teacher salary costs and therefore that central government should ensure that all increases in salary costs are covered by increased subvention. One instance indicates the power that LGs can exert. At the time of the creation of *gimnazjums* many LGs increased the employment of teachers and some had to borrow to fund the consequent salary costs because the subvention was insufficient. These loans were subsequently paid off by the state budget—with interest (MEN, 2001).

6.3.2.2. How Local Governments Finance Their Schools

Most local governments use an input-based system for determining schools budgets. This was the case in two small rural *gminas* visited, Czosnów and Lubicz (data were collected on the former). Each school's organizational plan, over which the *gmina* has limited influence since it must meet MEN criteria and be approved by the *kuratorium*, determines the main part of the school budget. The school budget is agreed between the school and the *wójt* (mayor) and approved by the council. In small *gminas*, with a handful of schools, the relationship between schools and the LG are close and school directors can make personal cases for resources.

Some LGs have introduced their own formulas for determining the funding of their schools. These are cities or mainly urban area LGs where schools are larger and differences in school size less marked than in rural or mixed areas. Świdnica *powiat*, Poznań and Kraków, for example, are LGs which have formulas. Kwidzyn is another city which introduced its own version of a 'voucher' in 1994 and operates a formula for determining school budgets.

6.4. The Implementation of the Funding Formula

6.4.1. Kwidzyn: Example of a Gmina Using Its Own Formula for Funding Its Schools

Kwidzyn is an urban *gmina* with around 38,000 inhabitants and is a city with the status of a *powiat*. The city has two major employers - an international paper company and a TV plant. In 2007 the *gmina* had 4,365 students in 4 primary and 3 *gimnazjum* schools. Kwidzyn took over the running of schools early, in 1994, and has experienced considerable political stability and continuity in education policy. From the start, Kwidzyn funded its primary and then *gimnazjum* schools using a per student formula, referred to in Kwidzyn as an 'education voucher'. Over a decade's experience of per student funding makes Kwidzyn worthy of study.

6.4.1.1. THE EDUCATION BUDGET

In 2006 Kwidzyn *gmina* received in state subvention for education 16.2 million *Złoty*[17] and spent 16.8 m zł directly on its primary and *gimnazjum* schools. As can be seen from Table 6.3, it spent an additional 7 m zł on other educational activities, including transport, capital expenditure, pre-schools and central administration. The *gmina*'s additional

Table 6.3. Kwidzyn *Gmina*: Education Budget 2006

Type of Expenditure	Złotys
Pre-school	3,747,493
Primary schools	10,155,854
Gimnazjum schools	6,681,324
Transporting children with disabilities to school	105,444
School administration (central)	673,793
Contribution to repairs to *liceum* (in *powiat*)	200,000
Teachers' professional development: salary bonus and services	238,355
Other educational activities (includes monitoring student attainment)	988,304
Miscellaneous current expenditures	571,976
Capital expenditures	416,328
Material help for students in tertiary education	157,923
TOTAL EXPENDITURE ON EDUCATION	**23,936,794**
Education subvention from state	**16,234,455**
Total expenditure on all activities	**85,474,300**
Education spending as a proportion of total public expenditure	28.0%
Education spending funded from own resources as a proportion of total education spending	32.2%
Gmina-funded expenditure on primary and *gimnazjum* schools as a proportion of total education expenditure	3.6%
Subvention as a percentage of total expenditure on primary and *gimnazjum* schools	96.4%

Source: Kwidzyn City Local Government Annual Finance Report.

contribution to direct spending on primary and *gimnazjum* schools was only 3.7% of the state subvention, but when all expenditures on education are considered, Kwidzyn funded 32 percent from its own resources. In 2006 education accounted for 28 percent of Kwidzyn's total expenditure.

6.4.1.2. How Schools Are Funded in Kwidzyn

Kwidzyn adopted per student funding because the *gmina* council believes in the principle of subsidiarity:

> "At the center we do not believe we know better than the school directors what their needs are. We tell them how much we can afford to let them have and they decide how to manage it." (R. Bera;[18] Deputy Mayor: interview).

Kwidzyn refers to its formula as determining the value of an education voucher, therefore this term will be used. Although referred to as an 'education voucher', the money for each student enrolled at a school goes directly to the school and not via parents. One of the objectives of introducing vouchers was to foster more competition between schools in order to encourage them to improve their quality.[19] School choice by parents is governed by rules that are common throughout Poland. Each school has a catchment or reserve area and pupils from this area are given first preference for admission to the school. Parents can send their child to a school outside their catchment area if it has a spare place. The school director can choose how many students to recruit, subject to approval of the annual organizational plan by the local government.

Kwidzyn bases the per student value of the 'voucher' on an activity-led model of its schools: it makes explicit the input standards it is funding. The calculation of the voucher is divided into three parts: (A) teaching staff salaries (81%), (B) non- teaching staff salaries (7%), and (C) non-staff expenditures (12%). Capital expenditure is allocated separately. The breakdown of the three parts of the 'voucher' for the 7 schools and their values are shown in Table 6.4. Parts B and C have the same value for all schools but Part A varies in value to take account of teacher salary differences in schools (due to the four teacher grades). Kwidzyn reckons that its schools need to have over 500 students to be financially viable. However, the council has decided to retain the smallest *gimnazjum* because it is needed on the city outskirts. It is therefore funded 15 percent more for Part A to cover its higher unit costs.

The allocation per student for teacher salaries for each school is based on an explicit input standard. The average class size funded for teaching is 26 pupils. This class size, given the number of students at the school, determines the number of classes (in fractions) needed in each grade. The number of classes is multiplied by the number of lessons per week students in each grade receive (24 for primary grades 1 to 3, 32 for primary grades 4 and 5, 33 for primary grade 6, 34 for the first grade of *gimnazjum* and 35 for grades 2 and 3). This gives the number of lessons a week needed for each grade. This is then divided by 18 lessons—the teaching load of a teacher—to derive the number of teachers needed for each grade and the total for the school is then derived. Additional teaching staff are added (see Annex A, Table 6.20) for director and deputies, educational psychologist, child carers and librarians, the full time equivalent posts varying with size of school. The average basic salary of the actual teachers in post at the schools is calculated (this is different for each school). This is multiplied by the number of teaching posts allocated by the formula to give total basic salaries for the school. To this is added teacher salary supplements for the number of years worked, additional responsibilities and motivation; there are further additions for school directors and deputies; to the total is added social insurance taxes. The grand total is divided by the number of students to arrive at Part A of the voucher shown in Table 6.4.

Primary school 6 has a higher value of Part A because it runs 'integrated classes' in which children with special educational needs are taught with mainstream pupils. There are 5-7 SEN pupils per class, which is kept at around 20 pupils, taught by two teachers.[20] School 6 is therefore funded for a lower average class size. In September 2007 one of the *gimnazjums* will have integrated classes as well. Parts B and C of the voucher are not based on explicit input standards and depend on what the *gmina* can afford. Kwidzyn also has a private *gimnazjum*, which is funded by the voucher.

Capital investment is decided separately. Kwidzyn has now refurbished and renovated all but one of its schools and intends to move the remaining school into new premises. It invested in a center for ICT skills that is used by all schools, as well as another sports center. The *gmina* greatly reduced the costs of kindergarten provision by turning it over the private sector where teachers work 40 hours a week, as the Teachers Charter does not apply. Kwidzyn only runs one out of 8 kindergartens. There are now 2.5 teachers per kindergarten class compared to 5.5 in the early 1990s. The *gmina* also provides scholarships for students, using a variety of criteria—low family income, academic and sporting abilities and for students in schools abroad. Other services funded by the *gmina* are home-to-school transport and teacher professional development. Kwidzyn's department of culture and education employs 3 full time staff.

Table 6.4. Annual Per Student Funding of Each School in Kwidzyn (2007)

	Primary Schools				Gimnazjums		
	SP2	SP4	SP5	SP6	G1	G2	G3
Number of students	600	816	525	765	261	931	467
	Złoty	Złoty	Złoty	Złoty	Złoty	Złoty	Złoty
Value of education voucher part A (teachers)	2,923	2,970	2,928	3,578	3,574	3,061	3,306
Value of education voucher part B (non-teaching staff)	286.8	286.8	286.8	286.8	286.8	286.8	286.8
Value of education voucher part C	454.8	454.8	454.8	454.8	454.8	454.8	454.8
Adjustment weighting	1	1	1	1	1.15	1	1
Total value of voucher (A+B+C)	2,199,000	3,029,000	1,927,000	3,305,000	1,295,000	3,540,000	1,890,000
Per student amount	3,665	3,712	3,670	4,320	4,962	3,802	4,047
Pensions	13,872	37,535	26,112	29,376	17,952	1,632	13,056
Total school budget	2,212,872	3,066,535	1,953,112	3,334,376	1,312,952	3,541,632	1,903,056

Source: Kwidzyn City Local Government.

6.4.1.3. Assessment of the Effects of the Financing Reform in Kwidzyn

Kwidzyn was concerned with creating a more efficient school network. For over 10 years it had been experiencing declining student numbers, as shown in Table 6.5. The city council decided to close the smallest primary school, which could not cover its costs if funded only via the voucher. This process took 3 years with many meetings with parents. A small primary school, where grade 6 results had been poor, was merged with a larger school with good results and, according to the deputy mayor, these have been maintained.

Table 6.5. Kwidzyn City *Gmina*: Number of Pupils, 1998 to 2006

	1998	1999	2000	2001	2002	2003	2004	2005	2006
Primary schools	5,267	4,313	3,479	3,424	3,292	3,123	3,013	2,871	2,706
Gimnazjums	0	700	1,340	1,879	1,761	1,721	1,692	1,625	1,659
Total	5,267	5,013	4,819	5,303	5,053	4,844	4,705	4,496	4,365
Percentage change		-4.8%	-3.9%	10.0%	-4.7%	-4.1%	-2.9%	-4.4%	-2.9%

Source: Regional data bank GUS 1998-2006.
Note: increase in 2001 due to additional grade in *gimnazjums*.

School-based financial management has also created incentives to improve the internal efficiency of schools. The school budget is determined by the value of the voucher multiplied by the number of students. The school director prepares an annual budget plan based, as in all schools in Poland, on the organizational plan for the delivery of the curriculum. The school director can determine the number of non-teaching staff constrained by health and safety regulations. The system promotes efficiency by enabling schools to vire (switch money between budget lines). Permission for this is a formality.

The staffing of the seven schools is shown in Table 6.6. As can be seen, the student-teacher ratio in three schools is close to the EU19 in 2004 of 15.3 for primary (apart from primary 6 with integrated classes) and above the EU19 of 12 for lower secondary (OECD 2006). The student non-teaching staff ratio is also relatively high in 5 of the schools. The vice mayor confirmed that the number of non-teaching staff had declined since the *gmina* took over the running of schools and introduced funding by voucher.

Table 6.6. Kwidzyn City *Gmina's* Schools: Teaching and Non-Teaching Posts

Type of school	Number of students	Number of full-time teachers	Number of part-time teachers	Secretarial and admin. staff	Janitors	Handymen	Cleaners	Student-teacher ratio†	Student-non-teaching staff ratio‡
Primary 2	600	39	1	2	0	2	5.5	15.2	63.2
Primary 4	816	48	4	2	1	2	6	16.3	74.2
Primary 5	525	34	4	1	1	1	3	14.6	87.5
Primary 6	765	57	0	2	1	2	6	13.4	69.5
Gimnazjum 1	261	17	4	1	2	1	2	13.7	43.5
Gimnazjum 2	931	49	18	1	2	2	7	16.1	77.6
Gimnazjum 3	467	30	6	5	0	2	5	14.2	38.9

Source: Kwidzyn City Local Government
† Estimated since full time equivalent teacher data is not reported. It is assumed that part time teachers are equivalent to 0.5 of a full time teacher.
‡ NTS = non-teaching staff.

Each school's income from the *gmina* is paid into a commercial bank account and the budget managed centrally by a team of accountants: schools have no financial staff of their own.[21] The chief accountant at the *gmina* therefore shares responsibility for the budget with the school director, an arrangement that reduces the possibility of fraudulent use of the budget. National law places severe sanctions on school directors who mismanage the budget—they may need to pay any over-spending from their own salaries and have to finance from their own pockets any transaction for which they cannot produce an invoice.

One school in Kwidzyn was visited: *gimnazjum* no. 2. This is the *gmina*'s best performing *gimnazjum* in terms of grade 9 results and student competitions. It recruits well outside its catchment area and can select these students by ability. The school has 931 students, distributed in grades and classes as shown in Table 6.7. It is interesting to note that grade 3 has the same number of classes as grade 1, despite having 49 fewer students. This is because the number of students in grade 3 had declined since grade 1 due to non-promotion of students. Between 30 and 40 students were held back in grade 1 and about 50 in grade 2. Some held back students left for other schools. The school director decided not to reduce the number of classes because when she had done this in a previous year there had been considerable student and parent dissatisfaction at the disruption to class membership. She therefore decided that the budget would bear the costs of the smaller class sizes by reducing non-staff expenditure—in particular on teaching materials.

Table 6.7. Kwidzyn City *Gmina*: Students and Classes at *Gimnazjum* 2

Grade	Number of students	Number of classes	Average class size
1 (year 7)	323	11	29.4
2 (year 8)	344	13	26.5
3 (year 9)	264	11	24.0

In addition to the voucher, the school collects a modest amount of own revenue. About 40 percent of parents pay a voluntary contribution of 30 zł per family per year. This money is managed by parents and used for school trips. The school has a sponsor for its handball team. Some rooms are rented out but the money goes to the *gmina*. The budget of *Gimnazjum* 2 is shown in Table 6.8. Once all staff costs are added together including social security taxes these amount to 88 percent of the budget, while 3.5 percent was spent on learning resources (teaching aids, materials and equipment). This is still a relatively high proportion on staff.

Kwidzyn also sees the formula as only one tool in a governance framework for improving the quality of its schools. Another tool is performance monitoring. Kwidzyn has commissioned additional tests in primary grade 5 and *gimnazjum* grade 2 so that it can have value added analysis of student's progress using grade 6 and grade 9 national tests. It has commissioned research from Warsaw University on assessing value added by schools and by individual teachers and uses this information to monitor schools and encourage improvement, through some targeted programmes. The vice-mayor is in favour of *gminas* having a stronger role in monitoring school quality and devising their own policies for school improvement. It was stated that Kwidzyn's results are the best in the *voivod* but this has not been verified. Generally in Kwidzyn, the *kuratorium* was seen as distant and not particularly useful. Another key strand is improving teacher quality,

Table 6.8. Kwidzyn City *Gmina*: Budget for *Gimnazjum* 2 (2007)

Expenditure item	Amount (zł)	Percentage of total
Rewards & expenses not included in salaries	10,700	0.3%
Salaries	2,330,890	65.8%
Additional annual pay	186,800	5.3%
ZUS (social insurance)	419,320	11.8%
Unemployment insurance	57,110	1.6%
PEFRON	2,800	0.1%
Personnel costs not related to pay	350	0.0%
Social fund	128,210	3.6%
Materials and equipment	82,111	2.3%
Teaching aids and books	43,500	1.2%
Energy	164,000	4.6%
Sanitation	2,400	0.1%
Other services	57,700	1.6%
Internet	10,761	0.3%
Mobile telephones	980	0.0%
Landlines	9,400	0.3%
Domestic services	5,000	0.1%
Other items	6,600	0.2%
Professional training	1,500	0.0%
Stationery and printing	6,000	0.2%
Licences	2,000	0.1%
Capital works and repairs	13,500	0.4%
TOTAL	**3,541,632**	**100.0%**
Salaries as % total		**88.2%**

Source: Kwidzyn, *Gimnazjum* 2 Krajowa Armia.

for example by encouraging professional development: when it was short of ICT teachers it set up a center where teachers were trained.

Among those interviewed in the *gmina* there was a consensus that the voucher is equitable because it is objective and cannot be subject to personal influence. The salary part is adjusted to take account of differences in costs due to size (for one school which the *gmina* considers necessary for its community), differences in teacher qualifications and due to integrated classes at some schools. Three of the four primary schools had very similar per student allocations ranging from 3665 *Złoty* per student to 3712 *Złoty*; the primary school with integrated classes cost 4320 *Złoty* per student. Two *gimnazjums* cost 3800 and 4050 *Złoty* per student but the smallest one with only 261 students was allocated 4962 *Złoty* per student. Therefore the formula is horizontally equitable in allocating similar amounts per student for schools in the same grade range and only allocating more if a school has integrated classes or is particularly small.

6.4.1.4. Kwidzyn: Concluding Remarks

Kwidzyn has a reputation as a progressive *gmina* that has developed an active and effective role in managing its schools. The *gmina* has responded to demographic decline by rationalizing its school network to some extent. Funding schools by voucher makes the per student costs of each school transparent and informed decisions about closing or retaining higher costs schools. The voucher method enables the *gmina* to allocate the primary and *gimnazjum* schools a lump-sum budget, which encourages efficient budget management by school directors who have to purchase the needs of their school within the budget allocated to them. The voucher together with a degree of parental choice and public information about test results places some competitive pressure on schools. By commissioning value added analysis of student attainment the *gmina* has appreciated the role of social factors in determining student attainment and is beginning to address some of these issues with targeted programmes.

Kwidzyn provides an example to other LGs of how horizontal equity and efficiency can be promoted through a system of formula funding and school based financial management. Its formula has evolved over many years and is now more sophisticated than earlier versions.[22] However, Kwidzyn was not able to adopt a voucher system for its upper secondary sectors—run by the Kwidzyn *powiat*—and had to withdraw it after one year because one of the two schools was not financially viable if funded by the voucher but also was not feasible to close. Kwidzyn therefore doubts that a 'voucher' system, even one that is not a pure per student formula, is suitable for *gminas* with very few schools or with schools that have widely dispersed unit costs.

6.4.2. Czosnów Rural Gmina: Example of Input-Based Budgeting

Czosnów is a rural *gmina* about 30 km from Warsaw, with 8,500 inhabitants in an area of 140 square kilometres. At 68 residents per square km its density is average for a rural *gmina*. It provides a good example of the most common approach to school financing used by Polish LGs—an input-based, individually negotiated school budgeting system. Mainly agricultural, Czosnów is experiencing an increasing an inflow of residents from Warsaw in new housing developments. In the 2006/7 school year there were 819 students in seven schools, or an average of 117 students per school. The *gmina* has experienced a sharp decline in the number of students, which has fallen by 16 percent since 2001.

Table 6.9. Czosnów *Gmina*: Education Expenditure and Budget Revenue

Budgetary Concept	1998	2004	2006
Total budget revenues	9,113,790	17,385,838	20,240,439
Receipts from education	124,357	46,512	234,963
Education subvention from state budget	2,315,095	3,909,769	3,863,785
Total revenue for education	**2,439,452**	**3,956,281**	**4,098,748**
Total expenditure	**8,903,084**	**16,507,157**	**20,860,975**
of which on education	3,638,378	6,048,365	8,285,049
of which on primary and *gimnazjum* schools	NA	NA	6,664,773
Total education spending as percentage of total expenditure	40.9%	36.6%	39.7%
Primary and *gimnazjum* expenditure as percentage of total expenditure	NA	NA	31.9%
Percentage of education spending funded by subvention	63.6%	64.6%	46.6%
Percentage of primary and *gimnazjum* spending funded by subvention	NA	NA	58.0%

Source: Data supplied by Czosnów *gmina*.

When the education system was restructured in 2001/2 the *gmina* decided not to create a separate *gimnazjum* but to create *gymnazjum* and primary schools in the same buildings as the previous grade 1-8 primary schools had occupied. There is a school for each settlement, the distance between the nearest schools being 5 km and the furthest distance 8 km. The terrain is flat and the roads in quite good condition. Czosnów is therefore a good example of a *gmina*, which chooses to maintain a costly school network.[23]

6.4.2.1. THE EDUCATION BUDGET

In 2006 Czosnów received 3.86 m zł in education subvention.[24] Table 6.9 shows that Czosnów spent 8.3 m zł on education that year, which made up 40 percent of its total expenditure. Spending on educating students in grades 1 to 9 in its seven schools was 6.7 m zł. The subvention funded 58 percent of spending on grade 1 to 9 students' direct education costs in schools: this is reduced to 47 percent of total education spending in 2006, compared to over 60 percent of education spending in 1998 and 2004. This decline is largely due to the steady fall in the number of students, which reduced the subvention while the *gmina* maintained class and teacher numbers.

6.4.2.2. HOW SCHOOLS ARE FUNDED IN CZOSNÓW

The method of funding schools in Czosnów is the one most commonly found in Poland. Each year the *gmina* agrees a budget with the school director, who initially proposes a budget. The number of teaching hours per school are determined by the school's organizational plan which reflects the subject hours specified by MEN and any additional hours determined by the *gmina* (e.g. school 4 receives 10 additional hours). *Gminas* have discretion in determining policy for the values of the additions to teacher pay, which are set out in the Teachers' Charter. Teachers' basic pay and various supplements are shown in Table 6.10.

Because the school is the only focus for social life in the village, schools remain open for after school extra-curricular activities. This is funded both by the *gmina* and by parents from voluntary contributions, which are around 50 zł per student. The number

Table 6.10. Czosnów *Gmina*: The Composition of Total Teachers' Salaries (2006)

Type of salary payment	Amount (złotys)	Proportion of total pay (%)
Basic pay	1,914,740	58.49
Annual bonus	305,608	9.34
Extra hours	377,503	11.53
Supplement for 7 directors	67,200	2.05
Supplement for form tutors	48,350	1.48
Supplement for professional development	4,840	0.15
Supplement for curriculum advisers	10,032	0.31
Supplement for a specialist	240	0.01
Supplement for motivation	74,388	2.27
Supplement for extra tasks	928	0.03
Other	69,733	2.13
Various rewards	399,861	12.22
TOTAL	**3,273,423**	**100.00**

Source: Data supplied by Czosnów *gmina*.

of non-teaching staff is determined by the *gmina* but is historically based on the number already in post at each school. For example school 4 with around 140 students has one secretary, two cleaners, and one handyman. Basic pay rates are set nationally. The non-staff part of the school budget is proposed by the school director and agreed with the mayor. The costs of utilities are estimated from the previous year's expenditure. For other items, such as teaching aids, equipment and library books, the school director has to make a case to the mayor. Schools also raise some revenue of their own. Apart from voluntary contributions from parents both in money and in kind (e.g. decorating their child's classroom), schools rent premises and obtain the revenue in their budgets or run a small shop. Sponsors are actively sought. For example school 3 had successfully applied to the national lottery fund for money to buy an interactive white board.

Each school director presents the annual budget plan to the school council, who discuss it. However, this is their only involvement as the school council has no decision-making powers with respect to budget planning or execution and does not monitor the budget through the financial year.

Total expenditure on primary and *gimnazjum* schools is shown in Table 6.11. Almost 89 percent of recurrent expenditure goes on salaries and only 5.2 percent on teaching aids, equipment, and library books. As in the rest of Poland, parents have to supply textbooks, though the *gmina* provides poor households with financial assistance for this based on MEN's funding for support programmes. The *gmina* spends generously on

Table 6.11. Czosnów *Gmina*: Total Actual Expenditures of Schools (2006)

	Primary grades		*Gimnazjum* grades	
Expenditure item	Amount (zł)	Percent of total	Amount (zł)	Percent of total
Welfare benefits	2,263	0.0%	0	0.0%
Salaries	2,200,416	45.5%	1,253,907	68.4%
Additional annual pay	168,914	3.5%	100,658	5.5%
ZUS (social insurance)	401,286	8.3%	234,677	12.8%
Unemployment insurance	54,619	1.1%	32,563	1.8%
Personnel costs not related to pay	4,472	0.1%	2,686	0.1%
Materials and equipment	125,860	2.6%	69,228	3.8%
Teaching aids and books	50,654	1.0%	26,562	1.4%
Energy	112,392	2.3%	62,073	3.4%
Repairs	19,474	0.4%	13,893	0.8%
Other services	41,982	0.9%	27,673	1.5%
Internet	5,196	0.1%	4,629	0.3%
Domestic services	5,733	0.1%	3,532	0.2%
Other items	2,831	0.1%	1,600	0.1%
Total recurrent expenditure	3,196,092	66.2%	1,833,681	100%
Capital works (investments)	1,635,000	33.8%	0	0.0%
TOTAL	**4,831,092**	**100.0%**	**1,833,681**	**100.0%**
Salaries as % total		58.6%		68.4%
Salaries as % recurrent		88.6%		68.4%

Source: data supplied by Czosnów *gmina*.

renovating schools, this being 25 percent of total spending on schools in 2006. All the school buildings have been refurbished in the last 10 years and, in contrast with the period before the *gmina* ran schools, are now in a good state of repair. Schools are able to meet their running cost but are limited in their ability to spend on learning resources and it is for these that the two schools visited felt inadequately resourced.

6.4.2.3. ASSESSMENT OF THE EFFECTS OF THE FINANCING REFORM IN CZOSNÓW

Czosnów runs a high unit cost school network because its school are small and have declining student rolls, as shown in Table 6.12. Due to housing developments the number of children is predicted to grow in the next few years with a rise in the demand for kindergarten places which the *gmina* does not yet supply in sufficient numbers. Because its schools are small, the *gmina* has low student-teacher ratios and relatively low ratios of students to non-teaching staff, as shown in Table 6.13. Its student-teacher ratio at 7.5 is just about half of Kwidzyn's. Similarly the student-staff ratio for administrative and other staff is also about half those of Kwidzyn. Basically, Czosnów could, if starting from scratch, educate all its students in a single school.

Table 6.12. Czosnów *Gmina*: Student Rolls, 2001/2 to 2006/7

School	2001/2	2002/3	2003/4	2004/5	2005/6	2006/7
1	151	154	154	152	145	151
2	161	152	150	140	141	120
3	166	173	167	157	136	139
4	143	143	144	131	139	136
5	139	130	133	134	129	123
6	123	114	108	89	84	73
7	97	89	90	80	74	83
TOTAL	980	955	946	883	848	825
Percentage change		-2.6	-0.9	-6.7	-4.0	-2.7

Source: Data supplied by Czosnów *gmina*.

Table 6.13. Staffing Ratios at Czosnów Schools Compared to Kwidzyn Ones (2007)

		Administrative staff		Other staff		Teachers	
School	No. students	FTE	Students per staff	FTE	Students per staff	FTE	Students per teacher
1	151	0.63	240	4.13	36.6	16.6	9.1
2	120	0.88	136	3.13	38.3	16.2	7.4
3	139	0.63	221	3.13	44.4	15.8	8.8
4	136	0.63	216	3.63	37.5	14.7	9.3
5	123	0.63	195	3.13	39.3	16.5	7.5
6	73	1.25	58	2.63	27.8	13.1	5.6
7	83	0.63	132	3.13	26.5	16.1	5.2
TOTAL	819	5.3	155	22.9	35.7	108.8	7.5
Kwidzyn	4,365		321		81.6		14.9

Source: Czosnów and Kwidzyn *Gminas*.

When Czosnów's and Kwidzyn's expenditures on primary and lower secondary schools are compared—as in Table 6.14—Czosnów was spending 59 percent more per student, while it received only 27 percent more per student in subvention.

Table 6.14. Comparison of Per Student Expenditure in Czosnów and Kwidzyn (2007)

	Czosnów	Kwidzyn	Ratio Czosnów /Kwidzyn
Recurrent expenditure on primary and lower secondary per student (see Table 6.9)	5930 zł	3719 zł	1.59
Education subvention per student	4556 zł	3586 zł	1.27

Source: Czosnów and Kwidzyn *Gminas.*

As already noted, Czosnów has experienced a reduction in the proportion of its education spending funded from the subvention from 65 percent in 2004 to 47 percent in 2006. Consequently, the *gmina* decided to close the *gimnazjum* grades in the two smallest schools which from 2007/6 will revert to being primary schools. This move had been foreseen a number of years previously but the *gmina* had been waiting for a sufficient number of teachers to reach retirement age. The students will be bussed to one of the remaining *gimnazjums*, which will cost a lot less than maintaining two more *gimnazjums*. In one of the affected schools there was little parental protest, but the parents of the larger school petitioned MEN and the *kuratorium*, which supported the *gmina*, even though there are many instances when it does not agree to a school closure. The money saved will be spent on a new kindergarten in the vacated space. According to the mayor no more schools will be closed in the next 4 years, though he envisages having to close another one in 6 years time.

6.4.2.4. CZOSNÓW: CONCLUDING REMARKS

It is evident from the Czosnów case that per student funding does exert pressure on *gminas* to reduce unit costs by closing schools but this pressure is moderated by the difficulty of firing teachers (due to the provisions of the Teachers' Charter) and the resistance of parents and residents to losing the school as the perceived focus of social life in the village. Even in an area where distance between villages is relatively small and communications by road quite good, the social pressures against achieving a more efficient school network are considerable. Local democratic choice is to spend a large share of local revenues on providing a school in each village. Given this policy, the distribution of spending between schools and students is relatively equitable because each village has a school, with similarly sized classes. This would not be the case if provision were concentrated in two schools of minimum efficient size.

6.5. Assessment of Outcomes

6.5.1. Efficiency

The introduction of per capita funding is expected to improve the efficiency of a school system which was previously funded on an input basis. An efficient school system is one where costs per pupil are as low as they can be for a given quantity and quality of education. If schools are not efficient then it is possible to reduce costs per pupil without lowering pupil attainment. It is difficult to make the definition of efficiency operational when applied to education—a major reason being the difficulty of measuring schools' outputs, even if one restricted the measure to tests of student attainment. This study lacks useable data on pupil attainment, consequently the assessment of the impact of per capita funding on schools' efficiency relies on interpretations of data on per pupil costs and on factors which affect these.

As in other ex-communist countries, school resourcing during the communist period had been based on detailed input norms, a method of resource allocation used in other sectors of the economy. Schools were accustomed to receiving funding for the inputs they employed. Over time, as different central government ministries, *kuratoria* administrators and school directors negotiated marginal changes to local resourcing, the norms became less standardized nationally and funding allocations were historically based, except when some change was negotiated in some part of the system. Consequently, 'per student expenditures came to vary dramatically across schools of different types and schools of the same type in different areas of the country' (Levitas and Herczynksi (2002: 3). Up to 1999 'per student cost differences between jurisdictions remained dramatic and unjustified' (Jakubowski and Topinska, 2006:8). Warsaw provides a good example of ad hoc differences in per student costs. It consists of 18 districts, which until 2003 were separate *gminas*, each with its own accounting system, finance office, and method of allocating resources to schools. When Warsaw became a single *gmina* in 2003, per student expenditure in the lowest cost district (Ursus) was half that of the city center district.

In the early 1990s schools experienced insufficient funding to match their historical expenditure as the MoF began to insist on budgetary discipline by approving an annual budget for education, which could not be increased within the financial year (MEN, 2001). Pressure was put on MEN to cut expenditure and many schools ran up debts, in particular for social taxes and utilities. Thus, the formula began from the base of an inefficient school network due to small rural schools, ad hoc differences in per student costs for the same types of school in different localities, reflected in some areas in over-staffed urban schools.

Inefficiency was further compounded by a strong decline in the number of students over the last 15 years, which has affected both rural and urban areas including Warsaw. Between 1990/91 and 1999/2000 the number of primary pupils declined by 9 percent (680,000).[25] According to data from MEN, between 2000 and 2007 the total number of students funded by the formula declined by 1.2 million or 16 percent. Local governments have been faced with considerable resistance from parents to school closures, especially in rural areas where the school is seen as essential to the continued life of the village and where many parents place a high value on access to a nearby school. Thus, *gminas* have often been willing add from other sources of revenue up to 50 percent or more of the subvention in order to maintain existing schools in place, as in the example of Czosnów.

The formula introduced in 2000 did exert pressure on LGs to rationalize their school networks because it was genuinely per student based, and did not fully protect *gminas* from a fall in student numbers as had the earlier version of the formula. It also contained a weight for students transported to school. MEN at that time was explicit about wishing LGs to create more efficient school networks, particularly for *gimnazjum* schools. However, from 2005 to 2007 when a coalition of parties with strong rural support was in power,[26] MEN and MoF adopted the stance that school closure was a matter for LGs to determine, though as already noted, they cannot close schools without the *kuratorium*'s approval. In the *gminas* visited all had in the previous few years closed one school and in the case of Warsaw, 5. However, school closure is a contested and politically fraught issue. For example, in 2006 the then Minister of Education gave prominent public support to a group of parents protesting at the *gmina*'s proposal to close their village school. According to the financial director of Warsaw education department, 50 schools could be closed on efficiency grounds due to the decline in student numbers by 20,000 over five years but they had succeeded in closing only five. Another important factor when examining data on the changes in the number and sizes of schools is that the school reforms resulted in more and smaller schools because primary schools lost two grades, *liceum*s lost 1 grade and new three grade *gimnazjum*s were created. In Figure 6.1, the number of primary schools (*podstawowa*) can only be compared between 1994 and 1998 and between 2002 and 2006. Over both periods there was a decline in their number. Also the number of upper secondary schools has fallen at a time when the decline in the age cohort was to some extent offset by more students attending grades 11 and 12. However, against this trend was an increase in the number of *gimnazjum* schools even though the student population fell.

The structural reforms, together with the declining student numbers, have resulted in a decline in average school size. As can be seen from Figure 6.2, the number of very small primary schools (1-20 pupils) has fallen but the number with between 50 and 100 has increased, while the number in the larger size ranges has fallen due to the double impact of declining demography and the removal of two grades from primary schools. Data from GUS from 2000 to 2005 show that the number of primary schools in *gminas* declined by 10 percent while the number of classes fell by 9 percent, indicating that *gminas* were taking steps to improve the efficiency of their school networks.

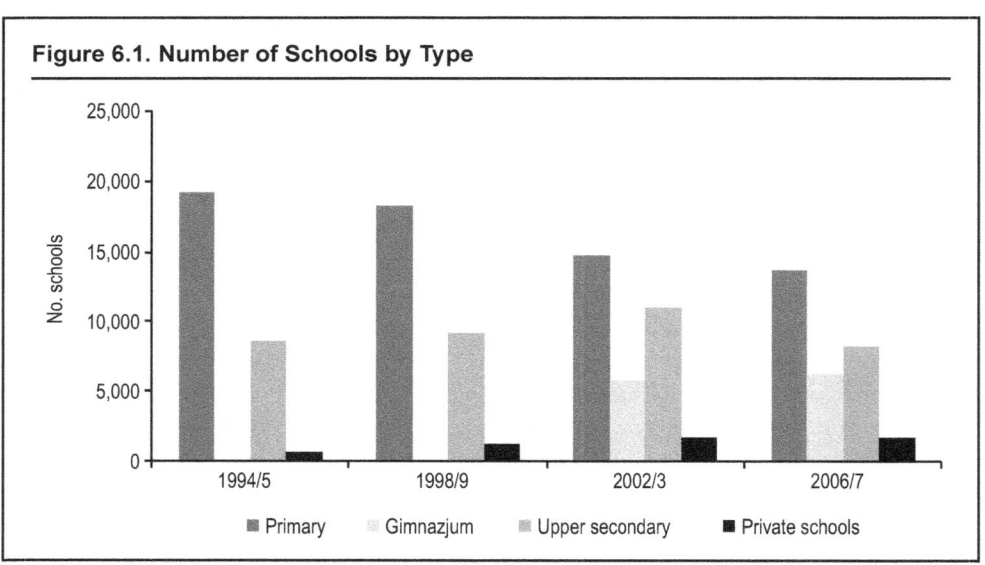

Figure 6.1. Number of Schools by Type

Source: GUS, provided by MEN.
Note: the structural reforms were complete by 2002. Private schools include all levels.

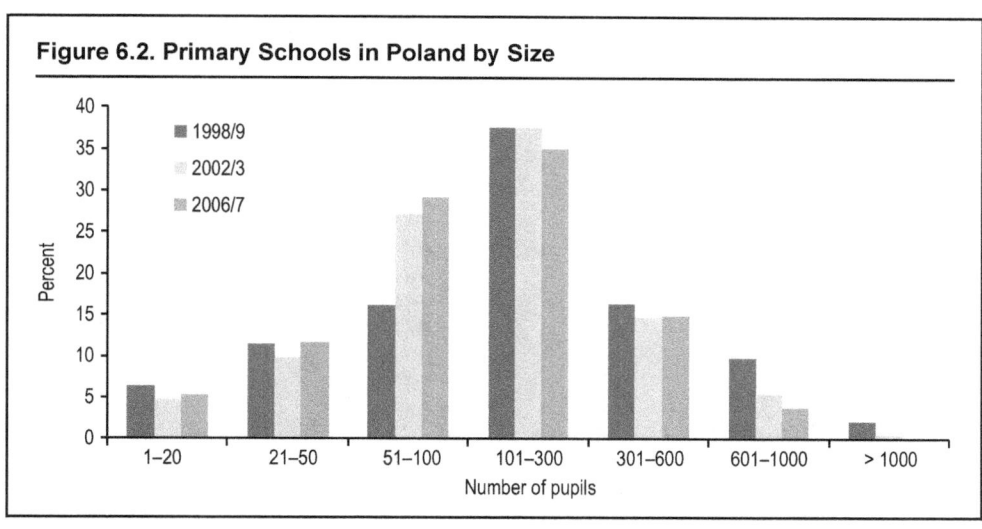

Source: MEN.

Another factor that can promote efficiency is that parents can choose a school outside their assigned area, provided it has a vacancy. This places competitive pressure on schools, particularly at upper secondary level for *liceum*s, for which there is selective entry. National examination results at the end of primary, lower secondary and upper secondary stages are now used by parents in forming judgments about school quality. Given the small size of many LGs there is considerable cross border movement of students, especially at secondary level.

As previously indicated, the Teachers Charter has made it difficult for LGs to improve the efficiency with which teachers are deployed as student numbers fall (OECD, 2006). Surplus teachers are then absorbed by creating more teaching hours by spitting classes. The data on teacher numbers are difficult to interpret because GUS (the national statistics office) has not collected data on full time equivalent teachers only on teachers with full time jobs (who could be working in excess of 18 hours).[27] MEN provided data on the total number of students from 2000 to 2007 and the total number of full time teachers but only for the current school year 2006/7. As can be seen from Figure 6.3, the ratio of pupils to teachers has declined over the period by 14 percent, while average class size over the system as a whole has remained at around 22 and has only fallen by 2 percent. 'Class' here refers to a form group (i.e. the main class to which students are assigned and not the smaller teaching groups for some subjects into which the form group may be split). These data suggest that the system has become less efficient due to the decline in the student-teacher ratio.

Overall, therefore, one can conclude that the formula, though influencing LG's decisions about school organization and resourcing, helped to counter other changes in the system which were making it more inefficient in terms of school and average class size and student- teacher ratios. However, the Teachers' Charter is seen by most experts as the main obstacle to making the Polish education system more efficient. The OECD (2006) report reflected the views of a number of experts interviewed for the study that:

> "...current regulations make the market for teachers very rigid and limit the room to manoeuvre of bodies running schools... Addition-

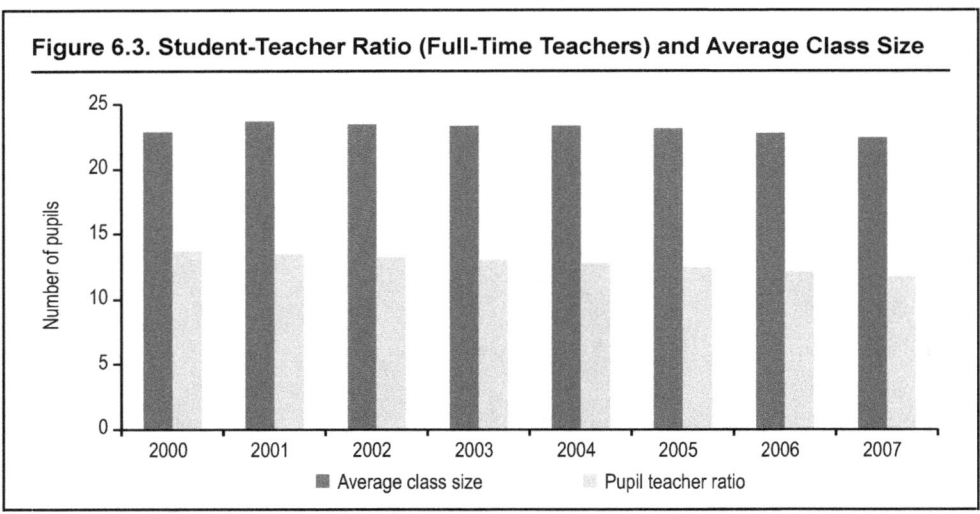

Source: MEN: teachers and students in general education in schools owned by local governments.

ally, existing rigidities in rules governing teachers' employment and incentives built into the Charter provide no monetary motivation for competition among teachers that could lead to improved quality of educational provision." (p.100).

LG management of schools has probably had more impact on improving efficiency in the use of non-teaching staff compared to the previous centrally determined norms as LGs are able to determine their own staffing. Due to the pressure on their budgets LGs have tended to eliminate unnecessary non-teacher posts and raise, for example, the work load of cleaners. Data at national level on numbers of non-teaching staff employed in schools was not available.

Generally schools are permitted to retain any underspending of the budget lines for utilities. and can shift the money to educational uses (with the permission of the *gmina*)—which is efficiency promoting. Accounting has also been rationalized and is done centrally by some LG and by schools in others. *Gminas* and *powiats* that use a formula to determine a global budget for their schools reported (e.g. Kwidzyn and Świdnica) that in the first few years school directors reduced overhead expenditures by up to 15 percent and shifted the money into learning resources.

A positive impact of decentralization is that *gminas* have invested in refurbishing, repairing, renovating and equipping their school buildings, for which central government had insufficient funds. It is generally acknowledged that Polish schools are in much better physical condition than a decade ago. However, the downside of this commented upon is that some rural *gminas* wasted capital resources by investing in new buildings for *gimnazjums*, which are under-utilized. *Powiats* are more constrained in investing in school buildings by lack of own resources. Alternative sources are private sponsors and some limited funds available from *voivods*.

There is also the issue of quality differences between schools, information about which is now becoming more available and better measured using the external test results. A particular issue of importance is whether the quality of small rural *gmina-*

administered schools is significantly lower than that of larger rural schools. This is a difficult issue to research as it requires good data on the family background of students, as studies from other developed countries show that these variables determine a much higher proportion of the variance in student cognitive attainment than school level factors. Research on attainment in Poland in relation to school size has now begun with the availability since 2002 of externally assessed and standardized attainment measures at the school level and using data from international assessments, such as PISA, in which Poland has participated. Using national test data, Herbst and Herczynksi (2004) investigated the relationship between primary school size and attainment at the school level in the grade 6 tests for schools in one *voivod*, Mazowsze. Family background was measured by parental financial contributions to the school budget per student and percentage of students in the school receiving social benefits. A non-linear relationship between school size and attainment was found, with the optimal size of primary school being about 600 students or 120 students per grade. The optimal size was reduced to 590 for schools in communities with below median average per student income, compared to 900 in richer communities. An increase in the proportion of students bussed to school had a negative association with attainment.[28] The authors conclude that there is a trade-off for attainment between the improved resources due to increasing school size on the one hand and, on the other, the negative effects of dysfunctional social interactions between members of larger and more disparate school communities and bussing more students for longer distances. Furthermore, this trade-off is different in different socio-economic contexts. However, as the average size of primary schools in Poland is around 200 students and 45 percent of primary schools have a 100 or fewer students, the evidence suggests considerable scope for further efficiency gains by closing small schools and thereby increasing the average size of school.

Clear evidence of improvements over time in the quality of education in Poland is found in the latest analysis of PISA 2006 results (OECD 2007).[29] Between 2000 and 2006 its average reading score increased by 29, with increases at all ability levels. Between 2003 and 2006 the maths score improved by 5 points and between 2000 and 2006 science rose by 9 points. Poland also found to have a relatively equitable education system in terms of PISA criteria.[30] This cannot be attributed to the school finance reforms alone (or at all) since, as summarized in the introduction, a whole set of major reforms to the curriculum, assessment and school structure were launched in the late 1990s.

6.5.2. Equity

In assessing what has been the impact of the formula on the equity of the distribution of resources, vertical and horizontal equity are considered separately.

6.5.2.1. VERTICAL EQUITY

Vertical equity is the 'unequal treatment of unequals' (Monk 1990). In particular, this term refers to providing additional funding to students with greater learning needs. The Polish formula attends to vertical equity by including a range of additional weights for pupils with various forms of special needs. However, such students are only funded if they attend special schools or centers or integrated classes in mainstream schools. Integrated classes are kept at 22 pupils or less and contain 5 to 7 children with special needs (SEN) and are taught by two teachers. The UK model of providing additional funding for individual SEN children in regular classes supported by a teaching assistant is not practiced in Poland. The weights for SEN students in the formula were generally regarded as satisfactory. However, as the OECD (2006:95) points out, weighing pupils for special needs only if they are in special schools or units encourages children to be placed in such schools or units when this may not be the best provision for them.

Additional weighting is also given to children from ethnic minorities who require additional language classes. However, there is no additional weighting within the formula for school students with learning difficulties due to socio-economic factors.[31] The influences of these factors on students' attainment are being recognized as the externally assessed test results in grades 6, 9, and 12, available since 2002, are analysed by researchers. Such evidence is beginning to be used by some LGs (e.g. Warsaw and Kwidzyn) to develop and fund special projects to improve the learning of lower attainers.

6.5.2.2. Horizontal Equity

Horizontal equity is the principle that all students with equivalent educational needs should have access to education of equal quality throughout the country (Monk, 1990). This principle is impossible to enforce when responsibility for managing and resourcing schools is decentralized to local governments who have the democratic right to determine their own level of resourcing of education, constrained by the requirement to maintain defined minimum input standards (or less frequently minimum output standards). When subsidiarity is privileged over national uniformity then the principle of horizontal equity requires that all local governments are resourced so that they are able to finance a common standard of education. Defining this standard involves an estimation of the normative need to spend on education in each LG unit, which takes into account differences in structural costs–these are costs that are beyond the control of the LG, for example due to population density, size, quality of roads, and socioeconomic conditions. Then fiscal equalization requires that each LG is resourced so that it can finance its needed expenditure. This creates a level playing field so that each LG can finance the common standard of education while its residents have the same fiscal burden as those in other areas but, in accordance with the principle of local democratic choice, can choose to spend more or less than the assessed amount of needed expenditure. Hence, when taxpayers' welfare is taken into account as well as that of the service recipients, the definition of horizontal equity is 'access to services of the same quality for the same price (tax) effort' (Bury and Swaniewicz, 2002, p.1[32]). Given the absence of a quantitative assessment of LGs' need to spend on education in Poland, other than that assumed by the formula, a rigorous assessment of the horizontal equity of the formula is not possible.

There is a process of fiscal equalization for local governments in Poland. LGs which receive in tax revenues more than 120 percent of the national average tax revenue per resident contribute to a fund which ensures that no LG receives less than 85 percent of the national average. However, fiscal equalization is restricted to revenue equalization so it is left to the formula for the education subvention to compensate for differences in spending needs.

A major cause of differences in LG spending per student is differences in school size and hence average class size between rural and urban areas. However, not all these differences are due to structural cost factors beyond the control of LGs; some are due to local choice, as with Czosnów. Therefore, one cannot use the existing school network structure in a country to assess LGs' need to spend as this makes no allowance for the potential for the school network to be rationalized, which depends on the closeness of settlements and the quality of road communications. Most of those interviewed acknowledged that the Polish formula is a relatively crude instrument for the assessment of LGs' need to spend. All rural areas and small towns of less than 5,000 inhabitants are funded the same per student amount, regardless of population density, dispersion of settlements or quality of communications or quality of the existing school buildings. Several witnesses commented that the formula is 'unfair' as in their view it allocates more to some LGs than they need and less than needed to other LGs. However, increasing the number of weights in order include more variables that cause structural cost differences between LGs would make the formula even more complex than it is. There is an inevitable trade-off between less complexity in a formula and greater inequity, because the formula fails to reflect sufficiently well differences in the cost of achieving an agreed common standard of educational provision and differences in the fiscal burden this places on local residents. Without an agreed common standard of educational provision, as is the case in Poland, it is not possible to devise a funding system that establishes, given its criteria are accepted, full fiscal equalization for local educational provision. Also, without a benchmark for a common standard of provision and how its cost varies according to structural cost factors in different LGs, it is not possible to undertake a rigorous assessment of the extent of horizontal equity (or inequity) of the funding system. All I have attempted with data readily available from the GUS website is to make a judgment about the extent to which differences in per student spending between LGs are indicative of horizontal equity or its absence.

Box 6.1. Non-Public Schools in Poland: Federation of Educational Initiatives

A promising development, which provides a solution to the high costs of *gminas* maintaining inefficiently small primary schools, is the possibility of setting up a NGO to own and run a school that the *gmina* cannot afford to maintain. This is promoted by the Federation of Educational Initiatives, an NGO set up in Poland in 1999 to sustain schools in villages. Its main objectives are to preserve the local school as the cultural heart of the village and to maintain access to rural schools near pupils' homes, rather than to run more efficient schools. The Foundation has a broader political purpose to develop civic society in rural areas through setting up rural associations, which own and manage the village school or kindergarten when the *gmina* is no longer willing to do so. By this means, active involvement of parents in running their village school is encouraged as a way of counteracting the power of the *gmina* wojts, who, it is argued, are not held sufficiently accountable for the use of their power by the electorate due to the lack of informed political engagement on the part of villagers.

A school owned by a NGO can be either public or non-public. It can be public if the NGO is supported by the *gmina*, in which case it will be funded on the same basis as the *gmina*'s schools and can receive capital funding from the *gmina*. Alternatively, an NGO can own a non-public school; in this case it can take advantage of the requirement that non-public schools, which teach the national curriculum and employ qualified teachers are entitled to be funded according to the financial standard that the formula determines for the *gmina* in which the school is located. This funding is paid to a non-public school via the *gmina*, which may contribute additional funding or resources if it so chooses. NGOs can manage a non-public school more cheaply than the *gmina* because they do not need to adhere to the Teachers' Charter. Rural association NGOs now run almost 70 kindergartens, for which EU funding is received to supplement the 75 percent of the cost that the *gmina* is required to pay, as well as around 250 small schools.[33]

(Box continues on next page)

Box 6.1 (continued)

Dłużew School is an example of a small rural school, which was taken over by an association in 2000 in order to prevent its closure by the *gmina*.[34] When the school was threatened with closure the Association of Friends of Dłużew School was established by a small group of professional people in Warsaw, whose families had originated from the village. This included descendants of the local aristocratic family, Dłużewski, who lost their lands after WWII. The Association now has about 100 members, many of whom give donations. The members elect the management committee of 11; this includes the village head—the soltis—who in Poland is directly elected by the village residents. At least 60 percent of the management committee must be from the village. When the school transferred to the Association the *gmina* gave them the school furniture and subsequently allowed the school to occupy the building rent-free. However, as the new school opened in September it received no state funding until the start of the financial year in January. In this situation appointing a school director, which is undertaken by the Association, was difficult. The director appointed has been in post since the school was founded. She is a retired director of a school in the local town who offered her services when it proved impossible to attract a suitable candidate through advertising. She is enthusiastic and dedicated to the school and its students. She spends very little of her time on financial management—this is done by the management committee who employ a private accountant (who supplied a summary of the 2007 budget).

Initially, the *gmina* was unco-operative, but since the Association has shown that it can run the school successfully the *gmina* has become supportive. It includes the school in local events and inter-school competitions and provides some financial support to the school in kind, for example it spent 50,000 zł on replacing windows in 2007. The *kuratorium* inspects the school to ensure that it teaches the national curriculum and employs qualified teachers.

The school has 40 students from Dłużew village in grades 1 to 6 organized as 5 classes. There are 9.1 FTE teachers. In addition, two hourly paid part time staff are employed—a handyman and a cook/cleaner. Parents also help in the kitchen. When the school was run by the *gmina* two more non-teaching staff were employed. Salary costs, at 2,526 zł per student, are considerably lower than in the *gmina* schools. As a comparison they are just under half of the 5,274 zł per primary student in Czosnów. Seventy six percent of Dłużew's budget is spent on salaries. Of the non-salary part, 13 percent goes on energy and 7 percent on maintenance. Thus very little is spent on learning resources and equipment for which the school relies on donations. The cost per student in 2007 was 3,332 zł. This compares with MEN's financial standard in 2007 for an unweighted student of 3,199 zł. Dłużew is located in Siennica *gmina* which has a population of nearly 7000. Siennica's subvention per student in 2007 was 3,700 zł and its expenditure per primary student was 6,276 zł. Allowing for additional *gmina* expenditure on Dłużew School of 1,250 zł (window replacement), the school costs around 4,580 per student, or about three quarters of the cost of a primary student in the *gmina*'s schools.[35]

The school director and president of the management committee maintain that the quality of teachers they employ is higher than in *gmina* schools, because they can dismiss an ineffective teacher. The teachers are said to be caring and interested in each individual child. The grade 6 results of the school in 2006 were the highest (by a small margin) of all small schools in the *voivod*.[36] Given the considerably lower cost per student at Dłużew School compared to the *gmina*'s schools and its ability to deliver good quality education, it is evidently more efficient than the local public schools. However, given the reliance on the enthusiasm and dedication of retired and part-time local teachers, who are paid less than those in public schools, it is unlikely to be a model that could be replicated on a wide scale under the current Teachers Charter.

6.5.2.2.1. Comparing Education Spending Per Student in Gminas by Type

The differences in average current expenditure per student on primary and *gimnazjum* schools (i.e. general education) in 2005 by type of *gmina* are shown in Table 6.15. Average current expenditure per student was 24 percent higher in rural than in urban *gminas* and 11 percent higher in mixed *gminas*. This compares with the subvention per student being 34 percent higher in rural *gminas* and 21 percent higher in mixed than in urban *gminas*. This shows that the relativities in spending assumed by the formula are altered by the actual decisions of *gminas*, which must reflect both differences in local preferences for education spending relative to other expenditures and in the size of *gmina* revenues. The last column in Table 6.15 shows the *gminas'* contribution to current educational spending per student (this is the difference between current general expenditure and subvention per student). In 2005, eleven percent of urban and rural *gminas* and 15 percent of mixed urban-rural *gminas* spent less per student on general education than the subvention per student.

Table 6.15. Educational Expenditure per Student (Primary and Lower Secondary) in *Gminas* in 2005, in zł

Type of *gmina* and indicator	Current general education spending per student	Capital expenditure per student	Subvention per student	*Gmina* contribution to expenditure per student
Urban: Mean	4,556	362	3,430	1,127
Range	(3,185 –10,749)	(0-3,754)	(2,770-6,146)	(-1,682 to 6,648)
Coefficient of variation	0.20 (0.23 in 2000)	1.57	0.15	0.83
Rural: Mean	5,663	546	4,605	1,057
Range	(3,638 –13,381)	(0-7,246)	(3,533-7,373)	(-2,102 to 8,048)
Coefficient of variation	0.20 (0.22 in 2000)	1.57	0.08	1.03
Mixed Urban- Rural: Mean	5,066	414	4,165	901
Range	(3,523 –11,007)	(0-5,483)	(2,992-6,411)	(-1,601 to 6,150)
Coefficient of variation	0.19 (0.18 in 2000)	1.76	0.16	1.07

Source: GUS.
Note: Current expenditure is the sum of expenditure on primary, *gimnazjum*, transport and special *gimnazjums*. MEN: subvention by *gmina*.

The range of spending per student in each *gmina* type between the highest and lowest spenders is large. As can be seen from Figure 6.4, the distribution of current spending per student has a long tail of high spending *gminas*, which spend well above the interquartile range. Comparing the coefficient of variation for general current expenditure per student in 2000 and 2005 in Table 6.15 shows that it has declined slightly over the 5 years, suggesting that the funding system has acted to reduce the dispersion of expenditure per student.

One of the main factors contributing to differences in education spending per student is differences in the amount that LGs fund from their other revenues.[37] Urban *gminas* tend to contribute the most as the average ratio of subvention to total education

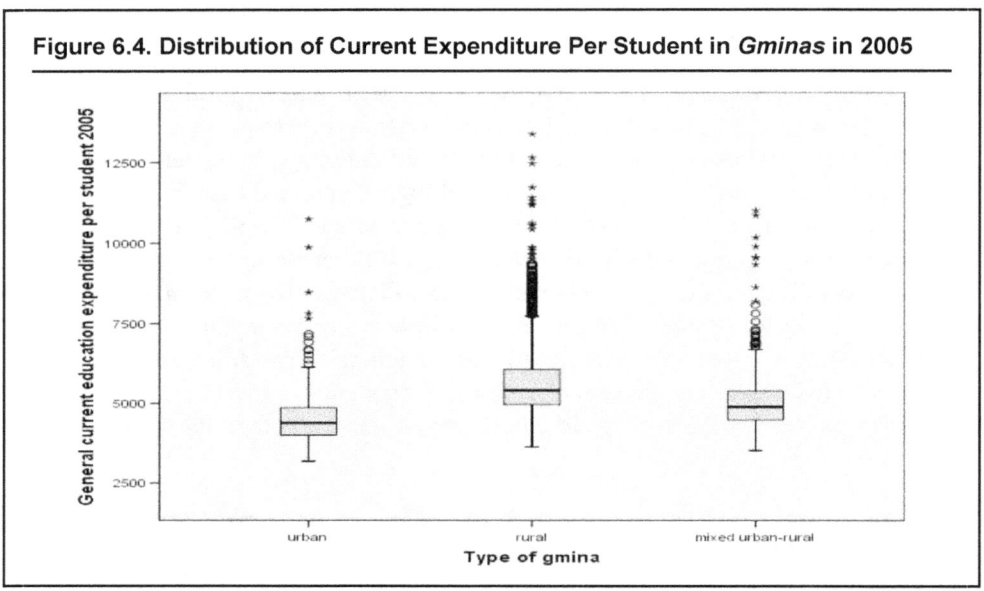

Figure 6.4. Distribution of Current Expenditure Per Student in *Gminas* in 2005

Source: GUS.
Note: the horizontal line through the box denotes the median and the vertical length of the box is the interquartile range. Observations beyond the whiskers—the vertical lines above and beneath the box- are outliers (defined to be over 1.5 box lengths from the whiskers).

spending is lowest for them at 55 percent: this compares to an average of 70 percent in mixed and 73 percent in rural *gminas*. The averages mask the considerable variation in the ratio of subvention to total education spending, which is shown for the three types of *gmina* in Figure 6.5. Here one can see that the median ratio of subvention to total edu-

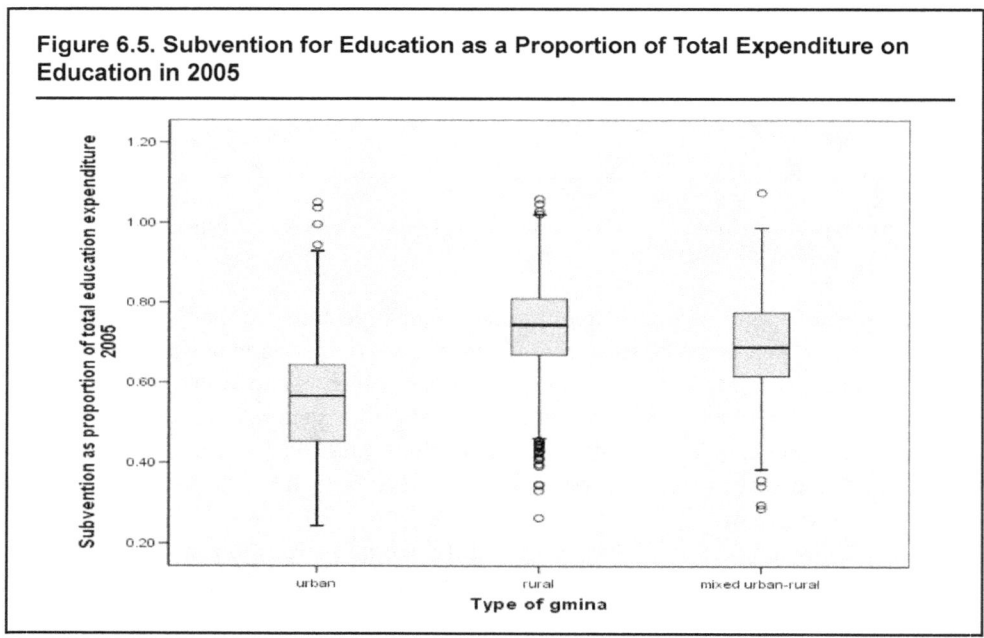

Figure 6.5. Subvention for Education as a Proportion of Total Expenditure on Education in 2005

Source: GUS and MEN.

cation spending is similar for mixed and rural *gminas* and higher than the median for urban *gminas*. But there is also considerable variation.

The extent to which *gminas* contribute to education from other sources of revenue is seen in Poland as an indicator of the success of school financial decentralization because *gminas* have been prepared to invest more in school facilities than central government was able or willing to in the past. It is observed that schools are much better maintained and physically resourced than a decade ago due to the contributions of *gminas* to capital expenditure and other non-staff expenditures. However, if *gminas*' additional spending on education over and above the subvention is related positively to their per capita revenues from their own resources, then there is a degree of horizontal inequity as the quantity of education resources that a student receives then varies according to income levels in their *gmina*.

Differences in spending per student can be consistent with horizontal equity if these differences are due only to structural cost differences. Differences in spending per student that vary directly with *gminas*' own revenues (from local taxes, share of national income and corporation tax, fees, rents and charges) are not consistent with horizontal equity. The same is the case with differences due to local preferences for collective spending, though it is usual to regard inequalities in consumption that are due to differences in income as indicative of an inequitable distribution and not to make this judgement about differences in consumption between individuals (or local governments) due to preferences.

The distribution of *gmina* income per capita (this is all sources of revenue including subventions) is shown in Figure 6.6. The interquartile range of incomes is compressed and the mean incomes of urban, rural, and mixed *gminas* are not dissimilar (at 2,015, 1,856, and 1,804 zł respectively in 2005) but there are some high outlying values.

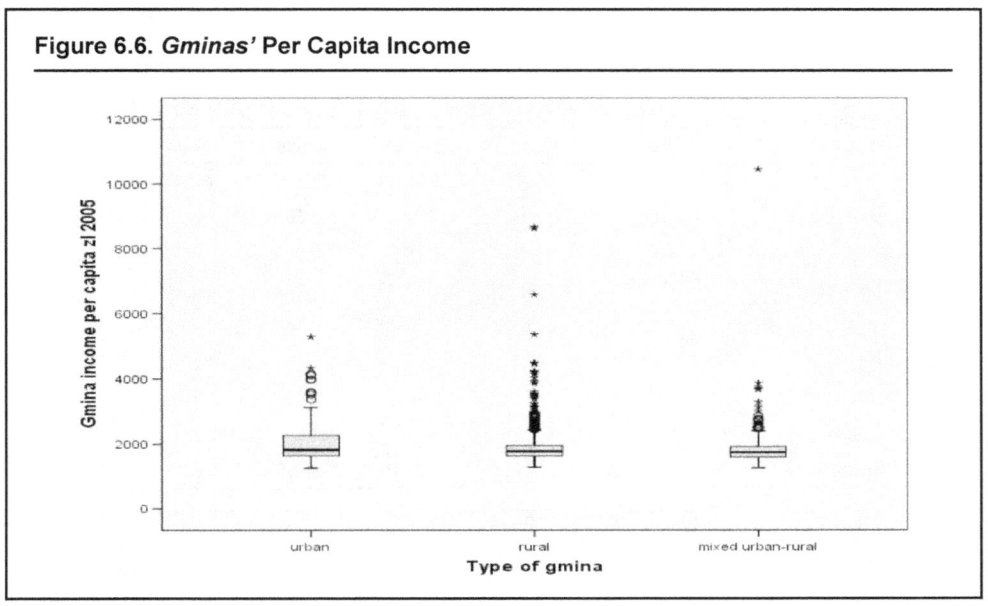

Figure 6.6. *Gminas'* **Per Capita Income**

Source: GUS. Note: the case number of outliers is given.

The extent to which variations in per student expenditure can be explained by differences in *gmina* own revenues per capita after controlling for structural cost differences can be tested using data available from GUS (National Statistical Bureau). These data include some indicators of structural cost differences, namely population density, size of *gmina*, average size of school, and the student-teacher ratio. The last two factors are amenable to local choice and therefore are not purely structural factors, but they were the best indicators of structural costs available. For this reason two sets of regressions were run, including and excluding these two variables. The data available from GUS on variables influencing *gminas*' structural costs are limited and do not include differences in local wage costs. However, there is 'in practice very little geographic variation in teachers' salaries' (OECD:2006). Given the lack of data on the regional wage rates, 15 dummy variables were included to take account of *voivod* fixed effects, which would include regional wage differences and Warsaw was excluded. Clearly, it would be preferable to have a wage index at *gmina* level had this been available.

A simple regression was run for each type of *gmina* to see whether differences in current general expenditure per student were associated with structural factors, or with financial factors, including the subvention per student and *gmina* own revenue per capita (i.e. per resident). The results are reported in Table 6.16.

Model 1 includes only structural factors (i.e. those that the *gmina* cannot influence)—total population and population density, which are likely to affect per student costs through resulting in small schools—as well as subvention per student and *gmina* own revenues per capita. In all three types of *gmina*, the association between per student expenditure and *gmina* own revenue per capita is statistically significant and positive. In rural *gminas*, expenditure per student is, as expected, higher when population density is lower. Also in rural *gminas* the size of the *gmina* in terms of population is positively

Table 6.16. Factors Explaining Current General Education Expenditure Per Student in Different Type of *Gminas*

Unstandardized coefficients reported	Model 1: Structural Variables and Revenues			Model 2: Includes Non-Structural Cost Factors		
	Urban	Rural	Mixed	Urban	Rural	Mixed
Constant	2546***	1456***	2974***	4995***	4514***	5285***
Population per square km	-0.047	-1.634**	-0.020	-0.004	0.024	0.51
Total population	-0.001	0.029***	-0.003	-0.001*	0.026	0.00
Subvention per student	0.198**	0.896***	0.465***	0.119	0.787***	0.39***
Own revenue per capita 2005	1.33***	0.258***	0.572***	1.16***	0.240***	0.58***
Student-teacher ratio	-	-	-	-110.2***	-166.7***	-129.8***
Average school size	-	-	-	-0.732*	-2.096***	-0.99
Number of *gminas*	290	1534	551	287	1532	548
Adjusted R-square	0.453	0.163	0.226	0.495	0.238	0.273

Note 1: 15 dummy variables for *voivod* fixed effects are included but the coefficients are not reported to save space; Warsaw is also excluded in to allow as far as possible, given the limitations of the dataset, for differences in regional wage costs.
Note 2: Student-teacher ratio is for 2002 since later data on teachers were not available from the GUS website. Number of teachers is full time teachers plus 0.5 x part time teachers.
*** indicates statistical significance at 0.001, ** at 0.05 and * at 0.10.

associated with higher per student expenditure. Model 2 controls also for cost factors that *gminas* are able to influence in the longer run: these are average school size and the student-teacher ratio. In all types of *gmina* and as would be expected, a lower student-teacher ratio is associated with higher costs. In rural and urban *gminas* differences in average school size are also associated with differences in per student spending. Of particular interest for assessing whether the funding system is horizontally equitable is the result that, controlling for factors that influence costs and the subvention per student, *gminas*' revenue per capita still had a strong influence on expenditure per student. In urban areas an increase in 1 zł in per capita own revenue was associated with 1.16 zł increase in spending per student. The size of the coefficient was smaller in mixed urban-rural *gminas* where the additional spending rises by 0.58 zł, but only by 0.24 zł in rural *gminas*. The smaller relative size of the coefficient in rural *gminas* compared to urban could be explained by the fact that some rural *gminas* with high cost school networks but comparatively low own revenues per capita, feel constrained to continue with relatively high per student expenditure. Differences in subvention per student have no association with spending per student in urban *gminas*, in contrast to mixed and rural *gminas*. In the latter the association is quite large, with a 1 zł increase in subvention being associated with 0.79 zł increase in expenditure per student. Running the same regressions for capital spending found it associated positively with own revenue per capita but not with the subvention or any of the other variables.

The evidence indicates that the school funding system is not horizontally equitable, since *gminas*' own revenues per capita influence spending per student, particularly in urban *gminas*. Similar findings are reported by Jakubowski and Topinska, 2006. The positive relationship between *gminas*' revenue per capita (fiscal capacity) and expenditure per student is what would be expected when the formula itself does not include weights for low income per capita or other indicators of social disadvantage.

6.5.2.2.2. Horizontal Equity within Local Governments

There is also the question of whether the funding mechanism has encouraged LGs to reduce inequalities in expenditure per student within their school system. With respect to upper secondary schools, the formula in 2000, rationalized funding by creating a more uniform set of weights for vocational schools and thus encouraged *powiats* to reduce per student funding differentials. The 2000 formula also reduced the differential between primary and upper secondary funding and introduced a small additional weight for post-*gimnazjum* students. Both the large urban *gminas* visited—Kwidzyn, by using a funding formula, and Warsaw—had reduced per student funding differentials between the same types of school.

Warsaw is an interesting case of a city seeking to equalize funding between schools. In 2003 the separate *gminas* surrounding Warsaw central *gmina* were amalgamated into one *gmina* with the status of a *powiat*. Since then Warsaw has around 250,000 students in 18 districts which administer its 1200 schools and kindergartens and manage the schools' accounts. The districts Warsaw inherited had quite different administrative systems, while the highest cost central district spent twice as much as the lowest spending outer district and even within the central district there were considerable differences in per student costs for equivalent types of school. The education department is working to reduce these differences year by year but it is quite difficult due to parental opposition when schools are threatened. The financial director estimated that it would take 8 years to even out spending between districts. At present Warsaw does not operate a formula because the cost differentials between schools are too great.

So while horizontal equity is not fully attained by the school funding system in Poland, it has worked to reduce horizontal inequities in funding between similar schools and has encouraged some LGs to do the same within their jurisdictions. Because expenditure data at the school level is not published nationally, but only reported in LG budgets, it is not possible to asses in how many LGs there has been a narrowing of differentials since the introduction of per student funding.

6.5.3. Transparency and Accountability

Another anticipated outcome of introducing per capita funding of education is better transparency and accountability. These are closely related. Transparency in this context is the degree to which information about how much is spent on schools individually as well as collectively, by whom and on the reasons for decisions about the amounts and types of resources schools receive. Accountability refers to procedures by which persons responsible for allocating and using school resources are required to justify their decisions to to others. Transparency, by putting informationn in the public domain, makes it easier to hold responsible persons to account. In examining transparency and accountability in the school finance system, first central govenment will be consdered and then the financial flows followed to LGs and finally to school level.

The formula and the processes by which it is annually reviewed have considerably improved the transparency of the allocation of finance from central governmment to local administrative units. In the communist period a number of ministries, apart from MEN, were involved in the administration of secondary education level institutions offering various vocational specialisms and the decision process was internal to the ministries and the *kuratoria* in the *voivod*s. In contrast, the major developments of the formula and its annual revisions are negotiated with the Commission for Central and Local Government. The intensity of its work varies from year to year depending on whether major changes are being considered. In 2005, for example, eleven different propositions were considered by the Commission. There is considerable disagreement within the Commission as the interests of the different types of local government differ[38] and the resolution of these differences are reflected in the final agreement on the weights in the formula. The Commission also decides on local governments' applications for additional funding from the reserve, which is 0.6 percent of the total subvention. The analytical requirements of the process of designing and maintaining a funding formula for education have led over the years to considerable improvements in the collection and use of data on school inputs and costs. For instance, in the past MEN did not know how many teachers were employed nationally or by each local government. MEN now has a statistical information system (SIO) and is able to provide data for the most recent year on full time equivalent teachers.

The total of the educational subvention is stated within the annual state budget and approved by Parliament (Sejm). This amount cannot be increased during the financial year unless this has been provided for in the annual budget law. MEN issues an annual regulation detailing the formula. It also sends a long letter to the local governments explaining the changes in the formula and produces a document detailing the subvention allocations. The Local Government website shows how the subvention for a local governmetn is calculated. At the end of the finacial year MEN prepares a report to Parliament on the execution of its budget. However, the complexity of the formula, with 46 weights in 2007, limits transparency as the formula is difficult to understand for those not intimately involved in it. For example, a wójt in a rural *gmina* was under the impression that rural areas did not receive an additional weighting. A further issue, raised by a number of interviewees, is the lack of an 'education standard', by which is meant a standard for the resources that a school of given type and size should receive. This has been under discussion for some time and a standard was briefly legislated for around 2001. It was found difficult to implement and was subsequently dropped. When there is no agreed national standard and it is maintained that the principle of local self-determination requires this to be determined locally and not set nationally, it is more difficult to hold *gminas* to account for the quality of education they provide via their financing decisions.

Transparency at local level is manifested through the local government budget setting. All LGs discuss the annual school budgets in council where they are agreed as part of the LGs annual budget. LGs that have their own formula, have a transparent method of allocation. In LGs with only a few schools, the budget of each school is agreed between the school director and the mayor (wójt in rural areas), who therefore has close knowledge of each school's finances. The school budget is largely determined by the annual organizational plan, which is a legal requirement and must conform to regulations regarding the curriculum. School councils are presented with the school's annual budget plan and ratify it, but they have no executive authority over the school budget and do not monitor it at regular intervals. This lack of involvement of school council members therefore limits transparency at local level. Information about the budgets of individual schools is therefore not widely publicly available and is not collected and published in any systematic way.

Accountability for education is a complex issue that cannot be adequately examined here. In Poland it is difficult to discern clear lines of accountability that link the quality of education to the spending of the public funds allocated for that purpose. There is a division of responsibility in that, in principle, MEN and the *kuratoria* are responsible for the quality of education, and local governments for the financing of schools. *Gminas* are held accountable for school resourcing by their electorates while the school and school director are inspected and evaluated by the koratorium. As the OECD (2006:101) comments "the position of *kuratoria* in the governance of education is ambiguous." As far as standard accountability for financial probity is concerned, LGs' education spending is audited along with other expenditures. Currently in Poland there is only internal auditing of local governments conducted by a regional accounting chamber in each *voivod*. An ICT system provides financial reports on LGs to the Ministry of Finance. LGs can contract private accountants for an external audit but this is not obligatory.

Since the introduction of national tests at the end of primary (grade 6) and end of lower secondary (grade 9) in 2002 and the nowa *matura* at grade 12 in 2005, and the publication of results at school level by the press, these measures are used to judge the relative quality of schools by parents and schools themselves.[39] As is well known, raw test results, which are not adjusted for prior attainment and/or home background factors, which are the major determinants of students' cognitive attainment', are misleading indicators of schools' effectiveness. Such value added analyses are beginning in Poland.[40] Some have been commissioned by larger LGs - Kwidzyn and Warsaw for example.

Kwidzyn has started to use value added test results in assessing schools and school directors. Both LGs are using value added evidence in order to inform the design of additional educational programmes for students from more disadvantaged backgrounds. Thus, the larger LGs are beginning to link educational and financial accountability and, in doing this, are utilising information on student attainment created by central government assessment policies. These developments result in the questioning of the usefulness of the current role of the *kuratoria* in securing educational accountability and prompt debates about how the current separation of financial and educational accountability can be reformed.

6.6. Conclusions

Every per student school funding system has a set of constraints that are binding in the sense that they determine certain costs or limit certain revenues at school level. Unless a per student funding formula can perfectly reflect the amount of funding that each school needs to be adequately funded, there has to be some flexibility that moderates the effects of the per student funding formula by adjusting school costs or their revenues or both to ensure that the school is financially viable. If there is not, the school either runs up debts or has to cut back on resources below the adequate amount or is rescued by being funded outside the formula, which undermines the formula's integrity. Some flexibilities are crucial to ensure that a per student funding system delivers adequate funding to most schools. If some schools do not receive adequate funding to cover their costs then these should be schools the education authorities wish to close, merge or change in some way to improve the efficiency of the school network. Table 6.17 summarizes these constraints and flexibilities for the Polish school finance system.

The most important flexibility in the Polish per student funding system is that *gminas* possess resources of their own, which they can choose to spend on education.[41] Other flexibilities are that *gminas* can determine non-teaching staff and non-staff expenditures. A further flexibility that has considerable potential for resolving the problem of unaffordable high cost rural schools is turning them into public schools run by NGOs or into non-public schools, which are funded from the formula.

Overall, one can conclude that per student funding has been generally successful in Poland. While there are continual arguments about the relative amounts that central and local governments contribute and how the weights favor different types of LGs, these debates are well institutionalized and a normal part of a plural society. There is no general desire to drastically reform the formula, though ideas from different perspectives about a voucher system or abolishing the subvention, or central government fully funding teachers are discussed. Per student funding was driven by the prior determination to decentralize power to local government units and not by educational imperatives. Thus, the main function of per student funding is to distribute a central pot of funding among LGs according to a negotiated agreement about legitimate differences in relative costs of different forms of educational provision. Though the formula has brought about greater fairness in local government funding for education through the applications of a consistent set of rules, the funding system remains horizontally inequitable due to a number of factors. The formula does not distinguish between rural and small town *gminas* with different structural cost characteristics, the local government finance system is not sufficiently equalizing, and LGs have different preferences for the priority given to education.

Table 6.17. Constraints and Flexibilities in the Polish School Funding System

Constraints	Flexible Elements
The total subvention made available by the Ministry of Finance and the amount allocated to each local government by the formula are fixed.	Local governments have their own resources, which they can add to educational spending, but *powiats* rely mainly on the subvention.
	There is a small amount reserved and allocated according to LG applications.
Students attending public schools are provided with free education.	Schools can collect voluntary contributions from parents and sponsors, and rent facilities.
The national curriculum specifies the number of lessons that each subject must be taught to students over a three year grade range (grades 1-3, 4-6, 7-9; 10-12).	LG can decide to provide additional lessons. MEN specifies no maximum class size.
	Small classes can be combined.
Teachers teach 18 lessons a week for a full time salary.	Local government can determine non-teaching staff expenditures.
Basic teacher salary that *gmina* must pay is determined by national legislation. Teachers can qualify for promoted posts,[42] which entitle them to higher pay, with no control over this process by the local government.	Teacher salary bonuses, representing a relatively small percentage of their salary, are determined by LG.
Only qualified teachers can be employed.	
The Teachers' Charter makes it difficult to dismiss teachers other than when a school is closed.	Schools administered by NGOs or private firms can be set up to replace a local government school and do not have to adhere to the Teachers' Charter.
Existing network of schools: A local government can only close a school if the *kuratorium* agrees.	*Gminas* can close pre-schools and can close other schools with *kuratorium's* permission.
Health and safety regulations.	

The formula has improved the transparency of education funding: the formula is publicized and is annually debated and subject to revisions in the Commission for Central and Local Government. In principle the information about the local government education funding is publicly available, however the complexity of the formula makes it inaccessible to wide audience. Local government budgets are transparent in that they are publicly debated. In local governments which use their own formula for allocating school budgets these are transparent to those who wish to get informed. Accountability has improved as local governments are accountable to their electorates for resourcing schools. As a result of external testing at grades 6 and 9, parents, *gminas* and school staff are more aware of the results achieved by individual schools. However, accountability for school outcomes is weakened by the separation of responsibilities between local governments and *kuratoria*. The former are responsible for resources but have no say over the content and delivery of education which is supervised by the *kuratoria*, who have no responsibility for resourcing schools.

A number of problems with the school funding system, however, remain unresolved. LGs have limited room to maneuver in containing school costs and creating more efficient school networks as *kuratoria* have considerable powers to determine staffing, school closures and teacher promotions. *Gminas* are also constrained by MEN agreements with the teachers' union on the level of pay, while LGs are left to foot the bill for increases in teacher salaries that may not be fully reflected in the subvention. The Teachers' Charter is an obstacle to improving the efficiency of the system. It protects teachers' jobs while teachers' pay by international standards is relatively low compared to other occupations and GDP per capita (OECD, 2006: 95), which means teaching is not an attractive profession for many graduates.

Another source of tension is ambiguity about what the subvention is supposed to cover. Unlike Estonia, there is not an explicit division of responsibilities for funding different kinds of inputs, such as teacher salaries by the government and non-teaching staff salaries and school buildings costs by the *gmina*. Local governments, therefore, complain that the subvention does not guarantee the payment of teacher salary costs, over which *gminas* and *powiats* have limited control because of the provisions of the Teachers' Charter and the need for *kuratoria* permission to close a school. There is also lack of clarity about what MEN assumes should be the cost of educating a student in specific types and sizes of schools. This ambiguity is advantageous for the central government as it does not reveal if the financial standard is insufficient for funding schools of below a specific a size because the government has not stated its view on the maximum size a school can remain financially viable. LGs would prefer the transparency of such a standard since it would assist them in making the case for school closures to local parents and laying the blame on central government.

Rationalizing the complex and differentiated funding system, especially of upper secondary schools, was a strong factor for MEN reforming the formula in 2000 so as to ensure it was based on a certain amount per student. At that period MEN did see the formula as a force for encouraging LGs to create more efficient school networks, and used the restructuring of the school system between 1999 and 2001 to reinforce this view. However, while the formula does provide efficiency incentives for LGs, especially since the buffers were removed, it is a relatively weak force to counter the political pressures from the rural lobbies for maintaining small rural schools and from the teachers' union interest in job security, which maintains higher staffing levels in urban schools. Consequently, Poland has a relatively large and poorly paid teaching force rather than a better paid but smaller one. At present there appear to be insurmountable obstacles to achieving fewer but higher paid and higher quality teachers.

Two main messages emerge from the Polish experience. Per student funding is given a strong impetus by the decentralization of the administration of schools to democratically elected local governments. When education becomes decentralized a new funding system is required and per student funding provides a fair means of allocating central government grants to local governments, into which can be built some efficiency incentives. The main role of per student funding is to function as a fair procedural rule for allocating central government grants, which are relatively objective and less subject to political-bias and non-transparent manipulation than discretionary and individually negotiated allocations. A per student funding formula can include weights for addressing vertical equity issues but it is less able to create a horizontally equitable school funding system as this depends on the rules for fiscal equalization, which govern the whole system of local government finance. Once established, the funding formula remains subject to continual change in the course of negotiations between different interests. It is to be expected that a funding formula will undergo changes–minor annual revisions interspersed by more substantive alterations.

The second message is that while per student funding can provide a stimulus to internal efficiency, this is considerably blunted when, in the context of declining student numbers, efficiency is inconsistent with other social objectives, in particular preserving rural schools and placating a strong teachers' union. The government in power at the time the data for this study were collected had little concern for the efficiency of the school system, as was indicated by ministry officials. A frequently expressed view in Poland is that decentralization implies the right of local government to operate an inefficient school network, if this is what they choose to do. By itself per student funding is a relatively weak tool for promoting efficiency: to do this it has to be accompanied by other measures which will not materialize unless there is a political will to pursue the internal efficiency of the school system at the expense of other objectives favoured by specific political interests.

References

Bramley, G. (1990). *Equalisation Grants and Local Expenditure Needs*: Avebury.

Bury, P. and P. Swianniewicz (2002). "Grant transfers in financing local government in Poland." *Paper presented at NISPAcee Annual Conference in Kraków, April 24-27, 2002. http://unpan1.un.org/intradoc/groups/public/documents/nispacee/unpan004538.pdf accessed 17/11/2007.*

Herbst, M. and J. Herczyński (2004). "Is large more effective than small beautiful? Size and performance of primary schools in Poland." *Warsaw University mimeo.*

Herczyński, J. (2004). Formulae for allocation of funds to individual schools in Poland. In R. Levacic and P. Downes, Eds. *Formula funding of schools, decentralization and corruption: a comparative analysis.* Paris: IIEP-UNESCO.

Huber, G. P., and Glick, W. H., eds. (1993). *Organisational change and redesign: ideas and insights for improving performance*: Oxford University Press.

Jakubowski, M. and I. Topinska (2006). *Impact of decentralisation on public service delivery and equity: education and health sectors in Poland: 1998-2003.* Warsaw: Centre for Social and Economic Research.

King, D. S. (1984). *Fiscal Tiers: the Economy of Multi-level Government*. London: Allen and Unwin.

Levitas, T. and J. Herczyński (2002). Decentralization, Local Governments and Education Reform in Post Communist Poland,. In Davey, Eds. *Balancing National and Local Responsibilities. Education Management and Finance in Four Central European Countries.* Budapest: OSI/LGI: 113-189.

MEN (2001). *Report on the Development of Education in Poland.* Warsaw: Ministry of National Education.

Monk, D. (1990). *Educational Finance: An Economic Approach.* New York: McGraw-Hill.

OECD (2006). *Education and Training: boosting and adapting human capital, Chapter 4 OECD Economic Surveys: Poland pp. 91-119.* Paris: OECD.

OECD (2006). *Education at a Glance.* Paris: OECD.

OECD (2007). *PISA 2006: Science Competencies for Tomorrow's World Vol 1.* Paris: OECD.

Annex A. Additional Statistics on School Funding

Table 6.18. Shares of the Education Subvention by School and Student Type in 2000

Student category	Number of students	Weight	Weighted students number	Amount per student	Total amount (thousands PLN)	% of the total subvention
Primary schools and *gimnazjums*						
Students	4,453,683	1.00	4,453,683	1,932.97	8,608,827	47.50
Students of rural schools	1,728,957	0.33	570,556	637.88	1,102,866	6.09
Students of schools in small cities	183,536	0.18	33,036	347.93	63,858	0.35
Special classes in regular schools	5,269	0.50	2,635	966.48	5,092	0.03
Integrated classes in regular schools	5,368	3.00	16,104	5,798.90	31,129	0.17
National minorities students	34,818	0.20	6,964	386.59	13,460	0.07
Students bussed to school	611,212	0.30	183,364	579.89	354,436	1.96
Sport classes and school	20,627	0.20	4,125	386.59	7,974	0.04
Sport mastery schools	556	1.00	556	1,932.97	1,075	0.01
Non-public school in rural areas	755	0.80	602	1,542.51	1,165	0.01
Non-public school in small cities	120	0.71	85	1,368.54	164	0.00
Non-public schools in cities	35,505	0.60	21,303	1,159.78	41,178	0.23
Adult students in rural areas	220	0.93	205	1,799.59	396	0.00
Adult students in small cities	71	0.83	59	1,596.63	113	0.00
Adult students in cities	5,931	0.70	4,152	1,353.08	8,025	0.04
Handicapped children in general classes	13,950	0.25	3,488	483.24	6,741	0.04
Revalidation for serious disabilities	4,050	0.50	2,025	966.48	3,914	0.02
Post *gimnazjums* school						
Number of students	2,483,132	1.00	2,483,132	1,932.97	4,799,815	26.49
Adult students in *liceums*	70,369	0.70	49,258	1,353.08	95,215	0.53
Adult students in professional schools	174,607	0.81	140,559	1,556.04	271,695	1.50
Special schools non-vocational	78,350	2.40	188,040	4,639.12	363,475	2.01
Vocational special schools	32,727	1.00	32,727	1,932.97	63,260	0.35
Vocational schools	1509,090	0.15	226,364	289.95	437,553	2.41
National minorities	2,240	0.20	448	386.59	866	0.00
Non-public *liceums* for youth	41,965	0.60	25,179	1,159.78	48,670	0.27
Non-public vocational schools for youth	38,078	0.69	26,274	1,333.75	50,786	0.28
Non-public *liceums* for adults	43,065	0.35	15,073	676.54	29,135	0.16
Non-public vocational schools for adults	121,548	0.40	48,923	778.02	94,567	0.52
Medical schools	26,903	1.00	26,903	1,932.97	52,003	0.29
Special sailors' classes	1,569	1.00	1,569	1,932.97	3,033	0.02
Teacher colleges	15,619	1.00	15,619	1,932.97	30,191	0.17
Non-public teacher colleges	1,843	1.20	2,212	2,319.56	4,275	0.02
Students of schools in rural areas	174,677	0.33	57,643	637.88	111,423	0.61
Students of schools in small cities	74,809	0.18	13,466	347.93	26,029	0.14
Non-school tasks						
Boarding houses	118,833	1.770	210,334	3,421.35	406,570	2.24
Special preschools	3,056	4.500	13,752	8,698.36	26,582	0.15
SOSW	32,990	7.370	243,136	14,245.97	469,975	2.59
Extramural education activities	7,470,892	0.010	74,709	19.33	144,410	0.80
Pedagogical advisory centers	10,080,490	0.011	110,885	21.26	214,338	1.18
Holyday centers for children	29,558	0.221	6,532	427.19	12,627	0.07
Methodological help for teachers	7,470,892	0.008	59,767	15.46	115,528	0.64
Total			9,375,445		18,122,435	100.00%

Source: Levitas and Herczyński (2002), Appendix B.

Table 6.19. Kwidzyn's Subvention for 2007 Determined by the Formula

GUS Number: 22701
Gmina: Kwidzyn   Financial standard   3,198.5263
Powiat: Pomorskie
Type of *gmina*: city   Index for teacher salaries   1.0491

		No. students	Value of weight	No. of student units	Total allocation
Pupils (of school age) attending public and non-public schools		4,409	1	4,625.5268	14,794,869.27
Adult students attending public schools		0	0.7	0	0
Adult students attending non-public schools		0	0.35	0	0
Total students for part SOA of formula (school provision)		4,409		4,625.5268	14,794,869.27
Primary and gymnazja pupils in rural local governments and town with fewer than 5000 inhabitants	P1	0	0.38	0	0
Students with moderate learning difficulties	P2	17	1.4	24.9688	79,863.44
Pupils who are blind or partially sighted, who are disabled or who have learning difficulties	P3	17	2.9	51.7211	165,431.40
Pupils who are deaf or partially deaf, or with severe learning difficulties,	P4	12	3.6	45.3216	144,962.20
Children and youths with very severe learning difficulties who attend special schools	P5	6	9.5	59.7993	191,269.57
Handicapped pupils who attend an integrated class in a mainstream school	P6	36	0.8	30.2144	96,641.47
P7 = 0.08 for pupils in post primary schools	P7	0	0.08	0	0
P8 = 0.15 for students in vocational schools	P8	0	0.15	0	0
Students from national minorities and local pupils who talk a regional dialect and need additional lessons in Polish	P9	0	0.2	0	0
The above students who receive additional lessons when there are fewer than 84 of such students in primary grades and fewer than 42 in *gymnazja* and upper secondary grades. If P10 is received then P9 is not included.	P10	0	1.5	0	0
Students in sports classes	P11	81	0.2	16.9956	54,360.83
Students in master of sports classes	P12	0	1	0	0
Students taking vocational course for the health professions	P13	0	1	0	0
Students in music schools grade 1	P14	0	1.01	0	0
Students in music schools grade 2	P15	0	1.7	0	0
Students in general in music schools grade 1	P16	0	2.01	0	0
Students in general in music schools grade 2	P17	0	3.36	0	0
Students in art schools	P18	0	0.92	0	0
Students in general fine art schools	P19	0	1.35	0	0
Students in ballet schools	P20	0	3.42	0	0
Students in teacher training schools	P21	0	1	0	0
Students in various vocational schools for medical occupations	P22	0	1	0	0
Students taking part in out of school classes organized in health institutes	P23	0	1.84	0	0
Catch up classes for pupils falling behind	P24	0	0.6	0	0
Bilingual pupils	P25	0	0.17	0	0
Students in *gimnazjum* schools	P26	1703	0.04	71.4654	228,583.92
Students taking maritime and inland waterways vocational courses	P27	0	3	0	0
TOTAL FOR CARE AND WELFARE (PART SOB OF FORMULA)				300.4861	961,112.83

		No. students	Value of weight	No. of student units	Total allocation
CARE OF CHILDREN AND YOUNG PEOPLE (SOC)					
Children who are deaf or partially deaf, blind or partially sighted, disabled, or who have severe learning difficulties who attend special kindergartens and special kindergarten classes in primary schools	P28	8	4	33.5715	107,379.41
Children cared for in boarding schools	P29	0	1.5	0	0.00
Addition to P29 if the pupils attend special schools	P30	0	0.5	0	0.00
Boarding students in various artistic fields	P31	0	3.64	0	0.00
Boarders in holiday homes	P32	0	0.2	0	0.00
Boarders in special educational centers and centers for social therapy	P33	0	6.5	0	0.00
Boarders in special care centers for young offenders	P34	0	11	0	0.00
Children attending day care centers for social therapy	P35	0	1.5	0	0.00
Boarders with severe learning problems in kindergarten classes in primary schools	P36	11	9.5	109.6320	350,660.88
Pupils who use school hostels based on number of places and months of occupancy	P37	0	0.02	0	0.00
Children who need help with development in schools and centers,	P38	2	0.84	1.7625	5,637.42
Students attending institutions providing out of school activities: based on number of students in the gmina's schools	P39	4,409	0.001	4.6255	14,794.87
Institutions providing out-of-school activities related to the national curriculum based on number of students in the powiat's schools	P40	0	0.03	0	0.00
Institutions for out of school activities based on number of students in voivod schools	P41	0	0.008	0	0.00
TOTAL FOR SCHOOL PROVISION FOR PART SOB OF FORMULA				149.5915	478,472.58
TOTAL ALLOCATION FROM THE SUBVENTION 2007					
(SOA + SOB + SOC)				5,075.6046	16,234,454.68

Table 6.20. Kwidzyn: Calculating Part A of the Voucher

TABLE 1 CALCULATING NUMBER OF TEACHER POSTS NEEDED

	PRIMARY SCHOOLS				GIMNAZJUMS		
	SP2	SP4	SP5	SP6	G1	G2	G3
Total number of students 2005/6	643	852	587	808	256	921	460
Total number of students 2006/7	600	816	525	765	261	931	467
No. lessons per week in grade 1, 2, 3 primary			24				
No. lessons per week in grade 4 & 5 primary			32				
No. lessons per week in grade 6 primary			33		Note: includes extra lessons for split classes		
No. lessons per week in grade 1 *gimnazjum*			34				
No. lessons per week in grade 2 & 3 *gimnazjusm*			35				
Number of lessons a week a full time teacher teaches is 18							

CALCULATION OF NUMBER OF TEACHING HOURS NEEDED

	SP2	SP4	SP5	SP6	G1	G2	G3
Number of students in grade 1	91	146	81	126	130	323	192
Number of classes in grade 1	3.5	5.62	3.12	5.07	5	12.42	7.38
Number of teacher hours in grade 1	84	135	75	122	170	423	267
Number of students in grade 2	103	127	81	120	70	345	120
Number of classes in grade 2	3.96	4.88	3.12	5.00	2.69	13.27	4.80
Number of teacher hours in grade 2	95	117	75	122	94	466	170
Number of students in grade 3	97	112	87	127	61	263	155
Number of classes in grade 3	3.73	4.31	3.35	5.08	2.35	10.12	5.96
Number of teacher hours in grade 3	90	103	80	123	82	354	209
Number of students in grade 4	103	140	75	132			
Number of classes in grade 4	3.96	5.38	2.88	5.28			
Number of teacher hours in grade 4	127	172	92	170			
Number of students in grade 5	110	145	94	124			
Number of classes in grade 5	4.23	5.58	3.62	4.96			
Number of teacher hours in grade 5	135	179	116	159			
Number of students in grade 6	96	145	106	136			
Number of classes in grade 6	3.7	5.6	4.1	5.4			
Number of teacher hours in grade 6	122	184	135	180			
TOTAL TEACHING HOURS	**653**	**891**	**572**	**875**	**346**	**1243**	**646**
Total number of posts	36.3	49.5	31.8	48.6	19.2	68.0	34.1
Other posts							
Librarian	2	2.5	1.8	2.5	1	2.5	1.6
Integrated class teachers	0	0	0	7	0	0	3
Child carers	1.9	2.5	1.7	2.5			
Pedagogues	1	1	1	1	1	1	1
Sports activities staff	0.6	0.8	0.5	0.8			
TOTAL TEACHING STAFF POSTS	**41.8**	**56.2**	**36.8**	**62.5**	**21.2**	**71.5**	**39.7**

TABLE 2 ALL TEACHING POSTS

	SP2	SP4	SP5	SP6	G1	G2	G3
Total number of students 2006/7	600	816	525	765	261	931	467
Total teaching positions	41.8	56.2	36.8	62.5	21.2	71.5	39.7
School directors & deputies: not <1 not >3	1.7	2.1	1.5	2.1	1	2.1	1.4
Replacement teachers	1	1.4	0.9	1.3	0.5	1.6	0.8
Total teaching posts	44.5	59.7	39.2	65.9	22.7	75.2	41.9
Others	2.2	3	2	3.3	1.1	3.8	2.1
Total teaching staff positions	46.7	62.7	41.2	69.2	23.8	79.0	44.0

TABLE 3 CALCULATING THE AVERAGE SALARY PER MONTH FOR TEACHING STAFF

	SP2	SP4	SP5	SP6	G1	G2	G3
Total number of students 2006/7	600	816	525	765	261	931	467
Basic earnings	79,254	97,760	65,782	110,267	41,468	106,606	66,608
Actual number of posts	43.8	51.3	36.5	58.3	23.5	58.6	38.1
Average basic pay	1,809	1,906	1,802	1,891	1,765	1,819	1,748
Allocated number of posts (staffing model)	46.7	62.7	41.2	69.2	23.8	79.0	44.0
Basic pay for allocated no. of posts	84,480	119,506	74,242	130,857	42,007	143,701	76,912
	84,501	119,484	74,253	130,883	41,997	143,718	76,923
Addition for number of years worked	11,250	14,778	9,431	17,638	6,749	15,149	9,419
% addition of basic pay	13.32%	12.37%	12.70%	13.48%	16.07%	10.54%	12.25%
Teacher salaries for additional responsibilities	3,466	3,669	2,655	4,219	2,514	4,671	2,550
School director supplement	1,641	1,641	1,641	1,887	1,515	1,641	1,641
Number of deputy directors	1.4	2	1.1	2	0	2	0.9
Supplement for deputy directors	1,420	2,028	1,115	2,332	0	2,028	913
TOTAL SUPPLEMENTS director & deputies	**3,061**	**3,669**	**2,756**	**4,219**	**1,515**	**3,669**	**2,554**
Form teacher supplement	1,154	1,599	1,010	1,471	502	1,790	898
Teachers' motivational supplement	3,968	4,888	3,289	5,513	2,073	5,330	330
TOTAL SALARIES	**107,379**	**148,109**	**93,383**	**163,917**	**55,360**	**174,310**	**92,663**

TABLE 4 PART A: CALCULATING PART A PER STUDENT

	SP2	SP4	SP5	SP6	G1	G2	G3
Number students	600	816	525	765	261	931	467
Total amount of basic salaries	82,232	120,802	74,880	133,188	42,007	143,701	76,912
Extra for years worked	11,250	14,778	9,431	17,638	6,749	15,149	9,419
Total supplements director & deputies	3,061	3,669	2,756	4,219	1,515	3,669	2,554
Form tutor responsibilities	1,154	1,569	1,010	1,471	502	1,790	898
Addition for motivation	3,968	4,888	3,289	5,513	2,073	5,330	330
ZUS,FP, ZFN. ZFSS (social security taxes)	41,657	52,274	34,240	61,594	23,355	63,213	36,018
Total	143,322	197,980	125,606	223,623	76,201	232,852	126,131
Anticipated increase	2,866	3,960	2,512	4,472	1,524	4,657	2,523
GRAND TOTAL	**146,188**	**201,940**	**128,118**	**228,095**	**77,725**	**237,509**	**128,654**
VALUE OF VOUCHER FOR PART A	**243.6**	**247.5**	**244.0**	**298.2**	**297.8**	**255.1**	**275.5**

Table 6.21. Czosnów's Subvention for 2007 Determined by the Formula

GUS Number: 141402
Gmina: Czosnów   **Financial standard**   3,198.5263
Powiat: Nowodworski:
Wojewodztwa: Mazowieckie   **Index for teacher salaries**   1.0933

Type of *gmina*: rural		No. students	Value of weight	No. of student units	Total allocation
Pupils (of school age) attending public and non-public schools		812	1	872.6296	2,791,128.68
Adult students attending public schools		0	0.7	0	0
Adult students attending non-public schools		0	0.35	0	0
Total students for part SOA of formula (school provision)		812		872.6296	2,791,128.68
Primary and gymnazja pupils in rural local governments and town with fewer than 5000 inhabitants	P1	812	0.38	331.5992	1,060,628.90
Students with moderate learning difficulties;	P2	1	1.4	1.504	4,812.29
Pupils who are blind or partially sighted, who are disabled or who have learning difficulties	P3	0	2.9	0	0
Pupils who are deaf or partially deaf, or with severe learning difficulties,	P4	1	3.6	3.8688	12,374.46
Children and youths with very severe learning difficulties who attend special schools	P5	2	9.5	0	0
Handicapped pupils who attend an integrated class in a mainstream school	P6	0	0.8	0	0
P7 = 0.08 for pupils in post primary schools	P7	0	0.08	0	0
P8 = 0.15 for students in vocational schools	P8	0	0.15	0	0
Students from national minorities and local pupils who talk a regional dialect and need additional lessons in Polish	P9	0	0.2	0	0
The above students who receive additional lessons when there are fewer than 84 of such students in primary grades and fewer than 42 in gymnazja and upper secondary grades. If P10 is received then P9 is not included.	P10	0	1.5	0	0
Students in sports classes	P11	0	0.2	0	0
Students in master of sports classes	P12	0	1	0	0
Students taking vocational course for the health professions	P13	0	1	0	0
Students in music schools grade 1	P14	0	1.01	0	0
Students in music schools grade 2	P15	0	1.7	0	0
Students in general in music schools grade 1	P16	0	2.01	0	0
Students in general in music schools grade 2	P17	0	3.36	0	0
Students in art schools	P18	0	0.92	0	0
Students in general fine art schools	P19	0	1.35	0	0
Students in ballet schools	P20	0	3.42	0	0
Students in teacher training schools	P21	0	1	0	0
Students in various vocational schools for medical occupations	P22	0	1	0	0
Students taking part in out of school classes organized in health institutes	P23	0	1.84	0	0
Catch up classes for pupils falling behind	P24	0	0.6	0	0
Bilingual pupils	P25	0	0.17	0	0
Students in *gimnazjum* schools	P26	306	0.04	13.1539	42,073.17
Students taking maritime and inland waterways vocational courses	P27	0	3	0	0
TOTAL FOR CARE AND WELFARE (PART SOB OF FORMULA)		X	X	370.5451	1,185,198.48
CARE OF CHILDREN AND YOUNG PEOPLE (SOC)				0	0

Type of *gmina*: rural		No. students	Value of weight	No. of student units	Total allocation
Children who are deaf or partially deaf, blind or partially sighted, disabled, or who have severe learning difficulties who attend special kindergartens and special kindergarten classes in primary schools	P28	0	4	0	0
Children cared for in boarding schools	P29	0	1.5	0	0
Addition to P29 if the pupils attend special schools	P30	0	0.5	0	0
Boarding students in various artistic fields	P31	0	3.64	0	0
Boarders in holiday homes	P32	0	0.2	0	0
Boarders in special educational centers and centers for social therapy	P33	0	6.5	0	0
Boarders in special care centers for young offenders	P34	0	11	0	0
Children attending day care centers for social therapy	P35	0	1.5	0	0
Boarders with severe learning problems in kindergarten classes in primary schools	P36	0	9.5	0	0
Pupils who use school hostels based on number of places and months of occupancy	P37	0	0.02	0	0
Children who need help with development in schools and centers,	P38	0	0.84	0	0
Students attending institutions providing out of school activities: based on number of students in the *gmina*'s schools	P39	812	0.001	0.8726	2,791.13
Institutions providing out-of-school activities related to the national curriculum based on number of students in the *powiat*'s schools	P40	0	0.03	0	0
Institutions for out of school activities based on number of students in *voivod* schools	P41	0	0.008	0	0
TOTAL FOR SCHOOL PROVISION FOR PART SOB OF FORMULA		X	X	0.8726	2,791.13
TOTAL ALLOCATION FROM THE SUBVENTION 2007 (SOA + SOB + SOC)			1,244.0474	3,979,118.29	

Annex B. List of People Interviewed for the Country Case Study

Ms. Grażyna Kida, Director of Economic Department, Ministry of Education

Ms. Zdzisława Wasążnik, Director of Department of Financing of Local Governments, Ministry of Finance

Ms. Alina Kozińska, Foundation for Education Initiatives

Mr. Sławomir Broniarz, Head of ZNP (Union of Polish Teachers)

Mr. Antoni Krężlewicz, Mayor of Czosnów *Gmina*

Ms. Katarzyna Grabska, Head of Education Department of Czosnów *Gmina*

Mr. Roman Bera, Deputy Mayor of Kwidzyń *Gmina*

Mr. Marek Olszewski, Mayor of Lubicz *Gmina* and Vice President of Związek Gmin Wiejskich (ZGW or Association of Rural *Gminas*)

Mr. M. Sielatycki, Deputy Director of Department of Education, Warsaw Municipality

Ms. Ewa Piotrowska, Director of Finance, *Kuratorium* Oświaty in Warsaw

Ms. Anna Nagraba, Director of Dłużew School

Mr. Michał Rzewuski, Chairman of Dłużew School Association.

Mr. Mikołaj Herbst, Expert on Economics of Education, Centre for Regional Studies, Warsaw University

Notes

1. I would like to thank Jerzy Wiśniewski and Małgosia Lepiech for organizing my study visit to Poland from June 12 through June 22 of 2007 and for all the people who gave so generously of their time to explain the Polish school funding system to me and show me around their schools. They are too many to name here and they are listed in Annex B. I also thank Maciej Jakubowski and Jan Herczyński for his comments. All mistakes and errors of interpretation are my responsibility.
2. In Poland, the formula is referred to as an *algorithm*. However, to be consistent with the other chapters in this book, the word *formula* will be used.
3. Initially this was 50 percent of the state subvention per student in the LG area in which the school is located and later became 100 percent.
4. The weights for pupils were for rural *gminas*: 1.86 for average class size <15, 1.44 for class size 15 to 18; 1.33 for class size >18 and 1.2 for urban *gminas* with average class size < 24; 1 for average class size equal or greater than 24 (Levitas & Herczyński 2001, p. 25).
5. The thresholds changed over time: in 1999 the upper threshold was eliminated.
6. The weight was 0.33 for pupils in schools in rural areas and 0.18 for those in small towns.
7. PiS stands for *Prawo i Sprawiedliwość* (Law and Justice Party). It was voted out of office in October 2007.
8. U_p is the sum of the number of each type of student multiplied by its weight.
9. In the rest of the chapter monetary values are given in current year prices. Inflation in the period 2001 to 2007 was 2001: 3.2%; 2002: 2.0%; 2003: 0%; 2004: 4.0%; 2005: 2.9%; 2006: 1.9% and 2007: 3.7%.
10. In 2007 *gminas* were allotted 6.71% of national corporation tax and 39.34% of national personal income tax allocated as a national average according to the number of registered tax payers. *Powiats* received 1.4% of corporation tax and 10.25% of personal tax and *voivods* 15.95% and 1.6% respectively. (Source: interview at MoF.)
11. The Union of Polish Teachers (ZNP) is regarded as strong: MEN failed to obtain an increase in the *pensum* in 2000 when the Teachers' Charter was revised.
12. All public sector employees have a legally defined basic salary for their occupation and grade. In the case of teachers there is further legislation, which permits the Minister of Education to define lower basic pay for teachers so that teachers' salary costs can be afforded within the subvention total agreed by the MoF. Teachers' salaries account for about 90% of the subvention though this varies substantially for individual LGs.
13. This evidence does not include evidence of effective teaching measured in terms of student progress in external tests or other indicators of teacher performance (OECD, 2006).
14. Nominated and diploma teachers have permanent jobs. If made redundant long-serving teachers get paid 6 months' salary. Novice and contracted teachers get nothing. Redundancy pay is paid by local government. After 30 years' work, 20 of it in class, teachers have the right to retire. If retiring and declared redundant, a teacher gets an additional 3 months' salary.
15. A case was reported of a *kurator* refusing to allow the closure of a school in his own village.
16. This may well be a desirable development.
17. The calculation of the formula for Kwidzyn is given in Table 6.19 in the Annex.
18. The Deputy Mayor, whose portfolio includes Education and Culture, used to be a teacher.
19. Interview with Mr Bera.
20. This is the way integrated special education is organized in Poland.
21. This is one of the two models of organizing school accounting practiced by local governments in Poland. It would appear to be the more common one.
22. For example compared to an earlier version described by Herczyński (2004).
23. The information on Czosnów was provided by the mayor Antoni Krężlewicz and the inspector of education, Katarzyna Grabska, as well as by the school directors and staff of the two schools, which were visited.
24. Table 6.21 shows how the formula calculated Czosnów's education subvention in 2007.
25. See Levitas and Herczyński (2002), Annex A.
26. This government failed to return to power in elections held in October 2007.
27. The GUS website accessed in June 2007 did not have data on teacher numbers after 2002.

28. This is of course not the same as estimating the effect of bussing on the students who are bussed. The variable used could be correlated with unobserved social factors, which lower attainment.
29. See OECD (2007), Tables 6.3a and 6.3b.
30. These are that the PISA index of the economic, social and cultural status of students explains relatively little of the variance in student attainment compared to other countries and that the between school variance in attainment is small relative to total variance.
31. Due to privacy laws schools cannot collect data on parents' education, occupation, or employment. However, it would be possible, as in some other countries, to use area socio-economic data. In 2001 the team of experts advising on the formula proposed replacing the weight for rural schools by a measure of relative poverty at the *gmina* level but this was rejected by the Minister.
32. They cite as sources for this definition King (1984) and Bramley (1990).
33. Interview with Alina Kozińska, Foundation for Education Initiatives.
34. The school director and two members of the management committee were interviewed.
35. Data on Siennica are from GUS tables and from MEN for the subvention. The GUS expenditure on primary education does not include capital expenditure whereas the window replacement is capital expenditure.
36. The *voivod* results by school were seen by the interviewer.
37. I.e. *gmina* revenues from all sources minus the education subvention.
38. Interview with Marek Olszewski, Vice-President of Union of Rural *Gminas*.
39. During interviews, school directors and LG leaders, used test results to back up judgements about the quality of a school.
40. Jakubowksi (2007) undertook value added analysis of *gumnazjum* test scores at year 9 for 2005, 2006 and 2007 with a random effects student-level model. As in many other studies, expenditure per student was not statistically significantly related to attainment.
41. *Gminas* have limited powers to change local tax rates and fees, and their share of central government tax revenues is fixed.
42. These are the posts of Nominated teacher and Diploma teacher which carry higher salaries (see section 4).

CHAPTER 7

Per Capita Financing of General Education in Russia: An Assessment of the Financing Reform in the Chuvash *Republic* and the Tver *Oblast*

Sachiko Kataoka[1]

7.1. Introduction

In Russia, school directors historically were strict executors of federal regulations on education with little, if any, management or financial autonomy at the school level. School budgets were determined according to the budget allocations of previous years and federal regulations on educational inputs. Each school formulated its budget estimate by using the norms on inputs such as the number of classes (regardless of the number of students per class), base salaries for the weekly teaching loads (*stavka*) and salary supplements for additional work, and the size of buildings (square meters). Schools then submitted their budgets to the regional administration by line item. Budget items were narrowly defined and tightly controlled by the government. Schools received their allotment, which was often subject to nontransparent and unpredictable bargaining and discretion, on a monthly basis by line item. School directors were not allowed to reallocate among budget lines. For instance, savings on wages and salaries could not be used on other budget items like teaching and learning materials. Hence, even though school directors were given decision-making authority over personnel management, including hiring and firing of staff, in reality, the input-based budget allocation method with tight control over budget items has provided them with no financial autonomy or incentive to economize on staffing or spending. On the contrary, there was an incentive for schools to inflate their needs, for instance, by hiring and retaining as many teachers as possible.

Facing the severe fiscal environment, falling education budget and rapidly declining student population in the early 1990s, the government realized that the traditional input-based financing method was no longer affordable and that it needed an alternative scheme for financing the education sector—per capita financing (PCF). The federal government set up the legal framework to introduce PCF in the early 1990s, but it was only in 2001 when the Federal Ministry of Education and Science (MOES) started introducing the PCF mechanism on a pilot basis as part of the Education Modernization Program (EMP).[2] This chapter explores how the federal and regional governments started introducing PCF as an alternative financing method, focusing on the cases of the PCF experience in the Chuvash Republic (one of the three pilot regions) and the Tver Oblast (one of the 22 grant-recipient regions).[3]

The rest of this chapter is organized as follows: Section 7.2 provides a brief background summary on the education system and the development of the legal framework for the PCF reform. Section 7.3 discusses the design of the PCF scheme in Russia, including the policy objectives and methodologies. . Section 7.4 discusses the implementation of the PCF system. It explains how the PCF scheme began on a pilot basis and was gradually expanded, and then describes the historical background of introducing the PCF scheme in the two case study regions and the methodologies adopted in the respective regions. Section 7.5 assesses the outcomes of the PCF implementation to date in terms of efficiency, equity, and transparency and accountability. The concluding section summarizes lessons learned.

7.2. Background

7.2.1. Education System in Russia

Eleven-year general secondary education[4] (GSE) in Russian is compulsory since September 1, 2007. The GSE school system of the Russian Federation consists of nine years of basic general education and two years of upper secondary education, which leads to the certification of complete GSE. In the school year 2007/08, there were 56,407 full-time GSE schools (in addition, there were 1,585 GSE evening schools). Of these, 65 percent offered complete GSE (grades 1-11),[5] 19 percent offered basic general education (grades 1-9), and 13 percent primary education (grades 1-4) only. Private schools accounted for about 0.5 percent of GSE enrollment.[6] Public GSE schools are financed by the regional and municipal governments.

7.2.2. Legal Framework for Education Financing

The federal government set up the legal framework to introduce per capita financing (PCF) in the early 1990s (see Table 7.1). As part of the overall education reforms and educational decentralization to the regional level, the federal government introduced the concept of PCF in the *Education Law of 1992*. The Article 41 of the Law stipulated that educational institutions would be financed on a per student basis according to the federally and locally established norms for financing all types of educational establishments. It was expected that the PCF scheme would bring greater efficiency and accountability to the education system by providing school directors with incentives to manage school budgets efficiently and improve the quality of education in order to attract more students. Despite the urgent needs for the reforms, in the absence of detailed regulations to implement the Law or strong political will, no serious attempts were made at the federal level to introduce the new financing scheme during the 1990s. In the meantime, the Samara *Oblast* and Chuvash Republic went ahead and introduced the PCF mechanism at the regional level in 1998.

Table 7.1. Key Events in Education Financing Reforms in Russia

Year	Event
1992	*Education Law of 1992* introduced the concept of PCF and provided schools with the right to conduct independent financial and economic operations, to keep separate balance sheets, and to open commercial bank accounts.
1992	The Budget Code and the Treasury system were introduced which contradicted with school financial autonomy by requiring schools to close their commercial bank accounts and to operate single budget accounts under the Treasury.
1998	*Samara Oblast* and *Chuvash Republic* introduced the PCF mechanism at the regional level (prior to the pilot project supported under the EMP).
2001	Education Modernization Program (EMP) began supporting three pilot regions, Chuvash Republic and Samar and Yaroslavl *Oblasts* in implementing the PCF mechanism.[10]
2001	Education Reform Project supported the implementation of EMP.
2003	*Education Law No. 123 (Educational Subventions Law)* made the regional governments responsible for financing the *minimum* inputs through subventions to the local administrations.
2004	*Voronezh Oblast*, replacing *Yaroslavl Oblast*, began introducing the PCF mechanism at the regional level.
2005	22 regions joined the PCF reform.
2005	*Law on Inter-governmental Transfers No. 131* obliged regions to earmark educational subventions for each municipality.
2006	*Law on Autonomous Institutions No. 174* allowed schools to change their legal status to become financially autonomous outside the Treasury system.
2007	The Federal Ministry of Education and Science started the National Project *"Education"* to support the remaining regions to implement the PCF by 2009.

In 2003, the federal government obliged the regional governments to provide towns and municipalities with earmarked education subventions (subsidies) to finance what they considered the 'minimum' inputs to deliver educational services. The administrative structure in the Russian Federation consists of two levels below the federal government: regions (including *oblasts* and republics)[7] and towns/municipalities (*rayons*). Education administration is generally in line with this structure.[8] Until 2003, towns and municipalities were responsible for financing the entire budget for general education.[9] Because many municipalities had difficulties in paying wages and salaries for teachers and support staff in a timely manner, the Federal government amended the *Education Law No. 123 (Educational Subventions Law)* in July 2003 and made the regional governments responsible for financing the *minimum* inputs through subventions to the local administrations. The subventions were defined to cover wages and salaries for teachers and support staff, the cost of educational materials, technical teaching aids, and other consumables (Article 29). The local administrations remained responsible for financing the cost of building maintenance and utilities according to their own norms. In 2005, the *Law on Inter-governmental Transfers No. 131* further obliged regions to earmark educational subventions for each municipality, leaving municipalities with no power to reallocate the education budget to other sectors.

The Treasury system has undermined school financial autonomy granted under the education law, and the government has been debating to what extent schools should be given financial autonomy. The *1992 Education Law* provided schools with the right to conduct independent financial and economic operations, to keep separate balance sheets, and to open commercial bank accounts. In the same year, the introduction of the Budget Code and the Treasury control of regional budgets contradicted with school financial autonomy by requiring schools to close their commercial bank accounts and to operate single budget accounts under the Treasury. Because the financial and budgetary legislation has precedence over the education law in Russia, the introduction of the Treasury system has weakened the principle of school financial autonomy: schools no longer have freedom to reallocate among budget lines, including non-budget revenues–such as parental contributions and own earnings–without approval from the municipal Treasury.[11] The degree of school financial autonomy is an important issue under discussion in Russia today–the questions being whether schools should have complete autonomy or some restrictions, and whether budget carryovers should be allowed. The *Law on Autonomous Institutions No. 174*, approved on November 3, 2006, allowed schools to change their legal status to become financially autonomous outside the Treasury system. However, most schools have very limited incentives to change their legal status to autonomous because once they become autonomous, they will lose guaranteed financial support from the state. A new Federal Law No. 83, introduced on May 8, 2010, supported changes in the legal status of schools. Yet, at the moment, implementation of this law is still at very early stage.

7.3. The Design of the Funding Formula

7.3.1. Policy Objectives

It was only 2001 when the Federal Ministry of Education and Science (MOES) introduced the PCF mechanism on a pilot basis as part of the Education Modernization Program (EMP). The EMP was the first effort since the early 1990s to develop and implement a comprehensive reform strategy for education in Russia, aiming to improve quality, access and efficiency of the education system.[12] The Program attempted to introduce a number of innovative ideas into a hitherto conservative education system, including a PCF scheme. A comprehensive education reform project, Education Reform Project (ERP),[13] was designed to support MOES in implementing the EMP. The overall objectives of the "efficient and equitable public resource management" component of ERP were to improve the *efficiency* and *equitable* use of public resources for education in three pilot regions. More specifically, this component aimed (i) to introduce and develop a transparent mechanism to allocate regional budgetary resources for education; (ii) to improve the governance and management capacity at the regional, municipal and school levels; and (iii) to promote an education quality assurance and management information and statistics system. The Project also supported an associated component for modernization and restructuring of the network of general education schools. This set of reforms beyond the introduction of the PCF system was expected to promote freedom of choice while preserving fair and equal access to high quality education for all.

7.3.2. Methodological Guidelines[14]

The National Training Foundation (NTF),[15] the Project Implementing Unit (PIU) for the ERP, developed methodological guidelines for the calculation of the *normatives*, the term used in Russia for the standard costs per student, and adjustment coefficients for factors affecting the cost of education. First, the *normatives* were estimated based on salaries for teachers, assistant teachers, administrative personnel and support staff according to the federal Unified Tariff System, educational materials such as visual aids, teaching aids and office supplies, and general expenses, but excluding utility costs. The *normatives* were differentiated for urban and local municipalities by adopting different wage rates (*i.e.*, extra wages for rural schools) and notional number of students (*i.e.*, a smaller number for rural municipalities).

$$R_i^{cl} = W_i^{cl} + P$$

where,
- R_i^{cl} = *normative*, or per student costs in the ith municipality by type of classes (c) and level of education (l)
- W_i^{cl} = wage expenses in the ith municipality per student by type of classes (c) and level of education (l)
- P = expenses on education process per student

R_i^{cl} is estimated by the formula:

$$R_i^{cl} = \frac{\frac{a}{18.7} \bullet b \bullet 1.262 \bullet 1.02 \bullet 1.33 \bullet 12}{m} \bullet 1.33 \bullet w \bullet c \bullet R$$

where:
- a = number of hours according to the basic curriculum;
- 18.7 = weighted average number of hours per wage rate;
- b = wage rate corresponding to the weighted average Unified Tariff System category in the ith municipality;
- 1.262 = single social tax index;
- 1.02 = index of wage fund increase related to the increase of length of service, upgrading of professional category, etc.;[16]
- 1.33 = index, wage fund increase due to additional payments and allowances;
- 12 = number of months in a year;
- m = number of 'notional students' in a class in the ith municipality;
- 1.33 = index, wage fund increase for administrative/managing staff;
- w = appreciation coefficients by level of education (see Table 7.2);
- c = appreciation coefficients by type of class (program) (see Table 7.3);
- R = regional appreciation coefficients reflecting region-specific additional wage rates and additional payments/allowances.

Notional students. To prevent dramatic changes between the *normatives* and the existing budgets, the guidelines allowed the regional governments to adjust the *normatives* during the transitional period by using the number of 'notional students,' or normalized enrollment, instead of the actual number of students. For example, if the average occupancy rate in municipality A equals 12 students per class instead of 25, the number of 'notional children' to be used as a basis for budget planning in this municipality will be calculated using the factor = 25/12. The notional students are expected to be lower for correctional classes, compensatory development classes, and all types of classes in rural schools in general.

Level of education. The first stage (primary) of education consists of grades 1 to 4, the second stage (basic) grades 4 to 9, and the third stage (senior secondary) grades 10 to 11. The adjustment coefficients by level of education are shown in Table 7.2.

Type of class (educational program). The formula includes appreciation factors by type of class, as shown in Table 7.3.

Table 7.2. Adjustment Coefficients by Level of Education

	Division of classes into groups	After-school groups	Club activities	Total ('w' in the formula)
	(A)	(B)	(C)	(A) x (B) x (C)
1st stage (primary)	1.04	1.4	1.03	1.50
2nd stage (basic)	1.12	1.0	1.03	1.15
3rd stage (senior)	1.22	1.0	1.03	1.26

Source: NTF (2002).

Table 7.3. Adjustment Coefficients by Type of Class (Educational Program)

Regular	1.00
Gymnasia and Lyceum	1.15
Special education	3.22
Compensatory development	2.27

Source: NTF (2002).

The regional governments were given some flexibility in adopting the guidelines. First, regional governments were not required to adopt exactly the same variables and coefficients as described in the guidelines, even though many regions followed the guidelines only with small adjustments. Second, the guidelines allowed regions to smooth the subvention to each municipality be within certain ceilings such as plus or minus 10 percent difference from the expenditures in the previous year. The guidelines did not specify how long the length of the 'transitional period' should be, and it seems that regions could continue using the provisional measure for some years after the implementation of the PCF scheme. Third, the guidelines were primarily prepared for regional governments to determine the amount of educational subventions to municipalities. Then, regional governments may or may not require municipal governments to use the same formula with some further adjustments to determine school budgets.

7.4. The Implementation of the Funding Formula

7.4.1. PCF Pilot Project and Its Expansion

In 2001, the Education Reform Project (ERP) began supporting three pilot regions—the Samara *Oblast*, Chuvash Republic and Voronezh *Oblast*—in implementing the PCF as well as other reform activities. The first two regions were selected because they had already started piloting the PCF at the regional level in 1998. The last one joined the pilot at the end of 2004.[17] As a condition for the participation in the ERP, the pilot regions agreed that 90 percent of schools in their regions would become financially autonomous and receive per capita allocations by June 2005.[18] The NTF provided intensive support for the pilot regions, including various training for education administrators and school directors, study tours, the provision of accounting software, and materials and equipment for school network restructuring and quality assessment.[19]

Given the successful outcomes in the three pilot regions, the federal government decided to gradually have the PCF system fully rolled-out nationwide. In 2005, 22 more regions, including the Tver *Oblast*, were selected based on applications as grant recipients to implement the PCF, on the condition that each would complete an analysis of education financing and the school network before the end of 2005 and introduce the PCF scheme to the school level in 2006. Those 22 regions received training from the NTF as well, but not as intensively as the three pilot regions did. Nor did they receive a comprehensive reform package such as resource centers to facilitate the consolidation of the school network and various training programs. The remaining regions in the country also benefited from the project by attending PCF workshops organized in neighboring regions. Despite the limited support they got, some of them started to implement the PCF scheme using their own resources. The PCF scheme has gradually, but steadily gained political support and interest among federal leaders who were interested in adopting the PCF for the overall public services beyond the education sector. As of the end of 2006, more than a quarter of the 88 regions in the country had adopted PCF down to the municipal level.[20] Furthermore, MOES started the *National Project 'Education'* to support the remaining regions to implement the PCF by 2009. In the academic year 2007/08, MOES provided grants for 20 selected regions to implement the PCF and teacher salary incentives (50 percent top-up of current salaries to motivate teachers to accept the reform),[21] and helped schools establish the School Governing Body. With this support, MOES expected that 50 regions in total would fully implement the PCF mechanism by the end of 2007 and that all regions would do so by 2012.[22]

7.4.2. Chuvash Republic

Even prior to the Education Reform Project (ERP), the Chuvash Republic had started piloting the PCF at the republic level primarily as an effective tool for restructuring the school network. The *Republican Law on Financing Normatives for Educational Institutions in the Chuvash Republic No. 16* dated June 26, 1998 required the Republic to shift its education financing mechanism in three years from input-based financing, based on the number of teachers and maintenance costs, to a per capita-based financing, based on the minimum expenditures required for the education process, operation of buildings, facilities, and equipment. It spent about three years between 1998 and 2001 for the preparation for the republic-wide implementation of PCF, including development of rules and regulations, norms and methodologies for the PCF and piloting them in three pilot municipalities.

Based on their own experience through the pilot stage, the Regional Ministry of Finance (RMOF) and Regional Ministry of Education (RMOE) modified the NTF's methodologies to better fit their needs and make them simpler. The list of republican adjustment factors and the procedures for the use of adjustments have been defined by the Regional Committee, approved by the RMOF, stipulated in a republican budget law every year, and published on the Internet. The republican government has modified the adjustment coefficients over the years. Table 7.4 compares the coefficients adopted in 2003 and 2007, according to the type of education and school size. The coefficient for rural primary schools was much higher in 2007 than in 2003, and that for rural basic and secondary schools with less than 100 students also increased. It suggests that the Republic government clearly is protective of rural small schools to secure easy access to education, particularly primary education, for rural children. Taking into these adjust-

Table 7.4. Chuvash Republic: Adjustment Coefficients, 2003 and 2007

Adjustment Indices	Adjustment Coefficients 2003	Adjustment Indices	Adjustment Coefficients 2007
Education Programs			
Special education	2.15		2.08
In-depth study of certain subjects, gymnasium	1.13		1.15
Individual study at home	5.00		5.00
Non-resident study	0.50		0.50
Family education	1.00		1.00
Urban schools with the number of students:			
Below 500	1.17	Below 900	1.00
500-1,000	0.99	901-1,300	1.01
1,000-1,250	0.97	1,301-1,500	1.01
1,250-1,500	0.95	Over 1,500	1.05
Over 1,500	1.04		
Rural primary schools with the number of students:		**Rural primary schools - kindergartens :**	4.40
Below 15	1.50		
Between 15 and 20	1.20		
Between 20 and 25	1.10		
Between 25 and 35	0.90		
Over 35	0.80		
Rural basic schools with the number of students:		**Rural schools with the number of students:**	
Below 40	1.90	Below 100	2.20
40-60	1.37	101-200	1.00
60-80	1.15	201-400	1.02
80-120	0.95	401-600	1.10
Over 120	0.69	Over 600	1.05
Rural secondary schools with the number of students:			
Below 120	1.43		
120-200	1.07		
200-280	0.92		
280-360	0.90		
Over 360	0.93		

Source: Government of the Chuvash Republic (2003, 2007).

ments for urban and rural schools, in real terms, the *normatives* increased between 2001 and 2007 by 66 percent for urban schools and 109 percent for rural schools, as shown in Figure 7.1. Note that the *normatives* dropped in 2005, but it was only because the *Education Law No. 123* made municipalities responsible for financing utilities, maintenance and repairs, which had been part of the *normatives* funded by the republican government until 2004.

Each municipality was allowed to flexibly adjust the Republican coefficients and the proportion between wages and education materials when allocating the subvention budget from the municipality to schools. As shown in Figure 7.2, the Cheboksary Municipality, for instance, did not differentiate the *normatives* between rural and urban schools. The Cheboksary Town reallocated the subvention budget between wages and education materials, and increased the proportion of education materials from 6.2 percent in 2006 to 7.0 percent in 2007. In the case of the Cheboksary Municipality, the proportion of education materials increased even up to 10.7 percent in 2007.

7.4.3. Tver Oblast

The Tver *Oblast* joined the Education Reform Project (ERP) as a grant recipient in 2005, but there was little progress in implementing the PCF during the first year. Tver is a typical rural region in which the number of students has sharply decreased in the last decade. Given the rapid demographic change, the restructuring of the school network had been an urgent matter for the regional government. In 2004, the Regional Ministry of

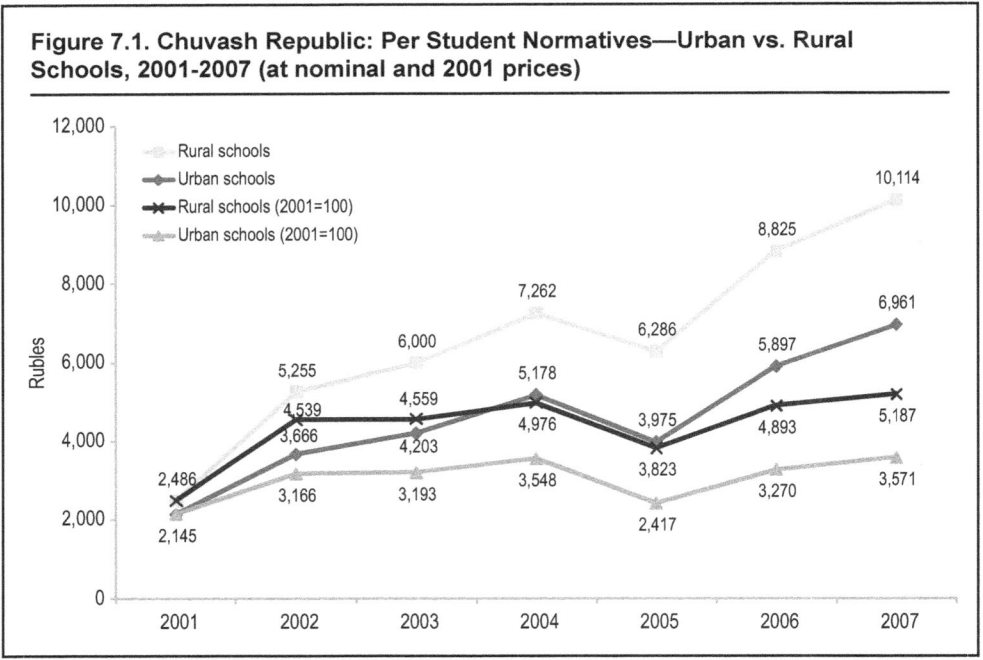

Figure 7.1. Chuvash Republic: Per Student Normatives—Urban vs. Rural Schools, 2001-2007 (at nominal and 2001 prices)

Source: Chuvash Republic.

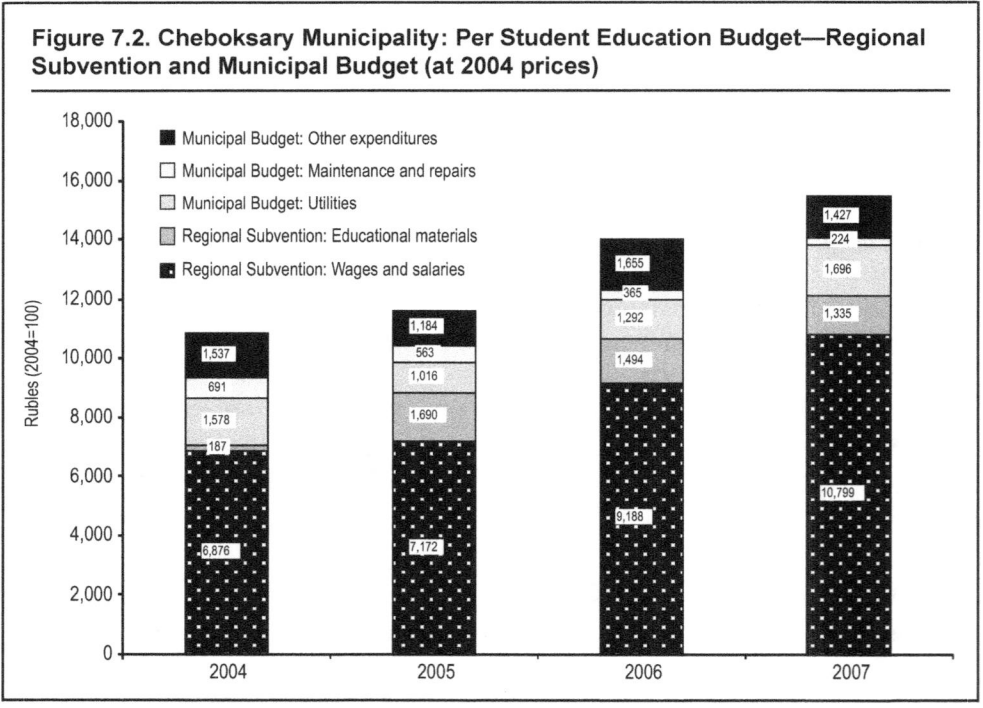

Figure 7.2. Cheboksary Municipality: Per Student Education Budget—Regional Subvention and Municipal Budget (at 2004 prices)

Source: Chuvash Republic.
Note: Other expenditures under the municipal budget include additional salaries, other payments to staff, taxes, communication, per diem and accommodation, other services, other expenditures capital increase, turn-over increase, investments.

Education (RMOE)[23] and Regional Ministry of Finance (RMOF) decided to apply for the ERP grants and began analyzing education budget allocations to municipalities, as required as part of the application. Through this exercise, they discovered wide variations in per capita allocations among municipalities. They also realized that developing one unified formula for every municipality and every school is not easy and that municipal and school geographical characteristics such as low population density and isolation from other schools needed to be taken into account when developing a formula. They informed municipalities that education budgets would be allocated to them on a per capita basis starting in 2005, but without clear guidance. Despite the commitment to the PCF and awareness of the problem, the RMOE and RMOF ended up adopting a formula with many coefficients and other adjustments in 2005, which made the municipal allocations almost the same as the historical ones. In much the same way, while some Heads of the Municipal Departments of Education were already also aware of the wide variations in the per student spending among schools in their jurisdiction (e.g. from 9,500 Rubles (US$350) to 90,000 Rubles (US$3,300) in the Zubtsov Municipality), they adjusted the formula so that the budget for each school did not deviate much from the historical allocations. There was little, if any, progress in school network restructuring or equalizing budget allocations among municipalities and among schools during the first year of the PCF implementation.

The PCF implementation began in earnest in the Tver *Oblast* only in mid-2005 when the First Deputy Head[24] of RMOE started to build consensus among stakeholders. As the Deputy Head of the RMOE observed inactions in implementing the PCF reform, he first tried to build consensus among various stakeholders at regional, municipal and school levels. The activities included awareness campaign for the Heads of municipalities and school directors through seminars and training. Through this consensus-building process, they came to share the same understanding of the objectives of PCF as an instrument (i) to facilitate the school network restructuring process; (ii) to improve access to good quality education and ultimately improve student academic performance (as assessed in terms of the Unified State Exam[25]); and (iii) to create a competitive system of education—schools compete for the best students and teachers, teachers compete for the best schools and students, and students compete for the best schools and teachers.

Between 2004 and 2007, per student education budget in Tver *Oblast*, on average, increased in real terms not only for salaries but also for teaching and learning materials. Table 7.5 shows that the total per student expenditures increased by 21 percent at the 2004 constant prices from 12,844 Rubles in 2004 to 15,537 Rubles in 2007, mostly owing to the increase of the subvention budget to meet the higher costs of teacher salaries. The non-budget revenues also sharply increased, even though the total amount is still small compared to the budget funds. A higher percentage of the subvention budget was allocated to teaching/learning materials (from 5.0 percent in 2004 to 11.2 percent in 2007), which was reflected in the considerable increase in the per student expenditures on those materials (from 315 Rubles in 2004 to 1,488 Rubles in 2007 at the 2004 constant prices).

In order to avoid the sharp budget cut for some municipalities, however, the Regional government invented provisional 'municipal coefficients' during the transitional period, taking a gradual approach to adopt formula-funding in a strict sense. The regional formula, which was designed based on the guidelines provided by the NTF, took into account the following adjustment factors: geographical locations (urban and rural),

Table 7.5. Tver Oblast: School Education Budget—Total for 43 Municipalities

	2004	2005	2006	2007	Changes 2004-07
Total Education Budget (Rubles mil.)	1,876,001	2,068,261	2,442,027	2,825,357	50.6
Oblast Subvention	1,299,599	1,475,696	1,734,360	2,078,451	59.9
Wages and salaries	1,234,597	1,398,980	1,595,654	1,845,050	49.4
Wages and salaries (percent)	95.0	94.8	92.0	88.8	
Teaching/learning materials	46,075	68,844	133,348	248,292	438.9
Municipality Budget	553,642	558,503	648,115	668,714	20.8
Utility	271,823	289,584	323,780	321,118	18.1
Maintenance	68,096	61,846	59,745	54,085	-20.6
Extra-budget Funds	22,760	34,063	59,552	78,193	243.6
Percentage					
Oblast Subvention	69.3	71.3	71.0	73.6	
Wages and salaries	65.8	67.6	65.3	65.3	
Teaching/learning materials	2.5	3.3	5.5	8.8	
Municipality Budget	29.5	27.0	26.5	23.7	
Extra-budget Funds	1.2	1.6	2.4	2.8	
Per student expenditures					
(Rubles at current prices)	12,844	15,303	19,339	22,626	76.2
(Rubles at 2004 prices)	12,844	13,581	15,648	15,537	21.0

Source: Calculated by the author based on data collected by the Tver Ministry of Education.

size of schools, types of classes, special education programs, individual education for disabled children and advance teaching. In addition, the Regional government decided to adopt a *municipal coefficient model* with a different but gradually converging coefficient for each municipality during the transitional period. As shown in Figure 7.3, the per student expenditures for municipalities ranged from 83 to 188 percent of the *normatives* (formula-based allocations) in 2005 without much change from the previous years, but

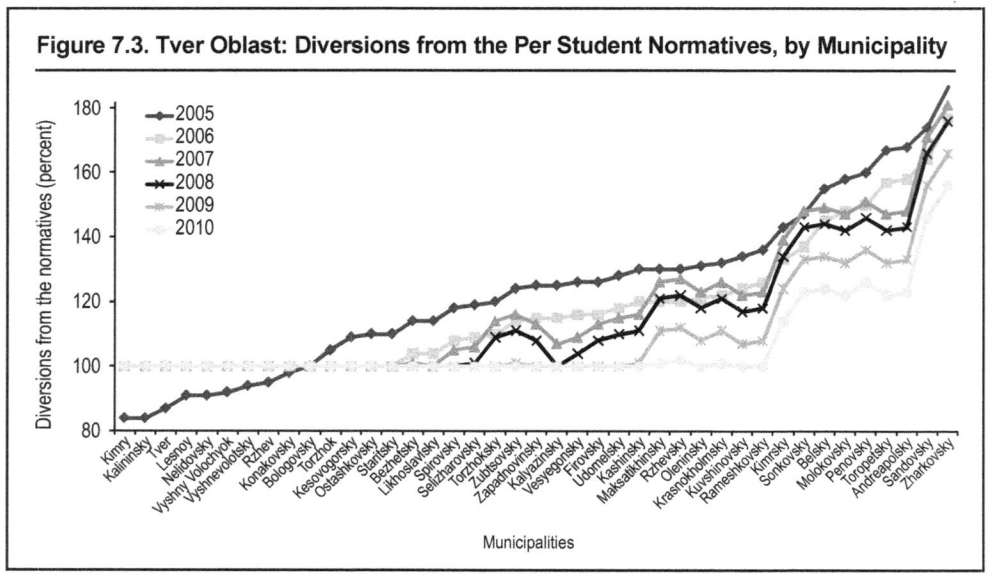

Figure 7.3. Tver Oblast: Diversions from the Per Student Normatives, by Municipality

Source: Tver *Oblast* Department of Education (2010).

the gap narrowed to 100-178 percent in 2006[26] and 100-158 percent in 2007 (not shown in the figure). Furthermore, the Regional authorities informed municipalities that they aimed to lower the highest municipal coefficient to around 130 percent in 2008 and, if possible, to 100 percent in 2009. Yet, they failed to reach the target value of 100 by 2009 and, as of 2010, they had only lowered the highest municipal coefficient to 156.[27]

In the same manner, the Regional government allowed municipalities to adopt a school coefficient model (a different coefficient for each school) for the budget allocation to schools during the transitional period. The Regional government set the minimum and maximum ceilings for the school coefficient. Given the imminent requirement from the RMOE to gradually conform to the *normatives* in a few years time, municipalities had no choice but to restructure the school network. This included closing down inefficient schools except for primary schools in rural areas. Municipalities generally close or merge schools only when can they offer alternative measures such as a bus program to ensure access.[28] As shown in Figure 7.4, the ceilings ranged from 55 to 570 percent of the *normatives* in 2006, which were narrowed to 80 and 350 percent in 2007, 85 to 300 percent in 2008, 90 to 250 percent in 2009 and 90 to 200 percent by 2010. Together with the introduction of municipal-to-school formula-funding, the RMOE required municipalities to prepare a municipal school restructuring plan. As a result, the Zubtsov Municipality narrowed the gap between the lowest and highest per capita allocations from 70 to 350 percent of the *normatives* in 2006 to 86 to 120 percent by 2010. In the case of the Vishny Volocheck Municipality, however, school coefficients got fully aligned with the *normatives* going from 65-350 percent of the *normatives* in 2006 to 100-100 percent by 2010.

The RMOF and RMOE required municipalities and schools to allocate a certain percentage of their total subvention budget to educational materials. Although the Education Law No. 123 (Subvention Law) does not specify how the subvention budget should be allocated between wages and educational materials, the Tver Regional government required municipalities and schools to allocate 11.3 percent of the subvention to educa-

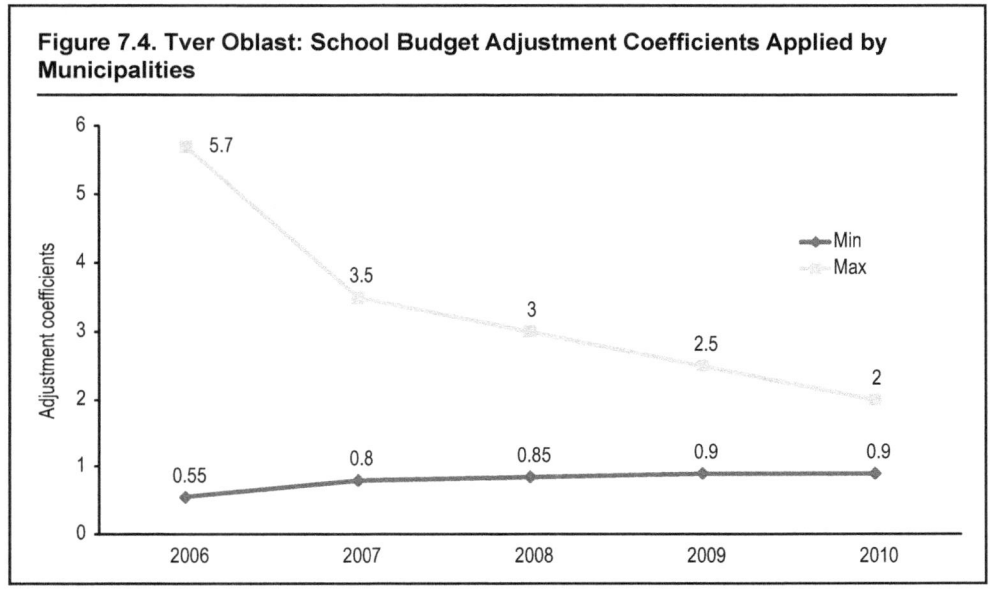

Figure 7.4. Tver Oblast: School Budget Adjustment Coefficients Applied by Municipalities

Source: Tver *Oblast*.

tional materials in 2006. Once municipalities receive the subvention, then, they allocate the earmarked amount for education materials to schools. The percentage increased to 15.4 percent in 2007 and planned to increase further in the future.

Municipalities do not use a formula to allocate municipal budgets for schools for utilities, maintenance and repairs based on a formula because it is difficult to develop norms. With regard to the municipal budget for education, many municipalities claim that while there are clear norms for utilities according to the types of heating, space, etc. (i.e., not on a per capita basis), there is none for maintenance and repairs, except that schools are entitled to receive their budget quota for maintenance and repair every five years. All of the municipal officials interviewed commented that budgets for utilities and maintenance and repairs are very difficult to allocate based on a formula, and also that there is not sufficient total budget for these items from the municipality. Because of the difficulties, the Head of a Municipal DOE expressed his wish that the regional subventions could also cover utilities, maintenance and repairs like.

7.5. Assessment of Outcomes

This section assesses the outcomes of the PCF implementation in Chuvash Republic and Tver *Oblast*. It will assess the impact of the reform in terms of efficiency, equity, and transparency and accountability, the latter including the area of school autonomy. This section, however, will not directly address the quality dimension.

7.5.1. Chuvash Republic

7.5.1.1. Efficiency

Investment support from the Republican government at the initial stage of the reform helped municipalities restructure the school network and improve the efficiency of the school system. In 1998, when the Republican government required all municipalities to prepare a school network restructuring plan, it also supported them by improving roads and providing school buses through the republican and federal programs. In other words, municipalities did not need to invest in buses using their own budget. The combination of systemic planning and financial support from the republican government helped most municipalities make considerable progress in restructuring the senior secondary level first, and then, the primary and secondary levels. Between 2001 and 2006, when the total number of students in the republic declined by 29 percent from 199,334 to 141,161, the total number of schools decreased by 18 percent, from 686 to 561.

It is difficult to close schools, but it is even more difficult to dismiss teachers and non-teaching staff. Even after the considerable restructuring efforts, about 10 percent of the schools (50 primary schools) in the republic still enrolled less than 100 students, 20 of which with less than five students.[29] These schools might remain if municipalities cannot offer village councils an acceptable alternative to assure access. Even when municipalities may close schools, they often try to avoid dismissing teachers and support staff as much as possible: highly qualified teachers can be transferred to bigger schools, while others retire or find different jobs within the school system. In Cheboksary Municipality, for instance, when the number of students sharply declined by 35 percent from 9,095 in 2001/02 to 5,893 in 2006/07, the municipality successfully managed to stabilize the average class size at 18 (see Figure 7.5). On the other hand, the number of class teachers declined only by 17 percent from 864 to 713, and non-teaching staff (including school

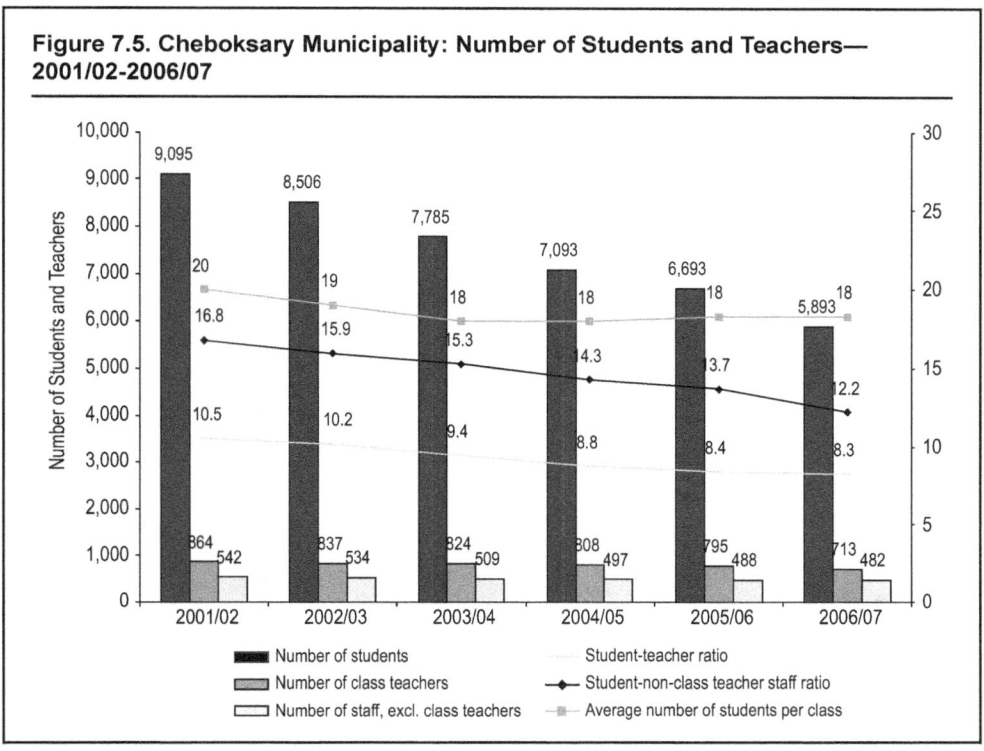

Figure 7.5. Cheboksary Municipality: Number of Students and Teachers—
2001/02-2006/07

Source: Chuvash Republic.

directors, non-class teachers, administrators and support staff) only by 11 percent from 542 to 482.[30] This data suggests two important points. First, while the school restructuring program seem to have considerably contributed to school and class consolidations, it was less successful in terms of reducing the number of teachers, and even lesser successful in reducing non-teaching staff, as clearly reflected in the low student-teacher ratio and the student-non-teacher ratio. Second, the combination of the flat average class size at 18 and the declining student-teacher ratio between 2003/04 and 2006/07 means that the number of teachers per class increased. Reasons for this may include that there are more extra curriculum courses being offered or there are more part-time teachers or a combination. In fact, the number of full-time equivalent teachers may be much smaller. More detailed analysis is needed to understand the various implications of the changes in staffing.

Overstaffing of non-class teaching staff seems to be contributing more to the high unit costs per student than that of class teachers. Figure 7.6 illustrates per student costs on wages and salaries (at 2004 prices) for 12 out of 85 schools in the Cheboksary Town.[31] The unit costs increased annually between 2004 and 2007 in all cases except one, and the variations among schools did not change much. Besides obvious reasons such as a low student-teacher ratio among small rural schools, there seems to be another important factor causing the high unit costs for some schools. There is a pattern that the high unit costs are closely associated with a very high proportion of non-class teaching staff (at the highest end, 62, 46, and 45 percent of total staffing regardless of the school size). This is consistent with the findings in Cheboksary Municipality above that the student-non-

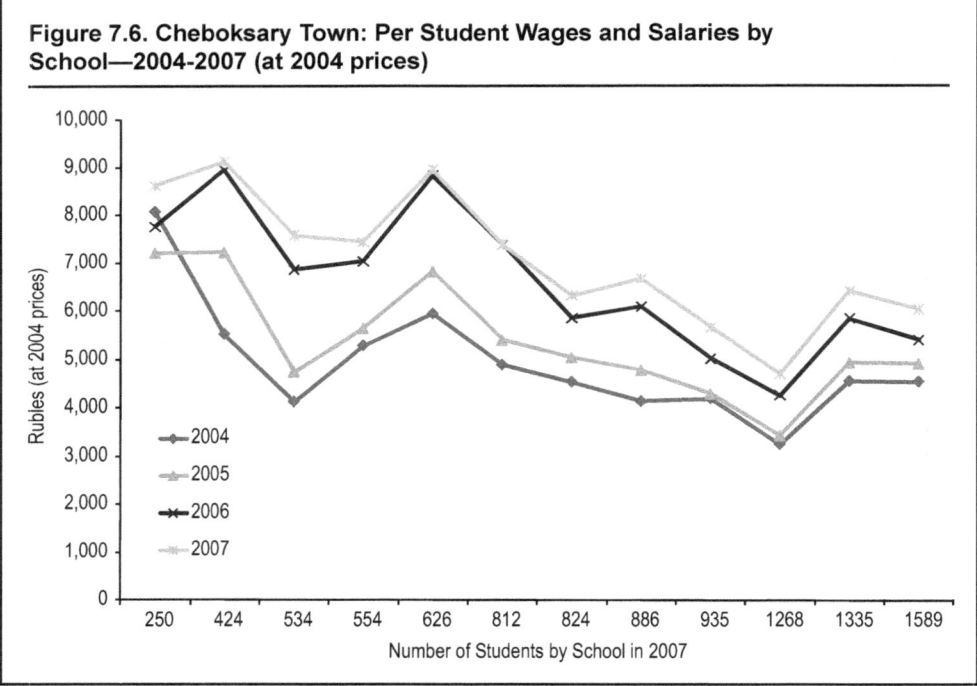

Figure 7.6. Cheboksary Town: Per Student Wages and Salaries by School—2004-2007 (at 2004 prices)

Source: Chuvash Republic Ministry of Education.
Note: Schools were ordered according to the number of students in 2007.

class teaching staff ratio dropped much more sharply than that student-class-teacher ratio. Although school principals have the authority to hire and fire not only teachers but also non-teaching staff, it seems they do not fully exercise their authority, probably because non-teaching staff may be less likely to find a job in the village outside the school. And, the municipal governments appear to support these principals, at least during the transitional period, to keep those redundant staff by providing additional budget outside the formula-based allocations, as reflected in the relatively higher unit costs.

7.5.1.2. Equity

The principle of equitable budget allocation for all children for better quality education is partially in place, so are measures both for vertical and horizontal equity. As shown in Figure 7.1, the relative per student normatives for rural schools compared to urban schools has increased between 2001 and 2007, indicating that the Republic government is more willing to maintain small schools to ensure access in rural areas (horizontal equity) even at the expense of efficiency. As shown in Table 7.4, vertical equity is assured in the higher coefficients for different types of student needs such as special education and home schooling. On the other hand, the equity principle is somewhat violated within each of the rural and urban categories; for instance, schools with more than 1,500 students are given a higher coefficient than those with fewer students. Such preferential treatment of bigger schools is partially mitigated by sharing their facilities with smaller schools. When the ERP provided 138 schools (about a quarter of all schools in Chuvash) with resource centers (well-equipped laboratories, science rooms, libraries, computers, etc.), those schools were required by the Project to maintain and share the various equipment and teaching materials with students in other schools and people in the community. Schools using those resource centers pay for the services (teachers' time and the costs for the courses) from the budget they receive from the government—money follows the students (or the service that they receive). In the Krasnoarmeiyskiy Municipality, for instance, there are monthly networking activities at the three resource centers in the municipality. In addition, students in six neighboring schools come each week to one of the resource center schools for special programs (preparation for exams) and specialized subjects. Hence, it appears that if access to town schools within a reasonable distance is guaranteed for rural students, and rural children are assured of nondiscriminatory treatment in urban schools, sharing of education resources among schools financed by the per student basis budgets may indeed result in more equitable provision of good education. In terms of vertical equity, the Republic government finances higher per student costs for individual study at home and special education.

7.5.1.3. Transparency and Accountability

While there are some positive aspects of the Treasury system and other federal rules, the strict control has limited schools' financial autonomy. In Chuvash, the Republic Treasury was introduced in 2001, even before the introduction of the Federal Treasury in 2003. The introduction of the Treasury system has had both positive and negative impacts on school financial management. On the one hand, the Treasury system has not significantly constrained schools and may even have eased their management burden. For instance, schools generally prefer to let the Municipal Treasury handle procurement matters rather than doing it on their own simply because it is easier. In some cases, the Treasury system has disciplined school directors to prepare a school budget plan more carefully in the first place because reallocations are allowed only once a quarter. On the other hand, the present Federal Treasury regulations can be insensibly inflexible. For instance, according to the existing procurement rules, schools may spend subvention budget to buy computers as educational materials, but not spare parts for computers which need to be purchased using non-budget revenues. A school director also pointed out that the government control over non-budget revenues is so tight that schools are unable to spend it flexibly. In terms of accountability, in Cheboksary Town, the Municipal DOE requires schools to publish school activity reports. In 2007, all schools submitted one. The school governing structure has been strengthened, too. Of the 73 general schools, 4 *gymnasiums*, and 4 *lyceums*, 53 schools had a Governing Board/Board of Trustees.

7.5.1.4. Summary

Chuvash's experience strongly suggests that PCF can be more effectively implemented when it is pursued not in isolation but tied with a set of comprehensive reforms, in particular, the rationalization of the school network at the municipal level. When the PCF scheme was first introduced in 1998, almost all the stakeholders resisted the reduction of coefficients in the formula which was perceived to lead to closures of rural schools, but they gradually realized that the old education system, with many small schools, was inefficient and unsustainable. Since then, it seems that many of those former opponents have accepted or have been forced to accept the reform, although a small group of opponents still exists, including some school directors, teachers and parents in rural areas who might be losing their jobs, village schools, or both. The case study shows that school consolidations have facilitated the introduction of PCF by reducing the number of small costly schools. The Treasury System has constrained school autonomy for financial management somewhat, but it has also promoted better planning, even though it may be limited to a few schools. However, the narrowly defined regulations on budget items and control over non-budget revenues limit the financial flexibility of schools. PCF could make school financing more efficient if schools are given more financial autonomy. The strict division between republican and municipal budgets, and within the republican budgets the division between the salaries and materials has an especially negative impact on efficiency.

7.5.2. Tver Oblast

7.5.2.1. EFFICIENCY

The introduction of PCF accompanied by the school network restructuring program has helped reduce the number of schools. As shown in Figure 7.7, for instance, in the Vishny Volocheck Municipality, the smallest schools with the highest per student school budgets have been closed, and the unit costs for the remaining schools have become more equal in terms of the percentage of formula-based norms. The Head of the Zubtsov Municipality DOE closed small schools—some of which had only 3-4 children—with the agreement of parents who were assured of school buses for their children. According to the DOE Head, even some parents who were not in favor of the closure of their village school in 2005 are now happy because their children are receiving better education in the town schools.

Nevertheless, various factors have constrained the school network restructuring process, and there still are many small, overstaffed schools in Tver. As of 2007, 51.8 percent of the 780 schools in the region had fewer than 100 students, enrolling only 11.4 percent of the students in total, as shown in Table 7.6.[32] The number of class teachers and other staff did not decline as fast as the number of students between 2004 and 2006 (by 10.6 percent, 4.8 percent, and 13.5 percent, respectively), reflecting the extreme difficulties or lack of incentives in dismissing teachers, and especially other staff. It is difficult to dismiss staff partly because they are protected by the Labor Law, but more importantly,

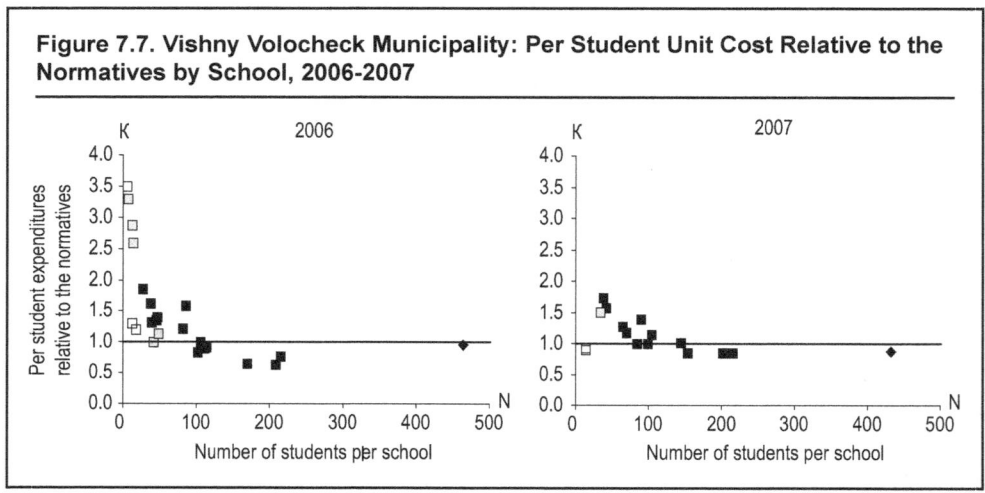

Figure 7.7. Vishny Volocheck Municipality: Per Student Unit Cost Relative to the Normatives by School, 2006-2007

Source: Vishny Volocheck Municipality.

Table 7.6. Tver Oblast: School Statistics—Total for 43 Municipalities

	2004	2005	2006	2007	Changes 2004-07
Number of Schools	926	865	808	780	-15.8
Of which small schools (percent)	54.6	54.8	53.0	51.8	-20.2
Number of Students	146,057	135,152	126,272	124,870	-13.5*
Of which small schools (percent)	13.1	12.5	12.2	11.4	-25.8
Average Number of Students per Class	11.9	11.7	11.6	11.5	
Of which small schools	10.0	10.7	10.4	9.6	
Number of School Staff	52,108	50,438	48,719	47,709	-8.4
Class teachers (percent)	29.7	29.1	28.3	n.a.	-10.6*
Other staff (percent)	70.3	70.9	71.7	n.a.	-4.8*
Student-Teacher Ratio	9.5	9.2	9.1	n.a.	
Student-Non-teacher Staff ratio	4.0	3.8	3.6	n.a.	

Source: Calculated by the author based on data collected by the Tver Ministry of Education.
* Changes between 2004 and 2006.

there are few other employment opportunities for them, particularly in rural areas.[33] Given the political and socioeconomic sensitivities, the DOE has, to the extent possible, tried to help those who have been made redundant to secure positions in other schools, to get different positions in the same school (such as librarian or school bus accompanying staff), or find other jobs outside the education sector. Only with no other options, have school directors and the Municipal DOE together decided to fire those passed the retirement age and low-qualified teachers in rural areas. No severance packages have been provided for these unlucky few. In the case of non-teaching staff, besides the fact the government norms are already generous, those norms are not always followed and some schools hire more staff than the norms primarily to create employment opportunities in rural areas.

7.5.2.2. EQUITY

The wide gaps in the municipal and school coefficients have gradually narrowed, but they still remain, leaving a question as to how to define horizontal equity. As illustrated in Figure 7.3, the wide disparities in the municipal coefficients narrowed from 84-181 percent of the normatives in 2005 to 100-156 percent in 2010, and the school coefficients from 55-570 percent of the normative in 2006 to 90-200 percent in 2010. Thus, the regional government and municipalities have addressed horizontal equity across the region, but at a slower pace than originally intended, and they aim to further narrow these gaps in the coming years. Their challenge raises a question as to what is the acceptable level of horizontal equity in terms of per student spending without harming access.

The persistent gaps in per student expenditures on wages and salaries among schools are likely to have been the result of trying to ensure horizontal equity, but allowing inefficiency among some schools during the transitional period may have also played a part. Of the regional subventions per student in the Zubtsov Municipality shown in Figure 7.8, wages and salaries are presented in Panel A (at the 2004 constant prices). Per student spending on wages and salaries gradually increased for most schools but the gaps among schools did not narrow down much between 2004 and 2007: they were highest among the schools with around 10 to 20 students (except an outlier school), but not the smallest ones, three of which closed down by 2007. This might have been because while one or two teachers taught multi-grades in very small schools, slightly bigger schools assigned a teacher per class with a few students in each.

The Regional regulation on the minimum spending on teacher materials ended up widening the gap among schools. Of the regional subventions per student in the Zubtsov Municipality, spending on teaching and learning materials are shown in Panel B of Figure 7.8 (at 2004 constant prices). Unlike the wage expenditures, per capita material expenditures were quite flat across schools in 2004, but no longer so in 2006 and 2007. This is because municipalities and schools were required since 2005 to allocate a certain percentage of their total budget to educational materials in the Tver Region. While it may sound like a good policy to secure the total budget for education materials,

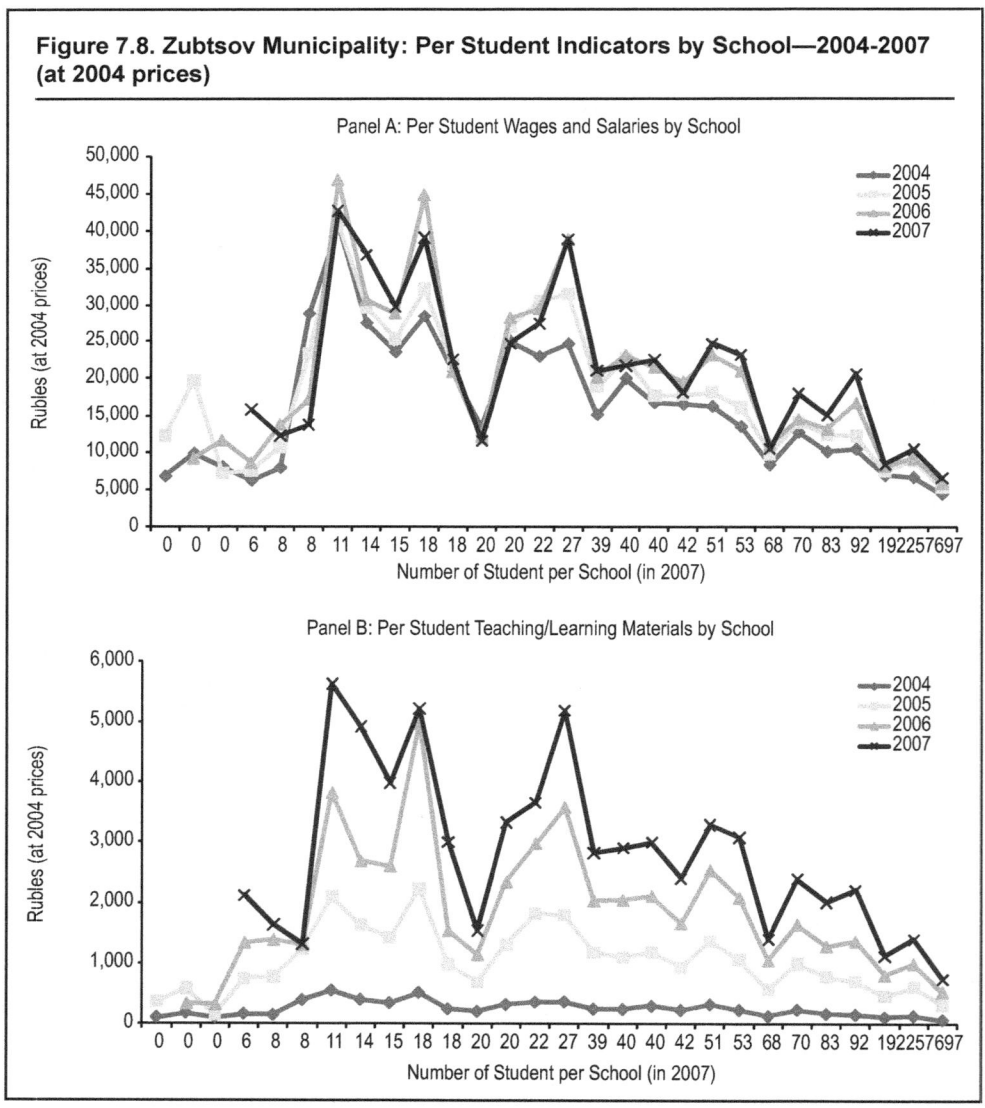

Figure 7.8. Zubtsov Municipality: Per Student Indicators by School—2004-2007 (at 2004 prices)

Source: Zubtsov MDOE.

the imposition of the fixed allocation has resulted in wide gaps in terms of per student expenditures across schools.

7.5.2.3. Transparency and Accountability

Schools are gradually developing budget planning and management capacities at the school level. While some town schools, for instance, in Tver City, prepare school reports as a public relation tool to attract students, most school directors still lack planning, financial management, accounting, and computer skills, and they typically involve deputy directors and accountants in the budgeting process. The role of accountants therefore is very important. In the Vishny Volocheck Municipality, for instance, accountants used to be staff of the centralized municipal accounting office and to work on school accounting among other sectors, but since September 2006, two schools share an accountant as their own staff member. Some accountants were transferred from the municipal accounting office, while others were newly recruited. The close communication between the school director and his/her own accountant helps him/her manage the school budget more easily.

Even though schools prepare their own budget, their financial autonomy is still limited. Schools prepare their budget according to their needs and may reallocate among and within salaries and educational materials with the RMOE's approval, but in reality, reallocation among these budget items rarely happens. The RMOF and RMOE want to protect non-salary budgets by specifying the proportion of budget allocated to educational materials while the restructuring of school network is in process. This has certainly contributed to the improvement of the teaching/learning process at the school level, but contradicted the concept of decentralization of education financing to municipalities and schools and also created a wide range in terms of per student allocations. As of 2007, the RMOF and RMOE planned to allocate the total subvention budgets as one envelope and let the municipalities decide how to allocate across budget items, once the restructuring process is more or less completed. This plan was yet to be seen.

The introduction of the Treasury system in 2003 made school budget more transparent than before, but might have had mixed impacts on management of non-budget resources. Unlike those in the three pilot regions, schools in the Tver *Oblast* did not have their own bank account prior to the introduction of the Treasury system in 2003, and most of them did not even know exactly how much budget they received from the municipality. Hence, schools did not feel particularly constrained when the Federal Treasury system was introduced. Rather, schools now know how their budgets are calculated and allocated to them and appreciate having more funds for educational materials. The federal law allows schools to procure goods and services up to 60,000 Rubles (US$5,300) without quotations, and for those over 60,000 Rubles, with three quotations. Schools usually submit procurement receipts to the Municipal Treasury for payment and rarely withdraw cash to make payments on their own, except for small petty purchases. On the other hand, even though a few school directors interviewed in the Vishny Volocheck Municipality explained that they do not collect cash from parents, it seems that many school directors might not be disclosing actual cash contributions because they would have to deposit them in a non-budget account under the Treasury. The supposedly transparent Treasury System may be making management of non-budget resources less transparent.

7.5.2.4. Summary

After the introduction of PCF in the Tver *Oblast* in 2005, dissemination of the new financing scheme and training of administrators and school directors resulted in the shared views and understanding of the objectives among various stakeholders at different levels. Together with the school network restructuring at the municipal level, the region and its municipalities started to move toward equalizing the per student expenditures among municipalities and within municipalities. They still have some ways to go to complete the school restructuring process, abandon the municipal and school coefficients–supposedly temporal measures–and equalize per student expenditures. Despite these limitations, the average number of students per class, pupil-teacher ratio and per student expenditures would have deteriorated probably even more than it actually had, had the school restructuring program not been in place. The gradual reform process, including consensus building among various stakeholders and negotiations with potential losers, together with clear plans for the future, build the foundation for further improvements in school financing.

7.6. Conclusions

The concept of the PCF was first introduced in 1992 in Russia, but it was not until the early 2000s when the federal government started earnestly implementing it as part of the Education Modernization Program. This study examined one of the three pilot regions that started the PCF reform in 2001 and one of the 22 grant recipient regions that joined the reform in 2005, both supported by the Education Reform Project along with a review of the overall policy objectives and the status of the subsequent nationwide expansion. This section summarizes lessons learned based on the two case studies on the implementation of PCF scheme. These findings reinforce the findings in the 72-region study summarized in Annex 1.

Clear legal framework and shared objectives under strong leadership at the regional level: In the two regions visited, it was striking that all the stakeholders interviewed at the different levels—regional, municipal and schools—shared the same understanding of the objectives of the PCF implementation and were supportive of the objectives. In both regions, there was a clear and conducive legal framework as well as strong and determined leadership at the regional level, not only by administration of the Ministries of Education and Finance, but also among political leaders, *i.e.*, the Regional Governor or President. Their dissemination strategy helped ease, if not completely eliminate, resistance against the reform among those who were going to be or perceived to be losers.

Interdependency between school network rationalization and the PCF reform: It is interesting that different regions took different paths in the implementation of PCF and restructuring of school networks. For instance, the restructuring was an initial goal in Chuvash, while the implementation of PCF was more important goal in Tver. What is common across regions, however, is that both these reforms need to interplay in order to see visible outcomes. Other reform programs such as the provision of equipment, computers, and educational materials for resource centers as well as school buses and road construction have facilitated the smooth implementation of PCF and restructuring because parents could expect some positive outcomes of the reform. Hence, the introduction of PCF scheme accompanied by school financial autonomy has facilitated the school network restructuring at the municipal level and class consolidations at the school level, and vice versa, but there is no way to evaluate the impacts of these reforms separately.

PCF not only from the region to municipalities, but also down from municipalities to the school level: The PCF scheme is not just about budget allocations from the region to municipalities, but also from municipalities to schools. As long as municipalities allocate budget to schools according to the input-based norms, efficiency gains at the municipal level will be very limited. Also, even though schools are given the authority to plan their budget according to their needs, the fragmented financing mechanism between regional subventions and municipal budgets and the Treasury system have constrained school's financial autonomy. Capacity building of school principals and accountants in school financial management is crucial to implement the PCF at the school level.

No rigorous evidence to prove that the PCF is effective to improve academic performance: Anecdotal evidence suggests that PCF has been an effective tool for motivating schools to improve the quality of education and student academic performance to compete for students, particularly in urban areas, but there is no quantitative data which can rigorously prove that the PCF scheme alone has exclusively contributed to such improvement, or indeed that such improvement has taken place at all.

Long-term perspectives: The implementation of a project takes time, at least a few years, starting from legal reforms, consensus building among various stakeholders, and technical capacity building for administrators and school directors. Therefore, mitigating measures such as municipal coefficients in Tver may be necessary and appropriate during the transitional period. However, the region and municipalities need to have a clear strategy and timetable for the transitional and post-transitional periods so that municipalities and schools can have sufficient time for adjustment with clear targets.

Monitoring and evaluation: The Federal MOES has not played to date a significant role in monitoring and evaluation of the PCF implementation. It is crucial to strengthen the role of MOES in monitoring and evaluation at the federal level, accumulating knowledge and experiences from various regions, and providing regions with technical skills and with opportunities for sharing experiences with one another.

References

Babko, N. and Klimanov, V. (2007), *Review of Regional Experience in Introducing Per Capita Funding Principles in General Secondary Education, Moscow. Seventy-two out of 88 regions responded to the study.* Unofficial translation is available for pp. 55-58 and pp. 185-190.

Canning, M (2004), *The Modernization of Education in Russia*, unpublished World Bank Policy Note.

Government of the Chuvash Republic (2003); *List of Threshold Adjustment Indexes Reflecting Ungraded Schools and Specific Characteristics of Special Education Schools, Gymnasiums for 2004*, approved by the Resolution of the Cabinet of Ministers of Chuvash Republic #336 date December 25, 2003.

Government of the Chuvash Republic (2007); *List of Adjustment Coefficients for 2007*, approved by the Resolution of the Cabinet of Ministers of Chuvash Republic #321 dated December 20, 2006.

Government of the Russian Federation (2001); *Concept of Modernization of Russian Education for the period up to 2010* (Protocol # 44, 25.10.2001).

Higher School of Economics (2010); "Education in the Russian Federation 2010 - Yearbook of Statistics", Moscow: Higher School of Economics.

NTF (2002); *Methodological Guidelines: Calculation and Implementation of Per Capita Budgetary Financing of General Education Schools,* Center for Social Consulting 'Stratosfera,' National Training Foundation, Moscow.

Tver *Oblast* Department of Education (2010); "Monitoring of Indicators of Transfer to Per Capita Financing of Municipal Educational Systems of Tver oblast in 2010", Tver *Oblast*, Russian Federation.

World Bank (2001a); *Agreed Minutes of the Negotiations between the delegations of the Russian Federation and the International Bank for Reconstruction and Development regarding Education Reform Project', March 22, 2001.*

World Bank (2001b); *Project Appraisal Document on a Proposed Loan in the Amount of US$50 million to the Russian Federation for an Education Reform Project, April 30, 2001.*

World Bank (2004); *Per Capita Financing of Education: Experience and Issues,* Report No. 29943, Moscow.

World Bank (2005); *Section II Methodological Guidelines: Calculation and Implementation of Budgetary Financing Normative for General Education Institutions,* Moscow (original in Russian, unofficial translation).

World Bank (2007); "Implementation Completion and Results Report (IBRD-46050) on a Loan No.:4605-RU in the Amount of US$50 Million to the Russian Federation for an Education Reform Project", Report No. ICR0000393, Human Development Sector Unit, Europe and Central Asia Region. Washington, DC: The World Bank.

Annex A. Factors Influencing the Implementation of PCF in 72 Regions

The progress of the PCF implementation varies between the three pilot project regions, 22 grant recipient regions, some other regions implementing the PCF without the ERP support, and the remaining regions which are yet to implement it. A study of the PCF implementation in 72 regions[34] has identified the following common factors that have affected the implementation process:

Positive Factors

- **Legal framework**: Appropriate legislation at the regional level, including budget laws.
- **Leadership**: Strong leadership at the RMOE, which was typically observed in the pilot and grant-recipient regions.
- **Regional strategies**: A clear regional strategy for stimulating municipalities to use PCF for allocations to schools, including a school network restructuring.
- **Strategies for the transitional period**: Gradual implementation of the PCF with clearly specified annual targets.
- **Dialogue among stakeholders**: Active dialogue and cooperation between the MOE and MOF at the regional and municipal levels, between the Region and municipalities, and between the municipality and schools.
- **Preparatory work**: Analysis on school mapping and restructuring of school network and analysis on school mapping.
- **School financial management capacity**: Capacities of school principals, accountants, and School Board members in managing school finance.

Negative Factors

- **Lack of clearly defined objectives and outcomes in the <u>federal</u> legislation**: Because the PCF was initially supported by a project without federal government's legal endorsement, many non-pilot project regions could not understand the objectives and methodology of the new financing mechanism at the initial stage.
- **Perceived loss of power and budget**: Some regional and municipal education and financial authorities resisted the introduction of PCF because a more transparent financing system reduced their control over education institutions. School directors who expected to receive smaller budgets also resisted it.
- **Expected negative outcomes of school network restructuring**: Municipal authorities resisted the restructuring of school networks because (i) schools are the center of life in many rural settlements; (ii) children must be assured of access to alternative schools, (iii) a school closure will create employment problems for the redundant staff, and (iv) the vacant premises need to be maintained.
- **Expected difficulties of more financial autonomy for schools**: Headmasters, especially in rural areas, resisted increased autonomy in school financial management because (i) they lack professional skills in budgeting and accounting or experience in mobilizing and managing non-budget revenues or both; and (ii) not all teachers understand the benefits of new opportunities provided by increased independence of the headmaster, and many of them tend to treat it only as an additional load.
- **Limited infrastructure**: In rural areas, access to financial infrastructure (banks, roads, cash collectors' vehicles, etc.) is limited.

Based on the experiences and evaluation findings to date, the MOES intends to define general principles and issue new recommendations on: (i) budget allocation methods from municipalities to schools; (ii) school financial autonomy; and (iii) methodology on PCF for pre-school education, disabled schools, stipend, and utilities[35]

Annex B. List of People Interviewed for the Country Case Study

Federal Level

Mr. Igor Remoienko, Deputy State Policy on Education Restructuring and Education Reform
Ms. Natalia Kondrashova, Deputy Executive Director, National Training Foundation
Ms. Tatyana Trofimova, ERP PIU Project Director, National Training Fundation (NTF)
Ms. Natalia Kondrashova, Deputy Executive Director, NTF
Ms. Aleksandra Velikanova, Financial Officer, NTF
Ms. Nadia Babko, Consultant (author of the 72 region study on per capita financing)

Chuvash Republic

Ms. Chernova Galina Petrovna, Minister of Education, Chuvash Republic
Ms. Petrova Svetlana, Deputy Minister, Pre-school and School Dept., Rep. MOE
Ms. Vanerkina Rimma, Head of Financial Dept., Rep. MOE
Ms. Gerdo Natalia, Project Coordinator, ERP (until December 2006)
Ms. Tsherbatkina Tatyana, Head of Department of Finance, Republic

CHEBOKSARY TOWN

Mr. Kudryashov Sergey, Head of DOE
Mrs. Chadkova Elena, Deputy Director
School Director and Chief Accountant

CHEBOKSARSKIY RAYON

Mr. Phomin Vickenti Genadyevich, School Director, Trenkassy Secondary School (Resource Center)
Fadeeva Galina, School Director, Opitniy Secondary School
Stepanova Lilia, Accountant
Krasnoarmeiskiy Rayon
Head of Municipal DOE, Krasnoarmeiskiy Municipality
Ms. Galina Yulmassova, School Director
Mr. Nikolay Antonov, Deputy Head of Municipal Administration

Tver Oblast

Ms. Irina Ivanova, Regional Department of Education
Ms. Marianna Shlinchyak, Regional Department of Education
Ms. Irina Maksimenkova, Deputy Minister, Department of Finance
Mr. Dmitoy Kulikov, Deputy Head, Unit of Education, Department of Finance

ZUBTSOV MUNICIPALITY

Mr. Anton Melnik, Head, Municipal Department of Education
Ms. Natalya Prokofyeva, School Director, Pogorelskaya School
Accountant, Pogorelskaya School
School Principal and Accountant, Staro-Ustinovskaya School

VISHNY VOLOCHECK RAYON

Mr. Anatoliy Irgistkin, Head, Municipal Department of Education
School Principal and Accountant, Solnechnaya School
School Principal and Accountant, Krasnoholmaskaya School

Notes

1. I gratefully acknowledge the research support of Kirill Vasiliev (Research Analyst, Human Development Unit, Europe and Central Asia Region, World Bank) and Natalia Tipenko (Consultant), who were part of the team that conducted this research, and of Dmitry Chugunov (Consultant), who provided me with the information to update some key sections. I would also like to thank the federal, regional and municipal officers, school principals and teachers, and members of the Project Management Unit for their generous cooperation during the field visits to the Chuvash *Republic* and the Tver *Oblast* in March 2007.
2. See Government of the Russian Federation (2001).
3. Research instruments include an analysis of government policy documents and materials produced under the Education Reform Project (ERP), interviews with officials of the Federal Ministry of Education and Science and staff of the central Project Implementation Unit for the ERP, and field visits to the Tver *Oblast* and Chuvash Republic in March 2007. The two regions were selected because they were considered 'successful' regions in implementing the PCF. In each of the two regions, the team visited two to three municipalities and two to three schools for interviews.
4. The term general secondary education (GSE) is a literal translation from a Russian expression that prevailed from former Soviet times. GSE refers collectively to the cycle encompassing both primary and secondary education. For purposes of consistency with the usage in Russian, however, the GSE expression is retained here.
5. About 4 percent of the GSE schools were either of *gymnasium* or *lyceum* type, specializing in certain subjects.
6. See Higher School of Economics (2010).
7. There are other types of political jurisdictions of the Federation: *krai*, autonomous territory (*okrug*) and two cities–Moscow and St. Petersburg. These are all treated as regions in this report.
8. Except for special education and special program schools, for which regions were responsible.
9. The Samara *Oblast* adopts an exceptional structure: it has established education districts between the *oblast* and municipalities, and shifted the municipal responsibilities to the education districts under direct control by the *oblast*. In other words, this structure made it easier for Samara to implement the PCF scheme up to the school level without another layer at the municipal level, but it is unclear whether Samara can maintain this structure even after the pilot project, or whether this structure may be expanded to other regions or both.
10. Initially, the Samara and Yaroslavl *Oblasts* and the Chuvash Republic were selected as the pilot regions, but the Voronezh *Oblast* replaced Yaroslavl at a much later stage at the end of 2004 because the latter could not reach a sub-loan agreement with the Federal government.
11. Since 2003, all schools in the Russian Federation have at least two separate accounts under the Municipal Treasury—one for the regional budget and the other for the municipal budget. Each school may have up to six accounts, including non-government revenues.
12. Canning (2004).
13. The ERP was funded by the World Bank and implemented from mid-2001 to December 2006. The ERP aimed: (i) to improve quality and standards; (ii) to promote the efficient and equitable use of scarce public resources for education; (iii) to modernize the education system (structure of network and institutions); and (iv) to improve the flexibility and market-relevance of initial vocational education. See World Bank (2001b) for a detailed project description.
14. This section largely draws from National Training Foundation (2002). Note that the methodologies were not formally adopted as MOES' official methodologies.
15. The federal government established the NTF in 1994 as a commercial organization to administer market oriented training programs and to act as a Project Implementation Unit (PIU) for the World Bank-funded Management and Financial Training Project (1994-2000). It served as a PIU for another Bank-funded Education Innovation Project (1997-2004) as well.
16. The index was obtained empirically based on the actual costs in several regions. When calculating the normative, regions are recommended to clarify these values according to the region-specific features.

17. Initially, the Samara and Yaroslavl *Oblasts* and the Chuvash Republic were selected as the pilot regions, but the Voronezh *Oblast* replaced Yaroslavl at a much later stage at the end of 2004 because the latter could not reach a sub-loan agreement with the Federal government.
18. World Bank (2001a).
19. World Bank (2004, 2005).
20. See Annex 1 for a summary of a study on the implementation of the PCF in 72 regions, some of which implemented the PCF without the ERP support (Babko & Klimanov, 2007).
21. The *National Project* began financing supplementary salaries for teachers from the Federal budget based on the number of students. In addition, regions are currently allowed to introduce a regional teacher salary scheme for top-ups, but only a limited number of regions have introduced it. In 2005, the Leningrad and Tumen *Oblasts* introduced such a scheme, and some others joined in 2006. The Tver *Oblast* also plans to introduce the regional salary scheme (10 percent top-up) in 2008. The MOES expects that all top-ups provided through the *National Project* will be replaced with regional governments' budgets in a few years.
22. As of 2007, the Federal MOES expected to complete the nationwide implementation by 2009, but MOES has delayed the deadline to 2012.
23. Regional-level Education Authority Bodies have different names in Russia, although their functions and responsibilities are very similar. In Tver, it is called the Department of Education, but for consistency and simplicity, in this paper we call all regional level education authorities Regional Ministry of Education (RMOE). Similarly, in Tver, each municipality has a department of education.
24. He was a staff member of the central Project Implementing Unit (PIU) for the ERP until mid-2005. After the case study was conducted, he was promoted to the Minister of Education and Science in August 2007.
25. In 2003, the Russian Federation combined the end-of-school exams and university admissions into a single Unified State Exam. Each candidate must take tests in mathematics and Russian Language as well as at least two other subjects relating to the courses they plan to take at university. Each test has three parts: a multiple-choice section, short-answer questions covering factual knowledge, and longer essays on more challenging questions. Marks are given out of 100. The highest level is so difficult that only one student in 10,000 will achieve the maximum score (Source: http://news.bbc.co.uk/nolpda/ukfs_news/hi/newsid_3485000/3485939.stm).
26. It should be noted, however, that the regional MOES/MOF ended up providing additional funds on top of the budget reflecting municipal coefficients for about five municipalities with small remote schools toward the end of the fiscal year as a transitional measure limited to one year.
27. See Tver *Oblast* Department of Education (2010).
28. Municipalities co-finance the bus program with the regional government, and the cost sharing proportion is decided based on the negotiations between the two levels of government.
29. Schools with less than 20 students are not legal entities, but branch schools of bigger schools.
30. The Head of the Municipal DOE and school directors together helped those made redundant find other opportunities: thirty were transferred to similar positions in other schools; two were pensioners; nine retired; eight looked for jobs with an employment agency. The fate of the rest is unknown.
31. The 12 sample schools are not necessarily representative of the entire population in the Cheboksary Town.
32. Generally, schools less than 100 students are categorized as small schools, but it could vary across municipalities because each municipality defines the size of 'small schools.' The Region defines small schools as those with less than 100 students.
33. In order to attract young teachers in rural areas, the regional and municipal education authorities provide scholarships for pedagogical universities for those who want to work in rural schools.
34. See Babko and Klimanov (2007). Because the study relies primarily on questionnaires, with in-depth interviews having been conducted in 12 regions only, it could not capture the complete picture of the implementation status of each region.
35. According to an interview with the MOES officers in March 2007.

CHAPTER 8

Per Capita Financing of General Education in Europe and Central Asia: Has It Delivered on Its Promise? An Overview of Six Country Case Studies

Dina Abu-Ghaida[1]

8.1. Introduction

The recent introduction of systems of per capita financing (PCF) in the Europe and Central Asia (ECA) region entailed a significant departure from the way most of the educational systems across the region had been financed for ages. The six country case studies (Armenia, Estonia, Georgia, Lithuania, Poland, and Russia) that make up this book have attempted to present a summary of the challenges that these countries faced in designing and implementing such schemes and an assessment of the main achievements in the form of concrete outcomes around three main areas: efficiency, equity and transparency/ accountability. This final chapter collapses all this wealth of information in an effort to contrast the experiences of each of them and derive a series of lessons learned over time.

The rest of the chapter is organized as follows: Section 8.2 covers the various objectives of the reform within the context of decentralization in each of the countries. Section 8.3 discusses variations in design, funding and coverage of these new finance mechanisms. Section 8.4 evaluates the impact of these reforms in terms of the set of outcomes mentioned above (efficiency, equity and transparency/accountability), also taking a brief look at what happened to the core goal of any educational system: improving the quality of education. Section 8.5 concludes by summarizing the main lessons learned for each of these countries.

8.2. Different Objectives of Per Capita Finance Reform in ECA—But in the Context of Decentralization

The case studies demonstrate the importance of decentralization reforms in ECA countries as drivers for implementation of per capita financing in these countries and for the reach of the per capita formula, i.e. whether it allocates funding to the local government or all the way down to the school. In addition, the case studies document a range of policy objectives of the per student finance reform (schematically summarized in Table 8.1) including improved equity and efficiency of education spending (the latter often expressed in terms of rationalization of the school network); increased competition amongst schools, leading to better quality education; increased school autonomy; and improved transparency and accountability of expenditures. While the discussion in this section relies on the case studies and highlights some objectives for some countries more than others, it must also be acknowledged that the lines are blurred among these different objectives, e.g. increased school autonomy can be expected to lead to improved efficiency if school directors reallocate funds to more productive inputs. In addition, since the implementation of per capita financing occurs over a period of several years, some objectives may rise to the forefront more than others at different times—an evolution that is documented in the individual case studies where applicable.

Decentralization of responsibility for general education to either local governments or directly to schools features prominently in the reforms implemented in tandem with, or as precursors to, per capita finance reform in the case study countries. This is, of course, similar to the experience in the West described above where countries experienced major advances in formula funding of schools as a result of decentralization to the school level and promotion of school-based management. ECA countries too were attempting to come to grips with financing schools in the context of ongoing decentralization reforms, and resorted to per capita financing of education as it promised to deliver on the many objectives policymakers hoped to achieve. In the case of ECA countries, however, the degree of decentralization and, by extension, the reach of the per student formula, varied. In some countries, recently elected local governments were charged with providing education services and the per student formula was used by the central government to allocate funding to local government, which in turn chose the approach by which it determined funding for individual schools. In other countries, the central government used the per student formula to determine the budget of individual schools, which it then either provided for all schools to the relevant local government or directly to the individual school.

Table 8.1. Policy Objectives of Per Capita Financing in Case Study Countries

Improvements in	Armenia	Estonia	Georgia	Lithuania	Poland	Russia
Equity				X	X	X
Efficiency	X			X	X	
-- in particular, rationalizing school network	X	X		X		X
Competition		X		X		X
School autonomy	X		X	X		X
Accountability	X					
Transparency				X		X
Quality				X		X

Note: As suggested by country case studies in this book. See chapters 2 through 7.

In the case of Poland, in 1990 around 2,500 democratically elected local governments, called *gminas*, were created and assigned a wide range of local social services, including education, for which they were assigned sources of tax revenues and grants.

This occurred after the election of the first non-communist government in 1989, leading to profound economic, political, and social changes for the country in the 1990s. Among them was the decentralization of political power, seen by many as essential to breaking up the centralized communist state (Levitas and Herczyński 2002). Thus, the main reason for decentralizing general education to local government was to promote local democratic institutions and diffuse political power rather than to use decentralization as an instrument for improving the quality of education. It was, however, hoped that local governments would be willing to invest more in school facilities than the central government and would have the incentive to reduce school debts.

Responsibility for primary schools was to be devolved to *gminas* from 1994 onwards, so the 1993 Law on *Gmina* Revenues introduced a new method of funding primary education: a general purpose education grant, or "subvention" as it is referred to in Poland, is allocated to *gminas* according to a per student formula to be developed by the National Ministry of Education as a contribution to the financing of their recurrent educational expenditures. The Ministry was faced with the problem of considerable differences in per pupil costs between rural and urban *gminas*, costs in the former often being three or four times those in the latter. Furthermore, the much higher per student costs in rural schools were in many cases not explainable based on external factors, such as a sparse population or poor road infrastructure. And finally, Poland is unique among the countries covered in this book in having very strong and active teacher unions that defend the Teachers' Charter (legislation that protected teachers under the previous regime). Thus, the Ministry had to grapple with two conflicting objectives for the formula: creating a funding system that was more horizontally equitable and efficient, on the one hand, and, on the other, a system that was politically acceptable to teacher and rural interests.

Since independence, Estonia has experienced rapid political and economic change under a post-independence government that has been liberal, pro-market and keen to foster decentralization. It revived the pre-war municipalities as units of local government so that today, Estonia has 227 municipalities, and although almost 70 percent of the population lives in urban municipalities, over 80 percent of local governments are rural. The Basic Schools and Upper Secondary Schools Act of 1993 assigned responsibility for general education to local governments. The new municipalities were keen to open schools, which they were able to do with little capital expenditure by bringing empty pre-war school buildings back into use. The Act specifies that a school shall have its own budget, may have its own bank account, and that grants for education, based on the number of students, shall be allocated to local governments from the state budget each year. The government in power in 1993 was led by politicians to whom per student funding of general education appealed for a number of reasons, primary amongst which was the desire to promote competition both among public schools and between public and private schools, whose growth would be encouraged by a per student state subsidy. There was, in addition, a desire to promote internal efficiency by inducing municipalities to reduce the number of schools, which had burgeoned since 1991.

The new Georgian government that took power following the "Rose Revolution" of 2004 undertook a systematic effort to improve governance in the country by minimizing the role of local governments, especially in the area of public finance. Thus, local governments were not only deemed to be administratively incompetent but also non-transparent and the Government took away most of their responsibilities, including health, social protection, and local transportation. Some functions were decentralized to the level of service providers, some were centralized, accompanied by a serious effort to privatize providers of social services. With respect to general education, the Ministry of Education agreed with the Ministry of Finance to take funds earmarked for schools away from the local government level and to allocate them directly to schools in the form of school vouchers. Therefore, in the area of school finance, decentralization was introduced down to the school level while other functions in the sector were centralized, e.g. opening and closure of schools was the responsibility of the Ministry. In addition to the introduction of per student funding, other important reform elements included enhanced school autonomy, including budgetary autonomy, and introduction of state exams for candidate school directors as well as introduction of a school accreditation process and teacher licensing system. Georgian reformers did not trust that vouchers will lead to school network consolidation, so they undertook major rationalization of schools just prior to implementing the vouchers.

In Armenia, promotion of school autonomy featured prominently too in the Ministry of Education and Science's adopted Strategy for Reform of the General Education System in 1997. In addition to promoting school autonomy, the Strategy proposed introduction of per capita financing for general secondary education as a tool for improving cost effectiveness (mainly by means of school consolidation), and reducing over-staffing. Thus, the Government's major objectives in introducing per student finance, as stipulated in the Government Decree No. 377 and Education Law of 1999, include: (i) establishment of favorable and promotional conditions by rationalizing and increasing the efficiency of the education system; (ii) implementation of education reform innovations, particularly decentralization of management and financing autonomy to schools and promotion of efficient and sustainable mechanisms for self-dependent schools; and (iii) establishment of the school board as an accountability mechanism by involving communities in school management.

In Lithuania, a working group was set up by the Ministry of Education in 2000-01 with the goal of assessing the inherited system of education finance, identifying the main problems and proposing reform measures. The report of the working group listed the main problems of the previous financing system as (i) education spending varies greatly in different regions or municipalities, although the education standards for pupil achievement are the same; (ii) network of schools of general education is not at its optimum, hence funds are used inefficiently; (iii) the largest share of funding is spent on running the schools and paying teacher salaries while the part for modernization of the teaching process or purchase of teaching materials is in decline; (iv) when distributing funds for implementing the teaching plans for a certain academic year among general education schools, the money is allocated per number of class sets, not per number of students, which leads to the funding of a large number of vacancies in classes; (v) schools have neither independence in planning their spending nor incentives to use the funds allocated efficiently and economically. Accordingly, the goals of the new system were defined as follows: (i) through more efficient use of education funds, to improve the quality of education services; (ii) to optimize the network of general education schools and to ensure equal opportunities to rural and urban students regarding access to quality education; (iii) to create conditions for the network of non-governmental general education schools to develop; (iv) to reduce the number of children who do not attend school;

(v) to strengthen the financial independence of schools; and (vi) to create a transparent education funding arrangement. Therefore, three key areas for reform may be outlined: quality, efficiency, and autonomy.

The Russian Federation (Russia) is a federal country with different institutional and financial solutions adopted by regional governments. The administrative structure in Russia consists of two levels below the federal government—regions (including oblasts and republics) and towns/municipalities (*rayons*) and education administration generally follows this structure. Until 2003, towns and municipalities were responsible for financing the entire budget for general education. Because many municipalities have had difficulties in paying wages and salaries for teachers and support staff in a timely manner, the Federal government amended the Educational Subventions Law in 2003 and made the regional governments responsible for financing the minimum level of education budgets through subventions to the local administrations (towns and municipalities). The minimum level of education budgets was defined to cover wages and salaries for teachers and support staff, the cost of educational materials, technical teaching aids, and other consumables. The local administrations remained responsible for financing the cost of building maintenance and utilities according to their own norms. Per capita financing in Russia had a wide range of objectives, including providing state guarantees of accessibility and equity to ensure complete education for all children; restructuring of the network of educational institutions to raise efficiency of spending; improving quality of education through competition for students; developing financial autonomy of institutions; and enhancing management of educational institutions by, inter alia, improving the transparency of budgetary and non-budgetary funds. An essential element of per capita financing was the decentralization of budget management to the school director, who was to receive a block grant, open and operate a bank account for the school, and flexibly manage a school budget (including funds obtained from non-state sources) without rigid budget headings. In all this, the school director would be accountable to a Board of Trustees at school level and there would be similar Boards at municipal and republican levels.

8.3. Great Variation in Design, Structure, Coverage and Reach of Funding Formulae

The case studies include countries that derived the per student amount in the funding formula using a bottom-up activity-led approach while others employed a more top-down approach based on historical actual expenditures. The funding formulae vary widely in their complexity, with the Armenian and Georgian formulae exhibiting the smallest number of adjustment factors to the per student amount based on school and student characteristics, and the Polish and Lithuanian formulae the greatest number. These school and student characteristics include geographic location, school size, school type, school language of instruction, student grade level, type of student, and type of special needs. The funding formulae also vary in their coverage of the school budget, with the majority excluding capital expenditures and some excluding certain types of recurrent expenditures. Finally, the funding formulae vary in their reach, i.e. whether the formula allocates general education funding on a per student basis to the local government or all the way down to the individual school.

Caldwell et al. (1999) write about phases in the evolution of formula funding based on the experience in Western countries. Accordingly, the first generation of funding formulae was simple pupil/teacher and staffing ratios and small per pupil allowances for consumable items. These formulae assumed that all pupils at a given grade level in a school have the same educational needs and hence cost the same to educate. The second generation of funding formulae was developed precisely in order to take account of differences in learning needs of students, i.e. some students cost more to educate than others. These funding formulae, e.g. the Ross Index in Australia, are indices made up of variables that reflect characteristics, such as economic disadvantage or lack of fluency in the language of instruction, which correlate well with student levels of educational attainment. The additional money per student delivered by these second generation formulae for supplementary educational need was not based on any analysis of the costs of educating students with particular learning needs to a given level of attainment. Rather, the formulae were used to distribute a politically determined sum of money to schools according to their concentration of educationally disadvantaged students. These second generation formulae have now been adapted and incorporated into the more comprehensive third generation formulae, which ideally have the following characteristics:

- *comprehensiveness:* includes all costs of educating students incurred at school level;
- *cost-based:* formula is derived from an analysis of costs of providing students with a specified educational program, differentiated according to student supplementary educational needs and specific costs of school they attend;
- *incentive appropriate:* formula encourages schools to act in ways which are consistent with agreed educational policy objectives.

The per student formulae encountered in the ECA country case studies arguably fall between the first and second generations of formulae described above, with considerable variation in their complexity and hence desire to accommodate the different cost structures of schools. In general, the per student funding formulae observed in the case studies begin with an amount apportioned for each student enrolled and subsequently incorporate adjustment factors, either based on school or student characteristics—see Table 8.2 and Table 8.3. Examples of school characteristics that feature in the different formulae include geographic location, e.g. mountainous, rural, urban, or island; school size; school type, e.g. primary, basic, or boarding school; whether a minority school or one with migrant students; and whether a school with multiple languages of instruction or integrated teaching. Examples of student characteristics that feature in the country case study formulae include the grade level; type of special needs, if any, e.g. students with learning difficulties, mental disorders, or sensory or physical disabilities; adult, evening, or distance learning student; and specialized student, e.g. sports, music, ballet, or art student. As Annex 1 shows, the funding formulae in Armenia and Georgia include the lowest number of adjustment factors based on school and student characteristics, whereas the formulae in Lithuania and Poland contain the greatest number—we will return to this distinction shortly.

The per student amount in the formula can be derived by relying on actual expenditures—a "top-down" approach—or using an activity-based model (Abu-Duhou et al. 1999)—a more "bottom-up" approach. The latter is a methodology for determining the

Table 8.2. Details of Per Capita Financing Formulae: Main Features

Features[1]	Armenia	Estonia		Georgia	Lithuania	Poland	Russia	
		Old Formula	New Formula				Chuvash R.	Tver O.
Scope & Purview[2]								
Entity receiving funding from central government[3]	school	municipality		school	municipality	local government	municipality	
Expenditure types included	all except capital	all		all except capital	teaching process	all except capital & preschool	mostly all, excluding capital and utility	
Flexibility in allocating received funding	substantial	partial		n.a.	partial	substantial	substantial	
Non-formula funding in education	vulnerable schools	recurrent expenditures	n.a.	vulnerable schools & teacher salary hikes	recurrent expenditures & non-teaching staff	varies	recurrent expenditures	
Formula in Action								
Derivation of formula (based on what?)	norm-based budget analysis	actual municipal expenditures	notional cost per student	actual school expenditure	standard per student amount	standard per student amount	standard per student costs & adjustment factors	
Buffers, adjustments or "hold harmless" clauses included	to schools with less than norm-based allocations	n.a.	to prevent large year-to-year funding reductions	to schools where teacher salaries exceed school revenues	n.a.	allocation per student has to be within certain level	municipal coefficients during transition period	

[1] See Annex 1 for a more comprehensive review of each cell in this table.
[2] All funding refers to formula funding unless otherwise stated.
[3] If Russia, then from the regional (oblast or republican) government.

Table 8.3. Details of Per Capita Financing Formulae: Adjustment Factors

Adjustment Factors[1]	Armenia	Estonia Old Formula	Estonia New Formula	Georgia	Lithuania	Poland	Russia Chuvash R.	Russia Tver O.
School characteristics								
Geographic location	x	x	x	x	x	x	x	x
School size					x		x	
School/institution type					x	x	x	x
Minority schools					x	x		
Multiple languages of instruction		x	x		x	x		
Migrant students					x			
Integrated teaching		x			x	x		
Student Characteristics								
Grade level					x			
Special education students		x	x		x	x	x	x
Adult students					x	x		
Home schooling/independent learning		x			x		x	
Vocational students					x	x		
Preschool students					x			
Sports students						x		
Music students						x		
Art students						x		

1. See Annex A for a more comprehensive review of each cell in this table.

resources needed to deliver a specified curriculum for particular students in specific school contexts.[2] Thus, activity-based funding focuses on the teaching and learning activities required by the educational program provided for students and costs the staff and non-staff resources required. It starts with assumptions about class size, number of hours students are taught per week or year, and the non-face-to-face hours teachers require for preparing lessons, curriculum planning, assessment, recording and reporting, etc. In addition, the number of support staff working directly to support teaching and learning can be estimated and included, and additional sums allocated for "curriculum support resources" such as books, materials, and equipment. Beyond these direct costs, other resource requirements can include management and administrative staff time, time for activities related to student welfare and career counseling, etc. Thus, the three aspects of activity-led funding analysis are: identification of the teaching and learning activities that are to be included, costing these activities, and the transformation of these "costings" into a funding formula for schools. Amongst the case study countries, only the new Estonian and the Lithuanian funding formulae employ the activity-based approach. The remaining formulae derive the per student amount, at least initially, based on analysis of actual past expenditures in the sector. In both cases, however, adjustments to the formula must take the available budget envelope into account and may employ elements of the other approach.

The funding formulae vary in the degree to which they cover the entire school budget, i.e. whether they include capital expenditures in addition to recurrent expenditures, and which elements of the latter. Thus, the formulae in Armenia and Georgia cover all recurrent costs–but not capital expenditures. Indeed, the Estonian funding formula alone includes a per student allocation for capital expenditures, though only as of 2005, having previously covered only teacher salaries and textbooks. Formula funding is arguably not suitable for allocating all types of public expenditure on schools, e.g. expenditures that have an uneven incidence over time, such as major capital projects, are not usually suited to allocation by formula to individual schools (Levačić and Ross 1999), as making adjustments that will complicate funding for temporary and often changing expenses remains impractical. Despite the inclusion of capital expenditures in the Estonian formula, not all recurrent costs are included, and municipalities are expected to pay for school operational costs and non-teaching staff out of own budgets. The situation is similar in Russia where municipalities are expected to cover utilities, maintenance, and repairs out of their own resources. Lithuania, on the other hand, distinguishes between expenditures on the teaching process versus the teaching environment, with only the first covered by the funding formula. The teaching process includes salaries of teachers, administrators, and professional staff, teacher in-service training, textbooks, library books, and teaching aids, while the "teaching environment" covers the salaries of technical staff (e.g. cleaners, drivers, gardeners, and cooks), and utilities and communications (telephone and Internet). Finally, Poland's formula is exceptional in that it does not stipulate what aspects of the school budget it is meant to cover, which may be interpreted as the formula covering the entire school budget in theory, but in practice municipalities supplement the formula allocation from their own resources (see more below).

A key distinction concerns whether, having calculated the general education allocation on a per student basis, the resources are transferred from higher-level government to municipalities or to schools directly. Here, only Armenia and Georgia have funding formulae that allocate funds to schools, which were transformed from budgetary institutions to autonomous legal entities.[3] For all other countries, municipalities receive the funds—in the case of Estonia, the funds received are earmarked for education, while in Poland they are not, and in Lithuania, although municipalities receive the funds, they also have prescribed to them by the central government the allocations for individual schools (with the caveat that municipalities may reallocate up to 5 percent of the total budget among schools). The fact that Armenia and Georgia also have the simplest funding formulae may therefore be a corollary of central government disbursing to schools with no involvement of local government and hence no discussion and dialogue between central and local government on the formula and its attributes. By contrast, in both Poland and Lithuania (the two countries with the most complex formulae) there is an annual review process that involves both central and local government where issues are raised and specific factors are taken into account. Whether schools receive directly their budgetary allocations from the central government or intermediated through municipalities is not merely a technical question affecting the design of the formula - it has instead important repercussions on the incentives for improvements in efficiency of spending in the system.

8.4. Assessing the Reform: What is the Evidence?

8.4.1. Assessment of Improvements in Efficiency

8.4.1.1. Improving the Efficiency of Spending: Local Governments are Key to Rationalizing School Networks

In their school-consolidation decisions, governments balance considerations of efficiency of the school network with considerations over the value and function that schools have in their respective communities. The case studies document a range of approaches to rationalizing school networks as a result of, in tandem with, or even as a precursor to implementing per capita finance. Thus, Georgia conducted a massive school network consolidation process in preparation for the implementation of per student finance reform. Lithuania and the Russian Chuvash Republic, on the other hand, succeeded in rationalizing the school network by a combination of the incentives inherent in their funding formulae and the obligation imposed on local government by the central and Republican government, respectively, to implement network consolidation plans. Poland stands out perhaps in having relied exclusively on the funding formula to achieve network consolidation, including introducing an adjustment factor into the formula to account for the cost of transporting students to school. Estonia's experience is noteworthy as well, in that the pressure felt by municipalities to close small schools led to a backlash and the adoption of a new formula that relieve much of this pressure. Finally, the Armenian central government priority to initially exclude small schools from the per student funding reform and the lack of budgetary authority over schools by regional governments meant the country has not been able to rationalize its school network. For considerable school consolidation to occur, there must be proper distribution of financial management authority among the various levels of government, as well as adjustments built into the reform, such as earmarked financing or bonuses, that facilitate school closings.

The country case studies demonstrate that closure of under-enrolled schools is by no means an automatic corollary of putting in place per capita financing. The 2000 ECA education sector strategy (Berryman 2000) highlights the problems of inefficient and inequitable education spending and goes on to state that "[i]t is almost universally accepted now that 'money follows student' is the preferred alternative" (p.48), where "money follows student" means that funding for education is a function primarily of the number of students. In theory, per capita financing permits local governments to find the most efficient means of providing education within the overall spending envelope provided by higher-level government. In particular, per capita financing imposes efficiency measures on jurisdictions with under-enrolled schools. Furthermore, under a per student formula, falling enrollment will cause a drop in school funding, forcing local government to close schools they can no longer afford. In practice, however, falling enrolments may not trigger a drop in funding, and local governments may lack the legal authority or political will to close schools, particularly if these function as an important center of village or community life.

The case of Poland demonstrates a gradual alignment of the incentives resulting from the funding formula as one way of achieving rationalization of the school network. In the initial 1994 design of the Polish per student formula, the commensurate legislation specified that any individual *gmina* must not receive less than 100 percent of its inflation-adjusted allocation in the previous year. This approach is of course more reminiscent of historical than per student funding. Consequently, in *gminas* where student numbers fell, as was often the case, allocation per student had to increase and efficiency gains were not realized. A major reform of the per student formula took place in 2000, which removed the guarantee to *gminas* of receiving last year's inflation-adjusted allocation, amongst other significant changes. Instead, *gminas* were given weaker guarantees, namely that the allocation per student could not be cut below nor increased above certain levels. This

---

Box 8.1. To Pilot or not to Pilot? Issues in Introducing the Per Student Finance Reform

By Jan Herczyński

Only Russia and Armenia chose to use pilots to introduce per capita financing mechanisms in education. Poland, Lithuania, Estonia, and Georgia were able to successfully design per capita financing systems, amend the laws to regulate the new rules and financial flows, and then introduce the new mechanisms in the whole country in one step. In Russia there was no transfer of experience between the pilot oblast and oblasts that introduced per capita financing at a later stage. Thus, in Russia the pilot mechanism was in fact a staggered, phased approach to implementing per capita financing, and not a trial and error exercise leading to adjustments based on an evaluation of results obtained and difficulties encountered. Armenia remains the only example of a successful pilot with a subsequent national roll-out. While systematically extending per capita financing, the Armenian authorities were also amending the formulas used, and most importantly adjusting the per student finance mechanism to protect small, vulnerable schools.

Two of the typical challenges for pilot projects are comparability with the rest of the country and the limited scope of the implementation of the reform in the selected locations. Typically, the pilot schools or districts receive additional financial or organizational support and often higher allocation than non-pilot schools. Therefore, the results of the pilot schools are not fully comparable to the results of non-pilot schools, which makes it difficult to formulate useful lessons. Furthermore, introduction of a formula itself, without changing the legal and procedural environment in which it operates, is unlikely to lead to practical changes in the way schools are managed (see, for example, Kataoka 2006). The key issue, therefore, is the scope of the pilot project. If the pilot amends the budget and education laws, increases the financial autonomy of local governments or of schools, and addresses the budgeting and management processes in the education sector, then it may have an impact on financing education. However, in this case, the allocation formula is unlikely to be the main element of such a serious pilot project. If, on the contrary, the pilot is restricted to the per student allocation formula, then its usefulness will likely be very limited.

Simulations at the national level can be more appropriate and are certainly a more cost effective instrument of testing different elements of the allocation formula and its coefficients than pilot projects at selected schools or municipalities. Indeed, the successful transition countries that did not use allocation formula pilots adopted the values of their formula coefficients only after analysis of simulation results. In the Georgian case, reformers conducted analysis and simulations with two goals. On the one hand, historical costs of schools were assessed to find the actual values and the relative differences in per student costs of schools of different type and environment. This first result was the basis for adoption of the categorization of school vouchers into city, rural, and mountain vouchers. On the other hand, the simulations were conducted to see what level of school vouchers was compatible with the funds available for pre-university education in the state budget. In general, simulations need to cover all the schools in the country in order to assess the effects of the overall budget constraints, and provide grounds, perhaps, for an increase in funding. Moreover, using computer simulations it is easy to analyze various allocation scenarios, or indeed completely different per student formulas, and compare them with each other. *Pilot projects by themselves can only implement one formula and one set of coefficients and values in only selected locations, and thus can never provide the richness of information and flexibility that can be attained from computer simulations.*

meant that jurisdictions with declining student rolls could experience for the first time a reduction year by year in total allocation. This clearly put pressure on these local governments to economize and so slow down the increase in costs per student as numbers fell by closing down under-enrolled schools. In addition, the 2000 revision of the funding formula included an adjustment factor for students transported to school, which further contributed to local government's ability to close under-enrolled schools. Indeed, data from the National Statistics Office indicated that between 2000 and 2005, the number of primary schools in *gminas* declined by 10 percent while the number of classes fell by nine percent, indicating that *gminas* were taking steps to improve the efficiency of their school networks. Finally, since 2005, *gminas* are not entitled to any guarantees regarding the per student allocation.

Lithuania, on the other hand, succeeded in rationalizing its school network by a combination of the incentives inherent in the funding formula as well as the obligation imposed on all municipalities by the central government to adopt network consolidation strategies. Initially, the Ministry decided not to be involved directly in the rationalization of local school networks. Instead, it used the funding formula as the instrument for achieving this objective by, among other things, decreasing the adjustment factor for small schools by 10 percent to motivate local governments to consolidate school networks. However, the Ministry reversed its decision in this regard when it found that municipalities were very slow in their school consolidation efforts. Instead, the Ministry introduced an obligation for all municipalities to adopt their own consolidation strategies and rewarded those who made the most progress by allocating school buses to them. In addition, school network consolidation was an important component of the World Bank-funded Education Improvement Project, which provided technical support to the Ministry in developing guidelines for local school network consolidation strategies. In 2004, the Ministry mandated the adoption of these strategies by municipalities, and by 2006, 58 out of 60 municipalities had complied. The result was, for example, a dramatic decrease in the number of small primary schools (grades 1-4) from 808 in the 2000/01 academic year to just 114 in the 2005/06 year. It is important to note that municipalities not only designed their local strategies but also implemented them cooperatively with school communities.

Similar to Lithuania, in the Russian Chuvash Republic, the Republican government required all municipalities to prepare a school restructuring plan, which it then supported by improving roads and providing school buses through Republican and Federal programs. As a result of systemic planning and physical support, most municipalities have made considerable progress to date in restructuring the senior secondary level first, and more recently, the lower levels. Consequently, the total number of schools decreased by 18 percent (from 686 to 561) between 2001 and 2006. Most municipalities have been in the final stages of closing very small rural schools, which only occurs in agreement with the rural council, and even when schools are closed, teachers and support staff are rarely laid off. Instead, highly qualified teachers are transferred to bigger schools, while others retire or find different jobs within the school system. Thus, while per capita financing may have provided the impetus for school network rationalization in the Chuvash Republic, several other factors, including a school restructuring plan and provision of transportation, contributed to its success.

Georgia, on the other hand, conducted a massive school network consolidation process in preparation for and as a precursor to implementation of per capita financing. Thus, in conjunction with decentralizing several aspects of school management down to the school, the closure and opening of schools was defined as one of the functions of the Ministry of Education. Therefore, prior to introducing per capita financing in the country, the Ministry began a process of reducing the number of schools from 3,153 in 2005 to a target of 1,800 schools (the number of schools in 2007 was down to 2,227). The target total number of schools was established based on a combination of a school mapping exercise and the introduction of some criteria for network optimization. Examples of these criteria include proximity to a large school (especially in the cities), unsustainable small schools with possibility to transport students to a larger school (in particular, availability of roads in the mountains and countryside), and small primary schools (which were transformed into affiliated schools subordinated to a larger full secondary institution). In this regard, the Ministry purchased a number of buses for transportation of children to consolidated schools.

Estonia is in the interesting position of having implemented a per student formula that put pressure on municipalities to close small schools and then deciding to design a new formula (as of 2008) that instead favors municipalities with 1,600 students or less. In other words, a particular concern in Estonia is that per student funding has put too much pressure on the financial viability of small schools during a period of marked demographic decline. Rural areas exhibit a great desire to preserve even very small rural schools. In addition, despite the concerns of some educationalists about the quality of education in small rural schools, they remain popular with many rural parents, and as a result, several of the political parties support the maintenance of small schools. The new formula therefore makes explicit the minimum school size that the government considers is to be maintained, and municipalities are free to sustain even smaller schools if they choose to allocate their own funds to that end.

Finally, Armenia, where local governments did not play a role in education, has not rationalized its school network because the central government opted to protect small schools and regional governments were not positioned to conduct or foster an efficient school reorganization. Despite the substantial reduction in the number of students in the period 2000-07, the total number of schools has declined very little (from 1,389 in 2000 to 1,362 in 2007). Most of the decline was the result of school consolidation in urban areas during 2003-05. In fact, as the central government excluded small, remote, and border schools[4] from the application of the per student formula, the proportion of schools with fewer than 300 students remained high at 55 percent in 2005. After the government piloted school management capacities at the local (*hamaink*) level and judged them to be inadequate, regions regained the management of those schools. Moreover, the regional governments–with deconcentrated offices of the Ministry of Education and Science–have no authority to reallocate budgets among schools or to arrange for transportation for students to schools. Thus, they have neither the incentives nor the tools to promote school consolidation.

8.4.1.2. IMPROVING THE EFFICIENCY OF SPENDING: INCREASING STUDENT-TEACHER RATIOS CANNOT BE ACCOMPLISHED BY PER STUDENT FUNDING ALONE

The case studies demonstrate the importance of having the correct incentives emanate from the funding formula (as in the case of Lithuania) but also of taking into account political economy considerations, e.g. assuring teacher welfare through provision of the right redundancy packages where necessary (as in the case of Armenia).

Armenia succeeded in increasing the student-teacher ratio primarily by making teachers redundant and providing a teacher redundancy package under the Education Sector Reform Program.[5] The package offered the following options: (i) professional training for new jobs; (ii) relocation grants for those who wished to move from urban to rural schools; (iii) small business start-up support; and (iv) a cash payment equal to six months' salary for teachers within five years of the official retirement age of 62 years. As a result, 7,200 teachers were made redundant during 2004-06, which fell short of the original 2003 target of 15,000 teachers, as a result of growing political opposition, amongst other issues. Nonetheless, Armenia achieved substantial internal efficiency gains during 2001-07: as the number of students, driven by demographic changes, declined by over 20 percent, the number of classes was reduced by 24 percent, teaching staff positions by 35 percent and non-teaching staff positions by 34 percent. As a result, the student-teacher ratio increased from 10.8 in 2003 to 13.9 in 2006 and the average teaching load increased from 18 to 22 hours per week.

Poland, on the other hand, has experienced a 14 percent *decline* in the student-teacher ratio over the period 2000-07, primarily as a result of the Teachers' Charter, which made it difficult to improve the efficiency with which teachers are deployed as student numbers fell by 16 percent over the same period. Initially in 1994, the design of the formula in Poland ensured that per pupil allocations were higher for *gminas* with low student-teacher ratios, with initial adjustment factors for *gminas* based on average class size. This arrangement gave perverse efficiency incentives, which were removed in 1996 when the class size criteria were abandoned. In response to the decline in student numbers, surplus teachers were absorbed by the system by creating more teaching hours by splitting classes. The Teachers' Charter includes regulations that make the market for teachers very rigid. On the other hand, local governments have had more impact on improving efficiency in the use of non-teaching staff compared to the previous normative approach since local governments are able to determine their own staffing. As a result of the pressure they felt on their budgets, local governments have tended to eliminate unnecessary non-teaching positions and raise, for example, the work load of cleaners.

Finally, the formula itself plays a role in putting in place the right incentives for declaring teachers redundant, as the case of Lithuania demonstrates. At 12 students per teacher, the student-teacher ratio was low and stable over the period 2000-05. Admittedly, this needs to be viewed in the context of the overall decline of student numbers by approximately 10 percent in the same period. At the same time, given the division of funding in Lithuania by teaching process (which includes teacher salaries and is centrally provided) and teaching environment (which is the responsibility of municipalities) and the fact that savings obtained under the teaching process cannot be used toward the teaching environment, it is clear that municipalities had no incentive to achieve savings under the teaching process, certainly not at the cost of entering the politically difficult terrain of teacher redundancy.

8.4.2. Assessment of Improvements in Equity

8.4.2.1. Improving the Equity of Spending: Funding Formula Provides the Incentives But the Role of Local Government is Again Key

The case studies document the myriad of ways that funding formulae attempt to address vertical equity by adjusting for student characteristics, such as special learning needs, or horizontal equity by adjusting for structural differences, such as school geographic location. However, none of the formulae studied adjust explicitly for student socioeconomic status—an important input into improving vertical equity. In addition, those formulae with the greatest number of adjustment factors allocate general education funding from central (or regional) to local government, leaving the decision up to local government (within boundaries) as to how funding is divided amongst individual schools. Thus, in Estonia and Poland not only do local governments, which have considerable authority as a result of decentralization reforms, often resort to input-based funding to allocate funds to schools, but they also often supplement the central allocation with their own revenues. In Poland, for example, the result is a wide variation in per student funding across *gminas*, which analysis shows are positively correlated with *gminas*' own revenues, above and beyond any schooling structural differences across *gminas*. This situation implies that per capita financing in Poland has not led to improved horizontal equity at the local government level. The result also illustrates the difficulty in achieving horizontal equity at the local government level when faced with a highly decentralized system where local entities have considerable jurisdiction and funding flexibility. Nonetheless, there is evidence of increased horizontal equity among the schools in Warsaw and Kwidzyn (i.e. equity among similar schools within these local governments), both large urban *gminas* where the local authorities have sought to equalize funding at the school level.

In general, per student formulae in the countries studied take into account student special educational needs and geographic location, but not their actual socioeconomic status. Thus, the per student formulae in almost all country case studies include adjustment factors based on whether schools are located in urban or rural areas, and some include other geographic criteria, such as mountainous or island regions (see Annex A). The principle here is that there are structural differences in education provision in different geographic locations that have cost repercussions that need to be taken into account, e.g. the smaller average size of rural schools, the extra cost of heating mountainous schools, etc. This is, of course, an attempt at ensuring horizontal equity of expenditures–defined above. In addition, several of the formulae take into account student special learning needs and disabilities, since such students require additional inputs, whether in terms of human resources or equipment. The Polish and Lithuanian formulae additionally provide adjustment factors for minority students, and Lithuania further takes into account migrant students. This "unequal treatment of unequals" (Monk 1990) is an attempt at achieving vertical equity of expenditures. Accounting for the minority or migrant status of students is probably the closest that any of the formulae comes to actually considering student welfare level. Of course, many of the above student and school characteristics may be correlated with student welfare level, but it remains the case that none of the formulae reviewed explicitly accounts for student socioeconomic status. From a vertical equity point of view, this is an important shortcoming.

Beyond the actual formula, a key issue in evaluating the horizontal equity impact of per capita financing is the role played by local government. On the one hand, it is arguably the case that per student funding allows the central government to ensure a *minimum* level of education financing in all jurisdictions (Berryman 2000). On the other hand, it is probably not realistic to expect the central government to take into account the different characteristics and needs of students in the allocations it makes. This fact seems to have been recognized by central governments in the countries studied, for the formulae for Armenia and Georgia—the only two countries where allocations are made from the central government to schools—include only geographic adjustment factors and none based on other student or school characteristics. In all other case studies, the central—or regional, in the case of Russia–government allocates funding based on the per student formula but dispenses it to the municipality. Once at the municipal level, different approaches are employed to allocating funding to schools, but even in the most restrictive scenario, i.e. Lithuania, where allocations to individual schools are determined by the central government, municipalities may reallocate up to 5 percent of the total received budget across their schools.

The leeway available to municipalities in allocating funds to schools varies greatly. The case of Lithuania is mentioned above. In Russia, the Chuvash Republic does not instruct its municipalities to apply the same adjustment factors that it has applied in calculating the municipal total allocation, and even the Republic's own adjustment coefficients are modified from those prescribed by the Federal level. And in the Tver Oblast, each municipality was allowed during the transition to per capita financing to adopt a school coefficient within minimum and maximum levels prescribed by the Oblast. In Poland, local government funding for education is not earmarked, and so municipalities are in principle free to reallocate to other sectors, as well as being able to add from their own revenues. In making the decisions as to the allocation to individual schools, *gminas* are constrained by several key regulations on, for example, the number of hours per week that students must be taught the national curriculum, and teacher working load and salary categories as stipulated in the Teachers' Charter. In Estonia, the central government education allocation to municipalities is intended to support recurrent spending on teaching costs, textbooks, and workbooks only, leaving municipalities to fund, at a minimum, non-teaching staff and non-staff costs. Several regulations set by the central government constrain municipal funding decisions, including, for example, provision of free education for all students in grades 1 to 9, the number of hours per week that students must be taught the national curriculum, and maximum class size. At the same time, municipalities have considerable flexibility in making resourcing decisions about their schools, including the power to establish, reorganize and close schools, discretion in determining the number and types of non-teaching posts at schools, and, perhaps most importantly, determining local policies for teacher pay above the statutory basic amount stipulated by the central government.

Municipalities that are free to do so choose a range of methods to allocate funding to individual schools, including input-based funding or what amounts to their own per student formula. In Estonia, most municipalities do not employ a per student formula, although the capital city Tallinn has developed not just one but two per student formulae: one for allocating central government funding to schools, which closely follows state guidelines, and one for distributing the city's own budget. In Poland, the majority of local governments use an input-based approach to determining school budgets, although an increasing number of cities are now experimenting with their own per student formulae for schools. One of the earliest such *gminas* is Kwidzyn, a city of 38,000 inhabitants that has over a decade's experience with per capita financing and designed a three-part formula for determining per student funding to its schools: (i) teaching staff salaries (81 percent); (ii) non-teaching staff salaries (7 percent); and (iii) non-staff expenditures (12 percent).

In Poland and Estonia, where municipalities supplement the central education allocation, there is a wide variation in the resulting per student allocation at the municipal level. In both countries, the central government undertakes a certain level of fiscal equalization across municipalities. For instance, in Poland, local governments that receive in tax revenues more than 120 percent of the national average tax revenue per resident contribute to a fund that ensures that no local government receives less than 85 percent of the national average. However, fiscal equalization is restricted to revenue equalization, so that actual education spending per student is not subject to any such equalization. Thus, in 2005, average current expenditure per student was 24 percent higher in rural than in urban *gminas* and 11 percent higher in mixed *gminas*. This compares with the central allocation per student being 34 percent higher in rural *gminas* and 21 percent higher in mixed than in urban *gminas*. This shows that the relativities in spending assumed by the formula are altered by the actual decisions of *gminas*, which must reflect both the differences in local preferences for education spending relative to other expenditures and the size of *gmina* revenues. Indeed, one of the main factors contributing to differences in education spending per student is differences in the amount that *gminas* fund from their own revenues, with urban *gminas* tending to contribute the most.

While differences in per student spending resulting from structural costs can be consistent with horizontal equity, in Poland the differences in spending vary directly with the *gminas*' own revenues. Relevant structural cost differences here may include population density, size of the *gmina*, average size of school, and the student-teacher ratio, although the last two are clearly amenable to local choice and not strictly purely structural. Using regressions that control for all four structural factors, the extent to which variations in per student expenditure can be explained by differences in the *gminas*' own revenues per capita was found to be statistically significant. The evidence therefore indicates that the Polish per student funding system has not achieved horizontal equity, as the *gminas*' own revenue per capita influences spending per student, particularly in urban *gminas*.[6] This result illustrates how it can be difficult to make gains in horizontal equity at the local government level because of the high degree of decentralization, which gives considerable rights and jurisdiction to local entities.

There is some evidence, however, of improved equity of per student spending within a few municipalities in Poland, although this result relies on strong local government leadership and does not originate from formula funding reforms. Warsaw is seeking to equalize funding among schools, and the trend toward the use of per student formulae in other Polish cities is inspired by their desire to equalize per student spending across their schools. The districts of Warsaw–until recently separate *gminas*–have quite different administrative systems, with the highest cost central district spending twice as much as the lowest spending outer district and even within the central district there are considerable differences in per student costs for equivalent types of schools. The Warsaw education department is working to reduce these differences year by year in the face of parental opposition–without the use of a formula since the cost differentials among schools are too great. The move to reduce inter-school per student cost differences is a step in the direction of improved horizontal equity since there are no apparent structural differences amongst the schools in question that would warrant the existing differences in per student expenditures. In addition, Warsaw educators are increasingly recognizing the evidence on the influence of socioeconomic factors on student achievement and see a correlation between the lower-funded schools and the socioeconomic background of their student bodies. As such, the move to equalize per student funding across Warsaw schools will also constitute a move in the direction of improved vertical equity of expenditures.

8.4.3. Assessment of Improvements in Transparency and Accountability

8.4.3.1. Improving the Transparency and Accountability of Spending: Per Capita Financing Has Made Positive Contributions but There Is Further Room for Improvement

The case studies document the improvement in transparency and accountability of budgetary allocation to local governments and schools as a result of the use of funding formulae (especially when they are simple), public availability of school budgets, and increased stakeholder participation and oversight. There remains, nonetheless, room for further improvement in transparency and accountability, for example by building capacity in budgeting, planning, and school management, expanding the role of school councils, and establishing linkages between financial and schooling outcomes data.

Simplicity of the per student formula contributes to its transparency, while its growing complexity deters technical debate and therefore public oversight. In the case of Estonia, strong features of the old funding formula were its simplicity and the stability over time of the adjustment factors in it. While the process for designing the new formula was transparent, with wide involvement of stakeholders and consultations with local governments and school directors, so that the general principles underlying the formula are understood, it is doubtful that the complex calculations entailed are equally comprehended. Such is the experience in Lithuania, where the complexity of the formula has meant that very few municipalities are able to conduct on their own the necessary calculations to check whether funds allocated to them reflect the results of the formula. In fact, all the main stakeholders, i.e. the Ministries of Education and Finance as well as the association of local governments, rely on the same experts for their information. In this manner, the country loses a vital element of transparency, i.e. the mutual checking and verification, leading to errors, as determined by the State Accounting Office for the first two years of formula implementation. Nonetheless, in Lithuania there is widespread, if incomplete, understanding of the main components of the formula and each year a consensus is reached regarding its amendments. Finally, in Poland the formula is hotly debated at the national level during sessions of a special commission consisting of representatives of central and local governments, despite the fact that the increasing complexity of the adjustment factors renders these discussions more and more difficult.

Accountability and transparency at the local level depend on the process by which the local government determines school budgets and the availability and publicizing of the relevant data. Thus, in Poland, all local governments discuss the annual school budget with school councils. Local governments that employ their own per student formula have a more transparent method of allocation, although this does not always translate into public availability of school budget data. More generally, school budgets are largely determined by the annual organizational plan, a school-level document detailing planned school activities and staffing levels that must conform to regulations regarding the curriculum. School pedagogical councils consisting of all school teachers are presented with the school's annual budget plan, but it is ratified by the local government. Only the school director has very limited executive authority over the school budget and can monitor it at regular intervals. A similar situation occurs in Estonia. In Georgia, school directors present the budget to school boards for discussion and approval; however, the real decision-making power within the school rests with the director. In Lithuania, some schools also have school councils, but their role appears to be even smaller with regards to budget decision-making. Overall, transition countries were arguably not able to develop strong and active school boards, and this clearly limits accountability at the local level.

While, generally speaking, schools and localities have greater financial authority and there is more availability of school-level information since the implementation of recent education finance reforms, the ability of stakeholders to fully exercise either their authority or oversight duties remains elusive because of their limited capacity or information. In Georgia, the budgeting and planning skills of school administrators are insufficient, which has led them to not take advantage of such opportunities as additional funding from donations or participation in projects (Shapiro 2007). School boards also do not have the necessary skills to be active participants and full partners in school management, which makes them rely heavily on school directors and limits accountability. Finally, parents not in the school board have a very poor grasp of school management and budget procedures (Shapiro 2007).

Beyond availability of relevant financial and educational data, accountability is enhanced by direct linkages between education spending and quality of education. Thus, in Poland, while local governments are responsible for financing education, the Ministry of Education and the *kuratoria*[7] are responsible for the quality of education. In other words, *gminas* are held accountable for school resourcing by their electorates while the school and school director are inspected and evaluated by the *kuratorium*. This arrangement does not foster accountability of either local governments or school-level officials for providing the population with high quality education efficiently. However, since the introduction of national tests at the end of primary (grade 6) and lower secondary (grade 9) in 2002, and the *matura* at grade 12 in 2005, as well as the publication of results at the school level by the press, parents and schools are using these measures to make their own judgments about school quality of education. In this manner, both the financial as well as learning outcomes information is available to the school-level actors. Furthermore, larger local governments, including Warsaw, are themselves beginning to link the available financial and education quality data in order to foster school accountability.

8.4.4. Assessment of Improvements in Other Key Areas

8.4.4.1. Improving the Quality of Education: Different Incentives Can Result from the Funding Formula with Different Impact on the Quality of Education

The case studies include the experience of Lithuania, which designed a funding formula primarily focused on improving the quality of general education and, based on available data on student learning, seems to have succeeded in accomplishing this objective. Lithuania also sought to foster competition for students between its public schools and its expanding private school network, all of which may have contributed to the observed improvement in education quality. At the same time, the efficiency objective of per capita financing, insofar as it leads to increased student-teacher ratios, for example, could be at odds with improving quality of education if the implementation of per capita financing is not properly monitored. In the case of Armenia, the efficiency objective has encouraged a form of multi-grade teaching that may not be conducive to imparting a quality education to students. At the same time, however, Armenia has not monitored student learning outcomes so any judgment on the impact of per capita financing on education quality remains conjecture at this stage.

Armenia has increased class size and the student-teacher ratio and fostered multi-grade teaching to reap efficiency gains from per capita financing without collecting, in parallel, data on student learning. While *regional* education departments monitor teacher and student performance according to the state educational standards for curriculum and teaching and learning methodologies, no data have been collected to examine whether per capita financing has resulted in any changes in student performance. Such changes may have potentially resulted from the increase in class size and student-teacher ratio, as well as the increase in multi-grade teaching, possibly negatively impacting student learning. For example, more than 40 percent of the 51 schools in the Vayots Dzor region make use of multi-grade teaching, which is often interpreted as the teacher dividing one lesson hour by half and spending each half with a different grade.

Lithuania does demonstrate improved education quality between 2002 and 2006, probably in no small measure as a result of its pro-quality per student formula. Thus, the funding formula expressly focuses on the teaching process, and apart from the basic amount for teacher salaries includes a number of components that contribute to the quality of the pedagogical process, including textbooks, teaching aids, teacher professional development, pedagogical and psychological services, career guidance, and cognitive development of students. Furthermore, the non-wage items' share of the per student amount increased over time, indicating a substitution away from pure teaching wages to the above-mentioned quality-enhancing inputs. Lithuania has collected data on student learning, which indicate that the percentage of grade 8 students achieving basic and high standards in Lithuanian, mathematics, science, and social studies rose by two to four percentage points over the period 2002 to 2006.

The promotion of competition for students among governmental schools as well as the expansion of the network of private schools is expected to contribute to improved quality of general education. Thus, the per capita financing approach, insofar as it rewards schools with greater enrolment, is assumed to lead to healthy competition among schools for students with a positive impact on the overall quality of general education. However, the other side of the coin was expressed by teachers and school directors in Georgia who spoke of a "vicious circle" (Shapiro 2007) in which schools in less competitive situations (e.g. poorer conditions of buildings and equipment or poorer student body served) may find themselves losing both students and funding, thus compromising education quality and leading to a further exodus of students and reduced funding. In the case of Estonia, Poland, and Lithuania, funding of private schools is included in the purview of the funding formula, again with an eye to promoting better quality of education. In Estonia, at 3 percent of total student enrolment, private schools remain a budding sector but seem to be carving out a niche for themselves in serving children with special needs as well as providing a second chance for graduates of academic upper secondary education who failed to qualify for higher education.

8.5. Main Lessons Learned

The aim of this overview chapter is to provide the lessons learned from the implementation of per capita financing of general education in six ECA countries from the point of view of achieving certain outcomes. The results achieved for the individual countries studied are documented in detail in the case studies and will not be repeated here. Instead, some broad lessons learned from the experience of these countries are summarized here in an attempt to inform future implementation of per student finance in the ECA region.

Regarding rationalization of school networks, the country case studies demonstrate that closure of under-enrolled schools is by no means an automatic corollary of putting in place per capita financing and that local governments play a key role. Given the fact that the different countries studied adopted different approaches to decentralization that led to a different role for local governments in implementing per capita finance, this lesson emerges quite clearly. Those countries that completely removed the local government level from the flow of funds from the center to the school either did not rationalize the school network (Armenia) or had to accomplish that task separately from and prior to implementing per capita finance (Georgia). Other countries that allocated funding for general education based on a per capita funding formula from the center to the local government were able to either rely exclusively on the incentives inherent in per capita funding to achieve network consolidation (Poland) or a combination of those incentives with other centrally mandated obligations (Lithuania). In sum, for considerable school consolidation to occur, financial management authority between the center, communities, and schools must be properly distributed, and the per capita financing arrangements must include earmarked financing, bonuses, or other adjustments that facilitate school closings.

Raising student-teacher ratios in an effort to improve efficiency of expenditures has proven particularly difficult to accomplish, especially given the decline in the school-age population in some of the countries studied. First, obviously, the funding formula needs to be designed to provide the right incentives to the relevant actors, which was not the case in Lithuania, for example, where local governments could not benefit from any savings achieved by letting redundant teachers go. However, the incentives put in place by the funding formula may be no match to the political economy pressures of simply keeping teachers on the payroll, transferring them to bigger schools, or finding alternative employment for them within the school system. The success of Armenia in increasing the student-teacher ratio hinged to some degree on the availability of World Bank funding for the teacher redundancy packages and to a large degree on strong political commitment.

The goal of improving the equity of education expenditures has also been difficult to achieve. In terms of vertical equity, while funding formulae adjust for such student characteristics as special education needs, minority or migration status, they do not account for student socioeconomic level. Regarding horizontal equity, the fact that implementation of per capita financing is inextricably linked with decentralization reforms has meant that *gminas* in Poland, for example, are at liberty to express local preferences and top up available funding for education, resulting in inequitable per capita funding across *gminas*. Nonetheless, this same leeway in funding, which resulted from strong decentralization efforts, has led to a process leading to improved equity within a few *gmina* in Poland that have chosen to adjust their per capita funding across their own schools.

As Lithuania's experience demonstrates, per capita funding formulae can be designed in such a way as to provide incentives that lead to desired outcomes: in this case, the focus of the funding formula on the teaching process has presumably contributed to observed improvement in learning outcomes. At the same time, however, if not properly monitored, it is possible for different objectives of per capita financing to be at odds with each other. For example, improving efficiency through multi-grade teaching in Armenia could have a negative impact on education quality, and it is imperative that the relevant learning outcomes data be collected and the trends monitored.

Per capita financing has led to improvements in transparency and accountability of general education expenditures, regardless of whether the funding formula is simple or complex. Arguably, however, a simple funding formula is more conducive to heightened transparency and accountability. A potential trade-off emerges here, nonetheless, in terms of improving equity, in that complex funding formulae are generally those attempting to make important adjustments for student and school characteristics. Among important further transparency and accountability improvements are building stakeholder capacity in budgeting, planning, and school management, expanding the role of school councils, and establishing linkages between financial and schooling outcomes data.

References

Abu-Duhou, I., Downes, P., and Levačić, R. (1999); "Component 1: Basic student allocation" in Kenneth N. Ross and Rosalind Levačić (editors) *Needs-based Resource Allocation in Education via Formula Funding of Schools*, Paris: UNESCO International Institute for Educational Planning.

Berryman, S. (2000); *Hidden Challenges to Education Systems in Transition Economies*, World Bank, Washington, DC.

Caldwell, B., Levačić, R. and Ross, K. (1999); "The role of formula funding of schools in different educational policy contexts", in Kenneth N. Ross and Rosalind Levačić (editors) *Needs-based Resource Allocation in Education via Formula Funding of Schools*, Paris: UNESCO International Institute for Educational Planning.

Kataoka, S.(2006); *Report on Implementation of Per Capita Formula Funding Projects in Tajikistan*, World Bank: Washington, DC.

Levačić, R. and Ross,K. (1999); "Principles for designing needs-based school funding formulae" in Kenneth N. Ross and Rosalind Levačić (editors) *Needs-based Resource Allocation in Education via Formula Funding of Schools*, Paris: UNESCO International Institute for Educational Planning.

Levitas, T. and Herczyński, J. (2002); "Decentralization, Local Governments and Education Reform in Post-Communist Poland," in *Balancing National and Local Responsibilities. Education Management and Finance in Four Central European Countries*, K. J. Davey (ed.), Local Government and Public Service Reform Initiative, Open Society Initiative, Budapest.

Monk, D. (1990); *Educational Finance: An Economic Approach*, New York: McGraw-Hill.

Shapiro, M. (2007); *Evaluation of the Ilia Chavachavadze Program in Reforming and Strengthening Georgia's Schools*, Padeco Co. Ltd.

Annex A. Per Capita Financing Formulae: A Comparative Analysis

	Armenia	Estonia	Georgia	Lithuania	Poland	Russia — Chuvash Republic	Russia — Tver Oblast
Scope and purview of the formula							
Entity receiving formula funding from the central (regional if in Russia) government	Funding for schools received directly by schools. Note: schools were transformed from budgetary institutions to autonomous legal entities.	Municipalities	Schools Notes: schools have become independent legal entities.	Municipalities, but with prescribed allocations for individual schools.	Municipalities	Municipalities	Municipalities
Types of expenditure included in formula funding	Excludes only capital expenditures.	Education grant comes in 2 parts: an allocation for basic costs of teaching, and an additional 10 percent for local governments to use according to their own choices for education spending. Also, there is a per student grant for textbooks, workbooks, and capital expenditures.	Whole school budget, including teacher and non-teacher salaries, and school maintenance, but not capital expenditures.	Teaching process, which includes salaries of teachers, administrators and professional staff, teacher in-service training, textbooks, library books, and teaching aids.	Excludes capital expenditures and mainstream preschools, but includes special preschools.	Covers salaries for teachers, administrative personnel and support staff, educational materials, and general expenses (excluding utility costs).	Covers salaries for teachers, administrative personnel and support staff, educational materials, and general expenses (excluding utility costs).
Flexibility in allocating received formula funding	School receives lump sum amount that it can allocate as it sees fit.	Municipality decides how to spend additional 10 percent of grant (see above).	Schools have full freedom to use the funds allocated to the school through vouchers.	Municipalities can reallocate among schools up to 5% of total received budget.	Local government funding is not earmarked for education.	Republic government does not instruct municipalities to follow Republic's coefficients for budget allocations from municipality to schools.	Municipality allowed to adopt school coefficient model within minimum and maximum ceiling specified by regional government.

	Armenia	Estonia	Georgia	Lithuania	Poland	Russia Chuvash Republic	Russia Tver Oblast
Education funding outside formula funding	Under pilot, schools with less than 100 students excluded from formula funding. Under national implementation, schools with no other school within 5km or in border areas excluded from formula funding.		Monthly grants for deficit schools. Moreover, the Ministry transfers supplements outside formula funding for 1) additional support to schools in conflict zones and 2) teacher salary increases, which are calculated by the number of teachers, not students.	Out of own resources, municipalities fund teaching environment, which includes salaries of technical staff, utilities, communications, maintenance, and student transportation. Municipalities can also choose to top up funds for teaching process.	A number of categorical grants are provided to municipalities for specific education needs (support to poor students, school safety programs, investments programs).	Out of own resources, municipalities fund utilities, maintenance, and repairs.	Out of own resources, municipalities fund utilities, maintenance, and repairs.
The formula in action							
Derivation of formula	Per student unit cost and fixed cost computed using regression analysis of norm-based budget of 154 pilot schools.	Formula calculates notional cost per student of providing teaching for an assumed number of classes at each school given the number of pupils in each of 4 grade ranges.	In 2005, and on the basis of actual expenditures in schools, average per student expenditure was calculated in city schools without capital costs.	Formula calculates the student basket, i.e. the standard per student amount for teaching process for a student of grades 5-8 in an urban secondary school with an assumed class size of 25.	The standard per student amount is derived by dividing the total amount of funding available nationally by the sum of weighted pupils and the teacher salary index.	National Training Foundation developed methodological guidelines for the calculation of standard per student costs and adjustment factors.	National Training Foundation developed methodological guidelines for the calculation of standard per student costs and adjustment factors.

	Armenia	Estonia	Georgia	Lithuania	Poland	Russia - Chuvash Republic	Russia - Tver Oblast
Buffers or "hold harmless" clauses included in applying formula	Adjustment amount applied to schools which would have received less than norm-based allocations.	Adjustment funding -- to prevent large year-to-year reductions in school's funding -- is triggered when school's annual increase in salary grant is less than national average.	Additional funding sent to deficit schools, i.e. schools where teacher salaries exceed the value of school revenues based on formula. No formal buffers or transition period.	No buffers.	Initially, local governments were guaranteed at least last year's allocation; changed to assurance (until 2005) that allocation per student not cut or increased beyond certain levels. Since 2005 no buffers.	During transition, instead of using actual number of students, regional government used number of "notional students" i.e. 25 students per class.	Regional government adopted municipal coefficient model with different but converging coefficient for each municipality during transition period.
Geographic location	Coefficients introduced in 2002 for schools in mountainous (1.02) and high mountainous (1.20) areas.	All island schools qualify as "regionally important schools" and are funded 20 percent more per student.	With city schools at 1, rural schools have coefficient of 1.5 and mountain schools coefficient of 1.8 (later reduced to 1.4 and 1.7, respectively).	Schools is in south-east region of country (with more than 1 instruction language) and in capital city have coefficient 1.21.	Additional weight of 0.38 for rural areas and towns with less than 5000 inhabitants.	Coefficients vary by urban vs. rural location (and school size for urban schools, and school size and type for rural schools).	Coefficients vary by urban vs. rural location.
School size				Coefficients vary according to 4 size categories (all urban schools fall under the largest category).		For urban schools, coefficients range from 0.95 to 1.17; for rural areas from 0.69 to 1.9.	Yes
School/institution type				Coefficients vary from 1.6 to 4 by grade for classes held in sanatoriums and hospitals.	Additional weight of 0.04 for gymnasiums; 0.001-0.03 for institutions providing out-of-school activities; additional weights of 1.5-11 for different boarding schools (special need, arts, young offenders, etc.)	For rural areas, coefficients range from 0.8 to 1.5 for primary schools; 0.69-1.9 for basic schools; and 0.93-1.43 for secondary schools. Gymnasium coefficient is 1.13.	Yes

	Armenia	Estonia	Georgia	Lithuania	Poland	Russia	
						Chuvash Republic	Tver Oblast
Minority schools				Coefficient is at 1.1.	Additional weight of 0.2.		
Schools with multiple languages of instruction		Maximum additional funding available is 3 times the standard per student amount.		Coefficient is at 1.36.	Additional weight of 0.2 for bilingual students.		
Schools with migrant students				Coefficient is at 1.36.			
Schools with integrated teaching				Coefficient is at 1.36.	Additional weight of 0.8 for handicapped pupils in integrated class.		
Adjustment factors¹ – Municipality characteristics							
					Additional multiplicative weight based on teacher qualifications.		
Adjustment factors¹ – Student characteristics							
Grade level				Coefficients vary according to 4 grade groupings (1-4, 5-8, 9-10, 11-12).			
Special needs student		Funded for being taught in smaller classes.		Coefficients range from 1.8 to 5.0 depending on type of disability, required special classes, and grade level.	Additional weights range from 1.4 to 3.6 for students with moderate learning difficulties, blind or disabled students, deaf students or those with severe learning difficulties.	Coefficient is at 2.15.	Yes
Adult student				Coefficient ranges from 0.5 to 1.4 depending on grade.	Enters directly into formula at weight of 0.7 in public, 0.35 in non-public school.		

	Armenia	Estonia	Georgia	Lithuania	Poland	Russia	
						Chuvash Republic	Tver Oblast
Home schooling/independent learning				Coefficient ranges from 2 to 3 depending on grade.		Coefficient is at 5.	
Vocational student				Coefficient ranges from 0.8 to 1.6 depending on grade.	Additional weight of 0.15; 1 for medical occupations; 3 for maritime vocational courses.		
Preschool student				Coefficients ranges from 0.6 to 1.9 depending on type of preschool.			
Sports student					Additional weight 0.2 in regular, 1 in master classes.		
Music student					Additional weight ranges from 1.01 to 3.36 depending on grade and type of school.		
Art student					Additional weight ranges from 0.9 to 1.4 depending on type of school.		
Ballet student					Additional weight of 3.4.		
Teacher training student					Additional weight of 1.		
Distance learning/evening courses		Coefficient is at 0.8.				Coefficient is at 0.5.	

[1] Adjustment factors can enter multiplicatively or additively into formula calculations.

Notes

1. I have benefitted from many exchanges and conversations with the authors of each of the country case studies during the period I led this project. Special thanks go also to Juan Diego Alonso and Alonso Sánchez for having taken over the project of the book and for thoroughly reviewing this chapter in order to help me sharpen some of the key arguments and conclusions, including the addition of some tables that were useful to make the chapter visually friendlier. A final thanks should also go to Jan Herczyński for substantially commenting on a first draft of this report and for contributing the box on piloting the reform. Needless to say, all mistakes, errors of interpretation and judgment are my sole responsibility.

2. In ECA parlance, the notion of "minimum standards," often referring to subjects and hours of teaching as well as other inputs, bears close resemblance to the activity-based model being described.

3. It should be noted here that in the case of Armenia, school budgets flow through regional deconcentrated offices of the Ministry of Education and Science.

4. Initially, during the pilot phase, this group of protected schools applied to those with less than 100 students enrolled. Later, as the PCF reform was rolled out nationwide, remote and border area schools, which tend to have low enrolment, were also considered protected.

5. The first phase of the Education Sector Reform Program was supported by the World Bank-financed Education Quality and Relevance Project. In parallel, conditionalities under a series of structural adjustment and poverty reduction support credits facilitated the implementation of teacher redundancy.

6. Differences in cost of living in different *gminas* were not taken into account due to lack of data and this would probably explain part of the differences in expenditure per student that are related to *gminas'* revenues.

7. Prior to the implementation of the decentralization reform, *kuratoria* were regional entities responsible both for financing as well as quality of education.

ECO-AUDIT
Environmental Benefits Statement

The World Bank is committed to preserving endangered forests and natural resources. The Office of the Publisher has chosen to print World Bank Studies and Working Papers on recycled paper with 30 percent postconsumer fiber in accordance with the recommended standards for paper usage set by the Green Press Initiative, a nonprofit program supporting publishers in using fiber that is not sourced from endangered forests. For more information, visit www.greenpressinitiative.org.

In 2010, the printing of this book on recycled paper saved the following:
- 11 trees*
- 3 million Btu of total energy
- 1,045 lb. of net greenhouse gases
- 5,035 gal. of waste water
- 306 lb. of solid waste

*40 feet in height and 6–8 inches in diameter

www.ingramcontent.com/pod-product-compliance
Lightning Source LLC
Chambersburg PA
CBHW080542230426
43663CB00015B/2680